Codeb

Codebreakers

The inside story of Bletchley Park

Edited by

F. H. HINSLEY
ALAN STRIPP

OXFORD UNIVERSITY PRESS

Oxford University Press, Walton Street, Oxford OX2 6DP

Oxford New York Toronto
Delhi Bombay Calcutta Madras Karachi
Kuala Lumpur Singapore Hong Kong Tokyo
Nairobi Dar es Salaam Cape Town
Melbourne Auckland Madrid

and associated companies in
Berlin Ibadan

Oxford is a trade mark of Oxford University Press

Published in the United States
by Oxford University Press Inc., New York

British Library Cataloguing in Publication Data
Data available

Library of Congress Cataloging in Publication Data
Memories of Bletchley Park: codebreakers / edited by
Sir Harry Hinsley, Alan Stripp.
p. cm.
Includes index.
1. World War, 1939–1945—Cryptography. 2. World War, 1939–1945—Secret service—Great Britain. 3. World War, 1939–1945—Electronic intelligence—Great Britain. 4. World War, 1939–1945—Personal narratives, British. 3. Great Britain, Government Communications Headquarters—History. 6. Bletchley Park (Buckinghamshire, England)—History. I. Hinsley, F. H. (Francis Harry), 1918– II. Stripp, Alan, 1924– . III. Title: Codebreakers.
D810.C88M46 1993 940.54'8641—dc20 92–42502
ISBN 0–19–820327–6

5 7 9 10 8 6 4

Printed in Great Britain
on acid-free paper by
Biddles Ltd,
Guildford and King's Lynn

PREFACE

THIS book is the inside story of the wartime work of Bletchley Park and its outstations, where German, Italian, and Japanese signals were successfully broken, interpreted, and summarized, and their essence distributed to Allied commanders in Britain and abroad. Unlike other stories—and there have been many—of the breaking of the German Enigma cipher machine, which formed one major part of that work, it is written by men and women who themselves worked at Bletchley, and in that sense it is the first account, and could well be the last, which is both authentic and fairly comprehensive.

Just before the outbreak of the Second World War the Government Code and Cypher School (GC&CS) moved from London to Bletchley Park. In this unpretentious place, variously known as War Station X, Room 47 Foreign Office, BP, the Park, or Government Communications Headquarters (GCHQ), it grew in numbers from under one hundred in 1939 to over seven thousand in 1944, and the scope and significance of its work expanded out of all proportion to its size. As early as the end of 1942 it was reading some four thousand German high-grade signals *a day*, with slightly smaller numbers of Italian and Japanese signals.

This success, on an unprecedented scale and against enormous odds, had an almost miraculous quality at the time and has since acquired almost legendary status. Its value in helping Britain to escape early defeat, and in ensuring and greatly hastening Allied victory, is now self-evident. But while cryptanalysis—the breaking of enemy codes and ciphers—was its *raison d'être*, Bletchley was led by the obstacles and opportunities of wartime to undertake many other tasks. Some of these, like the study of enemy wireless systems, preceded its successes against ciphers. Some followed upon those successes:

- the translation and elucidation of decrypts;
- the rapid summarizing and dispatching of their contents (Ultra intelligence) to Whitehall and operational Commands;
- the discussion with them of the significance of that intelligence;

- the meticulous indexing that formed the basis of the expertise needed for that discussion.

The Index was also at the heart of the successful struggle against ciphers—a struggle which was unremitting and which often had to be renewed every twenty-four hours. Most of these activities are dealt with in the following chapters, and it must be emphasized that the term 'codebreaking', used in our title and throughout the book, refers not simply to cryptanalysis but to the whole operation carried out at Bletchley.

The editors decided that the best order was to place the handling of decrypts—the producing of Ultra intelligence—first, as being more accessible to most readers than the description of the work of cryptanalysts. The more technical sections that follow are subdivided into the main programmes in which Bletchley was absorbed:

- the Enigma machine and the bombe;
- Fish and Colossus;
- field ciphers and tactical codes;
- work on Japanese codes—a programme which encountered different problems and in which Bletchley's efforts were subsidiary to those of its counterparts in the United States and the Pacific.

We must also emphasize three points. First, some activities which were connected with the work of GC&CS are excluded, because they were not carried out at Bletchley or were not under its immediate control. Examples are the work of intercept stations; that part of the exploitation of tactical signals which took place in the field and generally went under the name of Army or RAF Y; and the supervision, at every operational headquarters that received it, of the security of Bletchley's product—the SCU–SLU organization.

Secondly, for lack of contact with appropriate contributors, this volume does not do full justice to the contribution made by the United States to Bletchley's work, on German no less than on Japanese signals. This has restricted our discussion of the part played by the US Navy.

Thirdly, few of the events described here were chronicled at the time, and those who worked at Bletchley and its outstations were forbidden to talk or write about it—almost to remember it. The compiling of this book has rested almost entirely on personal memories; and that is unusual in an account which pretends to any sort of accuracy. Moreover, nobody who worked at Bletchley can now be under 65;

several contributors are in their mid-80s. For all of us the clear and accurate recollection of highly specialized Top Secret facts across fifty years has been a demanding task, requiring much cross-checking. There will still be errors and contradictions, for which we are sorry.

The particularly tight security which prevailed at Bletchley has added to these problems. Within each block, hut, or room there was little time and less encouragement to discuss matters of common interest unless the job specifically demanded it. Most of us had no idea 'what went on next door', especially as the variety of jobs increased and more staff arrived. A society which began with something of the collegiate atmosphere of a common room was transformed into a bustling headquarters with multiple assembly lines. The absolute secrecy preserved by all who worked there was and is an extraordinary achievement. Whilst wartime staff of Bletchley Park are now otherwise absolved from reticence about their work, the Government still requires them not to disclose details of some of the methods by which intelligence was obtained. This has meant having to disappoint some contributors by asking them to omit or alter certain details.

The editors are profoundly grateful to all their wartime colleagues, including three now in the United States and one in Israel, who have so generously given their time, searched their memories, and written their accounts. They have tirelessly endured our cross-examination on tricky details, and patiently accepted revisions and cuts. And we also thank, with apologies, those contributors whose chapters we had reluctantly to omit because, in the event, they overlapped with material we already had.

We have to acknowledge our debt to many others. Robin Denniston, the son of the first wartime head of GC&CS, originally conceived the idea of this book, recruited both editors, found us our publisher, and compiled the index. Sydney Wilkinson allowed us to use material from the privately printed autobiography by her husband, the late Patrick Wilkinson. We are grateful to the Institute of Electrical Engineers for permission to include Sir Harry Hinsley's article on Fish which appeared in *Electronics and Power* in July 1987; to the Editor of *After the Battle* for permission to use Diana Payne's article from issue 37; and to Frank Cass and Co. Ltd for allowing us to use articles which first appeared in *Intelligence and National Security*: by Noel Currer-Briggs in vol. 2, no. 2 of April 1987; and by Christopher Morris in vol. 1, no. 1 of January 1986, reprinted in *Codebreaking and Signals Intelligence*, edited by Christopher Andrew, in the same year.

We also thank those who have allowed us to use their photographs: The Science Museum and Anthony Sale for pictures of the Enigma, a bombe room, Colossus, and—we think—Hut 6; Dipl. Ing. Wolfgang Mache, of Siemens in Munich, and the Forsvars Museum in Oslo, for the Lorenz SZ 42; and Barbara Eachus, then Barbara Abernethy, for the group of rounders-watchers, complete with identifications. Pierre Lorain, of Paris, and Prof. Dr Jürgen Rohwer, of the Bibliothek für Zeitgeschichte in Stuttgart, have kindly provided other photographs; and Gilbert Bloch, also of Paris, has patiently answered many technical enquiries about the Enigma. We thank also two Cambridge friends in particular: David Wheeler, Professor of Computer Science, and Anne Stow, Librarian of the Scientific Periodicals Library. Our colleagues at Oxford University Press have given us generous guidance and encouragement in our preparation of the text.

Finally, both editors take this opportunity to thank their wives for their help and forbearance, and each other for a stimulating and satisfying combined operation.

F. H. Hinsley
Alan Stripp

Cambridge
October 1992

CONTENTS

LIST OF PLATES

(between pages 138 and 139)

LIST OF FIGURES

Tables

GLOSSARY AND ABBREVIATIONS

Abwehr	secret intelligence service of the German High Command (cf. *Sicherheitsdienst*)
additive	see 'key (3)'
ATS	Auxiliary Territorial Service (later Women's Royal Army Corps)
Banburismus	a method of attacking daily naval Enigma keys, minimizing the use of bombes, and using perforated sheets made at Banbury
bombe	British, and later American, electro-mechanical machine used to discover the wheel-settings for Enigma keys, and based on an earlier and simpler Polish *bomba*
Boniface	mythical agent used as an early cover-name for Ultra
book-breaking/ book-building	terms for reconstructing a code-book by cryptanalysis
BP	then meant only Bletchley Park
C (or CSS)	Chief of the (British) Secret Intelligence Service, M.I.6
cillies	procedural errors by Enigma operators, combining (1) a recognizable instead of random choice of message-setting, and (2) failure to alter the wheel position much, or at all, before sending a message; thought to be named after an operator's girl-friend 'Cilli', shortened to 'Cil'; sometimes erroneously called 'sillies'
cipher/cypher	(1) any system, other than a code, of substituting letters or numbers for the letters of a message, or of transposing them; in Royal Navy usage 'ciphers' were used by officers, 'codes' by ratings, regardless of

	their type; (2) a system using a numerical key to recipher an already encrypted text
code	a system of substituting groups of two or more letters or numbers for the words, phrases, sentences, punctuation, etc., of a message
code-book	usually in two volumes: one for encoding, arranged in alphabetical or similar order of words and meanings; the other in alphabetical or numerical order of code-groups, for decoding
codebreaker	literally someone who breaks an enemy code (or cipher) system; more broadly, the whole staff of a codebreaking unit, including those who collate, assess, and distribute the intelligence thus produced
code-group	a group of two or more numbers and/or letters carrying a specific meaning
Colossus	the first programmable electronic digital computer, used at Bletchley to solve Fish settings from February 1944, and followed by nine improved models
corrupt	different from the encrypted text because of errors introduced in interception or subsequent handling
crib	textual or other evidence which, by suggesting parallels of order, subject-matter, or expression, provides clues for breaking a code or cipher signal
cryptanalysis	the technique or profession of breaking codes or ciphers (a term not widely used before the 1950s)
cryptogram	a code or cipher message
decipher/decode/decrypt	transform a cipher or code text into plain language; a deciphered or decoded signal ('decrypt' was little used before the 1950s)
depth	to 'build (up a) depth' is to align two or more stretches of cipher text that have been reciphered by the same stretch of key; a conjectural key which makes sense

	of even two such texts is likely to be right (US 'super-imposition')
discriminant	in Enigma usage, a group of three letters (*Kenngruppe*) specifying which key is to be used on which day (see the Enigma description, Chapter 11); outside Enigma, a group denoting the use of a particular code or cipher system
encipher/encode/encrypt	transform a plain-language text into cipher or code
Enigma	the cipher machine used, in various forms, for most signals by the German armed services and several government departments from the late 1920s to 1945 (see the Enigma description, Chapter 11)
Fish	the BP cover-name given to German non-Morse traffic enciphered on a *Schlüsselzusatz* or *Geheimschreiber* machine, named 'Tunny' and 'Sturgeon' at BP
GAF	German Air Force; *Luftwaffe*
garbled	see 'corrupt'
GC&CS	Government Code and Cypher School
GCHQ	Government Communications Headquarters
Geheimschreiber	the Fish cipher machine cover-named 'Sturgeon' at BP, the Siemens T 52; literally 'secret writer'
group	generally a code-group or key-group of three or more letters or numbers
Grundstellung	a setting used to encipher the message-setting on types of the Enigma used by the *Abwehr* and railways in particular (see the Enigma description, Chapter 11)
hand cipher	the traditional method of enciphering a message, not by machine
Herivel tip	the particular chance that lazy or incompetent Enigma operators, after selecting the wheels specified in a new key and placing them in the correct ring-setting, might leave them in that position, or near,

	instead of turning them to a random setting—thus easing the cryptanalysts' task; named after John Herivel, who pointed it out
high grade	term referring to the high level of security which a code or cipher is designed to provide, rather than the traffic it carries
hiragana	the more cursive form of Japanese syllabary (cf. *katakana*)
Hollerith	punched-card equipment used for handling data quickly
Hut	at BP most of the early work was done in 'temporary' huts, of which the most important were: Hut 6: German Army and Air Force Enigma cryptanalysis; Hut 3: German Army and Air Force translating and processing; Hut 8: German Navy Enigma cryptanalysis; Hut 4: German Navy translating and processing (all these definitions are approximate; the designations became cover-names and moved with the teams when they moved into the more solidly built new Blocks A–H)
indicator/indicator-setting	see the Enigma description (Chapter 11)
JAAF	Japanese Army Air Force
JMA	Japanese Military Attaché
JN	Japanese Navy
kana	the Japanese syllabaries (cf. *hiragana* and *katakana*) used for writing verb terminations, postpositions, etc., as distinct from the characters or ideograms (*kanji*) representing names, nouns, verb-stems, etc.
kanji	the characters or ideograms borrowed from Chinese to denote the main elements in Japanese, which then had no script of its own
katakana	the more angular form of Japanese syllabary (cf. *hiragana*)
Kenngruppe	discriminant; one of four three-letter groups used on a particular day to specify

	the key in use; the German Navy had a wide choice of these, and they were enciphered
key	a cryptographic term with several uses apart from representing the key of an Enigma keyboard: (1) a set-up used in common by a group of Enigma-users, and designated Kestrel, Light Blue, etc. at BP; (2) the actual set-up for a particular day, specifying wheel order (*Walzenlage*), ring-setting (*Ringstellung*), and cross-plugging (*Steckerverbindungen*) (see the Enigma description, Chapter 11); (3) a subsidiary text of random numbers which can be added to or subtracted from a 'raw' numerical code-text to recipher it (hence 'additive' or 'subtractor' keys) or used in a more complex system, as in Japanese 6633
key-breaking	reconstructing the key (3 above)
key-stripping	removing a reciphering key (3 above) once reconstructed or captured, so as to expose the 'raw' code-text
lampboard	see the Enigma description (Chapter 11)
low grade	term referring to the level of security which a code or cipher is designed to provide, not the traffic it carries
Magic	US cover-name roughly equivalent to 'Ultra' and also covering high-grade Japanese signals intelligence
menu	at BP a deduced set of instructions, (1) for operators of modified Typex machines; and (2) for bombe operators, to establish the daily Enigma wheel selection and wheel positions
message-setting	see the Enigma description (Chapter 11)
MIRS	Military Intelligence Research Section
M.I.5	Security Service: intelligence operations in Britain, hence mainly counter-espionage
M.I.6	Secret Intelligence Service (SIS): British

	intelligence-gathering abroad, and counter-espionage abroad
M.I.8	signals intelligence service
NCO	non-commissioned officer
NID	Naval Intelligence Division
Offizier	a system of doubly enciphering confidential naval Enigma signals so that the first encipherment could be decrypted only by an officer
OIC	Operational Intelligence Centre of the Admiralty
OTP	one-time pad; a cipher which cannot properly be used more than once, since, after each page or part-page is used, it is torn off and destroyed; if used thus it is virtually unbreakable
Playfair	a substitution cipher, already superseded during the First World War, but used in a complex double-encipherment for low-grade traffic in the Second World War by the Germans (see Chapter 23)
RAF	Royal Air Force
recipher	disguise a signal text which is already in cipher or code form, by means of a key (3); US 're-encipher' or 'super-encipher' mean the same
RHV	*Reservehandverfahren*; see pp. 238–9
Ringstellung	ring-setting (see the Enigma description, Chapter 11)
rotor	wheel (of the Enigma)
Schlüsselzusatz	the Fish cipher machine cover-named 'Tunny' at BP, the Lorenz SZ 40 or 42; literally 'cipher attachment'
scramble	jumble deliberately
SCU	Special Communications Unit; responsible for distributing selected Ultra to overseas Commands, using hand-speed Morse; generally staffed by Army
Sicherheitsdienst	intelligence service of the Nazi Party (cf. *Abwehr*)

Sigaba	US near-equivalent of the Typex cipher machine
sigint	signals intelligence; the exploitation of code- and cipher-breaking
sillies	see 'cillies'
SIS	Secret Intelligence Service
SLU	Special Liaison Unit; responsible, like the SCU, for Ultra distribution overseas, but usually RAF-staffed and equipped with OTP or Typex
Stecker	German for 'plug' (see the Enigma description, Chapter 11)
stripping	in 'key-stripping': removing a broken re-ciphering key
Sturgeon	cover-name for *Geheimschreiber* 'Fish' traffic; cf. 'Tunny'
SZ	*Schlüsselzusatz*
traffic	a volume of signals possessing some common characteristic
traffic analysis	the exploitation of plain-language conversations, some low-grade codes and ciphers, signals procedure, and direction-finding
Tunny	cover-name for *Schlüsselzusatz* Fish traffic; cf. 'Sturgeon'
Typex	standard British cipher machine
Ultra	British cover-name, from June 1941, for all high-grade signals intelligence, derived not only from Enigma but from Fish and hand ciphers, and from Italian and Japanese codes and ciphers; later adopted, with some variants, by the US
Umkehrwalze	reversing wheel (see the Enigma description, Chapter 11)
WAAF	Women's Auxiliary Air Force; later WRAF
Walzenlage	wheel order (see the Enigma description, Chapter 11)
Watch	variously used at BP for specific functions within a hut
WEC	Wireless Experimental Centre

Wehrmacht	(German) armed services
WRAF	Women's Royal Air Force (formerly WAAF)
WRNS	Women's Royal Naval Section; 'Wrens'
WS	*Werftschluessel*; Dockyard Key
W/T	wireless telegraphy
Y Service	originally service covering signals interception, traffic analysis, and the breaking of low-trade signals; from October 1943 covering only interception and direction-finding; term also used as a cover-name for recruitment, language courses, etc.

INTRODUCTION
The influence of Ultra in the Second World War

F. H. HINSLEY

THE influence of Ultra—the code-name used in the Second World War for the product of the decryption of the more important enemy ciphers—is a subject that calls for two different kinds of enquiry. The records began to be available during the 1970s, so that we now have the essential evidence for the direct or the immediate influence it exerted; and, so long as we have proper regard for the rules of historical enquiry, we can establish what that influence was with reasonable accuracy. (This is not yet the case, at least in the United Kingdom, for the war in the Far East, which is therefore excluded from this analysis.) We know what information Ultra provided and when it reached its recipients. We know the nature and the extent of such other intelligence as was then at their disposal. And, although there are few *contemporary* accounts of what they thought of it and did with it, we know what appreciations, orders, and actions, and sometimes what discussions, followed its receipt. But because the very existence of Ultra remained a closely guarded secret until the 1970s, its influence was unknown to, or unmentionable by, the compilers of contemporary reports and the authors of the standard histories and the memoirs that were published before that time. These reports and these accounts already incorporate the contribution Ultra made to the course of events but they do not acknowledge it. The purpose of the historical enquiry is thus to identify that contribution and, to this extent, to put Ultra into the existing accounts.

But this cannot be the sole aim of the investigation. Over and above the direct or immediate influence of Ultra on events, we have to consider the effects or the consequences of its contribution for the course of the war. Let me give an illustration of this distinction. To identify Ultra is sufficient to establish that it alone made it possible in the last four months of 1941 to control the depredations of the U-boats and drive them temporarily out of the north Atlantic. But strict historical enquiry cannot establish the impact on the course of the war of the defeat of the U-boats at that time. As will be obvious from this example, this impact is, like Ultra's immediate contribution, already incorporated into, subsumed in, the record of the way the war developed. But if we are to assess its significance, we have to identify Ultra in order to be able to strip it out of existing accounts of the course of the war—in order to calculate how the war would have gone if Ultra had not existed. In the jargon of my trade, we have to engage in counter-factual history.

Counter-factual history is a difficult exercise, not to say a dubious one—as may be judged from such studies as those which have sought to reconstruct the history of the United States on the assumption that the railway had not been invented. It is certainly true that we should carry it out only if we are fully aware of what we are doing. But it is equally true that, unless we attempt it, we shall not grasp the significance of Ultra's contribution.

This contribution did not begin till the spring of 1941—eighteen months after the outbreak of the war. Although decrypts from the German Enigma were obtained regularly from the spring of 1940, they were confined for the next twelve months to an Enigma key used only in the Norwegian campaign and to two keys used by the German Air Force. Although the volume of decrypts was heavy during the Norwegian campaign and in the last phase of the battle in France, they could not be turned to practical use for lack of communications, security procedures, and expertise. Various claims have been made to the effect that Ultra was of some value during the Battle of Britain, against the threat of German invasion, or in the Blitz; there is no substance to them, though intelligence from other sources—prisoners; captured documents and equipment; agents; air photographic reconnaissance; the enemy's tactical radio communications—was improving.

The first Ultra which might have been turned to some advantage was that which from January 1941 first confirmed and then superseded attaché and agent reports about the scale and timing of the German build-up for the attack on Greece. It might have shown that the attack could not be stopped by any British force, however large, that could be spared from the Middle East; but for various reasons it was decided to take no account of this. The first developments to which Ultra made a contribution were the defeat of the Italian army in North Africa in February (which owed more, however, to intelligence from tactical codes than to Ultra) and the battle of Matapan at the end of March (a victory for the Mediterranean fleet that was made possible by the timely receipt of a few German and Italian high-grade decrypts).

These initial contributions were soon followed by others. Ultra in the form of German Air Force reports of the advance of the German Army positively assisted the British force in Greece to retreat in good order in April. In May the decryption in good time of full details of the German plan of attack did not enable the defenders to save Crete, but it enabled them to turn Germany's victory into a Pyrrhic victory. But Ultra did nothing to avert the surprise or the success of Rommel's first offensive, which took him to the Egyptian frontier by the middle of April, and it did nothing to avert the failure of Wavell's two attempts to drive him back—Operations Brevity in mid-May and Battleaxe in mid-June. The Enigma decrypts were still confined to those of the German Air Force, and all the Italian service cyphers had by then become unreadable.

In the second half of 1941, on the other hand, Ultra exerted a powerful, if not always a decisive, effect on the fluctuating fortunes of the desert campaign as a result of a significant expansion of its sources. At the end of June Bletchley broke a machine cipher which the Italians had introduced at the end of 1940 for communications about Axis Mediterranean shipping. It read it regularly and currently thereafter, decrypts rising from six hundred in July 1941 to four thousand in July 1942, the peak month. From the middle of September, though only temporarily, until the end of November, Bletchley solved the German Army Enigma keys in use within the Panzer Army and between North Africa and Rome and Berlin. It was sinkings of Rommel's supply ships, resulting directly from the Italian decrypts, that prevented Rommel from continuing his advance before Auchinleck opened his own offensive (Operation Crusader) in November; and those sinkings, rising before and during the offensive from 20 to 50 per cent of all ships sailed, combined with the receipt for the first time of Ultra about the state and the movements of Rommel's formations to enable Eighth Army to turn the tide during the Crusader battles and force him back to El Agheila by the end of 1941.

By the end of 1941 the tide was turning the other way. The shipping losses had forced the Germans to strengthen their air power in the Mediterranean and dispatch U-boats there, and these measures, by neutralizing Malta, cancelled out the value of the shipping decrypts. To make matters worse, the Army Enigma was lost from early in December, while Rommel's field intelligence, which continued to outclass that of the British forces, was boosted by an Axis success with Ultra: from January to June 1942 the Germans read the cipher used by the US Military Attaché in Cairo. It was in these circumstances that Rommel, surprising the British by resuming the offensive on 21 January 1942, forced them back to the Gazala Line by 6 February and then achieved a resounding victory in the battle of Gazala at the end of May. One of the Army Enigma keys that had been read during Operation Crusader was recovered in the middle of April. Together with Air Force Ultra, its decrypts gave a month's notice that Rommel intended to attack again towards the end of May. But Ultra revealed nothing about his operational plans or the redispositions which might have betrayed them. Until midway through the battle, moreover, the Army Enigma was being decrypted with delays of at least a week.

At that point, however, the situation changed again, and this time permanently. Bletchley began to read both of the Army keys with an average delay of twenty-four hours from the first week of June. From the same date it broke a new Army–Air Force liaison key, also with little delay; and from 11 July, in one of the rare exceptions to the wartime rules for Ultra intelligence, the authorities allowed this most voluble and valuable of Enigma keys to be decrypted in Cairo so as to minimize delay in getting Ultra to the Commands. In the middle of July another Enigma key was broken, that used by the Germans in connection with the air transport of army supplies and reinforcements to North Africa from Greece and Crete. With these additions to the Air Force Enigma, the British had acquired access, though with different degrees of speed and completeness, to every enemy cipher in use in the African fighting. Both directly in the shape of the decrypts and indirectly by the effect that Ultra had in raising the efficiency of British field intelligence, the Middle East Commands thereafter received more timely intelligence about more aspects of the enemy's activities than any force enjoyed in any land campaign in the whole war. They took some time to become adept at handling it—too long to avoid the loss of Tobruk and retreat to the Alamein Line. But an analysis of the use to which they put it during the retreat in

June and in the first round of fighting at Alamein in July fully bears out the view which Auchinleck expressed at the time—that, but for Ultra, 'Rommel would certainly have got through to Cairo'. It is certainly the case that Ultra showed that the Axis authorities expected him to do so: at the beginning of July the decrypts showed that the Panzer Army had requested maps of the chief Egyptian cities, that the Italian Navy was preparing to escort troop convoys to Egypt, and that Hitler had ordered exceptional steps to ensure that Rommel received additional troops.

Although Ultra was never again to be so crucial for the outcome in north Africa, it continued to be an enormous asset. The British authorities had appreciated before the end of July that Rommel must know that their situation was improving, and would want to attack again by the end of August, while he retained superiority in effective tanks; and on 13 August Montgomery had already appreciated that, if Rommel was to be thwarted, it was essential to garrison the Alam Halfa ridge. But it was still an enormous advantage that decrypts confirmed the accuracy of these appreciations from 17 August by disclosing the approximate date and the exact operational plans for the German offensive. Despite their foreknowledge, the British did not defeat Rommel in the field at Alam Halfa; but he was forced to abandon the battle after two days on 2 September, because a renewed offensive against his supply shipping, made possible by the replenishment of Malta and again guided by Ultra, had destroyed 33 per cent of the cargo dispatched—and 41 per cent of the fuel—in the second half of August. The intensification of the anti-shipping offensive, which sank no less than 45 per cent of the cargo sailed in October, had gravely reduced Rommel's freedom of movement by the time the British launched their own offensive from Alamein on 23 October, and Ultra further contributed to his defeat by establishing the precise effect of the shipping losses on his logistic and manpower situation and his defence preparations. But the influence of Ultra on the battle of Alamein was less than that of the decisive superiority—it was about 5 to 1—which the British had acquired in tanks and in the air; and the wonder is that, when Eighth Army was receiving a continuous stream of Ultra, it failed to cut off Rommel's retreat before he reached Tunisia.

During the campaign in Tunisia Ultra was much less complete. The new Enigma key for communications between the German Army and Rome was soon broken, but was read with considerable delay. The key introduced for use within the Army in Tunisia was not read till February 1943, and then irregularly. In March the old keys in use by Rommel's formations gave good notice of the enemy's plans before the battle of Medenine and full details of his strength and dispositions during the battle of Mareth. But their evidence was not decisive; other sources—field intelligence and air reconnaissance—were providing adequate information. And on the other fronts in Tunisia, where other sources were also performing poorly, Ultra exerted little influence on the fighting. On a quite different front, on the other hand, it was making a decisive contribution to victory in the battle of the Atlantic while the Tunisian campaign was being fought.

The first victory over the U-boats had already been achieved—and achieved entirely on the basis of Ultra—in the second half of 1941. The influence of Ultra in reducing Axis shipping in the Mediterranean had forced Germany to transfer twenty-one U-boats there, a third of her operational fleet, from the Atlantic during those months. Still more important was the fact that Bletchley had at last broken the naval Enigma at the beginning of June 1941 and was decrypting it nearly currently until the end of January 1942. At a time when the British anti-submarine defences were woefully weak and merchant shipping woefully scarce, and when the U-boat fleet was at last becoming a formidable force, the use of the decrypts to route convoys away from the U-boat patrols had a dramatic effect on the scale of the U-boats' depredations. In the four months to the end of June they had sunk 282,000 tons of shipping a month. Between the beginning of July and the end of the year the sinkings averaged 120,000 tons a month, and they had dropped to 62,000 tons in November, when the U-boats were temporarily withdrawn from the north Atlantic. It has been calculated that, allowing for the increased number of U-boats at sea, about $1^1/_2$ million tons of shipping (350 ships) were saved, and this intermission was invaluable for the level of British supplies, the building of new shipping, and the development of anti-submarine defences. Even so, it was less crucial than the second and final defeat of the U-boats, which Ultra helped to bring about in the spring and early summer of 1943.

When the U-boats returned to the north Atlantic in the autumn of 1942, after months in which they had been concentrated off the American coast, they were using a new Enigma key, Shark, that was unreadable. The result was reflected in a huge increase in Allied shipping losses on the convoy routes. Bletchley broke the new key in December, and the use of the decrypts for the evasive routeing of convoys secured a marked slump in sinkings until the end of February 1943, despite a continual increase in the number of U-boats on patrol. But in March 1943 Allied losses were again close to a level which, if sustained, would have disrupted the UK supply line; evasive routeing had been made impossible by the sheer size of the U-boat fleet. From the end of March, on the other hand, strengthened Allied escort forces went over to the offensive against the U-boats in the vicinity of the convoys, and did so to such effect that, while the number of ships sunk in convoy was immediately reduced by two-thirds, the U-boats suffered such heavy losses that they were withdrawn from the north Atlantic in May. Nor were they ever to return in strength. During June, July, and August 1943 the Allied offensive, extended to attacks on their refuelling points and their passage routes through the Bay of Biscay, finally crippled the U-boat command. In the last four months of the year Allied shipping losses were running at less than one-sixth of the insupportable level they had reached in March, and in 1944 they continued to fall.

Whereas Ultra had been solely responsible for the success of evasive routeing, it was only one of the factors underlying the success of the Allied offensive. This would have been impossible without the closing of the air gap in the north Atlantic, the introduction of improved radar and of high-frequency direction-finding for the escort vessels, and the deployment of aircraft-carrier support groups to hunt the U-boats. But the influence of Ultra on the offensive was enormous. By maximizing the effect of these technical and operational developments which came to fruition in 1943, and by enabling the Allies to pin-point their attacks in a huge theatre of operations, it ensured that the Allied victory was complete and decisive.

Since the middle of 1943 Ultra had meanwhile come into its own as an invaluable accessory in the planning of other Allied strategic initiatives. It had played no part in the preparations for the invasion of north-west Africa, which were marked both by excessive overcompensation in the size of the forces detailed for Morocco, and by lamentable underestimation of the scale on which Germany might dispatch forces to Tunisia. Such errors were thereafter avoided because first the growth of the Allied threat and then the extension of the theatre of operations produced a huge increase in the volume of

Ultra. Combined with the accumulation of Ultra about the German Air Force since the spring of 1940, about the German Navy since the summer of 1941, and about the German Army since the autumn of 1941, this gave the Allies the advantage that, when carrying out the landings in Sicily and Italy in July and September 1943 and the Anzio landing in January 1944, they possessed an accurate knowledge of the enemy's problems throughout the Mediterranean, of the condition and order of battle of his formations there, and often of his intentions. Especially in relation to his intentions, intelligence increased because Bletchley now solved some of the 'Fish' ciphers recently introduced by Germany for high-speed non-Morse transmission. The first important one to be read regularly, from the end of May 1943, was that used by Berlin and Kesselring as Commander-in-Chief South in Italy. These ciphers added a new dimension to Ultra, for, whereas the bulk of the Enigma was transmitted at and below Army level, the non-Morse ciphers were used between Germany's Armies and Army Groups and Berlin, and so carried statements of intentions, orders, appreciations, and situation reports of the highest strategic value.

As distinct from the assistance it gave to the planning of the Allied campaigns, Ultra was rarely of decisive operational importance during the fighting in Sicily and Italy. A notable exception to this statement must be made for the fact that, by revealing in advance the time, the direction, and the scale of Kesselring's counter-attack, it saved the Anzio beach-head in February 1944 and thus averted an Allied set-back of strategic proportions. But in Italy it provided full coverage of the strength and order of battle of the German divisions, as well as full knowledge of Germany's determination to yield as little ground as possible, and this conferred on the Allies a further strategic advantage; it enabled them not only to pin down a million battle-experienced German troops with a minimum effort but also to reduce that effort without sacrificing that objective as they prepared for the landings in France.

In the preparations for the cross-Channel invasion, the contribution made by Ultra was still greater, in proportion to the fact that, of all the Allied landings, Overlord, the first to be opposed by armoured divisions, was the most hazardous and the least certain to succeed. It is true that, of the three prerequisites for success, two were already in place—command of the sea and command of the air. The third was an assurance that Germany would be unable to concentrate first-class, especially armoured, divisions and then reinforce them in sufficient strength to prevent the seizure and the expansion of the beachheads. The limits to this strength that were acceptable in the light of the proposed scale of Allied assault and follow-up were laid down in the middle of 1943, early in the planning stage. Until the end of 1943 there was no Ultra to show whether the Germans were likely to exceed these limits, because their air and ground forces in the west were still using land-lines. All the evidence which suggested that they would do so, as also that they were intensifying their fixed defences, and which forced the Allies in January 1944 to double the length of the invasion front and increase the size of the assault force and the rate of reinforcement, came from other sources—the resistance movements, agents, captured documents, and photographic reconnaissance. But from early in 1944, partly from decrypts of Japanese reports from Berlin to Tokyo but mainly because Bletchley solved some of the new German Air Force and Army ciphers that were at last appearing on the air—and notably the non-Morse cipher introduced between Berlin and von Rundstedt, the Commander-in-Chief West, which was broken in March—Ultra confirmed and greatly added to the other intelligence about the identification and location of the German divisions.

As Ultra accumulated, it administered some unpleasant shocks. In particular, it revealed in the second half of May—following earlier disturbing indications that the Germans were concluding that the area between Le Havre and Cherbourg was a likely, and perhaps even the main, invasion area—that they were sending reinforcements to Normandy and the Cherbourg peninsula. But this evidence arrived in time to enable the Allies to modify the plans for the landings on and behind the Utah beach; and it is a singular fact that before the expedition sailed the Allied estimate of the number, identification, and location of the enemy's divisions in the west, fifty-eight in all, was accurate in all but two items that were to be of operational importance.

As luck would have it, one of the gaps in the intelligence related to 21st Panzer Division. Ultra revealed that it had moved to the Caen area in the middle of May; but neither Ultra nor any other source provided its exact location, and this proved to be the decisive factor in the Allied failure to capture Caen on the first or second day. The other gap was the unexpected presence of a good quality, partly mobile field division, 352nd Infantry, on the coast, where it delayed the break-out from Omaha and Gold beaches. But the consequences of these two deficiencies may give some idea of the significance for the success of the landings of the fact that the Allies otherwise knew from Ultra—and thus knew for certain—the whereabouts of the German armoured and mobile formations and could thus calculate the rate at which the enemy could build up counter-attacks and the directions from which they must come. It is by no means certain that, without this foreknowledge, the Allies could have proceeded when they did, or would have succeeded if they had proceeded. At the least, Ultra was prominent among the factors which undermined Germany's assumption that she had accumulated an adequate force against the landings.

The order of battle evidence, however crucial, forms only a part of the contribution made by Ultra to the success of Overlord. The decrypts were eloquent on other matters which only Ultra could reveal. They showed that, despite their growing anxiety about Normandy and their inclination to believe that the invasion would come in June, the Germans remained radically uncertain as to its place and time; and, while this was partly due to the Allied deception programme, that programme itself depended on Ultra's information about the enemy's appreciations. It threw much light on the preparations the Germans were making against the landings; on the exact areas of their mine-laying, especially in the Seine Bay; their plans for deploying the U-boats; their army chain of command; the state and strength of their Air Force; the condition of some of their offensive divisions; their fuel and manpower shortages. This advance knowledge was all the more valuable, moreover, because, although the naval and air Enigma showed that the landings had achieved tactical surprise, there was no Ultra about the German Army during the first critical forty-eight hours of the assault. Von Rundstedt's non-Morse link had temporarily ceased to be readable and the new Army Enigma keys were not read regularly until 17 June, by which date the bridgehead, as we can now see, had been secured. Between 8 and 17 June, however, decrypts of the German Air Force keys used by the Army–Air Force liaison officers and the parachute formations enabled the Allies to avert two serious threats. On the morning of 10 June they located the headquarters of the enemy's armoured striking force (Panzer Gruppe West), and its destruction later that day by air attack finally extinguished the German hopes for a concentrated counter-attack that would split the bridgehead in two. On 12 June they gave the advance warning which enabled

1st US Army to repulse the counter-attack south-west of Carentan by which the Germans had hoped to prevent the Americans from cutting off the Cotentin peninsula.

The volume of Ultra grew enormously from 18 June and particularly from the beginning of August, after the Allied break-out from Normandy. The destruction of German land-lines on all fronts kept it at a high level till the end of the war. But it was never again to be so valuable, either for its frequent vital contributions to operational intelligence or for its more pervasive influence on planning and strategic decisions. In the last nine months of the war, indeed, the Allies suffered operational set-backs like Arnhem and strategic reverses like Germany's Ardennes offensive which they might have avoided if Ultra had been more carefully considered; and strategic opportunities were missed which, like a more forceful prosecution of the bombing offensive against Germany's oil resources, might have shortened the war if the significance of the intelligence had not been disputed. But consideration of what Ultra might have accomplished in the last months of the war is irrelevant to an assessment of the consequences of the influence it had previously exerted.

In attempting that assessment we may at once dismiss the claim that Ultra by itself won the war. The British survived with little benefit from it before Germany invaded the Soviet Union in June 1941, as the Soviets survived the first German offensives without any benefit from it, so far as we know; and since those offensives were followed by the entry of the United States into the war in December 1941 we may safely conclude that the Allies would have won even if Ultra had not given them by that time the superiority in intelligence which they retained till the end of the war. But the end was then three and a half years away—such a length of time that we might be persuaded to jump to the opposite extreme and conclude that, far from producing on its own the Axis defeat, Ultra made only a marginal contribution to it. This second conclusion, however, can be equally firmly dismissed. To the question, why did Ultra not shorten the war, the answer is that it did.

By how much did it do so? In addressing that question we have to suppose that Ultra had not existed, and we cannot escape the risk of hypothesis and speculation which is inseparable from counter-factual history. But we can limit the risk if we depart as little as possible from the historical reconstruction of Ultra's actual impact. Even if it did not keep Rommel out of Egypt at the end of 1941 by its decisive contribution to the outcome of the Crusader offensive, as it probably did, it certainly did so in the summer of 1942, when it alone prevented Rommel from exploiting his victory at Gazala. And even if the Allies had still gone forward with the landings in French North Africa that autumn, the loss of Egypt, which would also have eliminated Malta, would surely have set back the conquest of North Africa and the reopening of the Mediterranean by at least a year—from May 1943 to at least the summer of 1944—and necessitated the deferment of Overlord.

The Allies might alternatively have cancelled those landings, turning their backs on the Mediterranean, and sought the earliest possible invasion across the Channel, which in any case always had priority in American thinking. But what would have been the prospects for that undertaking if Ultra had not existed? If Ultra alone had not prevented the U-boats from dominating the Atlantic in the last six months of 1941? If, after performing the same service again in the winter of 1942–3, it had not contributed heavily first to the defeat of the U-boats in the Atlantic in April and May 1943 and then to the Allied success in so crippling the U-boat command during the second half of 1943 that it could never return to the convoy routes? In the rate of shipbuilding and the destruction of U-boats, the Allies would no doubt have prevailed in the end. But they would not have prevailed in time to launch Overlord in 1944, and it is not unreasonable to believe that, even if it had been given priority over the clearance of the Mediterranean, Overlord would have had to be deferred till 1946.

It may be argued that, if only by stripping resources from the Pacific, this delay could have been shortened. But if the U-boats had delayed the invasion only by months, till the spring of 1945, other considerations would have come into play. As it was, the invasion of Normandy was carried out on such tight margins in 1944 that it would have been impracticable—or would have failed—without the precise and reliable intelligence provided by Ultra about German strengths and order of battle. Carried out in 1945, it would have failed more decisively—or, more likely, these other considerations would have necessitated further delay. Germany's V-weapon offensive against the United Kingdom, and especially against some of the invasion ports along the south coast, would have been in full swing, creating immense destruction throughout southern England. She would have finished the Atlantic Wall. From early in 1945, as Ultra revealed, she would have brought into service revolutionary new U-boats and jet and rocket aircraft. And, unless the Allies had incurred delays by undertaking diversionary operations, she would not have had to disperse large forces to hold a Mediterranean or a Norwegian front.

If not in these last directions then at least in others the Western Allies would not have been idle in these circumstances. Who can say what different strategies they would have pursued? Would the Soviets meanwhile have defeated Germany, or Germany the Soviets, or would there have been stalemate on the eastern fronts? What would have been decided about the atom bomb? Not even counter-factual historians can answer such questions. They are questions which do not arise, because the war went as it did. But those historians who are concerned only with the war as it was must ask why it went as it did. And they need venture only a reasonable distance beyond the facts to recognize the extent to which the explanation lies in the influence of Ultra.

PART ONE
The production of Ultra intelligence

1. Life in and out of Hut 3

WILLIAM MILLWARD

I ARRIVED on the doorstep of Bletchley Park (alias BP or War Station or Station X) on the afternoon of 1 April 1942.

From my present octogenarian watchtower I can perceive that this was a turning-point in my life, from a profession that was not quite in line with my capabilities to one that was: from teaching to intelligence. I sometimes think that the divinity that shapes our ends had been shaping mine with this change in view.

'Intelligence' refers to both skill and end-product. As a meaningful concept it has been spoilt by Fleming, le Carré, and many other less talented writers. In the present context I would define it as the method employed by Sherlock Holmes; not the sleuth on the trail with his magnifying glass, but the intellectual sitting quietly and consuming his ounce of shag. It means reviewing known facts, sorting out significant from insignificant, assessing them severally and jointly, and arriving at a conclusion by the exercise of judgement: part induction, part deduction. Absolute intellectual honesty is essential. The process must not be muddied by emotion or prejudice, nor by a desire to please. The skill is largely innate, but can be sharpened by a course of rigorous academic training. The Americans talk about 'intelligence analysis' and 'analysts' and the terminology is crossing the Atlantic. It is not ideal, since the process is as much synthesis as analysis.

After reading 'German with French' at Oxford, graduating in 1930, teaching at Dulwich College, adding Spanish to my languages, and getting married, I was commissioned in the RAF in August 1941. After training I was attached to 10 Group, Fighter Command, as Intelligence Officer, and served at Group Headquarters near Bath; at sector level (Portreath and Exeter); at station level (Predannack, night-fighters); and with a Czech squadron at Perranporth.

One day, when I was at Exeter, came a signal that I was to report forthwith to a named Squadron Leader at the Air Ministry. While I was waiting in his office a portly Group Captain came in flourishing a handful of papers and saying in a loud voice, 'He's no good, I don't want him, send him away.' My turn was next, and I wondered whether I should suffer the same fate. However, all was friendly and encouraging. I learnt later that the interviewer was one Group Captain Humphreys. He conducted the interview chiefly in Spanish, with an occasional break into German. I shall never know whether the Spanish was showing off on his part or to test the accuracy of my c.v. I left without any idea of what 'it' was all about or where it happened.

A fortnight or so later I was again bidden to the Air Ministry, to an almost identical experience. The interviewer was this time a Mr Cooper. I already knew his line of country, since he had lectured on an intelligence course I attended on the RAF Y Service. He gave me a relatively easy piece of German to translate at sight and nodded approval when I translated *Rundfunk* as 'broadcasting'. He told me that I was quite the most suitable person he had interviewed for some time. I was to be given some training and sent abroad. This was most unwelcome. My wife was recovering from a second miscarriage and needed all the support I could give. So I told him of my interview with Group Captain Humphreys. Came a pause, which I can only describe as pregnant. He then said, 'I know Group Captain Humphreys; I will speak to him,' and I was dismissed.

Back at Exeter I resumed my normal duties. A couple of weeks later, in the evening just as I was going on night duty, came a signal that I was to report immediately to the Air Ministry for service with Air Intelligence branch. I immediately consulted my superiors, who told me that they wanted to keep me and would try to have the posting cancelled; meanwhile I was to carry on as usual. Next morning they told me that I had encountered some very big guns indeed, and go I must. This time the trail led to a nondescript building which I later came to know as Broadway, near one of the entrances to St James's Park Underground. The lower floors were typical austere wartime, but the fourth floor, my destination, had red carpet and soft lights, and an air of comfort. I was paraded before an anonymous wing commander, who apparently only wanted to see my face. I found out later that this was Winterbotham, nominally my Commanding Officer. I was told to get into the shooting brake standing outside, and I should be driven 'there'. The driver at first refused to take my suitcase as well as me, being allegedly full up. The suitcase contained all my possessions and I insisted, and he finally agreed. We headed north up the A5, with me watching the route and surmising where we were going. We turned left at Fenny Stratford and had arrived.

The Security Officer on the gate used his telephone and summoned up a WRAF officer, with whom I had the following short colloquy:

ME. Who's got me; Humphreys or Cooper?
SHE. Humphreys.
ME. Thank Heavens.

She led me across a noble lawn, with on the left a Tudorbethan mansion, on the right a large lake; in front a group of wooden huts, our destination. In a small office in one of them I found Humphreys with his feet on the table—rheumatism, I was assured, not discourtesy. Since my interview with him there had been a revolution in Hut 3 next door, where I was to work, and Humphreys was on his way out. The three service officers formerly in charge had been eased out, perhaps because they had difficulty in agreeing with each other. Humphreys had lingered longer than the others, but I never saw him again. He handed me over to the officer in temporary charge of the RAF element in the Hut, one Squadron Leader Mapplebeck, who was soon also to disappear. He began my initiation, to be completed over the next few days by others. (It should be noted that the hut numbers not only designated the huts themselves, but were also used as cover-names for the work going on in them. When, towards the end of the war, the Hut 3 work was transferred to a brick building, it was still called 'Hut 3'.)

In my initiation stress was laid on the value of the work going out from Hut 3. It was 'the heart of the matter' and of immense importance and I was lucky to be associated with it: absolutely true. The cipher machine in universal use in the German Service, the Enigma, had been mastered; signals passing over interceptable channels in this cipher were being read in considerable quantity, and had already had a considerable influence on the course of the war. The process up to the production of 'raw' decrypts was carried out in Hut 6 next door. It was the task of Hut 3 to evaluate them and put the intelligence they contained into a form suitable for passing to the competent authorities, be they Ministries or Commands. I was to undergo a period of training, the method in use being 'sitting by Nellie'—that is, I was to accompany an experienced practitioner and he would show me how it was all done.

As befits a production unit, Hut 3 was set up like a miniature factory. At its centre was the Watch Room—in the middle a circular or horseshoe shaped table, to one side a rectangular table. On the outer rim of the circular table sat the Watch, some half-dozen people. The man in charge, the head of the Watch or Number 1, sat in an obvious directing position at the top of the table. The watchkeepers were a mixture of civilians, and serving officers, Army and RAF. I cannot remember any women involved in this part of the operation, presumably because it was still thought to be wrong for a woman to work on the night shift or because it was thought to be a man's job. At the rectangular table sat serving officers, Army and RAF, one or two of each. These were the Advisers. Behind the head of Watch was a door communicating with a small room where the Duty Officer sat. Elsewhere in the Hut were one large room housing the Index and a number of small rooms for the various supporting parties, the back rooms.

The processes to which the decrypts were submitted were, consecutively, emendation, translation, evaluation, commenting, and signal drafting. The first two were the responsibility of the Watch, the remainder of the appropriate Adviser. (I was a watchkeeper for the first couple of months, subsequently an Air Adviser).

The pieces of paper coming in from Hut 6 had on one side the original encoded text, on the other the decode, still in five-letter groups, in the form of gummed strip. 'Emendation' meant the division of the groups into German words or numbers, etc., and as far as possible the reading of corrupt passages and the filling of gaps. The skill was not unlike solving a crossword puzzle, and some people developed an amazing subconscious facility. An example: after the division into words, a short piece of text read: *die schon . e . a . . . . . Me 109 G4* ('the already—Me 109 G4'). The emender rendered the missing word on the basis of the two surviving letters and the force of 'already' as *veraltete* ('obsolescent'). This caused much discussion. The Me 109 G had only recently replaced the F variant. Could it be obsolescent already? The solution found with the help of an Adviser was most probably correct: the obsolescence applied only to the variant indicated by the '4'. The emendation was allowed to stand but qualified by a 'C%'. (The % sign was used to indicate reliability, or lack of it:

B% indicated some margin of doubt, C% caution if not confirmed, D% largely guesswork. In practice the recipients seem to have ignored the qualification.)

The next process was translation. This was mostly straightforward. New technical terms sometimes gave trouble. We had our back-room language expert in Trevor Jones, and he maintained a glossary of new terms as they appeared, having researched their meaning. Just occasionally he was defeated. I can remember his going round for several days with a worried look on his face murmuring *Drehkreuzachse*. I have forgotten whether he ever solved that problem and what the word meant in that context. Sometimes the exact flavour of a German word was important. Strength and stock returns, especially from North Africa, often finished with the statement that the situation was *untragbar*. Literally the word meant 'unbearable'; we translated it as 'intolerable'. Both renderings are too strong. The weight of the German word is probably best caught by 'unacceptable', but of course this changes the metaphor.

Before passing on his work, the watchkeeper had to devise and incorporate a notional source, so as to conceal the Enigma machine's vulnerability. Only a few people were told the true source, at least in the early days, and the idea was to put readers off as long as possible. The notional sources included many wastepaper baskets, drunken sailors, etc. Unreadable passages or gaps were ascribed to blots. Initially it proved a successful device: for example, in late 1939, when the first breaks occurred, one report included aircraft markings, allegedly seen by a little man looking over an airfield fence. It provoked an excited reaction from the Air Ministry officer concerned with order of battle, and precise and detailed instructions were given on what the little man was to look out for. Later the practice degenerated into little more than a gesture.

Having finished one task, the watchkeeper handed his work to Number 1, who carefully checked it and passed it to the appropriate Adviser. The watchkeeper then helped himself to a new task. It was customary to sort decodes as they arrived into piles according to priorities, and the new task would come from the highest priority pile.

The first task of the Adviser was to determine what new intelligence the message contained, and its significance. For example, in a long message the only point of interest might be the location of a flying unit, say a *Gruppe*, the equivalent of an RAF Wing. The Adviser would check with the Index. If the location was known already, its value might be slight. It would be greater if the location was new; greatest of all if, in the context, it might have strategic significance. The Adviser would insert a comment quoting what was known of recent movements of the unit and what significance attached to an apparent move. His justification was that his work obviated its being done again by the various recipients. Just occasionally he was able to perceive a most important development and draw attention to it. In the autumn of 1944 the closure of certain aircraft servicing units led, when collated, to a surmise that the German bomber force was being run down and the German Air Force was concentrating on fighter defence. In commenting we were supposed to restrict ourselves to our own source and to take no notice of 'collateral'. In practice, this was less of a restriction than it might be thought, since our source was far and away the most fruitful. We were, however, in close enough touch with the Air Ministry to draw their attention to possible tie-ups with 'collateral'. The volume of air intelligence was greater than that of Army intelligence, but the content, consisting more of bread-and-butter material, was less exciting. The really big stories, Alamein, etc., fell to the lot of the Army.

The remaining major task of the Advisers was to draw up a version for passing to Commands, mostly abroad, over signal channels. There were very few of these recipients when I joined. By the end of the war they numbered thirty or forty. The application of the 'need-to-know' principle and the need to take notice of Command hierarchies made distribution in itself quite an art. There were two reasons for the different version. First, the need to economize on signal space demanded concentration on essentials and the utmost brevity. Sometimes only a single fact, such as the relocation of the hypothetical *Gruppe* referred to above, would be included in a signal. Secondly, sending verbatim texts might help the enemy cryptanalysts by supplying cribs. I found it best to work afresh from the original German, but care had then to be taken not to produce discrepant versions. Finally the whole package was passed to the Duty Officer. He was in command of the Hut during his tour of duty and responsible for all 'releases'. Once they had reached the Advisers, the head of Watch had no responsibility for the output, and it fell to the Duty Office to check the Advisers' work, particularly with regard to distribution, precedence, and accuracy of the version for Commands.

Reports could be sent to London recipients by either teleprinter or bag. For Commands not well served by trunk communications, a network of hand-speed radio communications was set up, known as Special Communications Units (SCUs), provided by the Army. In the various Commands were Special Liaison Units (SLUs), provided by the RAF. Their task was security, to hold papers and control dissemination. Reports were in daily series under references of the form CX/FJ, the first digraph meaning 'agent's report', the second the responsible agent, notional or not. FJ was the first notional agent. After a short while he was killed off or otherwise disposed of by JQ. Another change took place shortly before my arrival, and JQ was replaced by MSS, who survived to the end. For signals, Commands were given an identifying digraph under which signals were numbered as originated for the particular Command. All signals were numbered as well under a general digraph which changed from time to time.

The daily rhythm was controlled by the successes of Hut 6. The commonest pattern was as follows. Keys changed at midnight and Hut 6 could start work as soon as messages started coming in from interception stations. Success with the most profitable line would be announced by late afternoon or early evening. About an hour later decodes would start to come in to Hut 3. First would come the traffic passed during the day, to be accompanied soon by the evening traffic as it was received. The evening was the busiest time for originators and our evenings could be fraught. By midnight things were beginning to slacken off, and sometimes, but not often, the trays would be empty by breakfast time. There was no sleep on the night watch unless involuntary, and no provision for it. It sounds as if there were nothing to do during the day, but this was not so. There were always left-overs to clear, belated Hut 6 successes to cope with, special problems to solve, and reading to do in order to keep up with the changing picture.

We worked in shifts on a pattern allegedly recommended by the medical authorities, its aim being to avoid painful changes in the circadian rhythm. It meant in practice destroying this rhythm. The three timings were 8 a.m. to 4 p.m., 4 p.m. to midnight, and midnight to 8 a.m. We worked the three in rapid succession, then had a longish free time. I worked these shifts for two and a half years with one week's leave a year, and have sometimes wondered whether working thus, with all the excitement and dedication which it involved, was perhaps a cause of the bad insomnia which hit me some dozen years later.

Towards the end of 1944 I gave up shift work and became deputy head of 3A. All the Air Advisers constituted 3A. The head and his deputy were responsible for reporting policy, organizing rotas, trouble-shooting, and keeping in touch with principal recipients, such as Air Ministry Intelligence (AI). Although I enjoyed working only days, I regretted losing the interest and excitement of watch work. For most of my time the head of 3A was E. J. N. (Jim) Rose, a man of great charm and ability. His deputy was Peter Calvocoressi, not unknown as a writer in post-war years. My move was caused by the transfer of Rose to Air Ministry Intelligence. Calvocoressi took his place as head of 3A and I moved in behind him. 3A was matched by a similar 3M (Military), headed for most of my time by Terry Leatham, with Alan Pryce-Jones as deputy.

Of the other back rooms, I have already mentioned Trevor Jones and his language studies. In another back room sat Professor Oscar Oeser with two graduate women assistants. As far as I can remember he was charged with a study of the techniques in use in the Hut. I remember his attempt to set up a comprehensive system of priorities driven by mathematics. Another back room housed F. L. Lucas (Peter to his friends), who was charged with the investigation of intelligence problems. He was known as a writer (*The Decline and Fall of the Romantic Ideal*), came from King's College, Cambridge, and was an 'Apostle' and our Guru. He probably produced the intelligence studies which, although outside our charter, were none the less welcome. Such a one was the study of German intentions in the early summer of 1941. It concluded that the Germans really meant to attack Russia, as against the Foreign Office view that they were building up pressure to exact more raw materials. Early in 1945, for reasons not known to me, I was charged by him with the task of investigating the complete failure of intelligence to give warning of the Ardennes counter-attack. My conclusions, I recollect, coincided with the later view of others that the signs were there but had not been brought together or evaluated correctly.

The most significant of the back rooms was the Index. It had been carefully designed by a refugee from Kelly's Directory, Wing Commander Cullingham ('Cully'). Some half-dozen young women, most of them graduates, were constantly at work. It registered everything, from every possible source, and by the end of the war had become a splendid instrument. It had two branches, corresponding to the two Services. The German Book Room had the task of compiling and typing up a daily German Book, a verbatim transcription of all the messages which had been emended, in the original language, with a record of the reporting action taken. The final process was 'squeezing the books', a close scan by the indexers for any reportable points that had been overlooked.

There was also a Day Watch, aimed at clearing the lower priorities and used as a training place. I cannot remember when it was set up. It did not impinge on the main Watch.

Three subjects were treated differently from the others. Anything with a scientific interest was extracted at the preliminary scanning stage and passed to a back room which provided a direct channel to 'ADI Science', i.e. Dr R. V. Jones. The reason for this was presumably the difficulty which the non-specialist would have encountered at the stage of evaluation. There was some contribution from the source to all the scientific problems which succeeded each other as the war progressed—navigational beams, radar, V weapons, etc. The work of Huts 6 and 3 was confined to Army and Air Force communications. For naval communications the Admiralty demanded quite different procedures, and the naval Enigma was tackled elsewhere in BP. There was, however, naturally, a certain amount of naval information in the communications of the other services, and to ensure that this was handled in a way acceptable to the Admiralty a small office manned by naval officers was housed in Hut 3. Lastly, special arrangements were made for the handling of any material which related to the success of Allied deception operations, especially important in the run-up to the Normandy landings. One other type of report was given special restricted treatment—anything that might have a 'gossipy' value with its increased risk of a leak to the 'media'. The causal case of this was a report that Rommel was ill and had returned to Germany for treatment.

The men and women of Hut 3 came from many backgrounds. Originally, a number of people, mainly academics, had been 'earmarked' in peace for this service in wartime. Bletchley Park had been acquired as a war station, and a practice mobilization had been carried out at the time of Munich. Many academics, either of this first wave or subseqently recruited, were still there when I arrived. Others had moved into back-room posts or left, being perhaps too used to and fond of controversy. My arrival was part of a second wave, many of which had been found by the process which produced me, a trawl through service records. In this wave were schoolmasters, business men, and odd bodies including an actor. It would be invidious to put the various professions in any order of usefulness, but teaching was certainly one of the best contributors. The agreement with the Americans, on their entry into the war, that the exploitation of Enigma traffic should be concentrated at BP, brought a reinforcement of American officers. There were never more than two or three on the air side of Hut 3, but they fitted in smoothly and made a good contribution. I am often asked if I knew the 'spy' John Cairncross. The answer is, 'Yes, I did.' But my acquaintance was fleeting and in memory limited to a single conversation, in which he told me that he had kept his roots in London and travelled up and down. I cannot recollect his ever appearing on the main watch. I found out later that he had transferred to the Secret Intelligence Service (SIS). My only reaction was 'nice work if you can get it'. I suspected nothing at the time, nor do I recollect any suggestion by others that he was doing anything improper. There was never any conspiracy of silence.

The interwar peacetime organization, GC&CS, had been part of the complex which also contained the SIS (or M.I.6). The head of GC&CS reported to the head of the whole complex, commonly known as C. The parent Ministry was the Foreign Office. Constitutionally Hut 3 was part of GC&CS and retained its relationship with the SIS. AI 1C, to which I belonged, was the AI (Air Intelligence) party detached to work with the SIS. One consequence was that we were paid London rates of allowance, unlike other RAF officers of different subordination, and this caused some jealousy.

Soon after my arrival the chain of command was clarified by the appointment as Head of Hut of Eric Jones, later to become one of the rare non-flying group captains, and in 1952, as Sir Eric Jones, Director of GCHQ. Jones reported to the Director, Travis, and through him to C. His qualifications for the post were not immediately apparent. He was a wholesale cloth merchant from Macclesfield and came to us after a spell in Air Ministry Intelligence. But he had the qualities of principle, strength of character, and a firm grasp of essentials which enabled him to settle most of the tiresome intrigues and controversies which, as I gathered, had in the recent past disturbed the smooth running of the Hut. He was ably supported by two people: F. L. Lucas, who advised him on Intelligence matters, and his deputy, Bill (Sir Herbert) Marchant, who placed his diplomatic qualities at Jones's disposal. I cannot resist telling an anecdote which illustrates the relationship between these two. A staff officer in Cairo was appointed to liaise with Hut 3. He did one piece of work, and Jones drafted an ambiguous signal which read: 'Delighted first fruits your liaison.' Marchant fielded it.

This pattern of organization did not apply to all parts of BP. Other activities came directly under the Service Ministries. The rationale of the Park as a whole was to concentrate in one place all activities in what came, under American influence, to be called 'signals intelligence' or 'sigint'. Both the Air Ministry and the War Office had establishments elsewhere which dealt with the tactical communications of the opposing forces, but in both cases the appropriate body at BP tended to take over some of their responsibilities as experience was gained. BP thus became a sort of university of signals intelligence, developing techniques which all might share. The formal organization of the whole was of less importance. However, the sharing process was sometimes thwarted by the 'need-to-know' principle. In view of the importance of security, the fences round Huts 3 and 6 were rather higher than some others. Sometimes this was bad for morale. Thus the decoding in Hut 6 was done by Wrens who were not allowed to know the relevance of what they were doing. There was a need to give them a pep talk from time to time without telling them much about the value of their material, an almost impossible task.

We still had some private life during these years. Shortly after my arrival at BP the end-shaper produced one of his happiest tricks. I discovered that Spanish linguists were wanted, a description which fitted my wife. She came at once to Bletchley and was interviewed by the head of Naval Section, Frank Birch, alias the Widow Twankey, because of his appearances in pantomime at the London Palladium in 1930. After the interview and before I had made contact with her, I ran into Frank Birch. He shouted across a large flower bed, 'She'll do.' and so, to the great content of both of us, we were able to continue living together until the end of the war in Europe. In the summer of 1945 I took part in the interrogation of the *Oberkommando der Luftwaffe* at Berchtesgaden, before returning to Bletchley. In 1958 I became Superintending Director of GCHQ, the post of Deputy Director having disappeared.

I am sometimes asked questions of the pattern: 'What was your most (adjective) experience?'—the adjective being a word such as 'exciting' or 'embarrassing'. Here are some answers:

Daunting: My first night as Senior Air Adviser, all by myself. It coincided with Operation Torch, the landings in North and north-west Africa. I had to cope with streams of air reconnaissance reports. Problem: should I pass these sightings to Commands? Would they find them of value or would they simply clutter up the signal channels? I decided to pass them on, and was not criticized for doing so; it cannot have been very wrong therefore.

Shameful: I invented a place called Senke, next door to Qatara. It is of course the ordinary German word for a geographical 'depression'.

Depressing: A one-off decrypt of a German intercept of a Russian message soon after the launch of the attack to the south-east in 1943 stated that 'the enemy was in Izyum'. Depression came when I discovered this place was well to the south-east of Kharkov. I did not, of course, then know that this was on the way to Stalingrad.

Valuable: The messages giving course and composition of the convoys taking supplies to Rommel in North Africa. These convoys and their surface escorts were Italian, the air escorts German. The messages were from the German liaison officer with the Italian Navy. It has been stated authoritatively that if these convoys, especially the tankers, had got through, Rommel must have driven Eighth Army out of North Africa. Destruction of the convoys was almost total. The affair illustrates to what extent the Enigma product could be used in operations. The rule was that other sources had to be available to which the intelligence could be ascribed. A sighting by reconnaissance aircraft was therefore essential, but the aircraft knew where to look. There was one worrying occasion when destroyers were sent to intercept a convoy without this safeguard, and the convoy was cancelled. As far as I know, this was the only occasion when a message was intercepted doubting the security of the Enigma cipher. Churchill is said to have sent a stinging rebuke to the Commander-in-Chief (Mediterranean). M.I.6 contrived a notional agent in one of the Adriatic ports. There was no follow-up by the Germans; their faith in the Enigma cipher remained unshaken to the end. I sometimes wonder, especially during the night, how many sailors I drowned. But *à la guerre comme à la guerre*.

Exciting: The night during Alamein when a long report from Rommel to Hitler showed that he had been comprehensively defeated and wanted permission to withdraw. I remember one phrase: *Panzerarmee ist erschöpft* ('The Panzer Army is exhausted').

2. The Duty Officer, Hut 3

RALPH BENNETT

Looking back, I can see that I joined Hut 3 at a turning-point both in the history of the Hut and in the history of British intelligence. In early 1941 no one could foresee that within twelve months Enigma would surpass all other sources and become the means of raising intelligence to a position in the directing of war which it had never held before. Nothing, indeed, seemed less likely to house great matters than the ramshackle wooden building (its atmosphere nauseating at night when the black-out imprisoned the fumes from leaky coke-burning stoves) to which I reported in February 1941. Yet within weeks its rise had begun, in consequence of breaks into first German Air Force and then Army keys by Hut 6; Hut 4 followed us a few months later, when Hut 8 broke the naval Enigma.

With war looming, Alistair Denniston had called for the recruitment of 'men of the professor type' to GC&CS. Conditioned by his 1914–18 and subsequent experience, he was thinking mainly of cryptographers, but also of translators. In Room 40 the former had lorded it over the latter, seen merely as necessary adjuncts; both were subordinate to regular naval officers. With cryptography now a separate department, 'professor-type' academic German scholars staffed Hut 3 when the first Enigma breaks occurred in May 1940, and this was still the state of affairs in the New Year. Since the invasion scare of September 1940, the only operational decrypts were from the beam-bombers' key, Brown, which was already the specialist province of Professor 'Bimbo' Norman in Hut 3 and Dr R. V. Jones at the Air Ministry.

What was eventually to prove a revolutionary change was heralded in January, when Light Blue, the German Air Force Mediterranean key, was added to the regular daily Red breaks. Wavell had just driven the Italians humiliatingly out of Libya; Hitler came to their aid, and Rommel landed in Tripoli in mid-February (on the same day as I arrived at Bletchley Park; I like to think that the conjunction was foreordained!). A month later Hut 3 was suddenly empowered to signal useful intelligence direct to Wavell in Cairo. This was an unprecedented step. Not foreseeing what they were letting escape from their control, it is to be presumed, the War Office and the Air Ministry allowed a Secret Service organization, hitherto staffed mainly by civilians, to handle operational intelligence.

Who was to judge what the Army and Air Force in Egypt might find useful, and who was to compose the signals? Small parties from the two Services, closely linked to the War Office and the Air Ministry by telephone, were already attached to the translation watch, and so the work naturally fell to them. A new member of the military section, a young Cambridge don with four months in an Officer Cadet Training Unit as my sole remotely military experience, my German acquired during a year's study of medieval history at Munich University—I was ill-qualified for the task which thus unexpectedly came my way. The other Military and Air Advisers (as we now came to be called) were no better prepared. Yet we were now to be the channel along which passed the intelligence which was to transform the basis of all operational planning.

By the autumn the War Office and the Air Ministry were beginning to regret their blindness of the spring: Greece, Crete, and the desert had shown what Ultra could do, and we had taught ourselves the job of intelligence officers tolerably well. But tensions in Whitehall were reflected in tensions within the Hut, and something like chaos sometimes reigned during the winter of 1941–2 under a regime of divided control. A complete reorganization in the spring restored a most welcome order. Under the firm but understanding rule of Wing Commander (later Group Captain Sir Eric) Jones, we could concentrate on our work undisturbed by internal conflict, and, by the time of Alamein (October 1942) the value of Ultra was becoming widely recognized.

At about the same time the flow of work and the division of labour within the Hut was gradually settling into its final pattern.

Decodes ('decrypts' according to modern usage, but the word was not used in the 1940s) arrived from Hut 6 in a trickle or a flood, depending on the number of keys 'running' at a given moment and how recent the break was. Hot off the decoding machines, they reached us in batches which went straight to the Number One of the translating watch on duty (the whole Hut worked round the clock in eight-hour shifts). The Number Ones became adept at instantly distinguishing the more from the less urgent in a handful of unemended and sometimes badly corrupt decodes, and distributed them among their team accordingly.

As soon as the Number One was satisfied that the missing letters and corrupt groups of a message had been sensibly reconstructed and that the whole had been fairly rendered into English, he handed it (according to its main tenor) to the Military or the Air Adviser, who sat at the next table in the crowded Watch Room. Elucidating the meaning from the voluminous indexes kept for the purpose, the Adviser would append notes to the translation (now on the way to becoming a teleprint) and draft an appropriate signal.

This was frequently a quite straightforward task: perhaps a particular division was moving from one sector of the front to another. But sometimes intricate problems arose. A former senior Military Adviser remembers puzzling over a very corrupt decode which mentioned 21st Panzer Division (half of Rommel's striking force in the desert) until he suddenly realized that a corrupt word could plausibly be emended to read *Auffrischung* ('rest and refit'). Having secured the assent of the Number One to the translation, he sent a signal on the lines of '(Fair indications) 21st Panzer to be withdrawn . . .'. (The alternative expressions of doubt were 'slight' or 'strong' indications.) On another occasion he deduced the possible replacement of Rommel at a time when he was known to be ill, from an apparently trivial message announcing that a room had been booked in a Rome hotel for a general last identified on the central Russian front. By a piece of insightful detective work, another Military Adviser sensed a connection between three outwardly unrelated messages and predicted the timing and route of Kesselring's final attempt to dislodge the Anzio bridgehead in February 1944, thus (but we did not know this until later) authoritatively contradicting an agent's report of a quite different route. Labour could on occasion be spent in vain, however. In the summer of 1942 Military Advisers and the topographical department agonized repeatedly over the arbitrary 'thrust lines' along which Rommel ordered his attacks, because they could not be correlated with British map references—it was frustrating not to know the time and direction of a forthcoming attack about which much else was known. Yet the Y Service in the desert was quite familiar with thrust lines and could usually discover their location. More frequent exchange of information would have saved time and increased efficiency, but this did not come until later.

So long as the war in Africa lasted, there was also a Naval Adviser. Hut 3 did not deal in naval intelligence as such; but the German Air Force provided escort for the Italian convoys which carried Rommel's supplies. Hut 4 had no direct communication with the Middle East (it fed the Admiralty, which signalled naval headquarters), but it had recently broken the Italian C 38m machine cipher, which carried shipping information. Between them, these two were mutually complementary sources of news about the convoys' routes and their estimated times of departure and arrival at designated ports. The combination was the basis of Ultra's first great contribution to the Mediterranean war. By the late summer of 1941 so many supply ships had been sunk that Axis operations were severely curtailed and indeed faced complete strangulation. For a variety of reasons pressure had to be relaxed during the winter, but the selective sinking of named tankers which Rommel was known to need to keep his armour on the move halted his last thrust towards the Nile at Alam Halfa in September and gravely handicapped him at Alamein in October.

When an Adviser had done all that he thought necessary, he passed everything to the Duty Officer through the glass hatch in the wall which separated his room from the Watch Room. The post of Duty Officer was an innovation of the 1942 shake-up, and proved to be the coping-stone of the Hut 3 edifice. I was one of four officers (three for the Army and one for the Air Force) who occupied the position for the rest of the war.

The Duty Officer's job was to draw together all the threads of Hut 3's intelligence activity, taking if possible a broader view of it than the specialism of an Adviser might permit, and to be responsible for everything. Nothing could be teleprinted to the Service Ministries, nothing signalled to Commands in the field, without his authorization. There were no formal bounds to his responsibilities, but he 'carried the can' if ever there were a can to be carried. His most important duties fell under two heads.

First, to satisfy himself that the papers in front of him faithfully reproduced the sense of the information in the original German, and of a soundly based interpretation of it if this was not self-evident; and also that the draft signal did not, by uncautious wording, inadvertently imply more or less than was warranted. The signal should tell recipients, who might use it in operations at once, all that we knew in unambiguous language of complete objectivity, with any explanatory comment of ours clearly distinguished from the telegraphese summary of the text. (This objectivity was facilitated by the fact that, until the last few months, we were told nothing of the fighting). To give a very simple example: when reporting a forthcoming air raid on a British position, it was essential to state the authority originating the order and the time at which the order was given. A lower authority's plans might be countermanded by its superior (e.g. a division's by its parent corps); a later order (which the Y Service in the field might have failed to intercept) would supersede an earlier one. A comment might draw attention to a recent similar occasion, where perhaps subsequent instructions had detailed a single *Gruppe* of thirty aircraft to carry out the raid.

The Duty Officer's second main responsibility was for security. Nothing must be said in signal or teleprint which might reveal the source; Ultra was far too valuable a prize to risk losing through a moment's carelessness. (A similar prohibition bound Ultra users, of course). Closely allied to this was the application of the 'need-to-know' rule: signals must be sent only to those who could use them in action. Those who might have merely an interest in them, however close the interest, were to be rigidly excluded. The Duty Officer addressed signals accordingly, observing any current directions fitted to particular circumstances and following the standard practice that, for instance, what went to Eighth Army went also to General Headquarters Cairo, and that Army and Air Force authorities which habitually co-operated were kept informed on an 'all-or-none' basis. When in 1944 there were forty or fifty possible addressees in two theatres of war, this was a considerable task in itself. Finally, the Duty Officer had to prevent over-enthusiastic Advisers from claiming excessive priority for their wares, lest the special wireless channels allotted for our sole use become overloaded and clogged, thus causing damaging delays.

Quiet reflection by the Duty Officer on all these matters before he passed signal and teleprint to the Signals Officer for onward transmission was promoted by his relative separation from the continual buzz of the Watch Room. An occasional few moments of peace kept one alert. There were many decisions to be pondered over in almost every signal, particularly if (as was usual during the last twelve months of the war) critical operations were taking place in two theatres at the same time, so that constant vigilance and rapid changes of focus were necessary—not to speak of a great deal of background reading (sixteen hours of one's predecessors' work) to be assimilated quickly at the beginning of each shift.

This account of the production flow of urgent operational intelligence has so far made no reference to the Military Section, to which I had originally belonged, or the far larger Air Section. This is because, in the strictest sense, they were outside that flow, although closely bound to it. Operational intelligence did not pass through them, but they provided it with indispensable nourishment. From one point of view they were the powerhouses of knowledge, driving the whole forward through the high-class specialist reference libraries which their indexes represented; from another they were the gleaners who came after the harvesters, garnering grains of information which had escaped notice and also acting as channels of communication to courts of appeal.

The Military and Air Advisers who owed them allegiance could not have performed their tasks without the elaborate indexes over which ATS, WAAFs, and civilian girls laboured tirelessly, never more than a few hours behind the moving front of events, meticulously recording even the minutest details mentioned in Enigma decodes. I seem to recall, to illustrate what the indexes could do (but can memory be accurate after fifty years?), that a pointer to the location of the research establishment for V1s and V2s was discovered from a message of 1942 or early 1943 indicating that a junior *Luftwaffe* NCO, known to have belonged in 1940–1 to an experimental signals regiment supporting the beam-bombers, had now been assigned for duty at a place named Peenemünde on the Baltic (perhaps to track the early rockets?).

In their other capacity the heads of the Service sections scrutinized each day's output and offered the Duty Officer draft signals culled from items which had been overlooked in the first rush, or which arose from the subsequent juxtaposition of items hitherto treated in isolation. They were in daily, sometimes hourly, contact by telephone with the War Office and the Air Ministry, who were in possession of more information about orders of battle, for example, and were therefore treated as courts of appeal on tricky matters like the affiliation of regiments from one number series to divisions numbered in a different series.

Behind these front-line troops there stood a number of specialist parties whose support was indispensable but which seldom took the limelight. The work of a few may be briefly outlined.

Fragments of recondite scientific vocabulary turned up from time to time, as did freshly-minted names for radar parts and other newly invented equipment. When Watch and Advisers were baffled to devise plausible equivalents, they had recourse to one or other of our two 'walking dictionaries', men whose capacious memories stored up obscure linguistic learning and who showed a remarkable gift for verbal invention. (Both were choleric men who did not bear contradiction with equanimity!).

Another section undertook longer-term research. It found clues linking the 'consignment numbers' of eastbound trains on the German State Railways in early 1941 with particular divisions, was able to demonstrate a massive movement of troops towards the Russian frontier, and so to predict that Hitler would soon attack his ally of the last two years. Later it broke the code under which units of Panzer Army Africa addressed each other by animal names when using the radio, and elucidated the subheadings of the changing proformas used for supply and ammunition returns and for reports of the battle-worthiness of tanks and other armoured fighting vehicles of different types. This last could be of enormous operational value if either side happened to be about to open an offensive.

As the number of Enigma keys which could be broken increased, they bred competition for bombe time before there were enough bombes (see Glossary) to satisfy all needs. It was, therefore, desirable to establish priorities between keys and to make sure that those which produced the most valuable information were decided first. A small party was set up to handle these matters. A notable example of the need occurred in the months before Operation Torch, the descent on the north-west African coast, which took place in November 1942. In January each *Fliegerkorps* had been allotted its own Enigma key; all were quickly broken, including Locust, that of *Fliegerkorps* II in the western Mediterranean. Since little of importance was happening there at that time, Locust was given only low priority on the bombes and on some days was squeezed out altogether. As Torch approached, the western Mediterranean attracted more attention, and Whitehall asked Hut 6 to give Locust greater priority. This gave an immediate intelligence yield: *Fliegerkorps* II was shown to be lending aircraft to the eastern Mediterranean Command up to seventy-two hours before the landings—i.e. it (and therefore other German authorities) had no inkling of the destination of the Torch convoys and the need to search for them.

Messages without addressee or signature were sometimes received; obviously each was self-evident to those concerned, but a signal could not carry much weight without either. Study of the external radio characteristics of such a message could show that, say, it had passed between the Afrika Korps and Rommel, or between the latter and his superior, Kesselring. Another party kept Advisers and Duty Officers informed of such things; a signal might then read 'Strong indications 1200 hours tenth Kesselring ordered . . .'

The very important research party linking Professor Norman in Hut 3 with Dr R. V. Jones at the Air Ministry has already been mentioned. There were several others.

A new Army–Air Force co-operation key, Scorpion, came into use when Rommel began his great drive eastwards from Gazala through Tobruk towards the Nile in May 1942. It contained much 'hot' operational news; it was easy to break, for the daily settings could be predicted in advance. It was decided to radio them from Hut 6 to Cairo and to send an experienced officer out to compose signals on the spot. I was that officer from October 1942 until March 1943; the work was interesting and presumably useful at first, but Rommel's retreat eventually carried the transmissions too far away to be intercepted. My temporary absence meant that among much else I missed the fierce indignation and dismay felt throughout the hut at Montgomery's painfully slow advance from Alamein to Tripoli, incomprehensible in the light of the mass of Ultra intelligence showing that throughout his retreat Rommel was too weak to withstand serious pressure. He had only eleven tanks on 9 November and still no more than fifty-four a month later, so that Montgomery, with 270 tanks in X Corps, including fifty-two Grants and Shermans in 7 Armoured Division alone, might have annihilated him either before he reached the Libyan frontier or when he took refuge behind the Mersa Brega defences in December, instead of delaying outside the Brega position on the pretext that Rommel had a hundred tanks and might mount a counter-offensive just as he had done in the same place a year earlier. His delay seemed to cast doubt on the whole point of our work.

Before long, however, there was something for the old hands in

Hut 3 to savour: an intelligence revenge, so to say, for Crete. Only six weeks after our very first signal in March 1941, Ultra had given Wavell the German Air Force's complete plan for the invasion of Crete, and had done so a fortnight before the air landings on 20 May. So many parachutists were killed in the first moments that Hitler never used them in their proper role again. The island was lost none the less, because Wavell had no reinforcements to send, so that the attack was stronger than the defence. Dramatic attention had been drawn to Ultra's potentialities, but it had not helped in battle. Now, nearly two years later, the defeat was avenged. Having dealt the Americans a blow at Kasserine in February 1943, Rommel turned quickly about and planned to attack Eighth Army, which had just reached Medenine on its way to Tunis. Ultra revealed his intentions a week before he put them into effect. Montgomery massed six hundred anti-tank guns at the precise point where he said he would strike, knocked out fifty tanks in quick time, and won a total victory. Rommel left Africa for good three days later. Intelligence is useless unless there is force to take advantage of it; now the force was at last available. As Churchill said, Alamein was 'the end of the beginning'; Medenine neatly drove the lesson home.

After my return it slowly dawned on me that this was a symptom of the tremendous changes which had occurred during my absence. Until Alam Halfa (September 1942) we had always been hoping for proper recognition of the value of our product; now the recognition was a fact of life, and we had to go on deserving it. I had left as one of a group of enthusiastic amateurs; I returned to a professional organization with standards and an acknowledged reputation to maintain. Success was no longer an occasional prize, but the natural reward of relentless attention to detail combined with continual alertness to the wider implications, something so regular from now on that we were far too busy to notice it. Yet we could not boast. Everything we did we owed to Hut 6; without them we could not exist, and our task was to continue deserving the prominence their skills had thrust upon us.

There is but one more change in Hut 3 to recall; otherwise it remains only to note a few intelligence highlights. No formal agreement to share Ultra with the United States was signed until May 1943, but the two allies (the one reluctant to part with its precious secret, the other not relishing the role of suppliant) continued 'walking round and eyeing each other like two mongrels who have just met' (in the words of the official US historian of the Americans in Hut 3) until January 1944. Only then did the first American recruits arrive. Some remained with us and were quickly and smoothly assimilated; others underwent a few weeks' training before being assigned to one or other of the US armies and air commands preparing for D-Day. The merger was peaceful and rapid; not a ripple disturbed the surface of joint endeavour.

The impact of at least three sets of Ultra signals can be traced at the highest strategic and political level during the early months of the Italian campaign. It had been expected that, Italy having changed sides in September 1943, Hitler would conduct a fighting withdrawal in Italy and retire to the Alps to economize manpower and effort. His decision to the contrary on 1 October ushered in the slogging match up the peninsula but also his willing though unconscious support for the strategy the Allies had already determined on: to erode German strength by attracting as many troops as possible away from Russia and the west to a profitless theatre. Brooke, the British Chief of the Imperial General Staff, whose necessary preoccupation with the broad lines of strategy normally prevented him from considering individual items, explicitly recognized the value of the signal recording Kesselring's decision in March 1944 to stop trying to drive the Anzio beach-head into the sea in favour of building more defences to cover Rome. The anxious, protracted, and occasionally heated inter-Allied debates over Anvil (later Dragoon), the landings in the south of France in August 1944, can be shown to reflect a series of Ultra signals.

Bombing and sabotage cut enough land-lines in northern France in the weeks before D-Day to force a proportion of useful intelligence on to the air. Ultra identified all the German divisions awaiting the invasion but was a little astray with one or two locations. In the first few weeks after the landing it demonstrated the deception-planners' success in suggesting that the Pas de Calais, not Normandy, was the real target: several armoured divisions were held there and away from the bridgehead which they might otherwise have crushed. No one who was in Hut 3 in August can forget the incredulity and excitement which greeted a decode on the tenth which conveyed Hitler's personal order for the renewal of the Mortain offensive: for a few moments before Montgomery and Bradley received it, we could sense on our own that three German armies might be surrounded and destroyed in what came to be called the Falaise pocket.

There followed a premature assumption among our superiors that victory was already won, and Ultra's influence unfortunately waned because of it. The risk of going 'a bridge too far' could have been foreseen as a possibility from scraps of Ultra, but Montgomery, over-cautious after Alamein, was over-bold before Arnhem. Three months before the surprise in the Ardennes on 16 December, Ultra detected the creation of a new Panzer Army east of the Rhine. A hint of its possible purpose (none was ever explicitly stated) could have been deduced from evidence which gradually piled up but which was never (it seems) brought together in a strategic assessment. Hindsight certainly makes its significance easy to see, but the contemporary blindness is baffling.

Army/Air Ultra undoubtedly changed the basis of military planning and the face of operations. The extent to which it did so cannot be measured with precision, however, because no general or air marshal was invited to set down how useful he had found Ultra. The crucial causal link between information and action is, therefore, often missing, and the gap has to be filled by cautious speculation. However, save for the cases just quoted, from late 1942 onwards no general seems to have disregarded the guidance of Ultra, provided he received it in time; by then it had proved its worth as an absolutely reliable source.

3. A naval officer in Hut 3

EDWARD THOMAS

BLETCHLEY PARK seems to have beckoned me from the very first. On the second day of the war the chairman of London University's Joint Recruiting Board nodded as he said, 'So you want to join the Navy: and you are a pupil of Professor Norman. I think we can use you.' Whether he knew the head of the German department at King's College, London, or was privy to the secret that he had made the dry run to Bletchley Park in September 1938 (as I discovered later), I shall never know. I was not surprised that Frederick Norman's name worked wonders: his brilliant mind had made a deep impression on me.

In July 1940, after my seaman's training, I was posted to Iceland as naval intelligence officer. Later that year I wondered how it was that a Norwegian gunboat, working from Reykajavík, so easily managed to find and sink certain small vessels which were trying to land German meteorological parties at various points in the Arctic. I had no idea at the time that she was acting on tip-offs from *Abwehr* ciphers broken at Bletchley. In August 1941 I was among the first to board U-570, a German U-boat which had been beached, virtually intact, on the south coast of Iceland. I wondered why the highly knowledgeable civilian intelligence officer (formerly of the Victoria and Albert Museum) who had been flown up from somewhere in England, and with whom I searched the nauseous interior of the U-boat, was so excited by the discovery of an empty wooden box, which he said had contained a cipher machine, with four slits on the shelf of one of its compartments. I found out later that this had been issued by the Germans in anticipation of the introduction of the formidable four-wheel U-boat Enigma which was later christened Shark by Bletchley's Naval Section.

A further experience in Iceland concerning signals intelligence of U-boats should be recorded here, since it was of importance to the battle of the Atlantic and appears in no published history of that campaign. I was in charge of the station installed there for taking high-frequency direction-finding bearings of enemy submarines. This had been sited in the north of the island, where it was intended to take bearings of Russian submarines! The Admiralty very soon decided that it should provide the urgently required cross bearings of U-boat transmissions, no other British-controlled territory being so suitable for the purpose. In the autumn of 1940 the order came for the station to be moved at once to a suitable site in southern Iceland. But it was then too late. The cables were immovably frozen into the ground and could not be shifted until May 1941. We thus lost six months' valuable direction-finding intelligence at a time when there was no naval Enigma, when the U-boats were attacking convoys at will, and when every scrap of intelligence that might locate them was of supreme value.

In early 1942 some half-dozen naval officers knowing German were summoned to Bletchley's Naval Section. Current gossip at the Park had it that there were two explanations for this. One was that the Section's head, observing that Hut 3 boasted several individuals in RAF and Army uniform, wished to have some navy-clad folk about the place to impress visiting VIPs. The other was that officers with first-hand experience of the naval war might be able to add a touch of verismo to the interpretation and analysis of the German naval Enigma decrypts then being done in Hut 4, mainly by men and women in civilian garb. We naval folk were soon to learn the supererogatory character of this second explanation. There was precious little that Hut 4's civilians did not know about how navies worked. Most of what I ever knew about the German Navy came from those who had been working on the naval Enigma since it was first broken a year earlier.

I vividly remember the sense of shock produced on my first arrival at the Park by the grimness of its barbed-wire defences, by the cold and dinginess of its hutted accommodation, and by the clerk-work we were first set to do. But this was soon swept aside by the much greater shock of discovering the miracles that were being wrought at the Park. In Iceland I had been interrogating the survivors of the many merchant ships sunk in the, at first, highly successful offensive against the Atlantic convoys launched by the U-boats in March 1941. I had spent many hours trying to analyse their strength and tactics. I could have spared my pains. For I now discovered that all this, and everything else about the U-boats, was known with precision by those privy to the Enigma decrypts. Leafing through the files of past messages—for the dreaded Shark key for U-boats, that had been introduced a week before my arrival, was to defeat Hut 8's cryptographers for another ten months—I shivered at seeing the actual words of the signals passing between Admiral Dönitz and the boats under his command whose terrible work I had seen at first hand. The stench of the filthy pap I had waded through on board U–570—a compound of bilge water, diesel oil, contents of latrine buckets, and Mosel wine—now acquired a quite different dimension. No less shocking was the revelation of the bestiality that underlay this sophisticated form of warfare. This emerged vividly from Dönitz's exhortations to his captains—'Kill, kill, kill!'—and the names given to the wolf-packs, such as *Gruppe Blutrausch* ('Blood Frenzy').

I can place the date of my arrival in Hut 4 pretty exactly. It was shortly before 11 February 1942, the day of the famous 'Channel Dash' of the *Scharnhorst, Gneisenau,* and *Prinz Eugen.* There was great commotion in the hut and cries of 'Where's Harry? Harry will be furious!' Indeed he was. Harry Hinsley, whom we naval newcomers had already pin-pointed as perhaps the most knowledgeable of all those in Hut 4, flew in late in the afternoon scattering smiles, scarves, and stimulus in every direction, exclaiming, 'It's happened again: whenever I take a day off something big blows up.' There had, indeed, been good indications that the ships were about to move; but the Enigma settings of 10, 11, and 12 February, by a stroke of the ill luck which precipitated tragedy from time to time, were not solved until three days later.

Hinsley was a key figure in Hut 4. His uncanny ability to sense, from tiny clues in the decrypts or the externals of the radio traffic, that something unusual was afoot was already legendary in the Park. He was well versed in the ways of navies, having more than once visited the Home Fleet in Scapa Flow to explain the workings of the Enigma to the Commander-in-Chief. He was a popular figure there and was known, as I later discovered when I joined the Home Fleet, as 'the Cardinal'. He was the chief channel for the exchange of ideas between the Naval Section and the Admiralty's Operational Intelligence Centre (OIC). This capable—but not infallible—organization had already in 1940 rejected a suggestion by Hinsley which, if adopted, might have saved the aircraft-carrier *Glorious*. On the other hand, during the 'Channel Dash' it was smart work done in the OIC which contrived to use the decrypts to have the *Scharnhorst* and the

Gneisenau mined off the Dutch coast with resounding strategic consequences. (I could not then have suspected that thirty years later I would spend twenty harmonious and productive years working with Hinsley on the official history of *British Intelligence in the Second World War*.)

This episode coincided with the onset of Hut 8's ten-month-long inability to break into the newly introduced Shark. Severe losses of merchant ships were to follow, largely in consequence of this. But already by the end of 1941 a turning-point had been reached in the battle of the Atlantic. The evasive routeing of convoys made possible by Hut 8's breaking of the naval Enigma in the spring of 1941 had, according to some historians' calculations, spared some three hundred merchant ships and so provided a cushion against the heavy losses yet to come. It also defeated Dönitz's offensive, which was intended to knock out Britain while the German armies disposed of Russia, so avoiding a two-front war. The six-months' long decline in sinkings also provided a crucial breathing space during which the Allies could develop anti-submarine weapons and tactics, and get on with building more merchant ships. This victory, which saved Britain, was based entirely on the work of Bletchley Park. It was also responsible, though I did not know it at the time, for the great reduction in the number of survivors who passed through my hands in Iceland, reducing my work-load and making it possible for me to be released to Bletchley.

Once there I was heartened by the resumption of contact with Professor Norman and two of his former pupils, one of them working on medium-grade German police ciphers, and the other on the *Abwehr* Enigma used by the shipwatchers at Gibraltar. Norman, as I discovered, had been one of the members of the original Hut 3 Watch set up by Welchman in early 1940. Since then he had become Dr R. V. Jones's principal researcher at Bletchley, scanning every type of decrypt for signs of German technological and scientific innovations. Jones owes him, and the fabulous index he maintained, an only partly acknowledged debt of gratitude. This is perhaps the place to clear up one of Group Captain Winterbotham's many mis-statements concerning Bletchley. He claims to have initiated the Hut 3 Watch and to have staffed it with German-speaking RAF officers. In fact, in early 1940, no such officers were forthcoming. That is why the Watch, concerned entirely with German Air Force and Army matters, was originally headed by Commander M. G. Saunders, RN—another colourful Bletchley character whose deserts have been insufficiently acknowledged—and manned by the likes of Norman, Bill Marchant, and F. L. Lucas.

We naval newcomers were at once impressed by the easy relations and lack of friction between those in, and out of, uniform. Despite the high tension of much of the work, a spirit of relaxation prevailed. Anyone of whatever rank or degree could approach anyone else, however venerable, with any idea or suggestion, however crazy. This was partly because those in uniform had mostly been selected from the same walks of life as the civilians—scholarship, journalism, publishing, linguistics, and so forth—and partly because these were the people who saw most clearly what stood to be lost by a Hitler victory. All at the Park were determined to give their all to see this did not happen. Service officers gladly served under civilians, and vice versa. Dons from Oxford and Cambridge worked smoothly together. There were exceptions. Certain fairly senior, but very able, service officers (regulars) took advantage of complaints from Whitehall at the turn of 1941–2 to bid for control of certain sectors of its now immensely influential output. Those at the coal-face sensed the tension; and there were mutterings in the corridors. But changes were soon made, and new lines of responsibility drawn.

The most sweeping of these affected Hut 3, responsible for translating and elucidating the German Air Force and Army decrypts from Hut 6, for supporting its cryptanalysts, and for signalling the gist of the decrypts to operational Commands in the Mediterranean and, later, in other theatres. These changes coincided with the introduction of Shark and a consequent slackening in Hut 4's demands on us naval newcomers. New, fascinating, and exciting work was found for us. Rommel, fighting in Africa, depended on shipments of fuel, ammunition, and other supplies sent across the Mediterranean in convoys controlled by the Italians. His fortunes waxed or waned with the adequacy, or inadequacy, of his supplies. His most notable victories came when his logistic position was good; and his defeats when he was weakened through want of supplies. They were adequate when the fortunes of war permitted his convoys to arrive safely and in sufficient number: but he faltered when the RAF and Navy contrived to prevent this. His final defeat owed much to the sustained sinking of his supply ships. Bletchley played a big part in bringing this about.

Hut 6's decrypts told us a great deal about these convoy movements. One source was the Air Force Enigma which throughout 1941 had been revealing, albeit somewhat spasmodically, the instructions for their air escort. This intelligence had, for example, resulted in considerable disruption of the transport to Africa of the first of Rommel's armoured formations. The second and more important source was the Italian administrative machine cipher, C 38m, broken by Hut 8 in the summer of 1941. This yielded, amongst other things, advance warning of the sailing dates, routes, and composition of virtually all trans-Mediterranean supply convoys. It also threw occasional light on Italian main-fleet movements. During 1941 the gist of the relevant Enigma decrypts had been signalled by Hut 3 to the Mediterranean authorities by the SCU/SLU channel, while that of the C 38m decrypts had been sent by a part-naval, part-civilian processing watch in Hut 4 separately to Malta and elsewhere. An outstanding result of these messages had been a spate of sinkings in late 1941 which played a big part in Rommel's retreat to El Agheila at that time.

It was probably a coincidence that, at the time of the Hut 3 reorganization of early 1942, a twenty-four-hour watch of naval officers—one of them a regular—was set up and became an integral part of that hut. Called 3N, one of its jobs was to provide advice, hitherto lacking, to the watch on naval problems arising from the Army–Air Force decrypts. Its other and more important task was to co-ordinate the shipping intelligence from these decrypts with what came out of the C 38m. To bring this about 3N and Hut 4's Italian watch became virtually a single team, the former being responsible for the final shape of the outgoing signals—and for taking on the chin any riposte from bewildered recipients at the other end (which was seldom). This development came at a bad time for the British in the Mediterranean. The Axis had greatly strengthened its convoy defences and Malta was all but immobilized by the attacks of the newly arrived Luftflotte 2. Axis convoys were getting through wholesale, and opportunities for attacking them were much reduced. Rommel's recovery in January 1942 was made possible by these developments. Every scrap of intelligence became doubly valuable. The co-ordination of the two sources came at the right moment.

Advance warning of a convoy movement came first normally, but not invariably, from the C 38m. An immediate signal would be drafted in Hut 4 and sent across to 3N, who would check that there was nothing to be added from the Enigma or, if there was, would add it. Elucidatory comments would be added where necessary and a signal sent off by the SCU channel after discussion of its priority with the Hut 3 Advisers. When a land battle was in progress, every signal was of the highest importance, and careful calculation was needed to decide in what order they should be dispatched. Sometimes, dependent on the Hut 4 originator (two of them were brilliant), amendments to the wording would have to be made by 3N to render it into naval signalese. This would occasionally evoke pained remonstrance from Hut 4. But by then it would be too late. 3N and the Hut 4 Watch were more fortunate than our RAF and Army colleagues. Their interpretations had frequently to be argued out with the appropriate indoctrinated sections of Air and Military Intelligence in Whitehall. We were entirely on our own. A regular naval officer in the Admiralty's OIC was supposed to check our signals for any conspicuous *bêtise*. But I remember his ringing up only twice—once about a *Times* crossword clue.

The voices I remember best from Bletchley are those of the Hut 4 watchkeepers. There would be long conversations on the inter-hut telephone comparing the contents of decrypts and trying to puzzle out obscurities. The Air Force Enigma helped greatly in determining the all-important convoy routes. In 1941 the C 38m had mostly expressed the positions through which they were intended to pass in terms of code-names: these had to be worked out on a chart by means of pins and lengths of cotton representing distances and steaming times. But in 1942 the Enigma used straight co-ordinates which helped to elucidate the code-names and save precious minutes. Enigma details of where there would be air escort, or—more importantly—where there would not, were of importance to those planning attacks, and even more to the reconnaissance aircraft which were always sent out beforehand to fix the positions of convoys known from the decrypts. This essential step was invariably taken to provide cover for the source. The Air Force Enigma was often the first to provide warning of the imminence of a convoy. At the end of each month the settings of the C 38m were changed. A gap of up to four days would then ensue while Hut 8 worked out the new ones. And on at least two occasions the Italians made more fundamental changes which would silence Hut 8 for up to a fortnight. During these gaps the Enigma, broken daily, was our only source of shipping intelligence.

The Air Force Enigma, unlike the C 38m, would sometimes indicate the importance—to the German Air Force, of course—of a given convoy, occasionally specifying that it carried urgent supplies of fuel or ammunition. Though these indications were made only in general terms, they were invaluable to the attack planners. From about August 1942 Hut 6 regularly broke the Chaffinch key of the German Army in Africa and this provided, as well as much else of the highest importance, precise details of cargoes. Ships carrying operationally urgent supplies could now be distinguished from those with routine shipments. This made selective attack possible and greatly increased the effectiveness of the anti-ship campaign. An example of its effectiveness may be found in the Allies' ability, which came as a surprise to some historians, to feed the 250,000 prisoners trapped in Cape Bon during the final phase of the war in Africa. Ships known from the decrypts to be carrying rations had been spared; while those with cargoes of tanks, fuel, and ammunition had been selected for attack.

The arrival of Chaffinch, supplementing the former sources, coincided with that of Rommel on the Egyptian frontier. It now became doubly urgent to deprive him of supplies. It also coincided, to our great good fortune, with the recovery of Malta as a base for anti-shipping operations, and with the breaking by Hut 8 of the naval Enigma key used by the Germans in the Mediterranean. Its yield made for much more efficient attacks on coastal supply shipping, on which Rommel, far from his supply bases and convoy terminals, now largely depended. All this sharply increased the pace of our work. Rommel clamoured for fuel, and attacks on tanker convoys were now given highest priority. Many were successful. Those during August 1942 were largely responsible for his failure at Alam Halfa. After the war I found my initials at the bottom of the signals giving details of three supremely important tanker movements at the time of the October battle of El Alamein. Their sinking was largely responsible for Rommel's long and halting retreat westwards. I well remember the frustration that exploded from our Hut 3 colleagues at Montgomery's failure to overtake and destroy him. I had not seen such a demonstration since the Knightsbridge fighting six months earlier, when Eighth Army advanced against an anti-tank trap at the so-called 'Cauldron' position and lost heavily. Hut 3 believed that it had provided full details of Rommel's intentions on this occasion.

The Hut 4/3N routine continued until the final victory at Cape Bon. It seemed scarcely credible that the Axis could have sufficient ships left unsunk to succour the fighting in Tunisia. But they did. And the pressure continued right up to the end. Somehow it always seemed to be greatest during the night watch (midnight to 8 a.m.). No greater contrast could be imagined than the evening drive to the Park through quiet countryside—and the hurly-burly of Hut 3 into which one was pitchforked at its end! The 3N evening watchkeeper would announce that he had two minutes in which to catch his transport and leave behind a sheaf of draft signals all requiring instant scrutiny and agonizing decisions about priorities: the current Chaffinch would just be breaking (as often happened just after midnight) and scatter further urgent papers on one's desk; a battle would be raging in Africa, and the watch, the Advisers, and the Index would be totally monopolized without a second to spare for one's problems. I remember one night when no fewer than thirty-two signals went out from 3N. How one longed for the 3 a.m. canteen break when, with luck, a few moments' calm might be enjoyed in the company of some totally unknown, but totally charming, girl from some mysterious corner of the Park. How one longed to meet her again! But seldom did.

But of all the girls at Bletchley the palm must go to the 3N indexers—an ugly word for a talented group of loyal and lovely ladies. Mostly Wrens and WAAFs, they were always on duty, keeping a record of every detail that might be needed for reference in solving some future conundrum. Often, with a gentle word, they would guide the harrassed watchkeeper to the solution that had been eluding him. One of them, a senior and impressive WAAF officer, introduced the Park to the Moped and to Nescafé—both then new to British life. She would 'take the watch' when one of the regulars was sick. They also lightened the burden of the main Hut 3 Index.

After the end in Africa I was posted as intelligence officer and signals intelligence adviser to the Commander-in-Chief Home Fleet in his flagship, the battleship *Duke of York*, based at Scapa Flow. In its operations off the Norwegian coast and on the Arctic convoy routes Bletchley's intelligence, filtered to us through the Admiralty's OIC, helped us to many a victory—and at least one fiasco. But that is another story.

4. The Z Watch in Hut 4, Part I

ALEC DAKIN

How was I recruited? In April 1940, about the end of the phoney war, Hugh Last, Camden Professor of Ancient History, asked me to come to his rooms in Brasenose College, Oxford. He explained in a roundabout way that there was important but highly secret war work to be done, and that my studies in ancient languages and Egyptology might make me suitable for it. He advised me to go to a house called Bletchley Park and offer myself. And so on 6 May 1940 I took a train to Bletchley and entered BP, where at some stage an oath of secrecy was administered to me which I observed faithfully, even to my wife when we were married in 1953.

The first thing I recollect is the sight of the wooden door of a hut on which had been inscribed in a bold cursive hand

German naval section

which gave my heart a great lift. From boyhood onwards I had been keenly interested in ships and particularly the Navy. My family summer holiday was regularly spent in New Brighton, and I vividly recalled how I saw the battleship *Rodney* sail down the Mersey after she was built at Birkenhead. So the prospect of being involved with the *Kriegsmarine* thrilled me at once.

I found myself among colleagues and friends. The group of translators on duty in Hut 4 was called the Z Watch, and the person in charge of it was Walter Ettinghausen, who has been Walter Eytan since the end of the war. He was the complete German scholar, from St Paul's and Queen's College, Oxford, and it seemed natural for him to become the co-ordinator from the first day he arrived in his Tank Corps uniform and brilliantly polished black boots. His leadership was exercised with gentleness and understanding, and all who knew him and worked with him loved him. After the war he emigrated to

Israel, where he became Director-General of the Ministry of Foreign Affairs, and later Ambassador to France.

The team which evolved round him consisted of three groups which provided a constant watch round the twenty-four hours. Whenever Hut 8 was able to break and decrypt a new 'day' of German naval Enigma signals, the Z Watch was ready to translate them and process the material for the Admiralty.

There was great diversity among the people who made up these three groups. The head of one group was Charles Leech, a business-like businessman and a 'trouble-shooter' in civilian life. He worked rapidly and decisively and never turned a hair. In his group Gordon Priest was a modern linguist who could always be relied on to plough through the masses of signals that sometimes descended on us. He was probably the youngest of us, and sadly died before realizing his full potential.

Another head could hardly have been more different. Eric Turner was an academic whose life before and after the war was devoted to Greek papyrology. His scholarship and reputation were recognized by a CBE in 1975 and a knighthood in 1981. Ann Toulmin, who worked closely with him, had joined up as a Wren direct from university, and as a German specialist had been sent to the intercept station on South Foreland. One day, as she was teleprinting her report to Station X (Bletchley), the answer was signed 'WGE'. This was her Oxford tutor Walter Ettinghausen, and the upshot of a teleprinter conversation was that she joined Hut 4.

The other member of Eric's group was Leonard Forster, who as Professor of German at Cambridge has done much valuable work in that field. I retain a vivid memory of him at his desk with a neat motto in front of him:

> The Emperor Pertinax
> Had a certain axe
> With which he used to strike
> Those whom he did not like.

The third group was blessed with a pair of prodigious workers in Ernest Ettinghausen, the younger brother of Walter, and Thelma Ziman, another WRNS officer, who had come from South Africa to serve in the war. She was later awarded an MBE.

I became the 'sorter' in Charles's group, and, as the product of a Yorkshire grammar school and Oxford, and an Egyptologist, was perhaps liable to make too detailed an examination of difficult signals.

As Hut 8's decrypts arrived in Hut 4, each group handled them as follows, exchanging jobs when necessary. A wire tray comes in, laden with decrypts in the form of sheets covered with tapes carrying the printed German text in five-letter groups like those in the original cipher text. The sorter, often Number 2 of the group, glances at them, quickly identifies those important for the Admiralty, and hands them to Number 3; who rapidly writes out the German text in word-lengths, staples it on to the decrypt, and hands it to Number 1; who translates it into English, stamps it with a number (e.g. ZTPG/4793), and passes it to a WAAF girl who teleprints it to the Admiralty, adding the initials of Number 1, e.g. WGE.

There were few naval Enigma decrypts before May 1941. Until then our watches spent twenty-four hours a day studying the masses of teleprinted signals spread out on a huge table. Messages of every kind, in various codes and ciphers, poured in from Chicksands and other intercept stations, so we began to recognize, for example, what we afterwards learnt was *Werftschluessel* ('Dockyard Key') on which John Barns spent desperate months working at 'those bloody bigrams' until he finally cracked it (see Chapter 24). Many signals were in code, but some in plain language: 'It is getting hot around here'—was that 'Jervis Bay'? We also recognized the three-letter German Naval Air code which we called GNA, and did some rudimentary wireless telegraphy (W/T) traffic analysis. Harry Hinsley had worked out a system of evaluating 'linkages', signals which were repeated by the German shore stations in Norway such as OLO (Oslo) and BNA (Bergen). These repeats could give warning that *Hipper* or other heavy ships were moving or about to move along the coast and could be a threat to units of the Royal Navy. Particular responsibility rested on the one of us whose job it was to keep watch during the night, when Harry was not on hand to assess their significance. We could ring him up, but how were we to discuss enemy naval movements on a public telephone? Here the most English of games came to our rescue: Christopher Morris and Charles Allberry were Cambridge cricketers, and a complex system was worked out which enabled Harry to be given a W/T situation report during the night in the form of a cricket commentary.

Naval Enigma signals sometimes started with an indication of urgency. In the early period there was SSD (*sehr sehr dringend* ('very

very urgent')); but gradually this was used less and the regular prefix was KR or KRKR (*ich habe ein Kriegstelegram* ('I have a war signal')). When an operator started with KR, that warned all others to keep the air clear. This warning, which started as a rare indication of extreme urgency, came to be used more and more often, though it still caused a frisson when it appeared.

Naturally, those who drafted or sent signals were warned against frequent use of the same words or phrases at the start of a signal, as that would offer any enemy a way of identifying its subject and thus breaking into the cipher. A phrase which often appeared at the beginning of the morning weather forecast and was thus tried as a possible crib was *Wettervorhersage Deutsche Bucht* ('weather forecast German Bight').

Signals normally began as either 'A to B' or 'B from A'. 'To' appeared as ANAN, 'from' as VONVON—short but vital words being repeated to avoid misunderstanding, like the services' 'not repeat not'. Common punctuation marks were X = full stop, XX = colon, Y = comma; and a proper name of person, place, or ship, would be marked by J's, e.g. JBISMARCKJ. X also appeared in abbreviations: EINS FDLX ZERSTX IN SICHT = EIN FEINDLICHER ZERSTOERER IN SICHT ('one enemy destroyer in sight').

A message from the *Bismarck* provides a sample complete signal in the series of five-letter groups as we might receive it from Hut 8:

KRKR FLOTT ENCHE FANAN OKMMM XXTOR PEDOT REFFE RACHT
ERAUS XSCHI FFMAN OEVRI ERUNF AEHIG XWIRK AEMPF
ENBIS ZURLE TZTEN GRANA TEXES LEBED ERFUE HRERX

Commander-in-Chief Fleet to Naval Headquarters: Most immediate. Torpedo hit right aft. Ship unmanœuvrable. We fight to the last shell. Long live the Führer.

Early in our history there was a remarkable signal that revealed that a group of whaling ships had fallen into enemy hands. This must have been sent from some remote area of the south Atlantic, so it was not surprising that it was somewhat corrupt. The name of one ship gave particular trouble because of its unlikely initial letter: it appeared as JXLELEGGERJ. But the translators were becoming practised researchers in *Lloyd's Register of Shipping* as well as *Jane's Fighting Ships*, and the unfortunate vessel duly appeared with her correct name *Ole Wegger*.

The first ZTP teleprint to the Admiralty was sent at 1131/12/3/41 and signed CTC/VC: C. T. Carr, later Professor of German at St

Andrews. Regular decrypting started somewhat later. Examples from the early ZTP messages may give a picture of the intelligence content.

ZTP/6 is a signal from Gruppe West to Fleet: Naval Attaché Washington reports convoy rendezvous 25 February. (But this was sent to the Admiralty only on 12 March, so there was no immediate operational urgency.) Other very early signals cover a wide range of topics: U-boats, supply ships, operations in the Baltic, frequencies and call-signs, and 'Fleet' mentioned above was presumably *Bismarck* and *Prinz Eugen* already working up for their later operation.

ZTP/77, dated 15/3/41, had to add a '*sic*' to 'U 552' when no U-boat number even approaching this had been known before.

ZTP/198, another signal decrypted very late, from *Hipper*, reported her arrival in Brest with propeller trouble, half main-armament ammunition expended, and twelve torpedoes fired with eleven hits.

ZTP/228 of 22/4/41 was a signal from *Tirpitz* in the Baltic, reporting that working-up was to start on 9/5/41.

ZTP/747 is from WOHLFAHRT to U KUPPISCH, and seems to be the start of what was later to be Dönitz's regular practice of referring to U-boats by their commander's name.

By now we are coming to the *Bismarck* episode, and at 1136/20/5/41 we find 'Fleet' reporting to Gruppe Nord, 'At 1300 passed *Flugzeugkreuzer* ('aircraft cruiser') *Gotland*; presume we shall be reported.' This and the following signals were decrypted after the *Bismarck* had been sunk.

ZTP/816 (1148/25/5) shows an interesting appreciation of the situation. Its sender is unclear: a corrupt group, then 'West to Commander-in-Chief. Am of opinion since *Bismarck's* fighting power has been demonstrated enemy will not attempt to force decisive engagement unless he can bring up *Rodney* or second *King George*.'

At 0028/25/5 Commander-in-Chief reports, 'Attacked by planes from aircraft-carrier. Hit by torpedo.' But at 0153/25/5 he reports, 'Torpedo hit of no consequence.'

ZTP 899 (2325/26/5): 'Gruppe West to *Prinz Eugen*; presume refuelling carried out.' This, after *Prinz Eugen* was detached, reminds us of the tragic mistake the *Flottenchef* made when he failed to top up with fuel before leaving Bergen. It seems in a strange way appropriate that *Prinz Eugen*, as the survivor of the *Bismarck* story, should have sent the last signal made by any German naval unit, a plain-language message sent from a harbour in Denmark after the war was ended: *Es lebe Deutschland und die unbesiegte Kriegsmarine* ('Long live Germany and the undefeated Navy'). Undefeated? It was not an unreasonable claim. Hut 4 intelligence shows how desperately anxious the Admiralty must have been at the end of the war as the new types of U-boat came nearer to war readiness and it became clear that, if the war went on much longer, we should not be able to guarantee access to the latest forms of the Enigma.

ZTP/902 is the signal in which *Bismarck* reports that she is unmanœuvrable. Was the *Torpedotreffer achteraus* ('Torpedo hit astern') accidental or providential? This shows how the one fatal spot was found—the Achilles' heel. The admirals must have thought it unlikely that this could happen again if and when *Tirpitz* should herself go out into the Atlantic. As these ZTPs show, we were sending intelligence to the Admiralty, which warned that, despite this great relief, the anxiety would continue. No wonder that long afterwards, when *Tirpitz* was hidden in remote fjords of north Norway, brave men were ready to give their lives in midget-submarine attacks on her.

What about our contacts with the Admiralty and the Navy? Regularly one of us would be sent to work for a short period in the Admiralty, sometimes as an exchange. When my turn came, a higher-ranking officer passed me in a corridor; I felt the force of his personality. Back in the room where I was working I asked who he was. 'That was Harwood.' So it was the victor of the Battle of the River Plate, which had been such a tonic in the black days of December 1939. It was he who so skilfully manœuvred the smaller ships *Exeter* (8"), *Achilles*, and *Ajax* (6") to neutralize and defeat the *Panzerschiff* ('pocket battleship') *Graf Spee* with her 11" guns. And there was a period when one of us at a time went to Scapa Flow for a week and lived aboard one of HM ships—a destroyer or a carrier. I was in *Punjabi* and came back from Scapa in the submarine P39 on the surface.

Often towards the end of the war we could not help feeling sympathy for German naval ratings. A signal would be sent to a ship or a U-boat at sea: name and rank would be given, and then the grim words *total ausgebombt* ('[Your home] has been completely bombed out').

From time to time there were others who joined us. I remember a remarkable man known as 'Daoud', a Muslim with a Scottish accent.

Was his name Cowan? One of my most vivid memories is of a night when not much was happening. I was the only one of my normal group of three on duty with Daoud. In addition to my usual role of sorter I was responsible for the teleprinted message to the Admiralty, but there were not many. Wire trays would come over from Hut 8 with only a few signals in the bottom which had 'come out' late, or corrupt ones which had been sent back marked, 'All again, please.' Nothing exciting—but then, in the next almost empty tray, one of the most exciting messages ever.

Some Top Secret signals were reciphered by the sender in another setting. This one was headed *nur durch Offizier zu entziffern* ('to be deciphered by officer only') with a special setting of the machine that would mean extra work for Hut 8. It began like this:

OKMMMANANALLEXX
EINSATZJWALKUEREJ
NURDURCHOFFIZIERZUENTZIFFERN
OFFIZIERJDORAJ
DERFUEHRERJADOLFHITLERJISTTOTXDERNEUEFUEHRERISTFELD-MARSCHALLJVONWITZLEBENJ usw.

Naval Headquarters to all. Operation 'Valkyrie'. Officer only. Setting D (Dora) The Führer Adolf Hitler is dead. The new Führer is Field-Marshal von Witzleben, etc.

At that moment Walter happened to come into the room, looked at the signal, and asked me to speak quietly. Did our ever-present Wrens understand German? He decided he would personally teleprint the signal to the Admiralty on a special secret line. As we walked off to our midnight meal in the canteen, Daoud said: *Der letzte Witz seines Lebens!* ('the last joke of his life'). How strange that the name of Hitler's successor, Witzleben, should mean 'Joke-life'; and that the first people to see that signal were a Jew, a Scottish Muslim, and a Yorkshire Primitive Methodist!

5. The Z Watch in Hut 4, Part II

WALTER EYTAN

I DO not know how people were recruited for Bletchley Park. Since hardly anybody outside the organization knew anything about it, or so much as suspected its existence, I cannot imagine that anyone actually applied for employment there. One day at Oxford, in the summer of 1940, I was asked by someone—I believe it was Alec Dakin—if I would be interested in intelligence work for the war effort, and I said I would. In September of that year I was called up in the regular way for service in the Royal Armoured Corps (RAC), vaguely supposing that, if anything came of Dakin's suggestion, I would in due course be moved to some other unit. For several months, as a trooper in the RAC, I trained as a tank gunner, until one day the call came. I was given railway vouchers that would take me the following day from Tidworth to Bletchley, about which I knew nothing. I was told to take my rifle and kitbag, and did as I was told.

At Bletchley, thus armed and equipped, I was assigned to the Naval Section. I wore my uniform for several days more; I had no other clothes with me. I was told that I could be promoted to full colonel (quite a jump for a simple soldier), but Frank Birch, the head of Naval Section, advised against this. He said I would be talking to admirals, and being 'only' a colonel would put me at a disadvantage. I would be best off—not personally but for the job in hand—as a civilian. This caused me no problem, but it was not always easy for really young people, who could feel themselves tempted, not always in reply to an outright question, to explain self-defensively why at the height of the war they were in 'civvies'. At least one breach of security occurred as a result, but since this was in an Oxford senior common room there were enough sensible people around to keep the secret to themselves.

Security was miraculously well preserved at BP. We were warned from the first moment never, under any circumstance, until our dying day, to reveal even by the most opaque hint what our work was; and we were taught how to handle awkward questions that might be put to us. As far as I know, apart from the single instance cited above, not one word ever came out about BP until Winterbotham many years later published a book about it. I was shocked to the point of refusing to read the book when someone showed me a copy, and to this day I feel inhibited if by chance the subject comes up, though Winterbotham's book naturally led to a spate of others. Security was second nature to us; my wife said she found difficulty in marrying a man who would not tell her what he did in the war. I did tell her that I had spent most of the time at a place called Bletchley, which meant nothing to her, and it was not until she read about Winterbotham's book in the *New York Times* that she put two and two together. We were employed nominally by the Foreign Office, which paid us our monthly wage, but even this I never spoke about. By the end of the war thousands of people were working at BP, and yet the enemy never knew.

I arrived at BP in February 1941 and do not recall finding many people in the Naval Section before me. Gradually others arrived; I never knew or even asked where they came from or how they were chosen. It must have been by recommendation. The Cambridge contingent was larger than Oxford's, but most came from neither place. They ranged from businessmen to scholars, with the odd Wren and ATS officer here and there. The Section was housed in Hut 4, and in practice 'Hut 4' and 'Naval Section' came to be synonymous terms.

It was in 1941 that Hut 4, with Enigma decrypts beginning to flow from Hut 8, began to expand and flourish and play a vital role in the war. Hut 8 was home to the mathematicians, at least one of them a genius, and others at the very top of their profession. It was the task of Hut 4 to exploit the fruits of their work and make them available in intelligible form to the Naval Intelligence Division (NID) in the Admiralty. The NID people, in their turn, decided what, and in what form, and with what comment or recommendation, to make available to the operational and other decision-makers up to and including the Prime Minister. Intelligence from this source was, for security reasons, restricted to the relatively few officers and officials who absolutely had to know. The material was transmitted to the Admiralty through Hut 4's own teleprinter room, manned by a dozen or more WAAF girls—curiously not by Wrens. Through our teleprinter we could also connect with W/T intercept stations along the coast.

Occasionally I visited one of these stations myself, and when need arose I would also go up to London and spend a few hours in the NID basement to find out any special needs it might have, clear up obscurities, and ensure effective liaison. When pressure was too great for the WAAFs to handle all the material, I would quite often, sometimes in the middle of the night, take my turn at teleprinting. There were always more machines than girls to work them.

Translating was more complicated than perhaps it sounds. Some enemy messages, once deciphered, were readable enough, in straightforward German which could be translated into English with ease. As often as not, however, there would be difficulties which it took a good deal of ingenuity and experience to overcome.

One difficulty arose from errors in transmission or interception. The Enigma machine could only decipher the texts it received, so that, if for any reason the text became corrupt and unintelligible between the German operator and Hut 8, the translator would have to do his utmost from his knowledge of the language, the context, and the operational background, to reconstitute it into understandable German. These could be puzzles which it would take several people to solve, and sometimes even many heads put together could not resolve them. All in all, the translators performed miracles in reconstructing corrupt texts and making them yield sense in English.

Another difficulty arose from the specialized vocabulary of German 'navalese'. None of us was a naval expert even in English; we would not ordinarily have known, in any language, the technical terms for parts of ships or their engines and armament or, for instance, for lighthouses and their operation. Even if we looked up an unknown word in a dictionary and learnt that the corresponding English word was 'occlusion', we could not know enough about lighthouses or lightships to judge whether in a given context 'occlusion' was the correct translation. Fortunately we had a special department in Hut 4, Naval Section VI, which over the years compiled a unique German–English dictionary of naval terms, and a first-class intelligence department, a library, reference works, card catalogues, and cartographical help, all linked directly to the Z decrypts. (The work of NS VI is described in Chapter 7.) The whole of Hut 4 was geared to the task of providing Admiralty with the most perfect Top Secret intelligence we could. We knew how much—for example, in the life-and-death struggle against Germany's U-boats—depended on the excellence of our product.

Files of fact and information were kept in every department, and the Z Watch had to be particularly scrupulous in this respect. Every 'Z' bore a number and soon the system burgeoned. A 'Z' transmitted by teleprinter was marked 'ZTP'; when we began branching out into other languages—e.g. Italian, French (Vichy), Spanish—a German signal teleprinted to Admiralty became 'ZTPG', an Italian 'ZTPI', and so on. By the time the war ended the volume of the various 'Zs' ran into the thousands, with the Germans easily in the lead but the Italians, if less numerous, often equally important when it came to the war in the Mediterranean. The Italian Navy used a Swedish cipher machine adapted from commercial use. The members of Z Watch had originally been recruited for their knowledge of German, but most of them must have been fairly competent all-round linguists, since I cannot recall that we had much trouble in tackling other texts—though we did have one member who was a Spanish specialist.

I should like to finish on a personal note. Our original family name (mine and my brother's, who was head of one of our three teams) was Ettinghausen, and we were both born in Germany. The security clearance must have been singularly perceptive, since such antecedents might so easily have disqualified us for BP, and in the United States certainly would have done. I suppose the responsible officer, knowing or discovering that we were Jews, must have concluded, correctly, that we had an extra interest in fighting Hitler, and therefore might be even more ardent than others at our BP work. There were altogether very few Jews at Bletchley, but at least five on the Z Watch, surely a far higher proportion than in any other section.

I may be the only one who will recall a peculiarly poignant moment when in late 1943 or early 1944 we intercepted a signal from a small German-commissioned vessel in the Aegean, reporting that it was transporting Jews, I think from Rhodes or Kos, *en route* for Piraeus *zur Endlösung* ('for the final solution'). I had never seen or heard this expression before, but instinctively I knew what it must mean, and I have never forgotten that moment. I did not remark on it particularly to the others who were on duty at the time—perhaps not even to my brother—and of course never referred to it outside BP, but it left its mark—down to the present day.

6. Italian naval decrypts

PATRICK WILKINSON

ONE day in the summer of 1938, after the Nazis had taken over Austria, I was sitting in my rooms at King's when there was a knock on the door. In came F. E. Adcock, accompanied by a small, birdlike man with bright blue eyes whom he introduced as Commander Denniston. He asked whether, in the event of war, I would be willing to do confidential work for the Foreign Office. It sounded interesting, and I said I would. I was thereupon asked to sign the Official Secrets Act form.

By now I had guessed what it was all about. It was well known to us that Adcock had been a member of Admiral 'Blinker' Hall's Room 40 at the Admiralty in the First World War, famous since its existence was revealed in 1928, which had done pioneering work on the decoding of enemy messages. A totally secret organization, the GC&CS, had carried on in peacetime, under the Foreign Office since 1922, and was now run by Denniston, always known as 'A.G.D.', a retired naval schoolmaster, whom I sensed to be a kind and civilized man. (Some time later he called on me again to ask about someone I knew: 'We know he's a communist, but is he the sort of communist who would betray his country?' I forget whether I said 'No' or 'I don't know'.)

When war broke out I was summoned to Bletchley Park and assigned to the Italian Naval Subsection. What we had to do was this. The Italian Navy used a book code, that is, an alphabetical dictionary in which every word or root was given at least one group of five figures as equivalent. Individual letters, numerals, and a large number of syllables ('spellers') were also given such equivalents. The encoder composed his message from these elements. But there was a serious complication. He had a reciphering book, a book of random groups of five figures, looking like logarithm tables, from which he selected at random a selection to add, group by group, to his message. (The Americans called these 'adders'; we called them 'subtractors', because what our assistant girls had to do was subtract them again without 'carrying', 'stripping' the message down to its original form.)

But the reciphering book was reconstructed, piece by piece with many gaps, by observing repeats I will not attempt to describe. The raw material that reached me was messages already stripped. Each group was to be indexed, and repeats then emerged. The object, of course, was to reconstruct the dictionary—the code-book.

How did one get a break-in? For a start, all messages began with a stereotyped formula of four groups: (1) *referimento* ('with reference to'); (2) the serial number of the message; (3) *corrente* ('of the current month', 'inst.'), or the name of the month; (4) date. So we knew that, if a group occurred in the third place several times in one month, occasionally in the next, but hardly ever otherwise, it probably meant that month. But more often *corrente* would be used. The dictionary might give a dozen groups for this, and the encoder would no doubt be instructed to pick one at random on each occasion, so that there would be fewer repeats to help the decoder ('cryptanalyst'). But such is the fecklessness of human nature that the encoders between them preponderantly used the first one in the list, so that it became familiar. I can still remember it: 76240. (When the war was over and the book was captured, the fact that this was the first on the list was confirmed.) In the case of the third group the identification was easy in any case. The fourth was more valuable. It would be provisionally identified in pencil in our index as a number between 1 and 31 (possible days of the month), and in due course it usually betrayed its exact value. Any identification so established was written over the group wherever it occurred in our folders full of past messages—in pencil while it was provisional, changed to ink when it was considered certain.

Such a break-in had not, of course, got us far. Much the greatest help was if we were fortunate enough to get a 'crib'. A crib becomes possible when a message is sent out by one authority, or repeated by another, in a different code or cipher which may have been broken completely or in part; or better still, when it is repeated 'in clear' (uncoded). The possibility of a crib may be perceived when messages of similar length are picked up which have gone out with the same sending call-sign at about the same time, or been repeated by recipients, in different codes.

'Spellers' are also a great help; and operators sometimes combined them with a word or root. For example, a group whose meaning had been guessed to be the root *grad* ('degree') was followed sometimes, we found, by a group we had identified with the speller IS and another unknown speller. Now we knew that there was an Italian hospital ship called *Gradisca*, so the unknown speller was identified as CA, and the group preceding *grad*– as 'hospital ship'. Further, it became clear that operators were syllabizing the name in different ways; so we soon had GRA, DI, and SCA. (It was a great thrill for my wife and me, visiting Venice some time after the war, to see moored at the Giudecca a ship with a red cross painted on its side and the name *Gradisca* in huge letters. It was like meeting a long-lost friend.)

Another useful source of speller identifications was the names of Italian naval officers. We had a copy of the alphabetical Italian Navy List, and if a group turned up that could be the first syllable of a surname on the list, soon followed by another identified speller, the remaining syllables of the surname and Christian name could yield several other identifications of syllables. (The list began intriguingly with a dozen Actons, from a family connected for many years with the Italian Navy and also with that of our historian Lord Acton.) There was, it will be seen, some rhyme and reason for a classical scholar to be allotted such work. He has been trained from his youth to wrestle in examinations with passages for unseen translation in which he has to guess, from his general knowledge and from the context, the meaning of unknown words. The same applies, of course, to all students of languages; but modern linguists tended to be used rather for translation work.

Our task was sometimes made more difficult, indeed ultimately futile, by lack of a sufficient number of 'stripped' messages. Groups had to occur sufficiently often in different associations with other already identified groups for their meaning to be deduced by a process of trial and error. As time went on we had made enough progress for the general sense of some current messages to be inferable. There was, however, another complication—'corruption' or 'garbling': somewhere along the line from the listening post a wrong digit might have crept in. The group would be wrongly indexed, unless the corruption occurred in a familiar identified group, in which case it could be easily recognized and corrected. Particular trouble could be caused when the corrupt group meant a numeral: a wrong numeral circulated in a decrypt could have incalculable consequences.

The most secret and general book codes of the Italian Navy were largely readable by GC&CS from 1937 to 1940, as was one of the two Naval Attaché codes.[1] The material we were working on was nicknamed 'Zag'. But with the entry of Italy into the war on 11 June 1940 everything was soon changed. The Italians had introduced either a new dictionary or, more probably, new reciphering tables (subtractors), if not both. The unfamiliar material was given the name of 'Zog'. Intensive indexing of the five-figure groups took place, to see if any pattern emerged which would relate Zog to Zag. I was put on to trying to see if anything seemed to fit. For a fortnight I toiled and caught nothing. Then one day I was asked to show what I was doing to a new recruit, the Cambridge historian Hrothgar Habakkuk. We had not gone far when up popped our old friend 72640, and what was more, as the third group of a message, just where *corrente* should occur. I took it along to show our new head, Wilfred Bodsworth, who immediately ordered all available hands to Zog. But, alas, little progress was made on this, or on its successor, 'Musso'. After July 1940 it was never possible again to read the main Italian naval book codes except for a few brief intervals as a result of captures after the middle of 1941; and further changes introduced in February 1942 caused all attempts to be abandoned.

Fortunately, however, the Italians began, from December 1940, to put more and more of their naval traffic on to a medium-grade Swedish cipher machine; this traffic was officially designated as C 38. It was broken into in the summer of 1941 and read almost continuously thereafter. The sinking of Axis convoys that resulted probably turned the scale against Rommel in North Africa. This development naturally changed the nature of the work in our subsection. The cryptanalysis passed largely to mathematicians, working under Vincent's direction; but the rest of us were still needed to deal with lower-grade codes, and also, because of our knowledge of Italian, for the reading of C 38 decrypts.

I had found relief from frustrating drudgery in a low-grade unreciphered code used by an Italian cruiser cut off in China, or by the Italian embassy in Pekin on its behalf—I forget which. The first assumption to make was that it was an alphabetical dictionary in which the words (or syllables or letters) were represented by groups of figures *in numerical order*. (Such a book would be convenient because the encoder could easily find the required group and the recipient the corresponding meaning.) Such a book it proved to be, called *Mengarini*. One had to guess at a few common words whose alphabetical differences corresponded roughly to numerical differences. When these were established, other identifications could be tried out around them; for example, if the group for *uno* was identified, the numerically preceding group probably meant *unità*. It was an amusing game. The subject-matter was generally banal routine; but at least some detail might strike a significant chord in some reader, and at best a message might be repeated from another code and so provide a crib for it.

With the breakthroughs in Enigma in 1940 it became clear that large numbers of assistant staff would be urgently needed. These were acquired on Churchill's express orders, but only after a personal appeal had been sent to him, most irregularly, by Turing, Welchman, Alexander, and Milner-Barry. A considerable number were WAAFs, rather fewer from the ATS; but by far the most were from the WRNS, heroic hand-picked girls who, having joined the Navy perhaps with thoughts of breathing the salty air of Portsmouth Docks or Plymouth Hoe, found themselves sent to about the furthest place from the sea in England. They were housed, initially, in the stateliest of homes—Woburn Abbey, Steeple Claydon, Beaumanor, Wavendon, and Walton Hall. They consoled themselves with calling the utility vans that brought them to work 'liberty boats', and 'saluting the quarter-deck' when they crossed the Wrennery landing. I remember going to a Wrens' party at Woburn, and, more vividly, arriving mistakenly for a dance at Walton (now the headquarters of the Open University) a week too early and asking a startled Wren at the door where the gentlemen's cloakroom was. Later in the war most of the BP Wrens lived and worked in purpose-built quarters at Stanmore in Middlesex.

Towards the end of April 1943, after the success of the 'Torch' landings in North Africa, I was about to announce my engagement to Sydney Eason, also in our Subsection, when I was summoned by Bodsworth and told that I was to take a party of half a dozen out to the Mediterranean. There were certain minor codes that we were reading which might be of some use out there, but which were more likely to be so if they were processed on the spot without the delay of transmission via Bletchley.

Bodsworth then began by saying whom he thought I could have. There was Pat Denby, a young man from Yorkshire, very clever and able. Then there was Sheridan Russell, a first-rate cellist (he had been spare man of the Lener String Quartet), no great cryptographer but a delightful, unusual personality of gypsy-like appearance—a genuine BP eccentric. From the girls he suggested Petronella ('Peta') Wise, Peggy Taylor, and—Sydney Eason. At this point I thought I ought to tell him of our impending engagement. He looked surprisingly disconcerted, then explained that we had an agreement with the Americans that men should not be accompanied in operational areas by their wives or fiancées. He decided, however, that it would be all right if we postponed the announcement of our engagement until it could be plausibly represented that it had all begun out there: 'Three months, say; it's a hot climate.'

The idea was that we should go out initially to Algiers, and then on to a hotel at a place called Bugeaud, high up in the Tunisian mountains near Bizerta, which was expected to be the base from which Cunningham would launch the assault on Italy. We were to go as civilians, though under the wing of one Commander Bradburne.

For work we were transported several miles out of Algiers to a picturesque French château with a fine view towards the mountains, built, if I remember, by Napoleon III for one of his mistresses. On the first day Bradburne dropped what to me was a bombshell. We were not merely to deal with low-grade codes, but to supply to Cunningham's Command the medium-grade cipher messages from the Italian C 38m machine. The cause of my embarrassment was this: I knew there was a long-standing tug-of-war between BP and the Commands abroad, the former being worried lest the secret that we were reading the machine traffic should be compromised by multiplication and exposure of the stations where this was done, the latter anxious to avoid the delays inevitable in transmission via Bletchley. I was a civilian employed by BP, and we were now being told to go beyond our brief. But I had no means of communicating with BP except through Bradburne, who was friendly and provided resourcefully for our welfare, but was also firmly ambitious. I had to assume that BP had been squared. The rest of my party were naturally delighted that they were to be given this far more exciting and responsible work.

The next thing that happened was the news that Cunningham had decided to run the assault on Sicily (Operation Husky) from Malta instead of Bizerta. This meant that we three men would cross to Malta with the troops, but the girls would have to come after us whenever they could. We crossed in June on the *Princess Beatrix*, a Dutch ship built shortly before the war for the Hook of Holland–Harwich crossing but now converted into a landing-ship.

The above developments are officially described by Hinsley:

The C38m was now decrypted in the Mediterranean theatre for the first time. As part of the preparations for *Husky* a small party of cryptanalysts from GC and CS was attached to C-in-C Mediterranean's HQ at Algiers to exploit on the spot Italian low-grade codes and cyphers which had hitherto been exploited only at GC and CS and at Alexandria. When the party arrived at the end of May, however, it found that, partly because of changes made by the Italians and partly for lack of interception facilities at Algiers, it could not work these codes and cyphers, but the presence of the party was turned to account: improved arrangements were made before D-day by which it moved to Malta with the C-in-C Mediterranean and decrypted the C38m there.[2]

Notes

1. F. H. Hinsley *et al.*, *British Intelligence in the Second World War*, I (London: HMSO; 1979), 199.
2. Ibid. III. i (1984), 90 n.

7. Naval Section VI

VIVIENNE ALFORD

I ARRIVED in Bletchley Park after a year as a member of the Voluntary Aid Detachment cooking ghastly food in army hospitals, followed by a brief interlude in Censorship, during which the only German letter I read was from the Empress Zita of Austria telling her son Otto to be sure to wear his winter woollies and a woollen scarf; followed by, until the beginning of 1943, a delightful period in the WRNS, keeping watch in intercept stations perched on cliffs from Hartland, north Devon, to Trimingham, north Norfolk. An interview with Frank Birch, Fellow of King's College, Cambridge, sent me to the GC&CS in Bletchley Park. I was allocated to Naval Section VI, housed in Block D, and headed by Lieutenant-Commander Geoffrey Tandy, RNVR, who had a degree in Forestry and was an expert not in cryptograms but in cryptogams: mosses, ferns, and so on.

NS VI existed for the purpose of solving obscurities in the text of decrypted and otherwise translated naval messages which, with the problem underlined in green, were passed down from the translators. They were known as the Watch and operated round the clock. Most frequently it would be a reference to a component of some new weapon, such as a heat-seeking torpedo, limpet mine, or direction-finding device.

The resources for identifying these objects consisted of a 'library' (at first just a few bookshelves) of Royal Navy service manuals, pilots, charts, etc., and such of their German, Italian, French, and (later) Japanese counterparts as had been obtained by capture; and also intelligence reports from many sources—diplomatic and commercial, espionage and refugees. These were systematically combed by lowly mortals, including myself—also known as the Watch—and a small library staff. Useful information—references to equipment, manufacturers, personnel (particularly U-boat commanders), geographical locations—was fed into a battery of index drawers, to provide useful material for the elucidation of problems of translation or identification by a small group of superior beings known as

'Research'. They were Leonard Forster, then Geoffrey Tandy's deputy and later Emeritus Professor of German at Cambridge; Alison Fairlie, later Emeritus Professor of French in the same place; Dione Clementi and Squadron-Leader Baghino (known and addressed as 'Bags'), as well as Bettina and Gioconda Hansford, English girls born and brought up in Italy, who dealt with Italian. On the Japanese side were Frank Taylor of the John Rylands Library of Manchester, and Peter Laslett, later co-founder of the University of the Third Age in Cambridge, both Sub-Lieutenants, RNVR, who had done the naval Japanese course.

As time went on I became increasingly involved in the technical-problem side, and, when the flow of captured documents became massive while the signals traffic diminished, I was put in charge of the section dealing with their registration, interpretation, and, where appropriate, exploitation, with a mixed civilian and service team. A curious and sometimes entertaining part of the job was that of interpreting the descriptions of weaponry written to help us by German scientists and engineers in what they took to be our native language. I particularly remember the delightful phrase 'and then the torpedoe do exscraze'. Of necessity the section occupied a large hut, the space being essential when collating and studying material like the construction drawings of battleships. It was, of course, particularly interesting to have the working drawings and manuals for the various hostile devices that had puzzled us for years.

With the end of the war and U-boats surrendering in Lissahally, the naval port of Londonderry, I was sent there with the task of identifying the material of interest to GCHQ and ensuring that it was sent there. Misunderstanding my mission, the authorities decided I had been sent to assist *them*, and would be there indefinitely. Unable to persuade them that this was not so, I borrowed the quartermaster's phone to ring the Admiralty on the day I knew Geoffrey Tandy would be there. Naval lines, at any rate then, had no amplifiers; so I found myself bellowing down the phone, 'SEND A SIGNAL ORDERING ME HOME', which prompted the Master-at-Arms to say, 'Ain't you 'appy 'ere, Miss?'—I was then Vivienne Jabez-Smith.

It worked. I returned, the required documents obtained, in an old Dakota in the centre of which was an enormous bomb, wrapped up like a parcel. On arriving at Manchester I was turned out, together with an Army officer. We became so engrossed in conversation that we all but missed the next stage of the flight; just making it, we finally landed somewhere in the Home Counties and got to Bletchley, through a thick fog, in a jeep.

My last, lasting, and chilling memory of BP was the evening when, while we were about to have supper in the cafeteria, someone came in and reported the dropping of the atomic bomb on Hiroshima. The news was received in dead silence, and conversation during the meal was subdued.

8. Anglo-American signals intelligence co-operation

TELFORD TAYLOR

When I joined the US Army Intelligence 'Special Branch' of Colonels McCormack and Clarke, early in August 1942, there was virtually no connection between the Branch and Bletchley Park. There had been a few contacts with the section of the Signal Corps which was breaking, and sending to our Branch, the Japanese diplomatic messages, but I knew nothing of that section until Christmas morning 1942, when Clarke asked me if I would be willing to go to England as representative of the Branch. I agreed to go, and was sent to the Signal Corps section, first under Colonel Bullock and then under Colonel Corderman, to be given a bit of training.

Meanwhile Clarke and McCormack (both men considerably older than me) were working with a British naval Captain Hastings to establish relations between the Branch and BP, primarily on matters dealt with in Hut 3. There was friction, and it was not until April 1943 that McCormack, Friedman, and I went to London.

We spent time mainly with C, with Alastair Denniston (at Berkeley Street in London) handling diplomatic stuff, and with Travis, by then running BP, and paid short visits to various outstations, M.I.5, etc. McCormack's main purpose was to get access to the fruits of Huts 3 and 6, and Denniston's diplomatics. This was fully accomplished as regards the diplomatics, but Nigel de Grey (and I think C for a while) were much opposed to sending BP's output to Washington. When McCormack and Friedman returned to Washington, I could not be at Berkeley Street and BP at the same time. I got a small office at the US Embassy (I was administratively under the military attaché) and a room at the Park Lane Hotel, and spent my time seeing that diplomatic material that our Signal Corps was not reading was duplicated and sent to the Special Branch. I was a bit lonely, but I became close friends with Denniston and his family. After about a month the Branch sent over a good man (Roger Randolph, I believe) to take over the diplomatics, and I transferred my main office to BP, and my habitat to the Hunt Hotel at Leighton Buzzard.

BP was certainly the end of feeling lonely. I cannot adequately portray the warmth and patience of the Hut 3 denizens (and to a lesser degree those of Hut 6 and other huts as well) in steering me around and explaining the many aspects of the work. At first I had no office, but Jim Rose and Peter Calvocoressi gave me a seat in their office, and they are still among my closest friends today. C, Travis, and de Grey were entirely civil, and Travis really friendly. The head of Hut 3, Group Captain Eric Jones, was personally impressive and at first all business, but eventually became a friend whom I greatly admired.

As my status in Hut 3 became taken for granted, the senior members told me that both fatigue and increasing production from Hut 6 were stretching the Hut 3 staff to the limit, and that they would welcome German-speaking American officers to be trained to join the British members. I was able to recruit several young officers awaiting assignments in London, including Landis Gores and Bob Slusser, and the Special Branch sent Lieutenant-Colonel Sam McKee as my deputy, so that I would not be tied to BP for the daily selection of German Army and Air Force messages received from Hut 3. This American gathering called for a room of our own, which was duly named 'SUS'. At about the same time the US Signal Corps Chief of Cryptology, Colonel George Bicher (pronounced Beecher), made contact with BP and arranged to send an American group to be trained and used in Hut 6. At BP, this group was led by Captain William Bundy.

During the autumn of 1943, the only 'rift within the lute' occurred when the US Army G-2 (General Officer for Intelligence), Major General Strong, came to England for a general look at how the American military intelligence activities were getting along. In the course of the general's visit to BP, de Grey somehow succeeded in convincing the general that there was no reason to send the output of Hut 6–Hut 3, etc., to the Special Branch or, indeed, anywhere else, since it was being sent direct from Bletchley to American Commands in Europe as well as to British commands. All that was needed, said de Grey, was regular reports on the information gained from the German messages.

That, of course, was not at all what the Special Branch wanted, and Travis went so far as to tell me confidentially that the Strong–de Grey agreement would not last. When Strong got back to the Pentagon, Clarke showed him his mistake, and soon Clarke appeared at BP and settled matters with Travis on the basis that all important messages would be sent daily by air to Special Branch, and that less urgent matters would be sent weekly. After this settlement, as far as I know, there were no disagreements of any importance from then until the end of the war.

During the winter and spring of 1943–4 preparations for the Allied landings in France included the creation of new Armies and Army Groups and top air headquarters, both American and British. I had observed that some of the British intelligence officers handling Ultra intelligence at the major air and ground headquarters, such as Wing Commander Robert Humphreys, were themselves graduates of BP. It occurred to me that the newly created US top headquarters would need officers trained in the use of Ultra.

Early in 1944 I was recalled to Special Branch for a few reporting and training sessions. I took occasion to present to Clarke and McCormack a memorandum proposing that some twenty Army intelligence officers, ranging from captains to lieutenant-colonels, should be sent to BP for six to eight weeks of training in the handling of Ultra traffic and presentation, and would then be attached to the intelligence branches of Army and Army Air Force top command groups. Clarke and McCormack were enthusiastic; the latter improved on my memorandum, and Clarke presented it to General Marshall for his approval. That was soon forthcoming, and was put into an order from Marshall to General Eisenhower in England. The missive was sent to Sam McKee, with orders to present it only to Eisenhower. Bedell Smith growled about what he called a Pentagon invasion, but Eisenhower welcomed the move, with the result that in a few weeks there was an invasion of BP by a train of young intelligence officers, passing through these closely guarded premises, and then flying off to their new assignments at the top headquarters.

Thus 'Special Branch in England' became 'Special Branch in Europe', and my duties rapidly became almost wholly administrative. With not more than three exceptions, the officers sent to BP fitted in personally and professionally with their British counterparts with ease and concord on all sides. I take no personal credit for this, but I take pride at the ease, goodwill, and success with which the merging was accomplished by Britons and Americans alike.

9. An American at Bletchley Park

ROBERT M. SLUSSER

My assignment to Bletchley Park was the final link in a chain of events comprising both good luck and good timing. For example, US military authorities in the autumn of 1942 were looking for recruits to a newly established military intelligence training centre at Camp Ritchie, Maryland, just as I was earning my officer's qualifications at the infantry centre at Fort Benning, Georgia. Since I had a working knowledge of German, I was sent to Camp Ritchie instead of being posted to a field unit.

My graduation from Camp Ritchie in December 1942 came at a time when US military intelligence was becoming aware of how much it still had to learn about German Army order of battle, a subject in which the British had a long head start. My next assignment, accordingly, was to the Intelligence Corps in the Pentagon, where a basic training text was the ill-reputed Pink Book on German order of battle, replete with errors and omissions. Nevertheless, work on this faulty basis gave me my first taste of order-of-battle research.

The British, meanwhile, had sent an expeditionary team to Washington, on the look-out for suitable candidates for a still-to-be established joint UK–US intelligence unit.

What the British had in mind was a documentary research organization, to be named Military Intelligence Research Section (MIRS), operating as a semi-autonomous part of M.I.14 and headed by Major Eric Birley. In May 1943 I was sent to London, where I reported to Major Birley in the MIRS quarters being established near Trafalgar Square.

Eric Birley's contribution to Anglo-American intelligence in the Second World War was of fundamental importance. Building on a pre-war foundation of research into the order of battle of the Imperial Roman army, Birley had used his expertise in this seemingly remote speciality to establish a formidable mastery of the structure of the *Wehrmacht*.

Major Birley was not, however, operating in the dark; from the very beginning of the war he was granted access to the Ultra decodes, many of which contained information directly applicable to order-of-battle intelligence. An important part of his functions, therefore, was to use the Ultra material as a touchstone, constituting first-hand reliability as a documentary source.

Under Major Birley's tutelage I wrote several reports on current developments—for example, the formation by Germany of a series of field divisions with personnel drawn from the German Air Force, a practice which Major Birley was quick to recognize as an early symptom of a manpower shortage in Germany which was to assume a significant limiting role in the later phases of the war.

I was not destined, however, to continue my work in MIRS, for in November 1943 I was assigned to Bletchley Park.

In September 1943 an Anglo-American agreement was signed providing for incorporation of US personnel into the existing British Ultra structure. The American team was headed by Lieutenant-Colonel Telford Taylor, with Major Sam McKee as his deputy. Recruitment of suitable personnel was one of the tasks to be assumed by the Americans. An American officer was to be assigned the task of choosing Ultra texts of long-term rather than current urgency for dispatch by diplomatic pouch to Washington. This was to be the task which I performed.

Later American recruits were given a guided tour of Hut 3, with information on the duties and functions of the staff officers. In his unpublished memoir of his work at Bletchley Park, Landis Gores has left a fascinating record of one such tour. The complete absence of such a tour, in my experience, constituted a limiting factor in my comprehension of the work performed in Hut 3 and its suppliers of data elsewhere in Bletchley Park. Lacking such an overview, I made an erroneous identification of my functions and responsibilities, believing that it was my job to serve as a connecting link between Bletchley Park and MIRS, whereas the real purpose for which I had been chosen involved not a closer integration into the work of MIRS but a clear-cut break with that organization. Those with whom I had been working were now to be avoided, because of their lack of knowledge of the Ultra world. It took me a couple of weeks to grasp the realities of my position.

Later, other tasks were assigned to me, especially supervision of index-carding of data from Ultra decodes—an important task, since the Hut 3 Index had become the primary research tool for evaluation of the day-to-day traffic prepared by the Watch. I was not, however, made a part of the team of US officers on the Watch.

Among the British officers at Bletchley Park was Elizabeth Burbury, a lieutenant in the WAAF, who was a member of the staff of 3N, the small naval contingent in Hut 3.

Just before my arrival at the Park, Elizabeth, restless at her seemingly routine job, had applied for transfer to other work. Luckily for me, Elizabeth's boredom passed fairly quickly with my arrival. We were married on 27 June 1944, and on 10 April 1945 our daughter Virginia was born.

After VE-Day (8 May 1945) the work of Hut 3 continued but at a much less intensive pace. At this time, it was decided to prepare a history of the war as seen from Bletchley Park. Topics were assigned as opportunity presented itself. I chose to write on the opening phase of the German assault on the Soviet Union in the summer of 1941. My basic research materials were boxes of decoded messages, texts of which had not been processed because of the time lag between decoding and the hectic pace of the German advance. Units shifted daily and the Ultra record, especially the messages sent by Air Force liaison officers (the so-called Flivos), provided a detailed record of the conflict. A useful research tool was an excellent German atlas, *Stielers Handatlas*, a copy of which I had bought at a London bookstore.

I do not know whether the post-VE Day essays have been preserved or whether their significance was purely local. For me, however, the essay I prepared marked the start of a new phase of my education as a historian, in which the detailed reconstruction of past events served as the basis for an interpretation of history at short range. I used this technique in *The Berlin Crisis of 1961* (Baltimore, 1973) and *Stalin In October* (Baltimore, 1983; Moscow, 1987). In the long run, therefore, my work at Bletchley Park helped shape my career as a historian, although along somewhat unorthodox lines.

10. BP, Admiralty, and naval Enigma

F. H. HINSLEY

I WAS pitchforked into Bletchley Park in October 1939 at the age of 20 and at the beginning of my third year at Cambridge, one of about twenty undergraduates who formed the first of the annual drafts of recruits which GC&CS took direct from the universities for the rest of the war. I believe this first draft all came from Oxford or Cambridge, where some of the colleges had been asked to select promising material for interview at short notice. I was interviewed in the rooms of the President of St John's College, briefly and informally, by two men I came to know very well: A. G. Denniston, the head of Bletchley, and John Tiltman, the chief cryptanalyst. I was formally invited to join GC&CS about four days later. It was all done with minimum fuss and maximum dispatch.

By the end of 1939 I was the leading expert outside Germany on the wireless organization of the German Navy. This may sound an arrogant claim, but it does not amount to much. Nobody had known anything about that organization at the outbreak of war and, on the other hand, until it expanded in preparation for the invasion of Norway in the spring of 1940, it remained so simple that little could be learnt from studying it. But its behaviour was one of the few sources of information about the German Navy, and my knowledge of it, such as it was, made me one of the few channels of liaison between Bletchley and the Admiralty's Operational Intelligence Centre, the OIC.

In keeping with the scarcity of intelligence, communication with the Admiralty was distinctly primitive. I used a direct telephone line which I had to activate by turning a handle energetically before speaking. On this I spoke, a disembodied voice, to people who had never met me—Commander Denning, who looked after Germany's surface ships, Captain Thring, who kept the U-boat plot, and occasionally the head of the OIC, Rear-Admiral Clayton. They rarely took the initiative in turning the handle to speak to me, and they showed little interest in what I said to them. Nor was this of any moment until, some time before the invasion of Norway, they paid no attention to indications from German wireless behaviour that something unusual was taking place in the Baltic. Somewhat later, a few days before the aircraft-carrier HMS *Glorious* was sunk by the battle-cruisers *Scharnhorst* and *Gneisenau* off Norway in June 1940, they showed some interest in indications that heavy ships were about to leave the Baltic, but were not sufficiently convinced to send a warning to the Home Fleet.

Looking back, I sympathize with the OIC. It must have seemed to them that GC&CS was intruding by watching enemy wireless traffic, which was an Admiralty responsibility. I was a young civilian who, as they correctly assumed, knew nothing about navies; and they were not to know that traffic analysis, as this activity came to be called, was an academic exercise which, like the elucidation of a Latin text or the wresting of deductions from the Domesday Book, called more for immersion in detail than for experience at sea. Except occasionally, moreover, it was not so sound a basis for reliable inferences as I no doubt believed it to be. I was and I remain, on the other hand, full of admiration for the alacrity with which the OIC responded to the loss of the *Glorious*. It immediately invited me to spend a month in the Admiralty. It sent me on the first of several visits to the Home Fleet at Scapa, where I stayed on board the flagship and walked the deck with Admiral Tovey and his staff. And on my return it did all in its power to ensure through the regular exchange of visits, and with the assistance of new scrambler telephones, that there should be complete collaboration between the OIC and the Naval Section at Bletchley.

Until the spring of 1941 my share in the collaboration was still confined to the study of the external behaviour of the German Navy's wireless traffic, which I undertook both for clues that might be of operational value to the OIC and in case it might give any help to the cryptanalysts who worked on the underlying cipher—the Enigma. I do not remember that it helped the Admiralty much beyond answering questions from its intercept stations—where, however, its remarkably resourceful naval and WRNS operators needed little guidance in their watch on the enemy's transmissions—and advising the OIC that things remained normal or that something untoward was afoot; thus, it enabled us to remain relaxed about a German attempt to cross the Channel until, at a surprisingly late date in the autumn of 1940, new transmitters and new frequencies suddenly sprang up in the Channel area. That relations were close and harmonious, however, is evident from two Admiralty signals of this period. The first is an enquiry from the Home Fleet: 'What is your source?' The second is the Admiralty's reply, of which the full text is: 'Hinsley.' To the cryptanalysts the work was of no value before a small amount of documentary material, captured in Norwegian waters in the early months of 1941, enabled them to decrypt naval Enigma messages for a few days in April and May 1941.

These messages gave greater precision to traffic analysis by disclosing the structure of the naval organization that lay behind the wireless networks. They also extended my collaboration with the OIC to discussions about the significance of the contents of the decrypts. Some of these, for example, revealed at the end of April, before the *Bismarck* left the Baltic, that she was preparing for a distant cruise. At the same time, the application of better traffic analysis to the cryptanalytical knowledge derived from the captured material was of some assistance in the struggle of the cryptanalysts to solve more of the daily Enigma settings. But their efforts by no means solved the problem of the naval Enigma. Its messages were still read on only occasional days and with considerable delays until the beginning of June.

The fact that the problem was solved from that date, so that the main naval key was thereafter read regularly for the rest of the war, was mainly due to the close relations that had been built up between Bletchley and the OIC. This development—the most important product of that collaboration—was brought about when the occasional decrypts revealed that the Germans were keeping trawlers permanently on station to make weather reports from the Iceland–Greenland area—and led me to conclude that, although they were not using it for their signals, the ships carried the Enigma. With this information, which included details of the varying patrol positions, the OIC arranged the capture of a trawler early in May. The documents taken from her gave the cryptanalysts the daily settings for the month of June. Later in May some additional cryptanalytical material was obtained fortuitously from a U-boat, U-110, but, because some difficulties still barred the way to the total solution of the cipher, it was decided to capture a second trawler at the end of June. She provided the settings for July, and by the end of that month Bletchley's mastery of the naval Enigma was complete. Apart from a new key used by U-boats that was unreadable between February and December 1942, all important naval keys were read for the rest of the war.

It is not possible to say when, or whether, Bletchley would have achieved this feat without these extraordinary measures. What can be said is that the regular receipt of naval Enigma decrypts from June 1941 to the defeat of Germany in May 1945 changed the course of the war by exerting a powerful influence on the outcome of most naval operations between the first defeat of the U-boats in the Atlantic at the end of 1941 and the Normandy landings in June 1944.

The flow of decrypts made life for me onerous and exciting, but did not greatly change the nature of my activities. With a few interruptions for visits to Washington to discuss collaboration with the United States in the production and distribution of Ultra intelligence, I continued to be engaged on liaison between Bletchley and the OIC till the summer of 1944, on the one hand debating with the Admiralty about the significance of the contents of the decrypts and, on the other, attempting to apply traffic analysis and operational information from the Admiralty for the benefit of the cryptanalysts in their daily struggle to solve the Enigma settings. After the Normandy landings, however, I became increasingly involved in negotiations with Washington until I returned to Cambridge in the spring of 1946.

PART TWO
Enigma

11. The Enigma machine: Its mechanism and use

ALAN STRIPP

THE Enigma machine, first patented in 1919, was after various improvements adopted by the German Navy in 1926, the Army in 1928, and the Air Force in 1935. It was used also by the *Abwehr*, the *Sicherheitsdienst*, the railways, and other government departments. From then until 1939, and indeed throughout the war, successive refinements were introduced, varying from service to service, and there were detailed changes in operating procedure until 1945. The following short description can therefore summarize only its main features and mention only a few of the Enigma variations.

The Enigma was used solely to encipher and decipher messages. In its standard form it could not type a message out, let alone transmit or receive it. From the cipher operator's point of view, it consisted first of a keyboard of 26 letters in the pattern of the normal German typewriter:

Q W E R T Z U I O
A S D F G H J K
P Y X C V B N M L

with no keys for numerals or punctuation. Behind this keyboard was a 'lampboard' of 26 small circular windows, each bearing a letter in the same QWERTZU pattern, which could light up, one at a time, from bulbs underneath. (The model with an A–Z keyboard, shown in several books on the Enigma, is a Polish-French replica, not an actual Enigma machine.) It measured about $13^1/_2$" × 11" × 6" (34 × 28 × 15cm), and weighed about 26 lbs (12 kilos).

Plates 1–3 show Enigma machines and wheels, and Plate 1 should be consulted in conjunction with Fig. 11.1. Behind the lampboard is the scrambler unit, consisting of a fixed wheel at each end, and a central space for three rotating wheels. The wheel to the right of this space is the fixed entry wheel or plate (*Eintrittwalze*), carrying 26

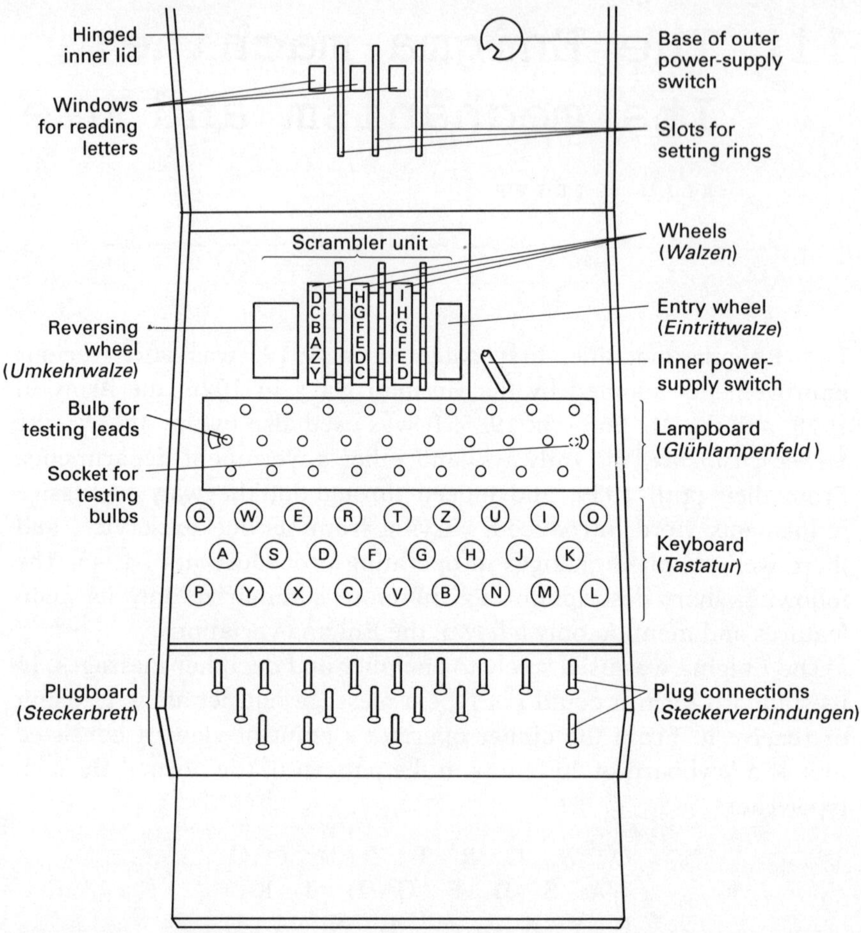

FIG. 11.1. 3-wheel Army Enigma machine (with plugboard leads omitted for clarity)

contacts round its left side, ultimately connected to the keys of the keyboard in ordinary alphabetical order. To the left of the space is the reversing wheel (*Umkehrwalze*), which scrambles the current it receives and sends it back by a different route from that by which it came. This wheel too has a circle of 26 contacts.

The three central wheels were selected from a box of five. Monthly orders specified a new choice every day, as well as their relative order in the machine, e.g. V–I–III or II–IV–I, etc. Each of these rotating wheels has a circle of 26 spring-loaded terminals on its right side and 26 flat circular terminals on its left, so as to provide an ever-changing series of connections as it revolves. Each contains a different internal wiring and carries the letters A–Z or the numbers 01–26 round its inner ring, which can be turned and locked in any setting before the wheels specified for a given day are inserted into the machine in the prescribed order, though they can still be turned bodily through slits in the inner lid, and the letters A–Z can be read one at a time in the window beside each slit. The specified setting of ring against wheel was called the *Ringstellung*.

Each time a letter key is pressed, the right wheel moves on one of its 26 places. Once during every 26 moves, at the 'turnover position' of the right wheel, the middle wheel will also move on one place; and when the middle wheel reaches its own turnover position it moves on again when the next letter is keyed, together with the left wheel.

Finally, the vertical front of the Enigmas used by the Armed Services contained a 'plugboard' with 26 pairs of sockets, again in the QWERTZU pattern. These could be connected by twin-cable leads—for example, coupling C to P, M to Z, J to S, and so on; but some sockets, usually six, were left unconnected. They were said to be 'self-steckered'. *Stecker* is a plug; *Steckerbrett* (usually called 'steckerboard' at Bletchley) is a plugboard.

Each time the cipher clerk keyed a letter, the right wheel moved on mechanically one place and, as explained above, from time to time the centre and left wheels also moved. As each new letter (e.g. P) was keyed, the current, normally provided by an internal 4.5 volt battery—although an outside power source could be used—flowed from a terminal under that key to a socket (e.g. P) on the plugboard. From there it either travelled via a lead to another socket (e.g. L), or, if the first socket was self-steckered, it stayed as P. Either way, it ran to the entry wheel, which did not alter it, through the pairs of terminals on all central wheels—each of which normally altered it again—to the *Umkehrwalze* or reversing wheel (with another alteration) and back through different circuits in all three wheels (hence still further alterations), out unaltered through the entry wheel, and back to the plugboard. Here its course again depended on whether that socket was self-steckered or cross-steckered; either way, it finally reached the lampboard and lit a bulb (e.g. W). Although the process, involving up to nine changes on the standard three-wheel machine, has taken some time to describe, it naturally took place virtually instantaneously. And it must be remembered that the moving on of at least one wheel, for every new letter keyed, introduced a new set of circuits for each new letter.

It is important to note that, if you press any key (e.g. B), any other letter may light up (e.g. T); but if you continue to key letter B, the lampboard may give, say, P, F, O, J, C . . . , but never B. The sequence will repeat only after 16,900 (26 × 25 × 26) keyings, when the inner mechanism returns to the same position. Messages were limited to a maximum of 250 letters to avoid this recurrence, which might otherwise have helped us.

In choosing a basic set-up for the machine, there was a choice from the 60 possible wheel orders, the 17,576 ring-settings for each wheel order, and over 150 million million stecker-pairings (allowing for six self-steckered letters). So the total number of possible daily keys was about 159 million million million. In each of these configurations, the machine had a period of 16,900 (26 × 25 × 26) keyings before the mechanism returned to its original position. But there were weak points. The Enigma is simply a swapping machine of an advanced type. All Enigmas of the same model, set up in the same way, will produce identical swaps. In any position where keying B gives T, keying T will give B. And keying B can never give B.

Although it was possible for one cipher clerk to carry out all the tasks of the enciphering procedure himself, this would have been a lengthy and confusing process; normally it called for a team of two. The cipher clerk would look at his signal text, which might begin *Panzer* ('tank(s)'). Typing P might give M on the lampboard; his Number Two would read this and write it down—and so on through the message. The radio operator would then transmit the resulting enciphered signal. But first the machine had to be properly set up.

Every month the operating instructions specified daily or more frequent changes to several variables (see Plate 4). A typical daily 'key' (taking examples from Plate 4) gave the clerk instructions for the first three steps of the enciphering procedure.

1. The wheel order (*Walzenlage*): the choice and position of the three wheels to be used (e.g. I–V–III).
2. The ring-setting (*Ringstellung*) of the left, middle, and right wheels (e.g. 06–20–24 denoting FTX).
3. The cross-plugging or 'steckering' (*Steckerverbindungen*) (e.g. UA PF etc.).

The cipher clerk would set his machine up accordingly. Until the end of April 1940, he then continued as follows:

4. He turned his three wheels to a position chosen *at random*, the 'indicator-setting' (e.g. **JCM**).
5. He twice keyed his own *randomly-selected* choice of text-setting, or 'message-setting' (e.g. **BGZBGZ**).
6. This came out as the 'indicator' (e.g. **TNUFDQ**).
7. He set his wheels at BGZ and keyed the clear text of the message, thus obtaining the enciphered text, letter by letter.

The message as transmitted included four elements, as follows:

(*a*) The preamble, transmitted *in clear* before the message itself, showing call-sign, time of origin, and number of letters in the text; this was followed by his chosen indicator-setting (e.g. JCM) (No. 4 above).

(*b*) A five-letter group comprising two padding letters (*Füllbuchstaben*) followed by the three-letter 'discriminant' (*Kenngruppe*), e.g. JEU, which distinguished various types of Enigma traffic and showed which of many 'keys' (sets of operator instructions) were being used. The latter were known at Bletchley by cover-names such as Kestrel, Light Blue, etc.

(*c*) The six letters of the 'indicator' TNUFDQ (No. 6 above).

(*d*) The enciphered text of the signal, in five-letter groups.

Once the signal had been transmitted in this form, and the text handed to the receiving cipher clerk—whose wheels would already comply with the same daily instructions Nos. 1–3—he would duly move his wheels to JCM (No. 4 above), key TNUFDQ (No. 6), and read the reciprocally enciphered result BGZBGZ (No. 5). He then turned his wheels to BGZ and deciphered the text by keying it out, with his Number Two noting each letter in turn.

After 1 May 1940 this procedure was changed. Presumably the German cryptographic authorities had belatedly recognized that the *double* encipherment of the text-setting represented a security risk which far outweighed the advantage of the double-check it provided. From that date the random choice of text-setting (e.g. BGZ as in No. 5) was keyed only once, giving TNU instead of TNUFDQ.

The reader should also bear in mind that the foregoing description of mechanism and procedure applies only to the standard Enigma used by the German Army and Air Force. The Navy provided three special wheels in addition to the five Army–Air Force wheels, and thus had a set of eight to choose from. On 1 February 1942 they added an extra settable wheel, next to the *Umkehrwalze*, resulting in the M4 model, often called the '4-wheel' Enigma. The railways, police, and post office used older Enigma models, while the *Abwehr* used an advanced but unsteckered one, and a different enciphering procedure, with a *Grundstellung* specified for each day's settings, instead of allowing a random choice (see Chapter 16). Certain other unusual models had a 28-letter keyboard and wheel system; a set of wheels for one such early model is shown in Plate 3. It seems clear that the '29-contact rotor' (wheel) suggested for this machine could not have existed.[1] The Enigma was essentially a *reversing* machine with an even number of wheel contacts, and Plate 3 shows that, although Ä and Ü have been added, there is no Ö. The 29-letter keyboard of this machine is thought to have had one letter, X, which bypassed the wheels and always gave X.

Note

1. C. A. Deavours and L. Kruh, *Machine Cryptography and Modern Cryptanalysis* (Norwood, Mass.: Artech House Inc.; 1985), 96–7.

12. Hut 6: Early days

STUART MILNER-BARRY

When the war broke out in 1939 I was in the Argentine, playing chess for the British team in the Olympiad. My great friend and rival, C. H. O'D. Alexander, was another member, as was Harry Golombek, late chess correspondent of *The Times*. We returned home immediately, and before long found ourselves at Bletchley Park, where we remained for the duration. We had been recruited by Gordon Welchman, an old friend of mine at Cambridge.

Welchman was a brilliant mathematician, a research fellow at Sidney Sussex. He and I came up to Trinity College, Cambridge, in the same term (October 1925). We became friends, and, as I lived in Cambridge with my mother (who was Cambridge born and bred, the daughter of Dr W. H. Besant, a well-known mathematical fellow of St John's College) we saw a lot of Gordon at our home in Park Terrace. In due course Welchman married and came to live in Cambridge himself.

Alexander was three or four years younger than Welchman and myself, but I had known him ever since, in 1924, he had beaten me at Hastings in the British Boys' Chess Championship, which I had won the previous year at the age of 16. Hugh Alexander was a scholar of King's and also a mathematician, though not, I fancy, in Welchman's class. He came from Birmingham, where my sister (the eldest of our family) was a lecturer in English and Anglo-Saxon at the University. When he left Cambridge he became a schoolmaster and taught mathematics at Winchester College. But before long he married an Australian girl some years older than himself. She was unhappy in the cloistered atmosphere at Winchester, and eventually he gave up teaching at which he was very good, and took up a business career in London for which he was ill-adapted; he was far too untidy even to look like a businessman.

Welchman had, I think, been recruited into intelligence work before the war broke out, and he had already done a good deal of research into the mysteries of the Enigma machine. These of course came easily enough to Alexander, but I am (in spite of my ancestry) almost innumerate. I therefore found Gordon Welchman's patient explanations very difficult to follow, and to this day I could not claim that I fully understood how the machine worked, let alone what was involved in the problems of breaking and reading the Enigma cipher. Fortunately this did not matter too much, as I was able to make myself useful in other ways—principally because I had a working knowledge of German.

To return to the beginning of the war: fairly early in 1940 we three found ourselves installed at The Shoulder of Mutton Inn, Old Bletchley, about a mile from the entrance to Bletchley Park. Here Hugh and I were most comfortably looked after by an amiable landlady, Mrs Bowden. As an inn-keeper she did not seem to be unduly burdened by rationing, and we were able (among other privileges) to invite selected colleagues to supper on Sunday nights, which was a great boon. Welchman moved out fairly soon to live with his wife in the town, but Hugh and I happily remained at the Shoulder until the end of the war.

When we first came to GC&CS, Bletchley Park was a tiny organization, probably not more than thirty strong. It consisted of a few old-time professionals who had worked in Room 40 at the Admiralty in the First World War, such, for example, as Dillwyn Knox, a Fellow of King's who died during the war, and A. G. Denniston, and new recruits such as Welchman and Alan Turing. Knox had, so I understood, been defeated by the Enigma, and the main credit for solving the Enigma and subsequently exploiting its success, should (subject to the Poles) probably go to the other two.

Turing was a strange and ultimately a tragic figure. But as an admirable biography of him has been written,[1] I shall say no more here. Welchman, on the other hand has, I think, never received his just deserts, quite apart from being ridiculously persecuted on security grounds for revealing, some forty years after the event, how the job of breaking the Enigma had been done. Welchman was a visionary, and a very practical visionary at that. In spite of Knox's failure, he always believed the Enigma could be broken. He also realized the enormous importance of the success, and took it for granted that, when the phoney war ended, the Germans would rely principally on the Enigma for their military communications. He foresaw much of what would be involved in the way of expansion of staff, machinery (the bombes), and all the other necessary substructure. And he had the fire in his belly that enabled him to cajole higher authority into supplying our wants. If Gordon Welchman had not been there, I doubt if Ultra would have played the part that it undoubtedly did in shortening the war.

The first essential, once the initial breakthrough had been made, was the expansion of staff. This was done to begin with on an 'old-boy' basis. Welchman knew a few undergraduate mathematicians whom he had supervised at Sidney Sussex. I lived in Cambridge and had the advantage of a close connection with Newnham College, where my sister Alda had been Vice-Principal until her untimely death in 1938. So I was able to recruit a few girls from both Newnham and Girton Colleges, such as Mary Wilson, Wendy Hinde, Margaret Usborne, and Jane Reynolds (later Jane Monroe), who formed, together with a number of undergraduates from men's colleges, the invaluable nucleus of the original Hut 6. At about the same time I made a very profitable foray to the Scottish Universities.

As a result of these efforts, we were able, even during the period of the phoney war, to put ourselves on to a three-shift basis, and there of course we stayed throughout the war. This was during the winter and spring of 1940, and the decrypts themselves were mostly practice by the Germans—nursery rhymes and the like. But the exercise gave *us* invaluable practice as well as the Germans, and provided us with a battery of cribs, of which we were able to make invaluable use when the war became real.

This happened, as I remember, with the invasion of Norway, about the end of April and beginning of May 1940. The keys we had been breaking were a practice key and the Red (general) key of the German Air Force. The Red key became of vital importance immediately, and remained so all through the war and in all the main theatres of war except Africa. Another key was the Army–Air Force key, the Yellow, used only in Norway.

The Red was the great standby that kept Hut 6 going. I cannot remember any period when we were held up for more than a few days at a time. Indeed, if we had been, it was by no means certain that we would have been able to get started again. The fact that we nearly always broke the Red, often quite early in the day, may give the impression that it was as easy as falling off a log; indeed Hut 3, our intelligence opposite numbers to whom all our decrypts were sent immediately, took it for granted that they would receive their daily ration. But there was in fact no certainty at all about it.

This leads me to stress how extraordinarily lucky we were. The Germans regarded the Enigma as a perfectly secure machine, proof against cryptanalysts however talented and ingenious they might be. Several times during the war, when it became inescapably clear that a great deal of intelligence was finding its way to the Allies, the Germans set up commissions of enquiry into the security of the Enigma. They always came to the conclusion that the machine was invulnerable and that the leakage must be due to secret agents. And the fact is that, had it not been for human error, compounded by a single design quirk, the Enigma was intrinsically a perfectly secure machine. If the wireless operators who enciphered the messages had followed strictly the procedures laid down, the messages might have been unbreakable. But of course that was the whole trouble. It is easy enough in principle to observe the relatively simple rules, such as, for example, avoiding enciphering the address and title of the recipient in the same way at the beginning and the end of the message. But if you are a harassed machine operator, it is so much easier to do what you have always done than consciously to force yourself to put your 'Xs' in different positions, or not to put 'Xs' in at all for punctuation, that it is very difficult to blame those concerned.

In claiming credit, as I have done, for Turing and Welchman for the initial breakthrough in the Enigma, I should stress the original and vital contribution made by the Poles. The Poles had always been brilliant cryptographers, and had been breaking and reading some Enigma ciphers since the early 1930s. When the war broke out, however, the Germans made a major change in the machine which put the Poles out of business; but shortly before the war and in anticipation of it, the French Intelligence Chief (Colonel Bertrand) and ourselves had got together with the Poles, who not only gave us an Enigma machine, but shared with us all their knowledge and experience. They had a group of distinguished mathematicians, including one Marian Rejewski and another, Colonel Langer, whom I met after the war. It was always a mystery to me that the Polish contingent was not incorporated at Bletchley during the war, where they would no doubt have made an invaluable contribution; but in fact they were side-tracked in France and had to be evacuated when the Germans overran the whole of the country. I can only assume there were security doubts, and I believe the Poles continued to operate their own organization; but I feel there must have been a sad waste of resources somewhere.

So much has been written on the technical side, including, of course, Gordon Welchman's own *The Hut Six Story*,[2] and many erudite productions by Polish cryptanalysts, that it would be pointless to add to it. But for the non-technical layman who would like to have some idea of what was going on, it might be of interest if, as a non-technical layman myself, I were to try to describe things as I saw them.

The Enigma, an electric machine, looked like a typewriter with a typewriter keyboard. But it could be set up in millions of different ways, so that if you typed out an ordinary sentence on it you would get nothing but a jumble of nonsense groups. In order to turn these nonsense groups back into the original German you therefore had to have a machine set up exactly as the original operator had it. Merely having a machine did you no good at all, and since the Germans changed their machine settings every twenty-four hours, you were helpless unless you knew in advance, or could in some way work out, what the new setting for the next day was to be, out of the millions available.

Since we did not know, we had to start from scratch every day; and the basis of breaking was known as the 'crib'. Take, for example, a routine message like *keine besonderen Ereignisse* ('no special developments'). This might appear in the enciphered version as:

Text:	KEINE	BESON	DEREN	EREIG	NISSE
Cipher:	ACDOU	LMNRS	TDOPS	FCIMN	RSTDO

This jumble would form the core of the message. But, of course, most messages had to have an address and a signatory; thus there would have to be two or three groups beforehand and two or three at the end, so that, even if you knew that somewhere in a short message (e.g. twenty groups of five) there lurked the five groups which represented *keine besonderen Ereignisse*, you did not know which five consecutive groups they were.

Here we were greatly assisted by an idiosyncracy of the Enigma machine. This was that a letter 'could never go to itself': in other words, if you tapped A on your machine, you might get any letter appearing except A.

As you will see, this was a great help in eliminating possible candidates. If you look back at *keine besonderen Ereignisse*, you will see that in the enciphered version beginning ACDOU there is nowhere a clash of letters between the German and the enciphered groups. But if, for example, you were looking for the most likely position in your twenty groups for the *keine besonderen Ereignisse* sequence, and you noticed that under the B in *besonderen* was another B, you would know for a certainty that that could not be the right position for the core of the message, and would have to look elsewhere.

Let us assume, however, that you have guessed the right position for the five *keine besonderen Ereignisse* groups. The problem is now to set up your own machine in an identical position in all respects to the German machine. If you could do that, you would have broken the Enigma Red key for that day; and then you could decipher all the messages sent over the air by the Germans for that day in that particular key. But how was this problem to be resolved?

In theory, of course, it could be done by running through all possible settings of the machine until, as by a miracle, the tapping of ACDOU LMNRS etc. produced KEINE BESONDEREN EREIGNISSE. But in practice this was completely impossible. It might have taken years to run through all the possible permutations and combinations, and the war might well have been over before we had succeeded with even one key for one day. However, given that we were confident that somewhere in a jumble of consecutive five-letter groups was concealed a text of intelligible German—twenty-five letters such as in *keine besonderen Ereignisse* should normally be quite sufficient—that would put us well on the road to success. So long a stretch would enormously cut down the number of machine settings that would have to be tried; and modern technology had, in fact, provided a machine (known as the bombe) which would normally provide the correct setting of the Enigma within a few hours or so.

In fact, the Germans used a number of keys every day. Some we were able to break and some not. As I explained earlier, the Red was the great standby, but at times others were of even greater operational importance. There was, for example, the Brown. The Brown was the key used by Kampf Gruppe 100, which was responsible for the so-called Baedeker raids on key targets such as Bristol, Birmingham, Coventry, and so on. My recollection is that the Brown was a relatively easy key to break, and that we often broke it fairly early in the day. Obviously, the earlier the better, so that countermeasures could be put in hand: sometimes even squadrons in the air, or at least such anti-aircraft ground measures as were possible.

Unfortunately, the Germans did not tell us what the targets were. They simply referred to them by numbers (*Ziel* so-and-so), and we might or might not be able to guess what town was intended. There was an obvious risk that, if we took countermeasures, we should give away that we knew from Enigma that X was the target that day. There was a story, which can still be heard from time to time, that it was known that Coventry was to be the target for a devastating raid, and that Churchill forbade any special precautions for fear of giving away the all important secret that we were reading the Enigma. What Churchill would have done had he been confronted with this terrible dilemma I have, of course, no idea. But it so happens that we did not know the target for that night until too late; in fact, as I remember, we were expecting a very heavy raid on London.

While Brown was, I suppose, the most dramatic of the various keys with which we were concerned, it was when Rommel invaded Egypt that Hut 6 really came into its own. The German expeditionary force had its own keys, which we named after particular birds, and the most important bird was Chaffinch. I think we read Chaffinch pretty consistently after the spring of 1942. And since the Germans had no other regular means of communication with their forces abroad, we were given a pretty complete picture of their strength and disposition, as well as their intentions; and, as a by-product, a lot of information about their U-boat movements in the Mediterranean. (This was quite distinct from the U-boat warfare in the Atlantic, which was looked after by Hut 8 under Alexander and which dealt in the U-boats' own naval Enigma key). I remember I made Chaffinch my own particular concern, if that day's key had not been broken by the time I came on deck.

Hut 6 was the cryptanalytical section; Hut 3 the intelligence section. We broke the keys, the messages were deciphered as they came in by our deciphering section, and the contents were passed immediately to Hut 3. It was Hut 3's responsibility to decide what they meant, to decide the degree of importance and urgency, and to report accordingly to London. Naturally, it was essential that we should keep in the closest touch with Hut 3, which was organized in watches just as we were; and the heads of our respective watches were in continual discussion about the priorities for breaking and deciphering. In the early days, before the production of bombes overtook the requirement, this sometimes produced very difficult discussions between

Hut 6 and Hut 8, because we shared the same bombes. But, fortunately, Alexander and I were such close friends as well as colleagues, that I do not remember any serious dispute ever arising. In any case, I took it for granted that ultimately breaking the U-boat cipher must take priority, for failure to read it could lose us the war. But naturally we took guidance from Hut 3 about which of our Hut 6 ciphers took priority in our sphere.

Once again, we were very fortunate. Hut 3 was staffed rather differently from Hut 6; whereas Hut 6 had a high proportion of undergraduates (even one or two straight from school), those in Hut 3 were for the most part older. They were, naturally, German scholars and not cryptanalysts, many of them schoolmasters or young dons of their University (predominantly Cambridge as it happened). But they were presided over by Group-Captain Jones. Jones was not a scholar or an academic; I suppose he must have had some knowledge of German, but primarily he was a business man coming, I think, from Lancashire. I do not know what brought him to Bletchley, but it proved a brilliant choice. He was a genuinely modest man who regarded himself as having little to contribute compared with the boffins with whom he was surrounded; in fact he was a first-rate administrator who was liked and trusted by everyone. After the war he stayed on in the service, and ended up as the head of GCHQ at Cheltenham.

I do not imagine that any war since classical times, if ever, has been fought in which one side read consistently the main military and naval intelligence of the other. Of course, the Germans read a fair amount of our own codes, but in nothing like the comprehensive and all-embracing manner in which we read theirs. It was rather like a game of bridge in which we were shown the opponents' cards before the hand was played. One might well have expected that, with the cards so stacked on one side, so big an advantage would be reaped by the reading side that the result of the contest could hardly be in doubt. But, although the intelligence balance was enormously in our favour, its only really decisive effect was in the battle of the Atlantic. It can, I think, be pretty confidently asserted that, had we not at the most crucial times and for long periods read the U-boat ciphers, we should have lost the war. I have seen it argued that, in the long run, it would have made no difference because the Americans would have more than made up any conceivable losses in our—and their—shipping; but this makes big assumptions about how the United Kingdom was to be kept from starving in the meantime. Certainly, when, as did happen in 1942, Hut 8 was held up for months on end on the U-boat ciphers, the losses in the battle of the Atlantic rose in the most alarming way. This was particularly so after the entry of the United States into the war, before the Americans had had time to organize a convoy system on the American littoral.

So far as the Army and Air Force were concerned, the advantage conferred on the Allies must have meant a very great saving of lives and, I imagine, a considerable shortening of the war. I would not suggest that it made the difference between victory and defeat. Indeed, in the early days the disparity in overall strength and readiness between the Germans and the Allies was such that no amount of knowing their intentions could prevent them carrying them out; only later, when the strengths became more equal, did the intelligence advantage become a match-winning factor, and remained so until the last days of Hitler.

I felt at the time—and looking back on it after more than half a century, I feel exactly the same—that I was extraordinarily lucky to have found myself in that particular job at that time; and I suspect that almost everybody concerned in the Enigma operation at every level felt the same. We were slightly ashamed, or at any rate unhappy, that we should be leading such relatively safe and comfortable lives when a large proportion of the population, whether civilian or in uniform, was in so much danger. But at the same time, we could not help realizing that our work, individually and collectively, was of enormous importance in the conduct of the war. For that reason alone there was a spirit of camaraderie which I think never failed us, even when the war generally seemed to be going badly, or when we found ourselves temporarily delayed in delivering the goods. There was a perpetual excitement about each day's breaks, at whatever time of day or night they might come. To the chess player, it was rather like a long-running tournament with several rounds being played every day, and never any certainty that the luck would continue to hold. The friendships that were formed during the war have in many cases survived fifty years later, and that applies equally to some of the small but very high-powered American contingent, headed on the cryptanalytical side by Captain (as he then was) William Bundy. No more admirable representative of our great new ally could possibly have been selected. Many of us feared, I think, that the Americans with their enormous superiority in manpower and resources of every kind, would quickly reduce Hut 6—and no doubt Hut 8 as well—to a very subordinate and minor role. Nothing of the kind happened. Bundy and his colleagues were anxious only to learn and to help. They learnt very quickly and their help was invaluable. Above all, able and high-powered as they were, they were modesty itself in their demeanour. There could have been no happier partnership.

It goes without saying that, since we were frequently reading the enemy's communications as soon as their intended recipients, some pretty dramatic messages were brought to me in Hut 6. I remember especially a message describing in considerable detail the German plans for the invasion of Crete in some fortnight's time, and also thinking to myself (quite wrongly, alas!), 'Now, we really have got them this time.' And also the desperate message from the German commander in the battle of Normandy in 1944, which heralded the collapse of the German resistance in the Cotentin peninsula and enabled the American tanks to break for Paris. This kind of message, shown to us maybe in the middle of the night, gave one an extraordinary sensation of living with history. But of course it was not individual messages of this kind that mattered most, though the Prime Minister took the liveliest interest in them and No. 10 had to be kept constantly in touch. It was the complete build-up which Hut 3 was able to construct of the whole German side of the fence that counted, and that could have been achieved in no other way.

The Cretan episode was, from the Hut 6 point of view, the greatest disappointment of the war. It seemed a near certainty that, with General Freyberg warned that the crucial point of the invasion was to be the airborne attack on the Maleme airport, and the time and every detail of the operation spelt out for us in advance, and given the appalling difficulty and danger of any airborne invasion in the best of circumstances, the attack would be ignominiously thrown back; and we awaited the operation with anxiety but also with a considerable degree of confidence.

In the event, it was a 'damned close-run thing'. The Germans took Crete from the air, and we lost a great deal of shipping in trying to save it. The best that could be said about it, from the Allied point of view, was that, though the conquest of Crete was ultimately achieved, it was so enormously expensive that the Germans never attempted an airborne invasion on that scale again. We fully expected, I believe, that Crete would be followed by Malta; but it never came. So, since the loss of Malta would have been an appalling catastrophe, we can at least be assured that the defenders of Crete lost their lives in a good cause.

Notes

1. A. Hodges, *Alan Turing: The Enigma* (London: Hutchinson, 1983).
2. G. Welchman, *The Hut Six Story* (London: Allen Lane, 1982; Penguin, 1984).

13. Hut 6: 1941–1945

DEREK TAUNT

I SPENT the Long Vac Term of 1939 in Cambridge, making some tentative passes at research problems in Divergent Series proposed to me by my prospective supervisor Professor G. H. Hardy, and playing cricket and tennis on the Jesus College Close. I had graduated in Mathematics that June, had spent three weeks at a camp for unemployed Welsh miners on Bredon Hill run by the University Scouts (though never myself a scout), and was trying to pretend that the worst was not about to happen. When it did, there was nothing for it but to register with the Joint Recruiting Board, wait for one's number to come up, and in the meantime to lead as normal a life as one decently could while the phoney war continued. Heroics were not yet the order of the day. The ghastly experience of the First World War had persuaded the Government that specialist training and talents should be applied to appropriate wartime tasks, and, as a well-qualified mathematician (though admittedly one of a markedly 'pure' complexion), I could expect that suitable employment in the war effort would soon be found for me.

Accordingly I reported early in December to the External Ballistics department of the Ordnance Board at Kemnal Manor, Chiselhurst, and was allocated to the 'low-angle' group. There were five of us in a temporary hut, where Captain Murphy, an ex-artillery man, led a team which comprised three other permanent civil servants and myself. Our task was to analyse test-firings and compute range-tables for surface-to-surface weapons. This work was undoubtedly important, and for a while seemed challenging. I learnt new methods and techniques (such as the dexterous use of a Brunsviga calculator, and the drawing of fifteen-foot graphs on the plotting-room table). But the gradual realization that the work could be done by any intelligent and conscientious youngster with a good O level in mathematics blunted any feeling I might have had (even after succeeding Captain Murphy as low-level chief when he replaced his immediate superior in the hierarchy) that it could justify my being kept out of the firing line.

After one abortive attempt to escape, foundering on the requirement of some specific experience in applied mathematics that I lacked, I found myself, in the middle of August 1941, transferred to GC&CS at Bletchley Park. It was shortly after the German invasion of Russia had greatly widened the scope for high-grade cryptanalysis, and the staff to deal with it was being expanded too. By good fortune I landed in Hut 6, two of whose leading figures—the Cambridge geometers Gordon Welchman and Dennis Babbage—had been known to me as an undergraduate. My new colleagues included several of my own mathematical contemporaries, and it was only later that it occurred to me that, had I been at either Marlborough or Sidney Sussex, instead of the City of London School and Jesus College, I might just have arrived at BP in its great pioneering days, rather than at 'the end of the beginning'.

I was allocated a billet in a railwayman's home at Stony Stratford, some six miles away by estate car (and later, as numbers increased, by superannuated coach), and assigned to Control. This section maintained constant contact between Hut 6 and the W/T stations intercepting the Enigma traffic. We were thus at the outer end of the production line which ended when the raw material, transmuted in the deciphering room into plain-text messages; was passed for interpretation to our neighbours in Hut 3. Between these extremes were the registration of the incoming messages, the breaking of the various daily keys in the Watch, the huts housing the bombes (electro-mechanical machines to test the 'menus' provided by the Watch), and the Machine Room; and the deciphering of traffic as each of the keys for the day was broken. The daily routine of breaking and deciphering occupied most of the staff on a three-shift basis, but others were concerned with external relations, administration, and research, for example on recalcitrant or never-yet-broken keys. The long, single-storey wooden hut buzzed with ceaseless and purposeful action, of which no memento or echo persisted when, fifty years later, I and other survivors from its great days revisited BP, at a time when the shell that had housed our historic exertions was derelict and under threat of demolition.

In Control we received hourly reports from the intercepting stations, of which those I most clearly remember were War Office Y Group at Beaumanor, RAF Chicksands, and (most surprisingly) the Police Station at Denmark Hill in South London, where there were machines for intercepting and recording high-speed transmissions.

Part of our job was to ensure that important frequencies were double-banked, both to avoid messages being missed and to provide confirmation of texts. A single false letter could wreck a crib or the accurate placement of a reciphered text. So messages of particular importance to the code-breakers in the Watch would be checked promptly with the original intercepts. We developed a healthy respect for the intercepting operators, whose task was to record with great accuracy messages in Morse code comprising up to fifty groups of five apparently random letters. There was no redundancy to spare, as with clear text. Some operators became so skilful that they could recognize their opposite numbers by their style of Morse transmission, just as one may recognize the handwriting of a friend or (perhaps a more apt comparison) the touch of a well-known pianist. This facility could be most valuable in identifying units when their frequencies or call-signs changed or they were moved around. It was commonplace for the operators to have identified the day's discriminants of important keys before we were able to tell them. The limited amount of chat in clear or in Q-code could also on occasion provide useful information, and no doubt relieved the tedium of receiving unintelligible messages whose importance they could only infer from our interest in them.

Although Control was not the most glamorous or exciting section in which to work, it gave a splendid overview of the whole Hut 6 operation. Its function involved being in constant touch not only with the intercept stations, but also with all the other sections of Hut 6, and often with Hut 3, who might ask for special attention to be given to emerging units or networks providing valuable intelligence. Our head was the scientist Professor John Colman, reputedly of the mustard family. He was in command of the strategy of interception; we of the day-to-day tactics. His deceptively laid-back manner remains a vivid memory, as does 'Titicaca', his accumulation of miscellaneous information, which he had named after the lake in the Andes fed by many rivers but with no outflow. The old hands in Control—Bob Baker, Reg Parker, Graham Lambert, Jack Winton—had worked in banks, and seemed older and more worldly-wise than the general run of staff. Of course the founding fathers—Welchman, Milner-Barry, and Babbage—were more mature, but the rest of us were like a bunch of enthusiastic undergraduates, our exuberance and in-jokes leavened by the civilizing influence of the women members of the team. The universal feeling of comradeship in a demanding but exhilarating enterprise was palpable, contrasting vividly with my previous experience of civil-service life, where formality and hierarchy were dominant characteristics.

The camaraderie we enjoyed and the justified pride we shared in our role and achievements were no doubt enhanced by the secrecy which surrounded our activities. Though the various sections in Hut 6 were kept aware of what was going on, we did not discuss our work outside its confines, let alone with family or friends in the outside world. An example of a prime snippet of secret knowledge which we had to keep to ourselves concerned the *Bismarck*, which had been sunk some three months before my arrival in Hut 6. I was told that its whereabouts at a critical moment had been revealed in an Enigma message to a high-ranking German Air Force officer, whose son was aboard the doomed ship. Thus our success in currently reading Red, the main German Air Force key, had played an important part in the drama. Though I have seen no explicit confirmation in print of this anecdote, it is compatible with Hinsley's account of the affair.[1]

Fifty years ago the use of a Christian name among colleagues usually indicated a considerable degree of intimacy. (I still remember my mother's disappointment when, after reading in my letter home that I had shared a pleasant punting expedition with a Cambridge friend, it dawned on her that 'Rose' was the surname of a fellow-undergraduate at my college.) Certainly I never learned the Christian names of Captain Murphy or the redoubtable Miss Hearn in the low-angle hut. But here all was different. The first time I lifted a telephone in Control I was greeted with the mellifluous announcement 'Sheila here', before I had even met any of the staff of the Registration Room (or was it the Machine or Decoding Room?—memory has lacunae, and, though the voice and persona of Sheila Dunlop are vividly retained, her precise place in the scheme of things eludes me). This typified the way we all treated each other as close and valued friends. When a given name failed to provide unique identification we resorted to other devices, such as distinguishing John Manisty from John Monroe as 'J.C.' and 'J.G.', or by calling David Uzielli by his second name Rex to differentiate him from David Gaunt. (These two possessed splendid, if rarely used, nicknames, namely 'The Unicorn-Zebra' from the telephone spellers he used for his surname, and 'The Mock Hurtle' from his energy. I suspect that these originated in some Carrollian skit dating from the unimaginable past before my own arrival on the scene.) Even the forms we used had nicknames—one was called a 'Hanky-Panky', or more briefly a 'Hanky', after its designer John 'Hank' Hancock; and the forms on which messages were registered were always known as 'Blists', which, as I discovered years later, were abbreviated from 'Banister lists' (after Michael Banister) rather than, as I must have supposed, from the unspoken feelings about them experienced by the girls whose task was to fill them in, day after day. So surnames *were* put to use, if not for specifying colleagues.

After a year or so I was transferred from Control to the Watch, the heart of the Hut 6 operation. The Watch, then led by Stuart Milner-Barry, had at its disposal a growing number of bombes, enabling it to exploit cribs and recipherments rapidly enough to make frequent current breaks of Red and Light Blue, the names by which the Enigma keys, used by the German Air Force generally and in North Africa respectively, were known in Hut 6. The early days, when 'female indicators' and 'Jeffreys sheets' made breaks possible, were a distant memory, but we still routinely scrutinized many-part messages for 'cillies'. (For this purpose I acquired a fluent knowledge of the 26-times table to add to the arithmetical dexterity I had developed at Kemnal Manor.) When firmly identified, cillies might help in reducing the number of wheel orders to be tested, and in extreme cases (aided by other evidence) could lead to a break by hand. I can remember the thrill when a key was coming out by the hand method perversely known as 'rodding'. This consisted of spotting consistent pairings of letters through holes punched in sheets of squared paper which we moved about over other sheets, full of letters representing the permutations produced by various choices of wheels.

Most of our effort in the Watch was expended on identifying cribs and recipherments and on writing menus for the bombes. Our main guide in fitting conjectured plain text to a message was the impossibility of any letter being enciphered into itself. But even with a cast-iron recipherment there could be variations of spelling and punctuation to contend with, and an additional complication was introduced with the rule that the first enciphered word of every message (or every part of a many-part message) should be an irrelevant insertion of random length. Given the most reliable crib, such as an early morning tuning message which might read ABSTIMMSPRUCHYYRESTXOHNEXSINN ('tuning message, remainder meaningless') followed by complete nonsense (or 'quatsch'), this text might begin anywhere in the first two or three groups of the intercept, and 'CH' might be changed to 'Q' and 'YY' to 'X' at the whim of the cipher operator. The Watch maintained detailed records of the behaviour of established cribs, searched continually for new ones, and studied the routes followed by recipherments—either from one key to another or from one day's key to the next. The number of keys under investigation soon extended beyond the available range of coloured pencils, and whole new families of key-names emerged, of which vegetables (leek, beetroot, endive, . . .) and birds (chaffinch, kestrel, . . .) were prominent. 'Post mortems' of failed menus also yielded valuable evidence. The limited bombe-time available made it important that the priorities of the various keys under attack, and the probabilities of success of particular menus, should be accurately assessed.

The chance of success of a menu depended not only on the reliability of the crib and of the intercepted text, but also on the compactness of the menu itself. Since the middle wheel turned over once every 26 letters, a menu using 14 consecutive letters of text had an even chance that this would happen somewhere in the stretch, ruining its possibility of success; but one using 21 consecutive letters would have a more than three-quarters risk of failure on this account. With a sufficiently long crib (especially one arising from a recipherment), it might be possible to avoid this risk by composing two menus using non-overlapping stretches of text. Much skill, ingenuity, and judgement could be expended on the composition of good menus from sometimes intractable material. With luck one might find several closed circuits among the letter-pairs available: thus a '6 and 4' menu, using only 6 letters but 4 closures, was preferable to a '12 and 1' or a longer chain without closures. We give an example to show how, in very favourable circumstances, a pair of runnable menus could be composed which would avoid the risk of failure caused by a middle-wheel turnover.

Suppose a message is received of which the first eight five-letter groups are

TVQLK IGWHB STUXN TXEYL KPEAZ ZNSKU FJRCA DVVTI

We suspect that the enciphered message begins WUEBYYNULLSE-QSNULLNULL ('Weather survey 0600'; *Wueb* is presumably an abbreviation for *Wetteruebersicht* and, as mentioned above, 'CH' as in

SECHS was often sent as 'Q'.) By sliding the crib along the text we find that positions at which the assumed plain text might start (i.e. those avoiding clashes between letters of crib and text) are 2, 5, 10, 17, 19 . . . Our experience of the initial nonsense-words suggests that the most probable of these positions is 10, so we set up our crib thus:

B S T U X N T X E Y L K P E A Z Z N S K U F
W U E B Y Y N U L L S E Q S N U L L N U L L

We find that we can compose a '10 and 2' menu from the first eleven letters and a '9 and 3' from the last twelve. Though this would have been regarded as unusually favourable, the prevalence of repeated letters in the crib makes it not implausible. Note that the overlap of a single pairing (L–S in the eleven position) does not invalidate the insurance against a simple middle-wheel turnover! Taking the last eight letters we have

1	2	3	4	5	6	7	8	9	10	11	12
L	K	P	E	A	Z	Z	N	S	K	U	F
S	E	Q	S	N	U	L	L	N	U	L	L

giving the menu shown in Fig. 13.1.

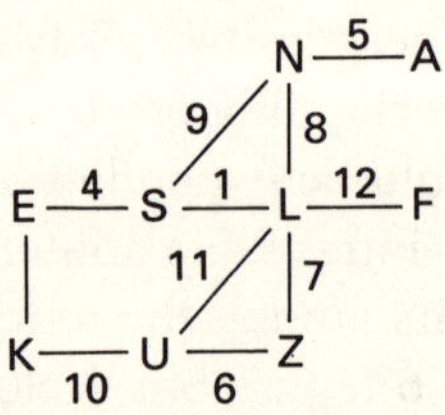

FIG. 13.1. Menu

When fed such a menu, the bombe would seek, for each of the wheel orders tested, those positions of the three wheels, from among the 26^3 (i.e. 17,576) possibilities, at which such a configuration could occur (with *any* set of nine different letters). The configuration with the actual letters of the menu might then be achieved by suitable stecker-pairings. The design of the bombes incorporated Welchman's invention of the 'diagonal board', which caused the bombe to reject any configuration, such as that shown in Fig. 13.2, which conflicted with the reciprocal property of the permutations effected by the

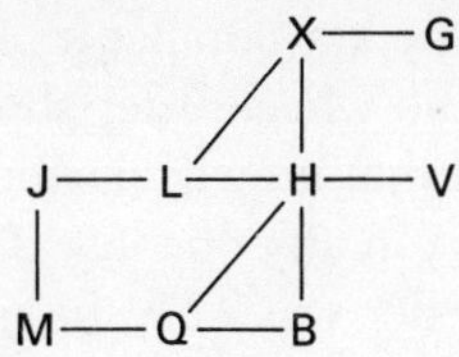

N–X, A–G, E–J, S–L, L–H, F–V, K–M, U–Q, Z–B

FIG. 13.2. Rejected configuration

stecker-board. When the bombe reached a position which gave no contradiction, it produced a 'stop', to be tested by hand in the Machine Room. Some stops would be more promising than others. For example, the configurations in Figs. 13.3 and 13.4 both imply consistent stecker-pairings. But it was known that every key contained ten steckered pairs of letters and six self-steckered letters. Hence the stop in Fig. 13.3, with six pairs and two self-steckers, would be more likely to be correct than that in Fig. 13.4, with eight pairs and no self-stecker, and would therefore be tested first.

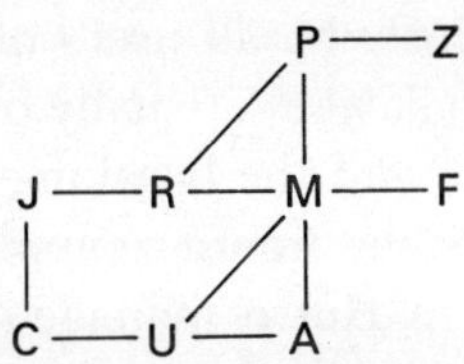

N–P, A–Z, E–J, S–R, L–M, F–F, K–C, U–U, Z–A

FIG. 13.3. Promising stop with two self-steckers

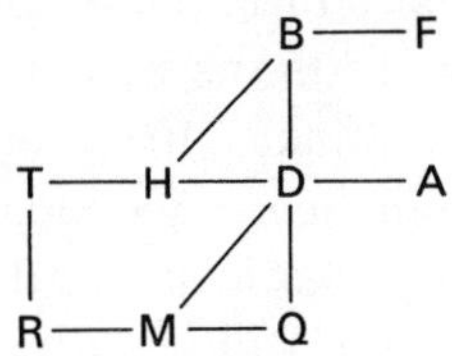

N–B, A–F, E–T, S–H, L–D, F–A, K–R, U–M, Z–Q

FIG. 13.4. Discouraging stop with no self-steckers

The unvarying number (six) of self-steckered letters in every key was only one of the ways that the key-composers helped the code-breakers. Another was the rule that no wheel order should be used twice on any monthly sheet of keys, and that no wheel should occupy the same position on two successive days in any one key. Thus if it were known that on Day 1 the Red wheel order was 123, the number of possibilities for its wheel order on Day 2 would be reduced from sixty to thirty; and further reductions would apply later in the month so long as continuity of breaking was maintained. As continuity was also crucial for the establishment of cribs and recipherments, the truism 'nothing succeeds like success' was notably valid here. The occasional full or partial key-repeats thrown up by Reg Parker's records also depended on past and current successes. But in other ways the Germans constantly sought ways to make life more difficult for us by introducing complications. These included the nonsense-words at the beginning of messages, the permuting of wheel orders during the course of the day, the 'pluggable *Umkehrwalze*', and another mechanical horror whose name and nature now escape me. The former pair of features were annoyances rather than serious threats, once we tumbled to what was going on. But the latter pair could have proved fatal to our efforts had either been introduced simultaneously by all users of the Enigma machine, or even by all using a particular key. Usually outlying units continued for a while on the old basis, and the breaking into their traffic could lead to a break-back into the more complicated version of the machine. At all events, we in Hut 6 managed to overcome all these hurdles, thanks to shortcomings both of the system and of individuals on the other side, and to the outstanding skill and inventiveness of Dennis Babbage and his team.

Thus life in the Watch was always demanding and never dull. Other members of the growing complement of Hut 6 had more humdrum but equally essential tasks, which they carried out meticulously and uncomplainingly, in the spirit of the girl in the Gracie Fields song who 'makes the nut that fits the bolt that holds the spring that works the thingamajig that makes the engine roar'. As numbers grew, so did the variety of our heterogeneous company. To the original team of mathematicians, classicists, and chess-players, some in the Intelligence Corps and some still civilians, were added graduates in other disciplines and school-leavers and men and women in varying uniforms—Army, RAF, WRNS, US Army—until in 1943 Hut 6 burst at the seams and we moved into purpose-built quarters in

Block D. The infusion of US blood brought us Bill Bundy—everyone's ideal of the New England gentleman, tall, slim, handsome, fresh-faced, and courteous—and others representing different traditions in American society, such as the exuberant Bill Bijur. The occasion when he celebrated his promotion to First Lieutenant by handing out cigars at midnight to all and sundry is a vivid memory, perhaps because it typified his generous, extrovert nature tinged with a touching naïvety.

The practice of restricting one's knowledge of what went on elsewhere in BP to what one *needed* to know helped to turn one's immediate colleagues into one's closest friends, although activities such as music, theatre, and the Home Guard brought outside contacts. It seemed to me that Hut 6 formed a sufficiently large and varied population to provide congenial company for all. Perhaps I was biased, being of the male minority in a community where the women were exceptionally intelligent and attractive. Certainly half-a-dozen male members of the Watch found their life-long partners from among their closest colleagues. Those of us who did not need never have been without female friends, to console us for the limitations of wartime existence and to help us appreciate our extreme good fortune in belonging to such a community, united in its commitment to an exciting enterprise of crucial importance.

After a long spell in the Watch I was moved over to the 'Qwatch' for the rest of the war. Our name—a pun on *Quatsch*, the German for 'rubbish'—was a typical Hut 6 in-joke, and our task was to cope with a variety of the less urgent but still important cryptographic problems. We were a close-knit group of three, working together in remarkable harmony, as our different talents seemed to complement each other. (In 1947 I acted as best man when the other two, Bob Roseveare and Ione Jay, were married.) My recollections of our activities are less vivid than are those of the Watch, but I recall a few items of our varied brief. We kept an eye on the key then known as Brown, used by boffins working at experimental stations on the Baltic coast who were interested in rockets and heavy water. But their traffic was sparse, and we made only occasional breaks. Another case we handled was that of the *Notschlüsseln*, emergency keys which could be constructed from long words, such as *Klostermann*. Though I cannot recall that we ever actually broke a key through prior knowledge of the keyword, we *did* identify some emergency keys and deduced the words from which they had been constructed. This was a satisfying exercise in ingenuity, which might well have led us to further successes. We constructed contingency plans to meet threatened new complications, which on one memorable occasion were rendered superfluous by the shortcomings of the enemy and the skill of Dennis Babbage. I went off to my family's New Year celebrations with the words 'I'm dreaming of the right scritchmus' running through my head to the tune of Bing Crosby's celebrated hit from *Holiday Inn*. I cannot now recall what technique was nicknamed a 'scritchmus', but whatever it was it was used to telling effect by Dennis, and the emergency was over by the time I returned a few days later.

Mention of Christmas reminds me of the incomparable John Manisty. Every community needs a railway timetable wizard, and J.C. was one *par excellence*. He also controlled the shift and leave rotas, and knew to a tee the preferences and alliances of the staff. You could save up your weekly day off until you had two or three days in hand, and could make the most of them by taking them after a night shift and returning on to an evening shift. John managed such arrangements with tact and finesse and certainly helped us to survive the traumas of wartime travel by rail.

Although we experienced all the shortages of wartime Britain and shared many of its hardships—with the notable exception of the Blitz, for BP was never attacked—life was eminently supportable. We had our immediate colleagues, whom we regarded as comrades-in-arms in a noble cause, and we could join in the varied activities of the large community inside the perimeter but outside the Hut. One activity which it is all too easy to mock at now was the Home Guard. Recruited from the male civilian staff, it included many members of Hut 6. The professional soldier Captain Shaw was Adjutant and F. L. Lucas was Officer Commanding, later succeeded by Michael Banister. At a time when an attack—perhaps by parachutists or fifth-columnists—was not unthinkable, we took our training seriously, priding ourselves on being more competent with weapons and manœuvres than the members of the armed forces in our midst. We practised rifle-shooting in the deep brickyard nearby, our officers went off on weekend courses involving tactical exercises without troops, and we thoroughly enjoyed the pretence that we were real soldiers. I recall two events with particular pleasure. In one we were challenged to infiltrate BP from outside without using our passes, and in the other we fought a pitched battle with the combined armed forces. The former exposed a serious security risk—lengths of metal fencing left lying around in the woods outside, which we used for scaling the perimeter fence. In the latter we achieved a satisfying victory over the Intelligence Corps and its allies. As the war ground on and the danger, first of invasion and later of a casual attack, faded away, it became more difficult to take ourselves seriously. The stand-down in December 1944 gave the welcome quietus to a survival that had outlived its relevance, but which in its time had generated enthusiasm, comradeship, and a great deal of harmless fun.

When VE-Day came the operational life of Hut 6 was over. Some of the staff stayed on to compile the official record of our achievements, and a few to join the post-war GCHQ at Cheltenham. Some of us dispersed to other warwork—I for a brief spell at the Admiralty Research Laboratory at Teddington disguised as a supersonic aerodynamicist. When VJ-Day followed sooner than we had expected, we returned to our pre-war modes of life, many in schools, universities, or the Civil Service. Some achieved great distinction in their professions: Howard Smith became Ambassador to Moscow; Asa Briggs a life peer, the Vice-Chancellor of Sussex University, and Provost of Worcester College, Oxford; David Rees Professor of Mathematics at Exeter University and an FRS.

Now that the veil of secrecy has been withdrawn from the war-time activities at BP, it is possible to discuss openly one's involvement there, in the mood of an objective *apologia pro vita sua*. When I am asked 'how much use was made of your mathematical training in the back rooms you occupied during the war?', I can only reply that, with the exception of some work at the Admiralty Research Laboratory after I had left Bletchley, nothing I did had any connection with my degree course in mathematics. But important facets of one's mental make-up are deeply influenced by the nature, if not the content, of one's education. Characteristics which were in great demand at BP were a creative imagination, a well-developed critical faculty, and a habit of meticulousness. While very specific talents were used by those, for example, who designed and built the bombes, the creative foresight of the founders of Hut 6, and the acumen and commitment of those who carried on their good work, were the consequence of their general rather than their specialized abilities. The three cardinal characteristics mentioned above were needed, and found in varying proportions, in the staff of Hut 6, which included not only mathematicians, chess-players, and classicists but also historians, modern linguists, bank staff, and actresses. We all contributed, in our diverse ways, to what we are entitled to regard as a highly successful and significant operation of war. Though I would not claim to have been exceptionally endowed with the first of the three characteristics, I believe that I was as well equipped as the majority of my colleagues in the second and third. To have been a non-passenger in a team of such a calibre and with such victories to its credit seems to me to justify some modest satisfaction. Our happy band may not have been with King Harry on St Crispin's Day, but we had certainly not been abed and have no reason to think ourselves accurs't for having been where we were.

Note

1. F. H. Hinsley *et al.*, *British Intelligence in the Second World War*, I (London: HMSO, 1979), 345.

14. Hut 8 and naval Enigma, Part I

JOAN MURRAY

I WAS recruited for GC&CS by Gordon Welchman, who had supervised me in geometry for Part II of the Cambridge Tripos. When he interviewed me, early in 1940, he said that the work did not really need mathematics but mathematicians tended to be good at it. Without breaching security he must have said enough to attract me, although the pay would be low, at £2 a week, I think; this had been increased by a cost-of-living bonus before I joined, which was after completing Part III.

I arrived at Bletchley Park on 17 June. After the routine administrative matters I was collected by Alan Turing, to work on naval Enigma in Hut 8, instead of with Welchman in Hut 6. This was because of the documents taken from the German patrol boat VP2623 in April, in the Norway campaign; they included a considerable amount of matched plain and cipher texts for two days. After a sketchy introduction to the workings of an Enigma, I was set to work testing the results of using the first British bombe on this material. A day or so later it was discovered that the plugging for one of the days was already available on a loose piece of paper, which meant that solution of that day's key could be completed by hand. (I realize that this conflicts with the statement in the published history, that the material from VP2623 had 'enabled GC&CS to read during May 1940 the naval Enigma traffic for six days'.[1] This was probably copied from a history of Hut 8 written after VE-Day, itself relying on memories, as there were no log books or regular reports of Hut 8 work at that time.) I have reason to be quite sure of my date, as it was my birthday on 24 June, and I then took the first leave to which I was entitled, on the basis of one day off in seven.

In my first week they put an extra table in for me in the room occupied by Turing, Kendrick, and Twinn. According to Good, I rose from the ranks of the girls in the big room; but this was obviously because of my degree, and before I had had any chance of proving myself. I think it was Kendrick who said, 'Welcome to the sahibs' room'—the only time that I met that term for it. Kendrick, exceptionally, never progressed beyond calling me Miss Clarke, and himself was known only by his surname. Another exception to the general use of Christian names was Turing, but this was not because of any need of formality with the head of Hut 8: he was widely known by his nickname, Prof., even during the short time when an actual university professor was working with us.

Very soon I worked a night shift, alone in Hut 8, and I felt quite important 'minding the Baby'. Peter Twinn lent me his alarm clock so that I could relieve him at 2 a.m. The Baby was a small special-purpose machine, made by the British Tabulating Machine Company at Letchworth, the firm which made the bombes: it was used to encipher a four-letter probable word, *eins*, at all positions of the machine with the day's wheel-order and plugging, punching the results on Hollerith cards. The minder had to make regular checks, and set the Baby for a new start when a cycle was completed. By sorting and collating the encipherments of *eins* with the message texts, the starting position could be obtained for a good proportion of the messages, which had to be set individually at this stage because of the complexity of the naval indicating system. This involved enciphering the message setting once on the machine, at a basic setting for the day (the *Grundstellung*), combining the result with an appropriate discriminator, and then applying a digraphic substitution. The choice of digraph table from the current set of nine was also part of the daily key. Using the *eins* catalogue and, at a later stage, 'twiddling' on messages for which part of the setting was known, were enjoyable jobs which were shared by everyone in Hut 8. Anyone could distinguish between German and a random string of letters.

My first promotion was to the linguist grade, still weekly paid, and I enjoyed answering a questionnaire with 'grade linguist, languages none', rather than mentioning school French and a smattering of German and Italian for reading mathematical books. My next promotion was apparently harder to negotiate, possibly because of my sex, although there was another female mathematical cryptanalyst, working in the Cottage. Commander Travis, later the top man at GC&CS, at this time had an office in Hut 8, and I remember that he stopped me in the corridor, to say that they might have to put me in the WRNS, to be adequately paid. Inevitably the duller routine clerical work was done by women, since only men with what were considered suitable qualifications for cryptanalysis or related translation and intelligence work could join GC&CS instead of being conscripted into the armed forces, or could be taken out of them for GC&CS; those in Hut 8 from the army became temporary civil servants, although in various parts of Bletchley Park there were uniformed officers and other ranks working alongside civilians. At one time there was a move to increase the pay of those who had qualifications which were not relevant, which I knew about through hearing some of the girls discussing whether one of them might benefit as a trained hairdresser; but I never heard the result.

It was probably early in July 1940, during a lull in the work which followed the solutions due to the VP2623 material, that Turing gave further consideration to 'simultaneous scanning'—that is, to finding a method of making the bombes test twenty-six hypotheses at each position of the wheels. Otherwise the best one could do with the first British bombe, as with the Polish ones, was to assume that the letter chosen as the input one was unplugged, with a probability of 6 in 26 of this being correct. Turing soon jumped up, saying that Welchman's diagonal board would provide simultaneous scanning, and he hurried round to Hut 6 to give the good news, doubtless with a circuit diagram to explain the method of testing. When he showed it to me, he had to tell me how relays work.

Some months before, when Turing discovered how the indicators worked for the German naval Enigma, he had thought of a method of using them for solving the day's keys. This became known as Banburismus, because the cipher texts were recorded as punched holes on long sheets of paper, made at Banbury. This attack was applicable only when the digraphic tables used in the indicators were known. About five days were identified as using the most fully recovered of these tables, and they were allocated to different analysts, for Banburismus. Eventually Hugh Foss, who had joined Hut 8 on returning from sick leave, was successful with his day. The next Banburismus was in fact for my day, when I had determined which wheel was on the right, although I had not got as far as Foss did. It was very important to reduce the number of wheel-orders to be tried on the bombes, because by the beginning of the war the German Navy had added three other wheels, each with two turnover notches, to the five used by the Army and Air Force, giving 336 possible wheel orders.

The method of Banburismus had been proved and to some extent refined, but it was evident that the digraphic tables had changed, I think in June. Work continued on the less favourable days, but the prospect of reading the naval Enigma currently, or nearly so, depended on another capture.

Soon Turing wrote an account—'Prof.'s book'—of Enigma theory and methods, which were still largely new to me. Doubtless this was used to introduce later new cryptanalysts to the work, although much of it was not needed in Hut 8. One chapter explained a method which could have recovered the wheel-wirings as well as the plugging, on material such as that from the captured German patrol boat VP2623. I was the guinea-pig, to test whether his explanation and worked example were understandable, and my task included using this method on half of the material, not used in the example.

The lack of profitable work on the naval Enigma meant that Hut 8 staff were available to deal with a different version, used by the German railway authorities. Initially, at least, this was used without security precautions. This gave a 'depth', which enabled Colonel Tiltman to recover the plain text of these messages, which consisted largely of numbers, with XX as a divider, forming timetables. After this the wheel-wirings were easily solved in Hut 8, using methods known before 1939, since this was a machine without plugging, similar to the commercial Enigma. The messages were decrypted by hand on Letchworth Enigmas, reading which bulb lit up, although adapted Typex machines were available for the Enigma used by the German armed forces (see Plate 5). On the Letchworth Enigmas the motion had to be applied by hand. Their wheels were as on the bombes, with sloping wire brushes to provide springy contacts, which meant that they should only be moved forwards, but some of the staff who were borrowed temporarily for this job forced the wheels backwards, thereby tearing out some of the wires. Much later I had a week working with the Wrens who operated the bombes, and learnt that the wires were regularly stroked back into position with tweezers before a set of wheels was returned to its rack. Improved Letchworth Enigmas were made, with wheels which could be moved in either direction, which was much more convenient for testing bombe results.

Work on the railway Enigma was passed to Hut 6 when captured naval material for February 1941 became available. After this came the heyday of Banburismus, with additional cryptanalysts, allowing three per shift. I believe it was harder to obtain the necessary support staff. Rolf Noskwith recently reminded me that Banburismus was often so enthralling that the analyst due to go home at the end of the shift would be unwilling to hand over the workings: he was too polite to say that I had been a particular culprit, being in a billet within cycling distance instead of having to catch official transport. We were working three shifts, and around midnight was a particularly interesting time, since the German naval keys changed at midnight, but results of analysis of most of a day's traffic began to reach us before then. The wheel-order changed only ten times in any month, so one success made it relatively easy to break the paired day, and thus we might read some of the traffic currently—as well as at the times when the keys had been captured. This meant that the analysts on duty might have little to do, particularly before methods were devised for solving *Offizier* messages. These used special plugging and a set of twenty-six starting positions. When these had been captured, Leslie Yoxall devised a statistical attack to recover the plugging. This was known as Yoxallismus. My own contribution, a day or two later, greatly speeded up the routine solutions, but my name was not attached to it: I was told, to my surprise, that I had used 'pure Dillyismus'. Chores performed in the slack periods included removing pins and tearing up the Banbury sheets for solved days, and other workings, as required for repulping. Occasionally we helped out in other sections, for example on the Italian naval cipher, but there were also times when we played chess or made up lost sleep, at our tables.

Most people did not take their weekly leave when working the midnight-to-nine shift, but I can remember Alan Turing coming in as usual for a day's leave, doing his own mathematical research at night, in the warmth and light of the office, without interrupting the routine of daytime sleep. Some, of course, found it very difficult to sleep during the day. As a slight consolation, shift work was some proof of the importance of the job. I can remember one girl in the big room explaining that she made a point of yawning ostentatiously and claiming that she had just come off night shift, when on leave, to keep up her end with friends who could say more about their war work. After a time the shift system for the big room was rearrranged, with the number on night shift only half that of the rest of the day, and avoiding a short change-over (off duty at midnight and on again at 4 p.m., or off at four and on again at midnight). The Pendered twins, who should have been excused night work because they were under 18 years old, did it uncomplainingly, perhaps as the only way to work in Hut 8 along with their brother. They also let others have a share, occasionally, of their allocation of Namco—national milk cocoa, which they were entitled to by their age.

Eventually the labour-intensive Banburismus was discontinued, because of the greater availability of bombes and improved knowledge of the beginnings of routine messages such as weather forecasts. In any case, Banburismus would have been impossible against the four-wheel naval Enigma, which was first introduced for the Atlantic U-boats early in 1942, and gradually spread to the other keys. The abandonment of Banburismus released staff for other work in Bletchley Park, and in fact soon made for more current reading. I was one of those who stayed in Hut 8.

Notes

1. F. H. Hinsley *et al.*, *British Intelligence in the Second World War*, I (London: HMSO, 1979), 163, 336.
2. I. J. Good, *Early Work on Computers at Bletchley* (National Physical Laboratory Report; London, 1976), 3.

15. Hut 8 and naval Enigma, Part II

ROLF NOSKWITH

I ARRIVED at Bletchley Park on 19 June 1941, my twenty-second birthday. Earlier that year, while at Cambridge, I had been recruited to Hut 8 by Hugh Alexander as a Temporary Junior Assistant (later Temporary Junior Administrative Officer) at the Foreign Office at a salary of £250 per annum. Alexander—the use of first names came only later—met me at the station and took me to the big room. There he introduced me to Michael Ashcroft who had arrived two days earlier and was therefore able to initiate me into the mysteries of *eins* catalogues, Banbury sheets, etc.

I was assigned to the Crib Room under Shaun Wylie. Hilary Brett-Smith, one of the cribsters, gave me a briefing about the successes of Hut 8, including its role in the sinking of the Bismarck. She mentioned that the significance of a crucial signal had been spotted by a bright young man in Hut 4 called Hinsley. I am sure that she had no inkling that he would one day be her husband.

At the time we were reading the naval traffic currently, thanks to the material from captured weather ships. We spent the next few days looking for future cribs in the form of regular messages, especially daily reports from weather stations at Boulogne, Hoek van Holland, Royan, etc. This state of affairs lasted till the end of July, when the captured material ran out.

1 August 1941, therefore, brought a fresh challenge for the Banburists and cribsters of Hut 8. By an apparent stroke of amazing good fortune the day produced two probable weather messages reported in 'depth'. Despite our high hopes the results were negative; 1 and 2 August remained among the very few days which were never read.

There followed an exciting period when almost every day was solved with varying delays, by a combination of Banburismus and cribs. Sometimes a depth crib would help the Banburists by confirming the relationship between the settings of two signals. Apart from the regular work I was told to look out for cribs for the *Offizier* messages (referred to by Joan Murray in Chapter 14). These had a short preamble, usually naming the addressee and sender, followed by the word *Offizier* and a name representing one of the letters of the alphabet (Anton for A, Berta for B, etc.). The letter identified one of twenty-six settings which changed every month. The rest of the message was then encrypted with a separate set of pluggings (*Stecker*), which changed every day.

During the later months of 1941, whenever a bombe was available, I tried a variety of cribs without success. Late in 1941 or early in 1942 it occurred to me that a certain message might contain instructions for the use or identification of ES cartridges, a system of coloured flares sometimes employed by the German Navy. I therefore tried EEESSSPATRONE as a crib for the start of the message: fortunately the connections between the letters produced a satisfactory menu for the bombe, which was not always the case with a crib of only thirteen letters.

I had had so little expectation of success that I had arranged to go home on two days' leave. Just when I had to run for my train we heard that the bombe had produced a promising result. Wylie agreed to send me a telegram where the name of a fish in the text would denote success. My father took the call when the telegram was read out over the telephone and was greatly mystified by an arcane message containing the word 'pompano'. I had to look up a dictionary to make sure that pompano is a fish.

The decrypt identified the P setting for the month (hence 'pompano'). There was only one other *Offizier* message on the same day, with setting X. This was solved fairly easily, probably by the *eins* method. A message with setting X on another day was then solved by Yoxallismus. This made use of the fact that the pluggings involved only twenty letters; the other six were 'self-steckered'. A trial decrypt at the correct setting but without pluggings would identify the letters paired with E, N, and other common letters, by means of a frequency count. From these the complete set of pluggings for the day could be deduced. Other settings used on that day could then be solved, leading to pluggings on other days, and so on until most of the month's *Offizier* messages had been decrypted.

The decrypts of the original month must have yielded more cribs, because I do not recall any great difficulty in solving later *Offizier* messages once the main key of the day had been broken. The subsequent proliferation of main keys (U-boats, Baltic, Mediterranean, etc., each with its own *Offizier* keys) was actually helpful, because the same message would often appear in several keys, sometimes on different days.

In February 1942 a fourth wheel was introduced into the machine used by U-boats, which prevented Hut 8 from reading their signals for the next ten months. Breaking of the U-boat keys was resumed in December 1942, based on the discovery that the 'short signals' used for weather and position reports were still enciphered, in effect, on the old three-wheel system. Much useful work was done in this connection by Michael Ashcroft whose promising post-war career at the Treasury was tragically cut short by his death from cancer in 1949.

The extension of the fourth wheel to home waters traffic in the summer of 1943 put an end to Banburismus and depth cribs. A correct crib became the sole means of solving a day's keys, but the growing number of bombes meant that alternative versions could be processed more and more quickly. Hugh Alexander and most of the cryptanalysts moved to other sections. Patrick Mahon was left in charge. During the last year of the war all the cryptanalytical work of Hut 8 (then moved into Block D) was done by him, Joan Clarke (now Murray), Richard Pendered, and myself. We still worked on a shift rota with a large supporting staff in the big room and the registration room.

After the bombes had identified a day's wheel order and pluggings there were still pleasant jobs for us in working out the *Ringstellung*—the position of the movable rim round each wheel—and the *Grundstellung*—the setting of the wheels at which a tetragram derived from the opening letters of each message had to be enciphered in order to obtain the setting for decrypting that message. Early in 1945 we learnt that the Germans planned to introduce a complicated new system involving a multiplicity of *Grundstellungen* for each day instead of a single one. We enjoyed ourselves in devising methods to meet this challenge, but the end of the war came before we suffered too much from the change.

Weather messages remained our most frequent source of cribs. The keys for D-Day in 1944 were solved in record time—before 2 a.m. if I remember correctly—by the crib WETTERVORHERSAGEBISKAYA.

At other times such cribs became less reliable because the Germans had a blitz on security after which the senders took care to vary the wording. During one such period, probably in 1943, we obtained our best cribs from messages with a warning of mines in stated grid positions. This led to a procedure known as 'gardening', whereby the RAF laid mines in specified positions solely in order to generate warning messages. The positions were carefully chosen to avoid numbers, especially 0 and 5, for which the Germans used more than one spelling in their signals.

I remember a day on which, being on day shift, I was asked whether 'gardening' during the night would materially improve the chances of an early solution of the following day: I said that it would. The night was stormy and I lay awake anxiously wondering whether my assessment had been correct or whether I had needlessly endangered lives. I was greatly relieved when I heard next morning that the bad weather had prevented any flights.

Among all the decrypts which I saw during my time in Hut 8 the ones which stand out most clearly are two successive messages at the time of the July Plot in 1944. Both were from Field Marshal von Witzleben; the first read: 'The Führer Adolf Hitler is dead.' The second mentioned 'a clique of party chiefs far away from the front line' but soon came to an abrupt end!

16. The *Abwehr* Enigma

PETER TWINN

No account has been published of the wartime enciphering methods of the *Abwehr*, the secret intelligence service of the German High Command, and this omission has left unrecorded a significant part of Bletchley Park's cryptanalytical success and of the Germans' use of the Enigma machine. Throughout the war the *Abwehr* employed not only Enigma machines but also the more old-fashioned and more familiar hand ciphers. This was not surprising, since the conditions in which the *Abwehr* and its individual agents sometimes had to operate were very different from those in the German armed services. It would have been embarrassing and inconvenient for an agent anxious, like some latter-day Ashenden, to slip across frontiers or arrive unannounced by parachute, to be encumbered by an Enigma resembling a weighty and antiquated typewriter.

These two methods had their organizational consequences in Bletchley, where it proved convenient to establish two teams to deal with these two very different cryptanalytical problems. The task of breaking the non-Enigma signals fell to the group originally headed by Oliver Strachey (a brother of Lytton Strachey); the other, headed after mid-1941 by Dillwyn Knox (universally known as 'Dilly' and splendidly pictured by Penelope Fitzgerald in her account of 'The Knox Brothers') was concerned solely with the Enigma. The two types of radio messages were known to our radio intercept organization officially as 'Intelligence Sections' and unofficially as 'Illicit Services', and it was natural to christen the two teams ISOS(trachey) and ISK(nox). Strachey and Knox were two of the very few survivors of our First World War cryptanalytical organization.

In pre-war days it was no easy task to design a high-security ciphering system that would satisfy the operational needs of armed services in time of war, and it was not necessarily an ill-judged decision by the German Navy in 1926 to try to do so by developing the commercial Enigma machine. Probably no practical Enigma-based system can be made which guarantees complete security, but it was not so much the fundamental weaknesses of the Enigmas which the Germans developed and used, serious as these were, but the way they used them and the indiscipline of the German operators, that led to such a catastrophe for German intelligence. This was true not only of the *Abwehr*'s use of the Enigma, but also of the German services' use, as is made plain in the detailed descriptions contained in Gordon Welchman's book *The Hut Six Story*[1] and in Andrew Hodges's book *Alan Turing: The Enigma.*[2]

It is interesting to speculate why the *Abwehr*, the secret intelligence service of the German High Command, decided to use a version of the Enigma which presented British cryptanalysts, in this case the ISK group, with problems substantially different from those facing the teams trying to break the German armed services' Enigma, although the differences between these two machines from the point of view of the operators using them were slight. It is possible that the German cipher authorities considered that the *Abwehr* machines, because of the conditions in which they were used, were more liable to capture than the military machines and, to avoid the risk of general compromise of the widely used Enigma, decided to use a specially designed and significally different machine. Keith Batey has suggested that, as the *Abwehr* needed to encipher long reports, they thought they needed a machine with a longer cycle. This the *Abwehr* Enigma provides, as described later. More simply, they may have thought that the new machine was more secure. If so, they were wrong.

The *Abwehr* Enigma differed from the services' machine (described in Chapter 11) in three ways.

First, the 'turnover' principle, which on other models affected the central wheels only, was extended in the *Abwehr* model so that the *Umkehrwalze* also moved.

Secondly, instead of having only one turnover position for each wheel, the *Abwehr* model had 11, 15, and 19 on the three wheels. As Plate 1 and Fig. 11.1 show, each Enigma wheel carried a ring round its periphery, labelled with each of the 26 letters as on many service Enigma wheels. These rings could be rotated to give the *Ringstellung*, which has already been described. It should be noted that it was this ring, and not the wheel itself, which carried the turnover mechanism. In consequence, if a turnover occurred as a wheel passed, say, from L to M as shown by the letter in the window, it would always do so irrespective of the *Ringstellung*. But the position had no bearing on the orientation of the internal wiring of the machine. This multiple turnover was a material difficulty for the cryptanalyst, but curiously, as explained later, it led Dilly Knox indirectly to the first break-through in solving the secrets of this Enigma.

Thirdly, the *Abwehr* Enigma had no plugboard at the front of the machine, and thus no *Steckerverbindungen*.

To sum up these differences: the *Abwehr* Enigma's rotatable *Umkehrwalze* was a matter of little real significance for us; its multiple turnovers on each wheel were a real headache for us, but the lack of *Steckerverbindungen* an enormous relief. In contrast, the services' Enigma had a non-rotating *Umkehrwalze* (a small bonus for us), only one turnover on each wheel (a great relief), but *Steckerverbindungen* (almost a disaster).

If the *Abwehr* thought, rightly, that having more than one turnover on each wheel was a valuable safeguard, why did the services not adopt it? It needed only a small manufacturing modification and in no way affected the operator's procedures. Again, if the services thought, again rightly, that the *Steckerverbindungen* provided powerful protection, why did the *Abwehr* not adopt this addition? My guess is that the *Abwehr* cipher authorities and those of the services were not in the habit of consulting each other. Whatever the reason, they certainly missed a trick in not combining multiple-turnover wheels with *Steckerverbindungen*.

But far and away the most serious example of lack of foresight is to be traced to a German decision, taken at least as far back as the 1930s, that cast a very long shadow into the war years, affected our success with both Enigmas, provided a distinguished Polish cryptanalyst with a glorious bull's-eye, and gave us the opportunity of recording our feeblest performance. As this is the bit of the Enigma story that remains in my mind most vividly, even after fifty-four years, perhaps I may be forgiven if I tell it in somewhat personal terms.

When I joined GC&CS in early February 1939 and went to join Dilly Knox to work on the German services Enigma traffic, the outlook was not encouraging. Before I arrived, Dilly was a lone hand (he always was) assisted by one secretary/assistant and enjoying a total lack of other facilities—though it is by no means clear that we could have used any. He was notorious for being very secretive about his ideas, and I am not sure whether he had any hopes of ultimate success. For my own part, during my first few weeks I felt we were no better than a pair of Micawbers. But I did learn something of great interest. It appeared that we were in possession of a message in cipher, together with its alleged plain-language version *and* the *Steckerverbindungen* in use on the date of the message. The fact that *Steckerverbindungen* were being used confirmed what we expected from other sources, that this message, if genuine, had been enciphered on a German services Enigma. A long time afterwards it was demonstrated that the message was indeed genuine. The provenance of this document was certainly not known to me, and probably not known in any detail to anyone on this side of the Channel. It must clearly have been stolen from a German office, probably by a Pole. The date of the message was roughly the middle of 1938.

At first sight this information seemed a likely basis for determining the all-important internal wiring of the wheels, but second thoughts showed this to be a vain hope. What we did not know was the order in which the letters of the keyboard were connected to the twenty-six input discs of the entry plate. In the commercial machine the order was QWERTZU, as in the German version of the keyboard order familiar to all typists, but it was obvious to us that the Germans would take advantage of the immense number of possible random orders from which they could choose. In fact, the number of ways of ordering twenty-six letters is an unimaginable number more than twenty digits long, each way being presumably an equally likely choice. It was immediately obvious that even the stolen message of more than two hundred letters could not conceivably provide enough evidence to reveal this all-important order, christened by Dilly, who had a taste for inventing fanciful jargon, as the 'QWERTZU' and by others of us, for more arcane reasons, as the 'diagonal'. Accordingly Dilly had, before my arrival, quickly decided that the stolen message offered us no hope and ceased even to think about it. After a little thought I agreed with him, although it left us no obvious prospect of how to proceed.

This was the position until Dilly was able to make a visit, with a French colleague, to the Polish cryptographers at Pyry in July 1939, a visit mentioned by Welchman.[3] It is reported that Dilly's first question to the Polish cryptographer Rejewski was, 'What is the QWERTZU?' I can imagine it was. Assuming that our stolen message was genuine, this was the only piece of information that we needed.

It is said that, after the meeting, Dilly returned to his hotel in a taxi with his French colleague, chanting, 'Nous avons le QWERTZU, nous marchons ensemble.' I can quite believe it; I wish I had been there.

On being given this information on Dilly's return, two hours' work enabled me to satisfy myself that the stolen message was genuine and to determine the wiring of the first two wheels which were in use. A further three days' work enabled me to read a few other messages sent by the Germans on that day in 1938 and intercepted by our radio operators and kept in our archives subsequently. I was interrupted in the last stages of this task by a visit from Josh Cooper, at that time a senior officer in Bletchley, who reminded me of what I knew only too well, that I was the first British cryptographer to have read a German services Enigma message. I hasten to say that this did me little if any credit, since with the information Dilly had brought back from Poland the job was little more than a routine operation. Indeed I had come out of my first few months in GC&CS extremely badly. If I had thought of making the guess, which in retrospect seems such a reasonable possibility, that QWERTZU was simply ABCDEFG, as Rejewski had done in 1933, I could have read a few messages within a fortnight of my arrival at GC&CS and made a début of unparalleled brilliance. Alas! I failed to grasp my chance. I can only say in defence—and it is not much of a defence—that Dilly Knox, Alan Turing, and Tony Kendrick did no better, and none of that trio was known as an unimaginative dullard. Of course, reading a few scattered messages on a single day in 1938 was a whole universe away from the problems that lay ahead, but it would have been some encouragement; had we thought of it in February 1939, we should have saved ourselves six valuable months.

The determination of a QWERTZU again figured prominently in the solution of the *Abwehr* Enigma which Dilly undertook in 1941. The problem first revealed itself as a growing volume of 'Illicit Service' messages which were plainly not enciphered on the services Enigma. The messages were distinguished by a group of eight letters separate from the message text, which was in the usual five-letter groups. This made it very probable that the traffic was encoded on some kind of Enigma with four movable wheels, since a standard method of indicating the initial message-settings for commercial types of the Enigma was to encode the setting twice at a given setting (the *Grundstellung*), which was given as part of the daily instructions to the operator. A typical example, given a Grundstellung of PZRF, and a message-setting ABCD, might be:

Grundstellung positions:	1	2	3	4	5	6	7	8
Message-setting:	A	B	C	D	A	B	C	D
Encoded message-setting:	E	T	Q	E	T	R	O	A

The amount of traffic intercepted increased to twenty or more messages a day in August–September 1941, which made it feasible to try to deduce the message-settings, since a guess at the decode of a selected message indicator might lead to decodes of parts of other indicators, enabling further guesses to be made.

Clearly this is a process which relies on brilliant guesswork and a good slice of luck but, on a lucky day, it was possible to finish up with a knowledge of several reciprocal pairs of letters (each the encoded version of the other) in the eight *Grundstellung* positions—assuming that one's guesses were right. In fact, as the guessing game proceeded, small bits of corroborative evidence encouraged the guesser, so long as the guesses were right. The process was, of course, much more uncertain than as described here, but Dilly's ever-inventive mind led him to devise a procedure which was an enormous help. This consisted of forming chains of letters from positions 1–5, 2–6, 3–7, and 4–8 of the indicators by selecting a letter in one of the coded message indicators in, for example, position 1, writing after it the letter corresponding in position 5, and, if that occurred in position 1 in another message, extending the chain by writing the corresponding letter in position 5 of the second message and so on. Before long, Dilly found a day on which the letter chains in adjacent positions (e.g. 1–5 and 2–6) were related, in that if the letters in the later chain were substituted by the letters immediately following in the sequence QWERTZU, large parts of the earlier chain were produced. This phenomenon he called a 'crab', on the grounds that 'things moved sideways'. Dilly's acute perceptions at once enabled him to make the following deductions.

1. The messages were encoded on an Enigma with a QWERTZU 'diagonal'.
2. Occasionally, between consecutive positions four places apart on the *Grundstellung*, all the wheels and the *Umkehrwalze* rotated together, producing a 'crab'.
3. The Enigma therefore had three wheels and an *Umkehrwalze* which rotated during encodement.

4. The wheels had numerous turnover positions, otherwise 'crabs' would be very rare.
5. There would be positions at which all the wheels and the *Umkehrwalze* turned over together without the same event happening four positions later. This predicted phenomenon Dilly christened a 'lobster', which he claimed was 'half a crab'.

Thereafter progress was rapid (although a number of problems had to be resolved *en route*) and the routine decipherment of *Abwehr* Enigma messages became a reality.

Sadly, on 27 February 1943, Dilly died—not before he had successfully broken into the *Abwehr* Enigma but before this, his last cryptographic task, had come to full fruition. Some time earlier, during his last illness, I was asked to slip into his seat, where I found a flourishing and productive section in the hands of a gifted trio—Keith Batey, Mavis Lever (later Mavis Batey), and Margaret Rock—whose distinguished contribution has not had the recognition it deserves, and who have added substantially to the text of this chapter. Much of the activity of the ISK group was then directed to determining the daily setting of the machine—the choice of wheels and wheel order, and the *Ringstellung* position. And of course the position of the wheels at the start of each individual message (the message indicator) had to be found and the messages deciphered.

There were then four *Abwehr* communication channels in use: two in Western Europe and two in Eastern Europe. As these networks used different daily settings of the Enigma, they represented different tasks. The messages from the Western networks were read rapidly and almost without interruption. The Eastern networks were much trickier and we seldom had much success, because the radio stations were far away and much of the traffic was almost inaudible. At the height of our activities the ISK staff rose to over a hundred, mainly female as was common in parts of BP, and the fact that the messages were intercepted, sent to BP, sorted, and distributed, the daily machine and message settings determined, and the messages finally deciphered and passed to our Intelligence colleagues, all usually within twenty-four hours, was not a bad record for a group whose success owed nothing to the canons of formal organization.

We continued in much the same way until the end of the war, living on a knife-edge because any small change by the Germans could have put success beyond our grasp. Such changes as they did make were relatively innocuous and indeed sometimes helpful. From time to time small groups were heard on the air using what turned out to be rewired Enigmas; their discipline was sometimes terrible. On one occasion Margaret Rock, who was looking at a collection of messages that had suddenly arrived, noticed that there was always a shortish message at the same time of day. This was an almost certain sign that it was a weather report. Usually, as the report was in standard form, the messages were of the same length; on this occasion they varied. However, as the letter X was noticeably absent from the last five to fifteen letters of the signal, and as the one letter that enciphering X on an Enigma will not give is X, she made the correct assumption that the operator or his superiors had decided to add an indeterminate number of Xs to the text before encipherment, just to fool us. Her guess was enough to enable Margaret to recover the wiring of this unknown Enigma, although, for various technical reasons, the analysis needed great mental dexterity. It was a pity that the rest of the messages turned out to be worthless.

Another time, dealing with yet another small group, we were amazed to be presented with twenty or more messages sent on the same day *with the same indicator*. Presumably the operator had not read his manual. This extraordinary lapse enabled us to recover the complete details of an unknown Enigma, using no other data than that the messages were in German. Again the information they contained was useless.

Oddities of this kind nevertheless kept us on our toes. In the last weeks of the war we noted the arrival of a quite new kind of ciphering system. We never made any headway with it, and I do not believe it forms any part of the Enigma saga.

As the war drew to its close, the *Abwehr* networks broke up and our story ended. Like their service colleagues, the *Abwehr* cryptographic security authorities had a bad war. Speculation remains why they made so many avoidable mistakes. Andrew Hodges suggests that the German authorities 'had assigned an *a priori* probability of zero to Enigma decryption, and no weight of evidence sufficed to increase it'.[4] I think I agree.

Notes

1. G. Welchman, *The Hut Six Story* (London: Allen Lane, 1982; Penguin, 1984).
2. A. Hodges, *Alan Turing: The Enigma* (London: Hutchinson, 1983).
3. G. Welchman, 'From Polish Bomba to British Bombe: The Birth of Ultra', Intelligence and National Security, 1/1 (Jan. 1986), 71–110.
4. Hodges, *Turing*, 201.

Editors' Note

Abwehr sigint was sent direct to M.I.6 for evaluation and use, and therefore falls outside the compass of this book. It was of major importance in counter-intelligence, including the activities of the Twenty ('Double-Cross') Committee.

17. The bombes

DIANA PAYNE

The breaking of the German Enigma cipher messages during the Second World War, and the effect it had on strategy, has been much publicized and debated since the secrecy restrictions were partially lifted in 1974. But the human side of the story of the WRNS involved in the soul-destroying but vital work on the monster deciphering machines has not been told in any detail. I want to try and describe my feelings as a young Wren thrown into this most extraordinary job, with all the tensions and isolation of not being able to talk about it to anyone until thirty years later.

My family were living in Cornwall, as our home in Hampstead had been destroyed during the Battle of Britain in 1940. I had taken my first job as a clerk in the Ministry of Labour, with a salary of £2 7*s*. per week, but my ambition was to join the WRNS, so I went to Plymouth to enrol. The centre of the town was in ruins after the German raids but, incredibly, the main department store was serving canteen lunches in a makeshift hut on its bombed site. I went on to Devonport and was interviewed by a WRNS officer. It seemed that I had been accepted for boats' crew category in view of my sailing experience, but suddenly she asked me if I could keep a secret. I answered that I really did not know as I had never tried. In spite of this unsatisfactory reply, she said that I would be considered for Special Duties X as a second choice. I did not take in the implications of this, as I was still dreaming of life at sea, with the romantic idea of marrying a sailor.

My call-up papers duly arrived, and informed me that my category was Special Duties X. Feeling very nervous, I reported for duty as a Probationary Wren at New College, Hampstead. After being enrolled we lined up to have our heads searched for lice, which seemed a depressing start to my naval career, but apparently this was a necessary precaution in all the Services. Then followed a strenuous fortnight learning naval etiquette, squad drill, and domestic duties, and marching up and down the Finchley Road—there was not much traffic in 1942. We had a final passing-out parade and inspection by the exiled King Haakon of Norway.

After being 'kitted-out', twenty-two of us were drafted to the mysterious Station X. On arrival at Euston station we had no clues as to our journey, so we enquired from the engine-driver where he was going. He replied with a broad grin that 'The Wrens get out at Bletchley'. From there we were driven to a remote part of the countryside, a beautiful Tudor house called Crawley Grange. This was our billet, one of several, including Woburn Abbey, which were used to house the workers of Bletchley Park at the headquarters of the GC&CS. It was now only too clear that we were not to be part of the Royal Navy, and my youthful dream was shattered, though I still had no idea that I was destined to live with five hundred women without a glimpse of the sea or sailors.

Next morning we were taken on the sixty-minute drive to Bletchley Park. It was a hideous Victorian mansion standing in grounds with several large huts. The first thing we noticed was a strange assortment of civilians going in and out of the main building. We were to find out later that they were Foreign Office cryptanalysts, mathematicians, chess players, to name but a few, who produced the vital menus which I will describe later. We were taken into one of the huts, where the conditions of the work were disclosed. It would involve shift work, very little hope of promotion, and complete secrecy. On this limited information we were given until lunchtime to decide whether we could face the ordeal. Only one girl tried to back out, warning us that she thought it would drive us all 'nuts'. However, we were young and patriotic, and there was only one thought in mind which unified the whole country—a rare moment in British history—and that was to defeat Nazi Germany. So we decided to face the challenge, and all signed the Official Secrets Act which committed us to the job for the duration of the war, and to keep the secret for ever—or so we thought then. The penalty for any breach of security was two years in prison.

Then the moment came when the heavily guarded secret of the German Enigma ciphers was revealed to us. This was the beginning of over three years working on watches of four weeks' duration: 8 a.m. to 4 p.m. the first seven days, 4 p.m. to midnight the second week, midnight to 8 a.m. the third, and then a hectic three days of eight hours on and eight hours off alternately, ending with a much-needed four days' leave.

Training was necessary to master the intricate complications of running the machines known as 'bombes'. These unravelled the wheel-settings for the Enigma ciphers thought by the Germans to be unbreakable. The bombes were bronze-coloured cabinets about eight feel tall and seven feet wide. The front housed rows of coloured circular drums, each about five inches in diameter and three inches deep. Inside each was a mass of wire brushes, every one of which had to be meticulously adjusted with tweezers to ensure that the electrical circuits did not short. The letters of the alphabet were painted round the outside of each drum. The back of the machine almost defies description—a mass of dangling plugs on rows of letters and numbers.

We were given a menu, which was a complicated drawing of numbers and letters from which we plugged up the back of the machine and set the drums on the front. The menus had a variety of cover-names; for instance, silver drums were used for Shark and Porpoise menus, for naval traffic. I also remember Phoenix, which must have been an Army key, because I associate it with names indicating tank battles at the time of El Alamein.

We only knew the subject of the key and never the contents of the messages. It was quite heavy work getting it all set up, and I now understand why we were all of good height and eyesight. All this work had to be done at top speed, and at the same time 100 per cent accuracy was essential. The bombes made a considerable noise as the drums revolved, each row at a different speed, so there was not much talking during the eight-hour spell. For technical reasons which I never understood, the bombe would suddenly stop, and we took a reading from the drums. If the letters appeared to be matching the menus, the Enigma wheel-setting had been found for that particular key. However, to make it even more difficult, the Germans changed this setting every twenty-four hours. The reading was hurriedly phoned through to the Controller at Bletchley Park, where the complete messages were deciphered and translated. The good news would be a call back to say, 'Job up; strip machine.' It was a thrill when the winning stop came from one's own machine; all were individually named after towns in the United Kingdom and Commonwealth.

Thanks to the generosity of the Polish authorities in handing over secrets of the early German Enigmas, the brains of Bletchley were able to evolve the more sophisticated bombes. These were built by the

British Tabulating Machine Company at Letchworth. We were taken there to watch them being made and to encourage the workers, although we thought their conditions were better than ours. It was a surprise to see the large number of machines in production.

The outcome of this complicated procedure was that the German High Command, Army, Navy, and Air Force messages were deciphered in a remarkably short time. It is now known from Group Captain Winterbotham's book[1] that during the battle of El Alamein Hitler sent a message to Rommel, but that Montgomery received it first because Rommel's was delayed.

All the Wrens took the job very seriously, and we felt the weight of responsibility that any mistake or time wasted could mean lives lost. An example of this tension was when I took a Wren out to visit some relatives. In the middle of tea she turned white and left the room, taking me with her. She thought she had made an error whilst on duty. We worked it out on paper and decided all was well. Panic followed while we wondered how to dispose of the secret piece of paper, which we burnt in a tiny bowl in the kitchen. My cousins, alarmed by the smell, thought we had gone quite mad. Another Wren, due to have an operation, was so scared of talking under the anaesthetic that she sought the advice of the Superintendent WRNS.

To keep our morale up, we were told that Winston Churchill was constantly on the line to his 'most secret source', and that our work was absolutely vital. Occasionally the monotony was relieved by news of our involvement in a past achievement, such as the hunting and subsequent sinking of the battleship *Tirpitz*. We had no status for this responsible job. My pay amounted to 30 shillings a week as an ordinary Wren, rising to £4 10*s*. when I later became a Petty Officer. We had no category badges, and were supposed to say, if asked, that we were just 'Writers'. Sometimes it was very difficult having so little to say about one's life, and this explanation did not always satisfy relatives and friends, so my wartime activities were considered unimportant and something of a failure. It was never clear who was in charge of us, as we were detached from the Navy, working under the Foreign Office, but the RAF provided technicians to service the bombes.

After a few months I was transferred to another fine country mansion at Wavendon. Here we worked on the premises—a building in the grounds with very little light or air from the high windows. This prevented the noise of the machines from being heard outside, but it would certainly not have passed the Factory Act. There were no security precautions at all—I suppose so as not to draw attention to what was going on in this small village.

A few miles away at Gayhurst another 150 Wrens lived and worked on the premises in conditions similar to Wavendon's—cold rooms, no transport, and, I am told, swallows nesting in the house and flying in and out through the broken windows. There, too, mice abounded, and one lunchtime a dead one turned up in the gravy-boat. It was a beautiful place dating back to 1086, and Sir Francis Drake owned it in 1581. The Wrens used the old church in the grounds every Sunday, and my friend remembers dutifully pumping the organ.

In 1943 a large establishment was built for the Wrens at Stanmore—and later another at Eastcote—to accommodate the ever-increasing number of bombes needed to cope with the flood of Enigma signals from the many theatres of war. I was transferred there, and it was a very different set-up after the casual country life. There were about five hundred Wrens plus headquarters staff. We slept in 'cabins', fifty Wrens in each, on double-decker bunks. Discipline was strict. Even after working all night we had to attend morning parade and squad drill.

We worked in a modern one-story building surrounded by barbed wire and high walls. We were issued with special passes, and Royal Marines guarded the entrance. There were about eight long rooms with ten bombes in each. At this stage I was promoted to Petty Officer, and was in charge of a room of ten bombes, with my own office and two Wren assistants. I took down details of the menus and drew them out for distribution. It was non-stop work, and any slip-up would cause the machines to go wrong and produce false stops.

The strain was beginning to show. Many of us developed digestive troubles with the constant change of hours. My friend collapsed unconscious, suffering from overstrain, and was invalided out of the Service. Another had nightmares, and woke up one night clutching a phantom drum. There were cases of girls going berserk on duty, and electric shocks from the bombes were another hazard.

I began to feel that this strange life of secrecy and semi-imprisonment would never end, but quite suddenly, as Germany crumbled, the bombes were idle and quiet, with no more menus coming through from the brains of Bletchley Park. Brilliant they were, but the outcome of their work was dependent on the unremitting toil and endurance of almost two thousand Wrens. The long chain began with the Y Service, which intercepted the cipher radio messages, and finished with the SLUs which distributed the information to the Allied Commanders, who, in the final reckoning, either used or misused it.

An appreciation came from Winston Churchill, thanking 'the chickens for laying so well without clucking'. I had buried this part of my life so completely in my subconscious mind that it was a shock to see the story suddenly shown on television over thirty years later. But it does seem that the Wrens made a great contribution to the Ultra secret, which has been described as the greatest intelligence triumph of all time. The fact that the secret remained intact both during and after the war is a triumph of integrity for the thousands of people involved. Without this priceless foreknowledge of German plans the war could well have been lost before the Allied forces were sufficiently well armed and trained to achieve complete victory.

Note

1. F. W. Winterbotham, *The Ultra Secret* (London: Weidenfeld and Nicolson, 1974).

1. Typical 3-wheel Army Enigma, with outer and inner lids open and apparently 18 steckers in use

2. Typical 3-wheel Army Enigma, with inner lid closed, showing the 3-letter setting; note the warning about secrecy

3. Box of five 28-letter wheels for early Marine Enigma (*Funkschlüssel* C, Mark II, used from July 1933), with separate A and Ä, U and Ü

Geheim! **Sonder-Maschinenschlüssel BGT** 0S ✲

Nicht ins Flugzeug mitnehmen!

Datum	Walzenlage	Ringstellung	Steckerverbindungen	Kenngruppen
31.	I V III	06 20 24	UA PF RQ SO NI EY BG HL TX ZJ	jeu nyq aqm nzo
30.	V II III	01 07 12	GF KV JM FB UW LX TD QS NA ZH	azs zds kck hye
29.	IV I V	11 17 26	CI OK PV ZL HX NB AW DJ FE ST	kap gwh lyx kvx
28.	III IV V	03 14 09	DX FR OJ ZL YT GK HM NC EZ IQ	plq vyj njv jlu
27.	IV II I	26 20 16	WK YX PD SC GV TI AO QZ JM ER	rbm cqr ynd pfo
26.	III V I	11 15 18	HD FZ TA WS MK XU EP CB GY LN	sqs vhf caj jjl
25.	V I II	09 17 26	SP LD WU HN BQ IE AT CX OZ FK	bsm vof rsp nle
24.	I V IV	12 23 02	CJ UH IE MQ SR BF XV OK TD WZ	brx vrm eng tvg
23.	II III IV	18 05 20	XD LS JU PV BI WA MF HG NE OZ	pnr tof osf iew
22.	IV V II	09 13 17	FO IW KV MD QL YX EZ SP CJ TB	kjt xrd trb oet
21.	II V IV	10 01 26	PV YX HR KD FT JM IU LZ BE OG	rrg gae iec lmk
20.	I III V	19 12 08	JS EH PB MD ZV UT WF NQ XK RA	oon gbz zky kjz
19.	V II III	10 20 15	HR TI UY SV NA EX ZB CW KG DF	kee urq eft gdp
18.	II IV I	22 18 02	OR CF JY EQ TB KL WX AI DN ZV	ako uzb xoq vhu
17.	III I II	14 09 16	UX TA ES WG CD VY ML PB OH RN	ofr nan ghy gac
16.	II I V	21 07 13	HI ZP UB JT ME AG DX OW SC FN	txm udr lpc tar
15.	V IV I	25 03 20	QJ CW OF UN XM RY ZI LE BT HD	snl adq rck tbg
14.	IV II I	02 12 21	EO KM VS XJ FG LT NU IC ZR BQ	nzn oxo ptl pcg
13.	II I IV	24 18 01	RQ WC OG LU PK DZ TA YH VN BS	efh vsa hld usg
12.	III I IV	14 07 11	LE TO JX VB FG WU QZ ND YM IA	xmv pow krj swe
11.	I II V	22 10 17	JY RQ MT DA KE IV BH LS PC NF	mrg nkl igy nkd
10.	II IV III	08 01 05	UX LE IK SM QH PN ZC WT RO GV	jpc lwj kqd ynp
9.	IV V II	13 21 19	SQ TY EO RM IK NJ AC ZX LW GP	ypz okr ibt jnl
8.	V IV I	25 06 22	HP AT IW SN UY DF GV LJ BO MX	nja zoe xay mjg
7.	I IV II	07 14 11	FO ID BW VY AS TP NH RK QX JU	vjp ftz kta yia
6.	IV II III	01 04 09	HT KI JV OE ZN MU BF YC DS GP	afn znv zot afb
5.	II III IV	16 24 15	TK PW ZG RC LB AJ US OX EY FM	mur vkd nwc rdf
4.	I V IV	10 08 04	HC BJ RU YE IL OM PK TG XD AN	mgt xcp gxf xwn
3.	II I IV	22 05 26	NR XU YF CA ZP KO GI EQ LJ BH	zxp bmn exv vxk
2.	III V IV	14 03 12	GU BH WL PA RT MV KJ XO CS DQ	ekr jdb bjw iqd
1.	II I V	19 15 04	AD LR ZJ XI BU KV SW FH EN MY	eqq czy mzi grg

4. Monthly list of instructions for Enigma operators, showing date, choice and position of 3 out of 5 wheels, their ring-settings, cross-pluggings (20 out of 26 possibles), and discriminants (distinguishing types of Enigma traffic, and showing which keys to use)

5. This almost certainly shows the decryption of Enigma in Hut 6; once the day's settings had been found, the signals could be decrypted on modified British Typex cipher machines; their output was on sticky tape, such as can be seen on the floor

6. Bombe room; probably a late installation at Stanmore or Eastcote; each bombe has its own console at the end, probably housing a small device for printing out the stopping positions and enabling them to be checked quickly against the menus

7. Part of Colossus (probably Mark II), which solved Fish settings, being adjusted by two Wrens.

8. Lorenz *Schlüsselzusatz* SZ 42, used for enciphering Tunny traffic

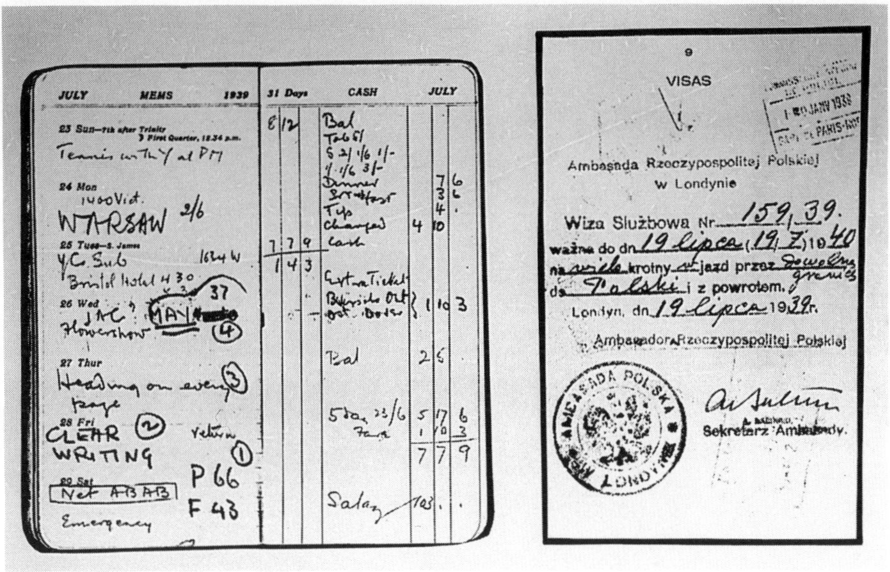

9. A. G. Denniston's diary and visa, showing the visit to Warsaw when the Poles revealed the progress they had made in breaking the Enigma

10. Group watching rounders at Bletchley Park, probably in 1940 or 1941; the five sitting are, rom left to right, E. M. Smith, Edmund Green, Barbara Abernethy (now Eachus), Patrick Wilkinson, and Alan Bradshaw; the back row, from left to right, are Philip Howse, Stephen Wills, Captain Ridley, John Barns, George McVittie, Marjorie de Haan, and A. G. Denniston, head of GC&CS.

	7452	飛	4906	
	1618		6430	飛脚
	4710	飛行	0258	
	4807	飛行隊	6240	航
	1614	飛行中隊	8351	
	2007	飛行戰隊	4770	航空
	5380	飛行師團	3935	航空路部
司令部	5271		4182	航空路部司令部
	8519	飛行集團	7036	航空軍
	3492	飛行場	0544	
	9023	飛行場中隊	3973	航空教育隊
部	0908	飛行場大隊	3782	航空地區司令部
	3006	飛行場司令部	0700	航空特殊無線隊
	1558	飛行學校	4698	航空特殊情報隊
團	0465	飛行家	9424	航空特殊通信隊
部隊	7599	飛行船	0670	航空通信司令部
	4511		3755	航空通信團
隊司令部	7057	飛行艇	6829	
	[illegible]	飛行機	7050	航空通信連隊

11. Part of a typical page from the Japanese Army Air Force 6633 code-book; the right column contains three groups of special interest, since they were known to refer to units engaged in intercepting and breaking American, British, Chinese, and Soviet signals:

0700 *kōkū tokushu musentai* (Air Special Radio Unit(s))
4698 *kōkū tokushu jōhōtai* (Air Special Intelligence Unit(s))
9424 *kōkū tokushu tsūshintai* (Air Special Communications Unit(s))

From: CinC Southeastern Air Fleet.

On 18 April CinC Combined Fleet will visit RXZ, R___ and RXP in accordance following schedule:

1. Depart RR at 0600 in a medium attack plane escorted by 6 fighters. Arrive RXZ at 0800. Proceed by minesweeper to R__ arriving at 0840. (____have minesweeper ready at #1 Base). Depart R ____ at 0945 in above minesweeper and arrive RXZ at 1030? (- - - - - - - -). Depart RXZ at 1100? in medium attack plane and arrive RXP at 1110. xxqxxxx - - - - - - - -. Depart RXP at 1400 in medium attack plane and arrive RR at 1540.

2. At each of the above places the Commander-in-Chief will make short tour of inspection and at _____ he will visit the sick and wounded, but current operations should continue. Each force commander - - - -

12. Extract from the decrypted signal, sent in the Japanese fleet code JN 25, which led to the shooting-down of the Commander-in-Chief, Combined Fleet, Admiral Yamamoto Ishiroku; shrewd guesses at the internal time-code and R— place-code enabled the Americans to intercept his aircraft at the extreme range of their fighters from Guadalcanal

PART THREE
Fish

18. An introduction to Fish

F. H. HINSLEY

GERMAN experiments in transmitting non-Morse teleprinter impulses by radio were detected before the war, but the pre-war transmissions were unenciphered. The first enciphered intercepts were obtained in the second half of 1940. They remained intermittent until the middle of 1941, but it was clear by then that Germany was developing on-line cipher machines to provide simultaneous encipherment and transmission and simultaneous reception and decipherment by radio, and presumably also by land-line, of messages based on the impulses of the international five-unit teleprinter code.

The first regular transmissions were intercepted on an experimental German Army radio link between Vienna and Athens from the middle of 1941. It used, as we now know, a cipher machine made by Lorenz (*Schlüsselzusatz* 40; SZ 40). The Army subsequently used several versions of a later model of this machine (SZ 42). During the remainder of 1941 it was established that another machine, in fact a machine manufactured by Siemens (T 52), was coming into widespread use in the German Air Force, and that some non-Morse radio traffic using yet another machine was being passed by the German naval authorities and the SS.

The GC&CS understood the design and method of operation of the Army machine (which it called 'Tunny') by January 1942, and was in the same position in relation to the Air Force machine (Sturgeon) by the summer of that year. By then, however, the signals intelligence authorities had taken the decision to concentrate the interception, cryptanalytical, and decryption resources almost wholly on the Army traffic. There were two reasons for this decision.

The first was that at every stage of exploitation—interception, solution of settings, decryption of messages—the non-Morse traffic, which came to be known as 'Fish' on the strength of a reference to the fact that one of the systems was named *Sägefisch* by the Germans, encountered problems of an even higher order than those that were presented by the Enigma machine which the Germans used for most of their Morse communications. At the level of interception, formidable difficulties arose because the transmissions were beamed, because the portions sent in auto-mode were at high speed, and because very accurate timing was required if their unbroken stream of elements was to be divided correctly into their components of mark and space.

These difficulties recurred at the level of cryptanalysis, which called for extreme textual accuracy, and also extended to decryption, which even after the settings had been solved was normally so laborious if undertaken by hand that the first step towards mechanization was the development of a decryption machine, delivered in June 1942. For all these reasons the available resources, which were limited, had to be carefully husbanded.

In the second place, the Enigma decrypts were by the beginning of 1942 supplying an immense amount of intelligence about the Air Force and the Navy, but little about the Army, on which, moreover, the need for intelligence was increasingly pressing as the war proceeded.

It would have become necessary to review this decision, and devote a larger effort to the attack on Fish if for some or other reason GC&CS had lost its ability to read most of the Enigma keys regularly. This situation fortunately did not arise; and for the remainder of the war the effort applied to Fish was concentrated on the German Army (Tunny) network. But it was an effort which never ceased to expand.

The Tunny network proliferated steadily from the middle of 1942; by July 1943 it had six links, by autumn 1943 ten links; and from early in 1944 it comprised twenty-six links, each using different cipher settings, between Berlin and the chief Army Commands throughout occupied Europe. The decryption was also increasingly successful; with two serious interruptions, in February 1944 and from June to October 1944, GC&CS solved a growing proportion of the ciphers and decrypted more or less regularly the growing volume of traffic passing in them. The number of decrypted transmissions rose from an average of only three hundred a month in 1943, so that more were decrypted in the six months from October 1944 to March 1945 than in all the period from the summer of 1942 to September 1944.

My main concerns are to describe the nature and illustrate the value of the decrypts. But I should first say something about the contribution made to this achievement by Colossus, the cryptanalytical machinery—as distinct from the decrypting machinery—that was specially devised for the work. The first success against the Fish keys, the solution of the Athens–Vienna experimental link in the spring of 1942, was made by hand methods; and it was by these methods that, overcoming various cryptographic and procedural improvements made by the Germans, GC&CS kept abreast of the still limited number of Fish links until May 1943.

By December 1942 it was clear that the German programme for increasing the security of the ciphers would before long win the day in all but a small proportion of the traffic unless high-speed machinery was developed. The first outcome was the 'Heath Robinson' prototype machines, the first of which became available in May 1943, and these were then superseded by Colossus Mark I, which came into use from the end of 1943, and the fully developed Colossus Mark II, which was brought into commission on 1 June 1944.

The decision to embark on this programme was soon to be vindicated. From May 1943 to January 1944 most Fish settings were solved by a combination of the hand methods and the machines. In February 1944 the introduction into general use of yet another German security device threw the task almost entirely on to the machines, and it was thanks to them that from this time, when the Fish network was just completing its planned expansion, the British success against it was able to continue till the end of the war.

I have mentioned that the effort against Fish complemented the work on Enigma by being concentrated against the German Army, whose Enigma keys were always more recalcitrant than those of the Navy and the Air Force. But its product also complemented the Enigma decrypts—those of the Navy and the Air Force as well as those of the Army—in a more general way. The Enigma was used for operational and tactical communications within Commands; in the Army, for example, it carried traffic within Armies, occasionally between Armies but never above Army level. Fish was used only for communications between the highest authorities in Berlin and the headquarters of the theatre Commanders-in-Chief, of Army Groups and, when occasion required, of Armies.

The difference was reflected in the volume of decrypts. As compared with the figures already given for the Army Fish, the volume of Enigma decrypts for all three services rose from thirty-nine thousand a month at the beginning of 1943 to about ninety thousand a month between the end of 1943 and the end of the war. But this discrepancy was offset not only by the fact that an individual Fish transmission commonly incorporated a large number of separate messages, but also by the difference in the nature and intelligence value of the messages.

As might be expected, the Fish decrypts, far from being tactical, carried discussions, orders, situation reports, and strengths and supply returns which were of exceptional significance for the light they threw on the intentions and the condition of the German Army and on the thinking and planning of the whole of the German High Command. Their significance was so exceptional, so strategic, that they lost nothing of their intelligence value from the fact that, whereas Enigma was commonly decrypted nearly currently, Fish transmissions were individually so troublesome that, even when the setting was solved, and even with the aid of the decrypting machinery, they were usually decrypted with a delay of several days.

Their value to the Allies will become clearer if I provide details of the dates from which the Fish links were broken and of the circumstances in which their signals were read. The first operational link to be broken was that between Berlin and Army Group E in the Balkans, with its headquarters at Salonika. It came into use on 1 November 1942, was broken almost immediately, and was read regularly until the volume of traffic dwindled from the summer of 1943. In January 1943, within a month of its inauguration, GC&CS broke the link between Army Group C in Rome and the headquarters of Panzer Army in Tunisia; with only one brief interruption in March, this was read regularly to the end of the Tunisian campaign in May 1943.

The decrypts were particularly valuable not only for being related, for the first time, to a theatre in which the Allies were operating, but also because they were obtained in the wake of the reorganization, and subsequently the disorganization of the Axis Commands in North Africa, when changes of keys and wireless routines were depriving the Allies of German Army and Air Force Enigma decrypts in that theatre. And at the end of May 1943 the link between Berlin and Army Group C and Kesselring, the Commander-in-Chief South, was added to the list of successes. For the rest of the war the decrypts of this link furnished comprehensive intelligence not only of German intentions and dispositions in the Italian campaign but also—and more and more as the Germans were forced back—on Germany's strategy on all the fronts.

Meanwhile, at the end of April 1943 the first link on the Russian front had been broken, that between Berlin and Army Group South. Its earliest decrypts gave full details of the plans for the German counter-offensive against the Kursk salient. Other links to this theatre soon succumbed—those to Army Group A, to the German Headquarters at Memel, and the German Mission in Romania in May, and those to Army Group Centre and to Army Group F at Belgrade in the summer of 1943. These links were broken at a time when, largely as a result of the difficulty of intercepting more localized transmissions from Eastern Europe, none of the Army Enigma keys on the Soviet fronts, and only a few of those used by the Air Force, had yet been solved. It was thus from the Fish decrypts that the Western Allies obtained the comprehensive intelligence about developments on these fronts which they enjoyed, with the interruptions already referred to, from the middle of 1943 to the end of the war.

The need for, and the value of, signals intelligence from Western Europe was even greater than for the Soviet fronts, or even the Italian theatre; and they of course increased from the beginning of 1944 as the Allies prepared for the landings in Normandy. It was here that Fish decrypts—and Colossus—made their outstanding contribution. In the whole of this area, from Denmark to the Pyrenees and from Calais to the Alps, intelligence from signals—though not from other, but inferior, sources—had hitherto been non-existent. The German Navy had made continuous use of radio, and all the naval Enigma keys had been readable since 1941. But inland, on account of the lack of fighting and the reliance on land-lines, the Army and the Air Force had not been on the air since the defeat of France in 1940. It was foreseen that this situation would change as the Germans prepared to meet the invasion, and great vigilance was applied to watching for new wireless frequencies and massing for the attack on new Enigma keys. To some extent the vigilance was rewarded; from February 1944 the expected wireless traffic was intercepted, mostly in practice exercises, and by April some of the newly introduced Air Force Enigma keys were solved. But the far stricter cipher security and wireless discipline of the Army successfully defied the attack on the new Army

Enigma keys except on an occasional day until 8 and 9 June, two and three days after the Allied landings. In January 1944, however, the Germans opened a non-Morse link between Berlin and von Rundstedt, the Commander-in-Chief West, and the link was broken towards the end of March.

From then to D-Day in Normandy all decrypts on this link, supplemented by those on the link between Berlin and Kesselring, supplied intelligence of crucial importance on Germany's appreciations of the Allied invasion intentions and on its own plans for countering them, together with much information about the state and dispositions of its divisions. Some of the intelligence was disturbing. It included indications from early in May that Allied deception had not wholly succeeded in persuading the enemy that the landings would not come in Normandy. The news, as late as between 24 and 27 May, that they were reinforcing the Cherbourg peninsula in a redisposition that was larger and more purposeful than any they had previously made came as a shock. But at least it came in time to permit the Allies to make essential last-minute alterations to the Overlord plan and to introduce effective modifications into their deception programme.

It is ironic that, having made so great a contribution to the success of Overlord, and perhaps even to the confidence necessary for the decision to proceed with it, the decrypts on Commander-in-Chief West's link were lost four days after the landings, within ten days of the commissioning of Colossus Mark II, because of a major change to the link's cipher system. The Allies were sufficiently assured by then that they would not be thrown back into the sea, and the Fish decrypts on Kesselring's link continued to supply some important intelligence for the Normandy campaign. But that link and almost all of the others succumbed to the same cipher change in July. Without Colossus, on the other hand, the Fish decrypts would not have been recovered, as they were in stages by the end of September 1944—after the longest black-out since the breaking of the first operational link in November 1942. From the beginning of October all the previously functioning links were again read regularly, the greatly increased cryptanalytical burden resulting from the German cipher improvements being offset by the steady growth in the number of Colossus Mark II machines in operation. Additional links introduced by the Germans since July or after October were also broken; and with active operations taking place on every front—in the west, in Italy, and on the Soviet fronts—all the links carried heavier and heavier traffic.

The consequent rise in the output of Fish decrypts went on unchecked until the end of March 1945, the month in which their volume was higher than in any other month of the war. If it declined thereafter, it did so only slightly and only because a number of the links were closing down as the Germans retreated and retracted their fronts. The rise was pronounced in the case of the Soviet fronts, where, despite the fact that the opening of new links was offset by the closing of others, all the links carried an enormous load and kept the Western Allies fully informed of the main developments during the Soviet advances. No additional links were established on the southern front, but the traffic carried by Kesselring's link expanded with the extension of his command and the increasing involvement of his problems in Italy with the German retreats in France, Yugoslavia, Hungary, and Austria. On the western front, however, the proliferation of the links and the increase in Fish decrypts were the outstanding developments in signals intelligence during the last seven months of the war.

As compared with the single link set up for Commander-in-Chief West before D-Day, several new links were opened between June and December 1944, and all were solved from October, or thereafter as soon as they appeared on the air. The most important were those between Berlin and the main Army Groups (Army Groups B and H), one between the headquarters of those two Army Groups and one between the two parts of Army Group B when that was broken up into Army Group B North and Army Group B South towards the end of the year. The load of traffic on all these links was all the greater because of the severe disruption of Germany's land-line and telephone communications by Allied bombing from the autumn of 1944. And the value of the decrypts was all the greater for the reason that while, as we have seen, there was no serious decline in the volume of Enigma decrypts, the solution of Enigma keys was frequently delayed from the autumn of 1944, and more so from February 1945, in consequence of the security precautions which the Germans were by then applying in the Enigma networks.

If the availability of the Fish decrypts was, thanks to Colossus, the outstanding signals-intelligence achievement in this last phase of the war, the outstanding operational and strategic feature of those months was the tenacity with which the German armed forces maintained their resistance to the advances of the Allies on all fronts. Whether or not the enemy would have been able to prolong that resistance even further if the Allies had lacked the advantage of possessing the signals intelligence is a question on which it is difficult to pronounce; but it is certain that the advantage was of enormous benefit to the Allies for the light it threw on German intentions, dispositions, and resources and for the ability they derived from it to plan their own moves with a view to achieving the maximum effect at the cost of the minimum expenditure of Allied resources and lives.

19. Enigma and Fish

JACK GOOD

DURING the Second World War the Germans used two kinds of high-grade cryptographic system: Enigma, and what we called 'Fish'. There were various forms of Fish. The official name for one was the *Schlüsselzusatz* ('cipher attachment') SZ 40 and 42, made by Lorenz (see Plate 8); this we called 'Tunny'. The other was the Siemens T 52, which the Germans called the *Geheimschreiber* ('secret writer') or *Sägefisch* (sawfish) and we called 'Sturgeon'. I worked on Enigma and on Tunny.

Before going into details, let us consider a few generalities concerning the art or science of cryptology, the two main branches of which are cryptography and cryptanalysis. The aim of the cryptographer is to produce a system that is convenient or simple to use legitimately but is too expensive, complex, or impossible in principle for the cryptanalyst to break (or to break too often or too soon). Systems of the latter type (using large quantities of 'one-time tape') are liable to be inconvenient for the legitimate users, especially if these users form an intercommunicating network. The Enigma and Tunny were both finite-state machines with a large number of possible states. But the number of possible states is not necessarily a good measure of the security of a cryptographic machine. It measures only the cost of an exhaustive or 'British Museum' attack. The cryptographer has to consider also whether there are cryptanalytic attacks that break down the problem piece by piece, and also whether there might be probable mistakes by cipher clerks that would be helpful to the cryptanalyst. For example, a simple substitution system has $26 \times 25 \times 24 \ldots 3 \times 2 \times 1$ (called 26!) $= 4.03 \times 10^{26}$ different possible substitution alphabets, yet such a system can be easily broken by a 12-year old, given a message of, say, two hundred words. The cryptanalyst's task, even for a simple-substitution system, is helped a lot if he has a correct *mot probable* or 'crib', a very elementary concept.

We can regard a cryptographic machine of given design or architecture as a device that converts the input (plain language, P) into cypher (Z) by means of a function f, Z = f(P,K) where K denotes the key. Or, in the language of statistics, K represents the parameters. A sensible cryptographer will assume that the function f is known to his 'enemy' the cryptanalyst. Suppose that K has N possible values. Then we can think of N as the British Museum work factor for the analyst.

As a 'thought experiment', let us imagine a cryptanalyst who is able to carry out a British Museum attack on one cipher message. That is, he knows the function f but decides to try all possible values for K for that message. For each of the N assumptions he has to see whether $f^{-1}(Z,K)$ produces plain language, where f^{-1} is the deciphering function which produces P if K is correct. Thus the cost to the analyst is N times the cost c of testing whether the output is plain language, for any given assumption about K. The cost c might be low if the beginnings of the plain-language messages are stereotyped. Otherwise a cryptanalytic machine could recognize, say, German language, by probabilistic discrimination between German and flat-random material. A flat-random sequence is one in which the probabilities of the 'letters' of the 'alphabet' are all 1/t when t is the size of the alphabet. For the Enigma, t = 26, whereas it is 32 = 2^5 for Tunny. If only the monograph (single-letter) probabilities $p_1, p_2 \ldots p_t$ are taken into account, then the expected weight of evidence per letter for the discrimination is $p_1 \log_{10}(tp_1) + p_2 \log_{10}(tp_2) + \ldots$ bans. For German this is only about 1 deciban per letter, so a text length of about 10 $\log_{10}$ N would be required. This can be reduced a lot if more than monograph frequencies are taken into account.

The Enigma and Tunny, the two main German cryptographic machines during the war, both attain a high value for N, partly through containing suitable wheels, but the wheels are entirely different for the two machines. The Enigma has been described in Chapter 11; let us look at Tunny.

Tunny was a cryptographic machine used by the German Army. It was used for transmitting even higher-grade secrets than the Enigma and sometimes contained messages from the megamurderer to his generals. Although the two machines had a little in common, the design of Tunny was very distinct from that of the Enigma, and was used for sending teleprinter messages, where a message often contained thousands of letters (whereas an Enigma message was seldom longer than a few hundred letters). The number of symbols in the teleprinter 'alphabet' is thirty-two. This alphabet is known as the

International Teleprinter Code or Baudot code and is illustrated in Fig. 19.1 in what I called 'reflection order' and in Fig. 19.2 in normal alphabetical order for easy reference. A transmitting machine can be fed either from a five-unit tape (see Fig. 19.3) or by a keyboard. Each plain-language 'letter' is combined with a key letter (or additive key) to produce a cipher letter. Let us denote these letters generically by

•	•	•	•	•	All space	X	X	•	•	•	A
•	•	X	•	•	Word space	X	•	•	X	X	B
•	•	X	•	X	H	•	X	X	X	•	C
•	•	•	•	X	T	X	•	•	X	•	D
•	•	•	X	X	O	X	•	•	•	•	E
•	•	X	X	X	M	X	•	X	X	•	F
•	•	X	X	•	N	•	X	•	X	X	G
•	•	•	X	•	Carriage return	•	•	X	•	X	H
•	X	•	X	•	R	•	X	X	•	•	I
•	X	X	X	•	C	X	X	•	X	•	J
•	X	X	X	X	V	X	X	X	X	•	K
•	X	•	X	X	G	•	X	•	•	X	L
•	X	•	•	X	L	•	•	X	X	X	M
•	X	X	•	X	P	•	•	X	X	•	N
•	X	X	•	•	I	•	•	•	X	X	O
•	X	•	•	•	Line feed	•	X	X	•	X	P
X	X	•	•	•	A	X	X	X	•	X	Q
X	X	X	•	•	U	•	X	•	X	•	R
X	X	X	•	X	Q	X	•	X	•	•	S
X	X	•	•	X	W	•	•	•	•	X	T
X	X	•	X	X	Figures	X	X	X	•	•	U
X	X	X	X	X	Letters	•	X	X	X	X	V
X	X	X	X	•	K	X	X	•	•	X	W
X	X	•	X	•	J	X	•	X	X	X	X
X	•	•	X	•	D	X	•	X	•	X	Y
X	•	X	X	•	F	X	•	•	•	X	Z
X	•	X	X	X	X	X	X	X	X	X	Letters
X	•	•	X	X	B	X	X	•	X	X	Figures
X	•	•	•	X	Z	•	X	•	•	•	Line feed
X	•	X	•	X	Y	•	•	•	X	•	Carriage return
X	•	X	•	•	S	•	•	X	•	•	Word space
X	•	•	•	•	E	•	•	•	•	•	All space

Note: This teleprinter code can be written with X and •, as above, or X and O, or 1 and 0. The variations have no significance.

FIGS. 19.1 & 2 The International Teleprinter Code in reflection order on left, and in alphabetical order on right

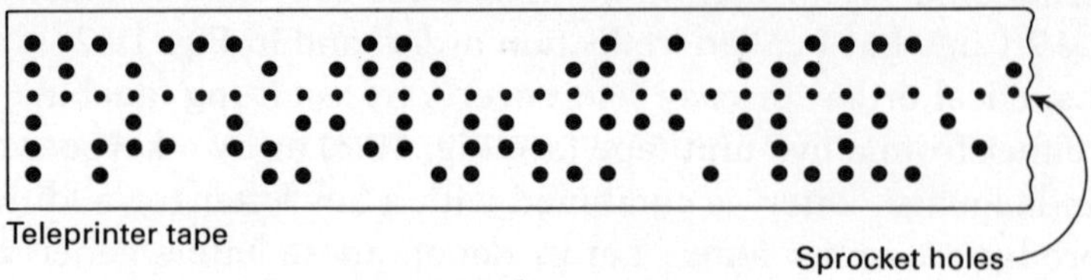

FIG. 19.3. Teleprinter tape

P, K, and Z. The method of combination is known as modulo-2 addition, or just addition for short, and is illustrated in Fig. 19.4. Modulo-2 addition is defined by the equations $0 + 0 = 0$, $0 + 1 = 1 + 0 = 1$, and $1 + 1 = 0$, or by dot + dot = dot, dot + cross = cross, cross + dot = cross, cross + cross = dot, and is applied to each of the five components separately, as illustrated, and we write P + K = Z. By adding K to both sides of this equation we see that P = Z + K because K + K = (0,0,0,0,0) or (. . . . .). Hence decipherment is the same process as encipherment; in other words, Tunny has the convenient reciprocal property that the Enigma has, but for a very different reason. Tunny does not have the non-crashing property; that is, a letter can encipher to itself as well as to other letters.

• • x • x
x • x x •
―――――
x • • x x
―――――

FIG. 19.4. Modulo-2 addition

Tunny has twelve wheels used for producing the additive key sequence, one key letter for each plain-language letter of a message. These wheels, known as pin-wheels, are completely different from the wheels of the Enigma. Instead of being wired they have 'pins' on their circumferences, where each pin can have two distinct states. Thus the pattern of a pin-wheel can be regarded as a circular sequence of 0s and 1s. As far as I can recall, these patterns were changed every day (or once a month at first), unlike the permanent wirings of the Enigma wheels, and the patterns were different on different links, such as Jellyfish, Bream, and Gurnard. The number of pins on the circumference of a pin-wheel is called the length of the wheel. Unlike the Enigma, Tunny needs no 'library' of wheels because their patterns can be changed without calling in an electrician. But, as in the Enigma, the keys that determine the settings of the wheels for individual messages are lower in the hierarchy than the keys that determine their patterns. The hierarchy has only two levels. The two corresponding cryptanalytic activities are known as 'wheel-breaking' (finding the patterns) and 'wheel-setting'.

The wheels fall into three categories known as the five chi wheels, the five psi wheels, and the two motor wheels called $\mu37$ and $\mu61$. The chi wheels move regularly and produce a sequence of teleprinter letters called $\chi = (\chi_1, \chi_2, \chi_3, \chi_4, \chi_5)$. The psi wheels all move together, but not regularly, and produce a letter called $\psi = (\psi_1, \psi_2, \psi_3, \psi_4, \psi_5)$. The psi wheels are driven by $\mu37$ in the sense that, in the original design, they all rotate one place when $\mu37$ shows a one (or 'cross'), and do not move when $\mu37$ shows a zero (or 'dot'). Likewise $\mu37$ is driven by $\mu61$ in the same sense, while $\mu61$ itself moves regularly. There were modified designs in which the motion of the psi wheels were affected by $\mu37$ + a component of χ_2 one back or even, as an autoclave, by P_5 two back. These minor modifications did not increase the cryptographic security much. Owing to imperfect transmission (garbles) the use of the autoclave[1] lasted only for a few months as far as I can recall.

The key letter K is produced by modulo 2 addition of χ and ψ, thus $K = \chi + \psi$ and $Z = P + \chi + \psi$.

The 'lengths' of the chi wheels are 23, 26, 29, 31, and 41. Being relatively prime (having no common factor) the period of the chi wheels is the product, which is 22,041,682, and of course no message could be long enough to 'bite its own tail'.

The lengths of the psi wheels are 43, 47, 51, 53, and 59, while the lengths of $\mu37$ and $\mu61$ are respectively 37 and 61. The period of the entire twelve wheels is the product of the lengths of all twelve wheels, which is about 1.6×10^{19}. This would be the work factor for a cryptanalyst wheel-setter from the British Museum. The number of pins to be positioned by a cipher clerk, on a given day, or month, is the sum of the lengths of the wheels, namely 501, which gives the cipher clerk a lot of trouble. But the German cryptographers must have thought that this inconvenience was acceptable and would keep the cipher clerk out of mischief. The work factor for a British Museum wheel-breaker is 'only' about $2^{501} \div (1.6 \times 10^{19})$, or about 4×10^{131}, because a rotation of a pattern is the same pattern as far as the wheel-breaker is concerned. Such a work factor could never be achieved, even if the moon were completely converted into an electronic computer.

Clearly the British Museum attack is out of the question, both for the Enigma and for Tunny. The cryptanalyst has to find some way to break the problem down.

After the outbreak of war I had to wait more than a year before I obtained suitable war work. My personality is not that of an officer and a gentleman, rather that of a philosopher and a mathematician, so I was not expected to join the Army (other than the Home Guard). Eventually I attended an interview run by Hugh Alexander and Gordon Welchman. Alexander had thrice been British chess champion and I knew him in the chess world.

A few weeks before I joined Bletchley Park, when I was playing in a chess match where the chess master Stuart Milner-Barry, later knighted, was probably playing on the top board, I was tactless enough to ask him whether he was working on German ciphers. He replied, 'No, my address is Room 47, Foreign Office.' Shortly thereafter, when I joined BP, he was there, working on German ciphers.

I joined BP on 27 May 1941, the day that the *Bismarck* was sunk, and was met at Bletchley railway station by Hugh Alexander. As we walked across a field, on the way to the office, Hut 8, he told me the exciting news that we were just beginning to read the German naval cipher system (the Enigma). It was a breach of security to discuss such secrets outside the office, but being secretive was somewhat out of character for Hugh.

The main activity in Hut 8 was the analysis of the naval Enigma. When I joined Hut 8, Alexander was the deputy head, while the head was the famous mathematician Alan Turing. I regarded myself as his main statistical assistant. Hut 8 was divided into two sections, a linguistics section, headed by Shaun Wylie, and a somewhat mathematical section in another room. There was a large third room where young ladies did clerical work. There was a hatch connecting the two smaller rooms for rapid communication. Once Hugh Alexander bounded towards the hatch, in some excitement, and banged his head badly at the top of the hatch, almost knocking himself out. He always worked with great energy and enthusiasm.

The linguistics section built up more and more knowledge about potential cribs (*mots probables*), so it was a case of success leading to more success. In the mathematical section, during my time there, the emphasis was on a technique called Banburismus, so-called because the stationery for it was printed in the town of Banbury. This was also the origin of Turing's names 'ban', 'deciban', and 'natural ban' as units for expressing 'weights of evidence.' Banburismus was an elaboration of a method called the 'clock method' by Rejewski, who attributes that method to Jerzy Różycki.[2] Banburismus depends largely on the indicating system (for the initial settings of the rotors for individual messages). I shall now describe that system as used for the naval Enigma that we attacked.

The German operator would haphazardly choose the settings for the three wheels as shown by the rings, say ASC, but he would not send ASC in clear. Instead, he would first set the wheels at $G_1G_2G_3$, the so-called *Grundstellung* which was part of the daily keys. Then he would tap out ASCASC (repeating ASC to provide a check). This would give him a hexagraph, say LQRCPY. He would write this in the pattern

```
L Q R
  C P Y
```

and fill in the rectangle with two letters that he chose haphazardly. For example,

```
L Q R T
O C P Y
```

Next he would encrypt the vertical digraphs LO, QC, RP, and TY by using a secret 'digraph table'. There were ten possible digraph tables (fixed for an appreciable time, perhaps of the order of a year), and which of the ten he was to use would be shown by part of the keys of the day. For example, LO might become TU, QC might become AH, RP might become LS, and TY might become IU. Then his rectangle would become

```
T A L I
U H S U
```

Then at last he would transmit TALI UHSU. The legitimate receiver would use the same procedure in reverse order to recover the true initial wheel-settings for the message, and he would get a check because of the repetition. He was unlikely to make a mistake because each digraph table was 'reciprocal', so that, for example, if LO becomes TU, then TU becomes LO in the same digraph table. Also he would obtain a check because the wheel-setting trigraph had been enciphered twice starting at the *Grundstellung* setting. I noticed on one night shift that about twenty messages were enough to identify which digraph table was in use, because the 'haphazard' letters (T and O in the example) were not 'flat random'. I do not think this discovery was of much importance because the wheel-settings chosen by the German cipher clerks often had enough other 'human-random' features.

If we, the cryptanalysts, know enough of the digraph tables, possibly through theft or capture, we can work back to the hexagraph LQRCPY and infer that LQR is the 'encipherment at $G_1G_2G_3$' (more precisely at $G_1G_2G_3$, $G_1G_2G_3 + 1$, and $G_1G_2G_3 + 2$) of the true settings ASC. We say then that (R,C) is part of the right-wheel (or fast-wheel) 'alphabet'. The first aim of Banburismus is to discover the right-wheel alphabet. Because of the reciprocal property of the Enigma, the number of possible alphabets is not $26! = 4.0 \times 10^{26}$ but 'only' $25.23.21.19 \ldots 3 = 26!/(13!2^{13}) = 7.9 \times 10^{12}$. It was, therefore, necessary to find about 129 db (decibans) from somewhere. This aim was achieved mainly by comparing pairs of messages whose hexagraphs started with the same (horizontal) digraph (and therefore had the same digraph at the fourth and fifth letters) such as LQRCPY and LQNCPV. (Of course we could not know the hexagraphs if we had no knowledge of the 'vertical digraph' table.) The cipher texts of messages were punched up on Banbury sheets (each consisting of the alphabet repeated again and again in columns) by the young ladies in the big room and related pairs of these sheets were compared at all slides from –25 to +25. At each slide or stagger the numbers of 'vertical repeats' (monographs, digraphs, trigraphs, etc.), observed as holes through both sheets, were converted into scores in decibans and entered on other stationery. Further information was obtained by sorting *all* the traffic (using Hollerith equipment) which found all repeats of four letters or more (tetragraphs, pentagraphs, etc.). The longest 'incorrect' repeat ever found (incorrect in the sense that it did not correspond to a pair of messages 'in depth') was an octagraph (corresponding to two messages whose 'hexagraphs' did not have even their first letters identical). If a coincidental cipher repeat had been much longer than eight, I would have called it a miracle.

On one night shift, when I was helping out in the big room by sliding one punched Banbury sheet against another one, I became so sleepy that I put my head down on the table and had a snooze. As soon as I woke up I shifted a sheet one place to the right and was amazed to find a twenty-two-letter repeat, a record. This repeat was of course 'causal', not a miracle. The young ladies were jealous, especially as I had gone to sleep while working. There is no justice.

If there are say 200 messages on a day, each of 150 letters, the number of pairs of messages is 20,000 and the number of places where a non-causal repeat might occur is 150 × 20,000 = 3,000,000. Therefore the expected number of non-causal octagraph repeats is $3{,}000{,}000/26^5 = 1/70{,}000$. In a year the expected number is about 1/200. This argument is only approximate, but it verifies that the non-causal octagraph repeat was not a miracle. A probabilist will notice the similarity to the famous 'birthday problem' (given twenty-three people chosen at random, it is 'odds on' that some pair have the same birthday). Compare also the concept of 'multiple comparisons' in statistics.

The method of scoring had been worked out by Turing. The topic is developed in greater detail by Good,[3] where Turing's contribution to the theory is given. At Alexander's suggestion I computed more accurate scores in decibans for tetragraphs etc., corresponding to various pairs of sources. The more accurate scoring system was known as ROMSing, where ROMS stood for the Resources Of Modern Science—Alexander's joke.

Given all this information, or just some of it because we would start work before all the information was in, the Banburists would get to work on the recovery of the right-wheel alphabet. A typical piece of evidence would be expressed as 'R = N + 7 with a score of 2.1db', or perhaps 'R = P + 5, certain' (where 'certain' meant odds of at least '50 to 1 on'). Thus we would have thousands of pieces of information to be chained together to try to build up a reciprocal right-wheel alphabet of high probability. The position of the turnover notch would also be found at the same time, because a turnover could 'kill the depth'. The right-wheel alphabet could serve the same purpose as a crib in providing a menu for a bombe, a cryptanalytic machine discussed below.

The game of Banburismus was enjoyable, not easy enough to be trivial, but not difficult enough to cause a nervous breakdown. I was quite good at this game, but Alexander was the champion. If he was on a working shift (we worked on a three-shift system, each shift being eight hours), he usually had broken most of the right-wheel alphabet by the time the next shift came on duty. I obtained the most probable *wrong* alphabet; it was about 3000 to 1 on at its peak and then gradually slipped back.

When I first arrived at BP, the scores were being calculated and recorded as decibans to one place of decimals. My first reaction was to think, why not drop the decimal point and call the unit the centiban? But I then noticed that most of the entries would be single digits if they were entered to the nearest half-deciban (hdb) and I calculated that not much information would thereby be lost by this 'rounding'. So I did not merely propose a new unit. This proposal led to a very great saving in time in Banburismus, perhaps of the order of 50 per cent. It exemplifies how valuable a very simple idea can be. John Pierpont Morgan had a point when he said, 'I don't want it perfect, I want it Thursday'; but perfectionism also has its place of course, especially in engineering.

As I said above, Banburismus would identify the position of the right-wheel notch (which caused the motion of the middle wheel). If the right wheel was one of numbers I–V, the position of the notch would identify the right wheel. By the time I arrived in Hut 8, the number of wheels available had risen to eight. Wheels VI, VII, and VIII each had two notches on their rings, and these notches were in the same positions for all three of these wheels. Hence the discovery of the notch positions would not distinguish between these three wheels. The notches for these wheels were Q–R, E–F, V–W, J–K, Z–A, for which the mnemonic was Royal Flags Wave Kings Above. The identification of the right wheel reduced the number of possible wheel orders from $8 \times 7 \times 6 = 336$ to 42 or 126. This reduction of work was especially valuable when bombe time was scarce.

The bombe was named after the Polish *bomba*. Both were electromechanical rather than electronic, but the bombe was much more elaborate. The *bomba* depended on there being plenty of self-steckers, and was defeated when the Germans increased the number of pairs of steckered letters to ten and the number of wheel orders from six to sixty. The bombe was of course named in honour of the *bomba*, but a less dangerous code-name should have been selected.

The bombe depended in the first place on the following obvious fact. If a plain-language letter X can be correctly matched with a cipher letter Y, in which case we say that X and Y are paired and write X↔Y or equivalently Y↔X, and if the wheels of the Enigma are in a known state, then the correct assumption for the 'stecker' of X implies the stecker of Y, and conversely. A correct crib of say twelve plain-language letters, correctly placed, would provide a menu for a bombe containing twelve simulated Enigmata. A 'closure' in the menu is exemplified by A↔B, B↔C, C↔A. A closure is valuable because it provides a good opportunity for a confirmation when the rotors are correctly positioned and when the initial stecker assumption is correct, and a refutation otherwise.

Gordon Welchman had the important idea that the reciprocal property of the steckers could be cryptanalytically used by means of a diagonal board, as discussed in his book.[4] In retrospect it is surprising that Turing missed this idea (for more than a day) which now seems so obvious, almost as obvious as that acceleration is proportional to force! Turing was a deep rather than a fast thinker, and his IQ was therefore not especially high. Shortly after Welchman suggested the diagonal board, Turing had an ingenious idea analogous to the logical fact that from a contradiction you can prove anything. According to Hodges,[5] Turing had previously argued with the philosopher Wittgenstein, who believed that the principle was of no importance. (Being a first-rate mathematician, Turing would use the method of proof known as *reductio ad absurdum* three times before breakfast. Wittgenstein was probably not quite so familiar with it.) In the application of a similar principle to the bombe, if a menu were rich enough (roughly speaking, if the crib had enough closures), then any assumption concerning the stecker of a letter on a closure, say E, would lead to all possible steckers for E, unless the wheel order and the positions of the wheels were correct. In this case the one stecker that would *not* be inferred for E, starting from an incorrect assumption, would be the *correct* one, whereas, if the assumption made for the stecker of E happened to be correct, then no incorrect inferences would be inferred. So the *number* of implied steckers for E provides much information. This ingenious concept saved a factor of about twenty-six in the running time of the bombe.[6]

Some of the more official messages were doubly enciphered. The superior officer would encipher a message using the same wheels and *Ringstellungen* as the cipher clerk, but with different steckers and with wheel-settings from a special list of twenty-six possibilities, one setting for each letter of the alphabet. He would pass this cipher text to the cipher clerk preceded by the words OFFIZIERGELB (if he had chosen the settings labelled G, or GELB). The cipher clerk would not know the settings nor the steckers used by the officer, but would re-encipher, on his own keys, what the officer had given him. Sometimes we would know the settings corresponding to GELB (or whatever) but not the officer's steckers, and then it was possible to recover the steckers by using a statistical procedure invented by A. L. Yoxall. On one occasion we thought we knew the wheel-setting *and* the steckers, but the *Offizier* message would not come out. This was indeed 'a riddle wrapped in a mystery inside an Enigma'. That night I dreamt that the two enciphering operations had been performed in the wrong order (which required that for once the superior officer and the cipher clerk were the same person). The next morning I checked that my dream was correct. Probably no one will ever know whether that message was important.

In about April or May 1943 I was transferred to Hut F, to work on Tunny. I have previously said it was October 1943 because that date was written on the book by Uspensky[7] which was a present from former colleagues in Hut 8. But I have since remembered that the publishers took several months to deliver the book. The book is autographed by Candida Aire, Hugh Alexander, Michael Ashcroft, Hilary Brett-Smith (now married to Sir Harry Hinsley), Arthur Chamberlain, Joan Clarke (now Murray), Al Clifford, Sylvia Cowgill, Pauline Elliott, A. P. Mahon, Rolf Noskwith, Richard Pendered, June Penny, Alan Turing, and Shaun Wylie. This book is one of my treasured possessions. The section was known as the Newmanry because M. H. A. Newman, FRS, was in charge. Its function was to work on machine attacks on Tunny, and it complemented the Testery, where hand and linguistic attacks were used. Some of those who worked or had worked in the Testery, apart from Major Tester, were Roy Jenkins (later Chancellor of the Exchequer), Alan Turing, Peter Benenson (founder of Amnesty International), Peter Hilton (now a well-known mathematician), and Donald Michie (well known to the artificial intelligentsia and previously Curator of the Balliol Book of Bawdy Verse). Peter Hilton once spent a sleepless night composing the masterly palindrome DOC NOTE, I DISSENT. A FAST NEVER PREVENTS A FATNESS. I DIET ON COD. This palindrome has often been incorrectly attributed to others.

Michie had been a major scholar in classics at Balliol College in Oxford but his wartime experiences converted him into a scientist. After about two or three months we were joined by Shaun Wylie, and later by about another twelve mathematicians. One of them was the extremely famous topologist, J. H. C. Whitehead (Henry). Some others, in alphabetical order, whose names I recall with clarity, were Michael Ashcroft, Oliver Atkin, Howie Campaigne (US), Michael Crum, Sandy Green (for a short time), John Herivel (mainly in administration), Walter Jacobs (US), Kenneth LeCouteur, Tim Molien, Gordon Preston, and David Rees. Wylie married one of the Wrens, Odette. They were both exceedingly thin but healthy. After the war Wylie wrote a well-known joint book with Peter Hilton on Homology.

About the time that Wylie joined us, we moved into part of a large brick building, called Block F, and later we had yet another brick building called Block H. We needed plenty of space to house the ten Colossi that were ultimately built.

The original break into Tunny had occurred because a German cipher clerk had enciphered two long messages at the same initial settings of the twelve wheels. By placing one cipher text under the other, and adding modulo 2, the common additive key was eliminated. (Recall that when working modulo 2, addition and subtraction are the same thing.) Thus a stream of P + P' was obtained. This stream was given to Brigadier John Tiltman, who succeeded in inferring what the two plain-language messages were. Next, one of the P streams was added to both cipher streams, to provide one useful stream of pure additive key K, and another useless stream that was effectively flat random. These two streams were given to W. T. Tutte, who, after a few months, was able to deduce the entire structure of the Tunny machine, including the lengths of all the wheels.

Of course, a part of Tutte's original break-in was the recovery of the wheel-patterns from a long stretch of key. Along with other techniques, this process was called 'wheel-*breaking*', and it was, of course, more difficult than wheel-*setting*, when the patterns of the wheels were known.

Naturally a section of GC&CS was then started up to exploit the new knowledge. Its head was Major Tester, and its function was to use methods similar to those used by Tutte, when opportunity presented itself, but with the enormous advantage of already knowing the wheel lengths, etc. Some of the members of the Testery were mentioned above.

One of these members was Maxwell ('Max') H. A. Newman. He felt inferior in the Testery, where he probably compared his efforts, in particular, with those of Peter Hilton. Hilton had exceptional powers of visualization and could see two teleprinter characters merging modulo 2 in his mind's eye. Newman judged that much of the purely non-linguistic work done in the Testery could and should be mechanized and that electronic machinery would be essential. He convinced Commander (later Sir) Edward Travis, by then the head of BP, that work on such machinery should be begun, and so the Newmanry was born. Its purpose, at first, was to set the chi wheels for individual messages after the patterns of the chi wheels had been recovered in the Testery.

First there was a machine called Heath Robinson, the name of the British artist famous for his cartoons of absurd machines (corresponding to Rube Goldberg in America). The main designer was C. E. Wynn-Williams of the Telecommunications Research Establishment, assisted by E. A. Speight, Arnold C. Lynch, D. A. Campbell, and F. O. Morrell, all at the Post Office Research Station in Dollis Hills on the outskirts of London. (In Britain the Post Office was then responsible for telephones.)

The input to Heath Robinson was a pair of teleprinter tapes, one containing cipher and the other one some function of the chi wheels. The tapes would be stuck into closed loops and driven partly by pulleys and partly by their sprocket holes. Both tapes would be read photoelectrically and the innards of the machine would count the number of times that some Boolean function was equal to a dot. The cipher tape would have a length prime to that of the key tape, so that in the course of a 'run' all possibilities were examined.

The machine had perhaps about two dozen vacuum or gas-filled valves or tubes. When I joined the Newmanry, Heath Robinson had recently been installed.

The main weakness of the design was the driving of the tapes partly by their sprocket holes at about a hundred times the speed of the tapes in normal teleprinter usage. This would cause these holes to stretch and the tape to have a tendency to tear. The stretching was a nuisance largely because the distance from the sprocket driving to the photoelectric reading was not as short as it might have been. Also, from time to time the machine would begin to smoke. It was not perfect but it was completed by 'Thursday'.

There were other reasons why progress was slow when I joined the Newmanry, two or three weeks after Michie's arrival, and the future of the Newmanry was in jeopardy. One trouble was that the best runs were not being made. Michie and I did research in the evenings on the statistics of plain language and wheel patterns, and that improved matters. Another problem was that mistakes were made in the manufacture of further key tapes owing partly to incorrect input to a simulated Tunny machine. We did not capture a German Tunny until the last days of the war in Europe. I soon adopted the motto, 'If it's not checked it's wrong.'

Progress improved to the point where a big investment in an improved cryptanalytic machine became clearly justified. So Heath Robinson had achieved its purpose. Tom Flowers, known as an electronics wizard, was called in by Newman, at the suggestion of Turing.[8] Tom Flowers and his 'band of brothers',[9] worked at the Post Office Research Station in Dollis Hill. Flowers pointed out that the stretching of the tapes could be avoided if the key tape were represented internally. Then only the cipher tape would be used in a run and it could be driven by pulleys alone, and the photoelectric reading of the sprocket holes would reliably provide the 'clock pulses'.

To represent the key tape internally would have the further advantage that errors in tape preparation would be eliminated and time would be saved. The cost would be that far more 'tubes' or valves (actually gas-filled thyratrons) would be needed than had been used in Heath Robinson. In fact, the first model of Colossus, installed in 1943, had about 1,500 tubes and later models had about 2,500 (see Plate 7). This was presumably far more than any previous electronic machine in the world and many people thought that such a machine could not be reliable, but Flowers knew that tubes were reliable if the machine was left switched on all the time. I regard that as one of the great secrets of the war, another one being that ordinary teleprinter tape could be run on pulleys at nearly thirty miles per hour without tearing. The Colossus Mark 1 was built by 'Thursday' and was nearly perfect too, apart from some teething troubles. Later, I estimated that, at its best, a Colossus could do about 10^{11} Boolean operations without making an error that would affect the outcome of the runs. Some especially important assistants to Flowers were S. W. Broadhurst, W. W. Chandlers, and later A. W. M. Coombs. A few years after the war Coombs told me that he had been deprived of credit by the Dollis Hill Administration for his contributions to trans-Atlantic communication, and that he felt like committing suicide. Flowers and the other engineers cannot be praised enough.

The programming of Colossus was done by Boolean plugging and toggle switches. The flexible Boolean nature of the programming was probably proposed by Newman and perhaps also Turing, both of whom were familiar with Boolean logic, and this flexibility paid off handsomely.

For a time, the mode of operation was for a cryptanalyst to sit at Colossus and issue instructions to a Wren for revised plugging, depending on what was printed on the electromatic typewriter. At this stage there was a close synergy between man, woman, and machine, a synergy that was not typical during the next decade of large-scale computers. But, after some experience, I worked out some decision trees, with Michie's co-operation, so that Wrens could operate Colossus in a more routine manner. (Otherwise we would have needed more cryptanalysts.) When the decision tree failed in its aim, a record from the printer was presented to the cryptanalyst on duty, called a 'duty officer', to make suggestions for further runs. The record contained all the high scores in the runs together with a frequency count of the best partial 'de-chi' with the alphabet in 'reflection order' (see Fig. 19.1). Reflection order was more likely than alphabetical order to be convenient for a cryptanalyst. In this reflection order, the third level was treated as the 'least significant' of the five because it usually contained less information than the other levels. I thought of the reflection order by a weak analogy with the sequence .xx.x..xx..x.xx.x..x.xx..xx.x..xx..x.xx..xx.x..x.xx.x..xx..x.xx. etc., which Euwe had used in an article on infinitely long games of chess (with a modified rule for a drawn game).[10] After two signs, four signs, eight signs, etc., in Euwe's sequence, all is repeated with dots and crosses interchanged. The Euwe sequence contains no subsequence repeated three times in succession. The reflection order is now called the Gray code and is useful for analogue-to-digital conversion. (Gray thought of the reflection order independently.)

The original function of Heath Robinson and of Colossus was to find the settings of the chi wheels. For the first few months of operation of Colossus this was its sole function, the rest of the work being completed in the Testery, and we got into the habit of thinking that wheel-breaking should be done by carbon units. But one morning Donald Michie came into the office with an idea for programming Colossus to help with that operation. With a little help from me we verified that he was right and, from that time onwards, Colossi were used both for setting and for speeding up the breaking of the chi wheels. Once again then, a simple idea that we had been overlooking led to a major saving of time. Since the mid-1960s, if there is a laborious calculation to be done, everybody thinks of programming it for a computer; but the mid-1940s were not the mid-1960s.

The organization of the Newmanry cryptanalysts was somewhat democratic. There were so-called 'tea parties' that could be called by any cryptanalyst by writing an idea in the current research log-book, and a note on the blackboard in the research room. By the end of the war five or six research log-books had been filled with notes.

Soon after the victory in Europe, Shaun Wylie showed that Colossus could have been used for breaking the motor wheels. (He was unaware of my hand-breaking of the motor wheels for BR 5521). Thus Newman's dream could have been completed. Also after VE day it was shown that multiplication to base 10 was almost possible on Colossus, by complicated plugging; I say 'almost' because the calculation could not be completed in the time between 'clock' pulses, but the exercise was interesting in showing how flexible was the Boolean plugging of Colossus. It was further evidence that Colossus could be regarded as the first large-scale electronic computer, albeit for a specialized purpose.

Most of the cryptanalysts in the Newmanry dispersed into various universities and most of us achieved some measure of success in our unclassified work. But the success of our efforts during the war, and the feeling that we were helping substantially, and perhaps critically, to save much of the world (including Germany) from heinous tyranny, was a hard act to follow.

Notes

1. D. Kahn, *The Codebreakers* (New York: Macmillan, 1967), 143–7, 206, 754.
2. M. Rejewski, 'How Polish Mathematicians Deciphered the Enigma', *Annals of the History of Computing*, 3/3 (1981), 223.
3. I. J. Good, 'The Joint Probability Generating-Function for Run-Lengths in Regenerative Markov Chains, with Applications', *Annals of Statistics*, 1 (1973), 933–9.
4. G. Welchman, *The Hut Six Story* (London: Allen Lane, 1982; Penguin Books, 1984), 77–83, 110, 137, 301–7.
5. A. Hodges, *Alan Turing: The Enigma* (London: Hutchinson, 1983), 154.
6. Ibid. 183.
7. J. V. Uspensky, *Introduction to Mathematical Probability* (New York and London: McGraw-Hill, 1937).
8. T. H. Flowers, 'The Design of Colossus', *Annals of the History of Computing*, 5 (1983), 239–52.

9. A. W. M. Coombs, 'The Making of Colossus', *Annals of the History of Computing*, 5 (1983), 253–9.
10. M. Euwe, 'Set Theory Observations on Chess', *Proceedings of the Academy of Sciences, Amsterdam*, 32 (1929), 633–42 (in German).

20. The Tunny machine

KEN HALTON

'TUNNY' was the word used at Bletchley Park to describe the traffic on certain of the Fish links which radiated from the German High Command in Berlin out to the various Army Commands. It was also the name of the equipment which was used at BP to decipher the messages picked up from those links. It is the use, function, and physical arrangement of the Tunny equipment which will be described here, after indicating where it fitted into the system of things. First of all, however, it is necessary to explain something of the actual enciphering system which involved the coding, in the cryptographic sense, of characters which were already coded in the telegraphic sense. This is totally different from the way in which the Enigma machine substituted one character for a different one (albeit in a very complex way) and where the word 'coding' had only one meaning.

The entire Tunny system had its foundations in the Baudot system of telegraphy, the derivatives of which had replaced the Morse system in many applications between the First and Second World Wars. Unlike the Morse code, where the characters varied in length from one dot (letter E) to five dashes (figure 0), each character in the Baudot code was represented by a group of five equal-length elements. Each code-element could be either of two states and, because of their Morse ancestry, these states were known as mark and space. Taken in groups of five there were thirty-two combinations and nowadays they would more readily be accepted as the binary numbers 00000–11111. The Baudot assignment of the combinations to the various characters was subsequently revised and a world-wide standard, the International Teleprinter Code, was in use by the 1930s. It is essential to realize, however, that the characters were encoded for telegraphic purposes in accordance with an international standard which was not secret in any way. That was exactly the opposite of any form of encoding that intentionally hides the true identity of the character and which, perhaps, we should refer to as encryption.

In the system of encryption used for Tunny traffic, known as the Vernam Cipher, each of the five elements of the telegraph code was operated on individually and was either changed into the opposite state or was not changed. The group of five elements then represented a new character, i.e. the encrypted one, but the process was repeated again on the new character to produce yet another, which was the one which was finally used.

The intercepted Tunny traffic was assembled at Knockholt, in Kent, and sent from there to BP. Some of it came by motor-cycle dispatch riders and some was transmitted over Post Office land-lines directly into Room 11 in Block F, which was in Newmanry, the name by which Professor Newman's section was known. Because, in the latter case, there was the possibility of introducing errors into the retransmitted messages, each was sent from a single transmitter into two separate lines at Knockholt and received on two separate receivers at BP. Six lines were provided and, used in pairs, they enabled three different messages to be sent at the same time. At BP they were reproduced on perforated paper tape and the pairs of tapes thus received were visually compared to detect any differences between them. Up to six might be tolerated but more than that meant that the message had to be restarted. Therefore, by line or by motor cycle, reliable tapes became available at BP.

The tapes were, of course, of encrypted messages, and two distinct processes had to be carried out on them before their clear texts could be seen. The first process was to find the encryption pattern that had been added to the clear text, and the second was to strip that pattern from the encrypt to reveal that clear text. Colossus was used to assist in the first of these operations and Tunny in the second, but other devices were also used and there was still the need for a good deal of human intervention.

When the German operator sent the message, he did so by typing it out on the keyboard of a teleprinter, that keyboard being similar to the one on a typewriter but restricted to thirty-two keys. Twenty-six of those were for the letters of the alphabet and the other six were used to control non-printing functions of the receiving teleprinter. These were letter shift, figure shift, carriage return, line feed, word space and all space. (The last of these was the condition usually received if the line went dead, and hence it was often used only to ring an alarm bell.) Each of the thirty-two characters was produced as a sequence of five electrical pulses, in which each pulse could be either of two conditions—called positive or negative, on or off, present or absent, etc.—allocated in accordance with the International Teleprinter Code (see Fig. 19.2). Thus the message left the operator's machine in clear and understandable form (plain text) and encryption was carried out subsequently in a separate machine, the Lorenz SZ 40 or SZ 42—the *Schlüsselzusatz* or 'cipher attachment' (see Plate 8).

The most significant parts of the SZ 42—of which the Tunny machine (Fig. 20.1) was an equivalent—were two sets of five coding wheels or rotors. Each of the five digits of the character code was passed through one of the coding wheels in the first set and emerged either unchanged or changed into the opposite condition. The five digits leaving that set of coding wheels then represented a different character from the one put in (unless, by coincidence, it happened to be the same) and the process was repeated through the second set of coding wheels to produce the encrypted character which was actually transmitted to line. Whether or not a coding wheel reversed the sense of the digit passing through it depended on the setting of a tooth on its circumference, the tooth being either erect or folded down. The wheels all had different numbers of teeth, which were set

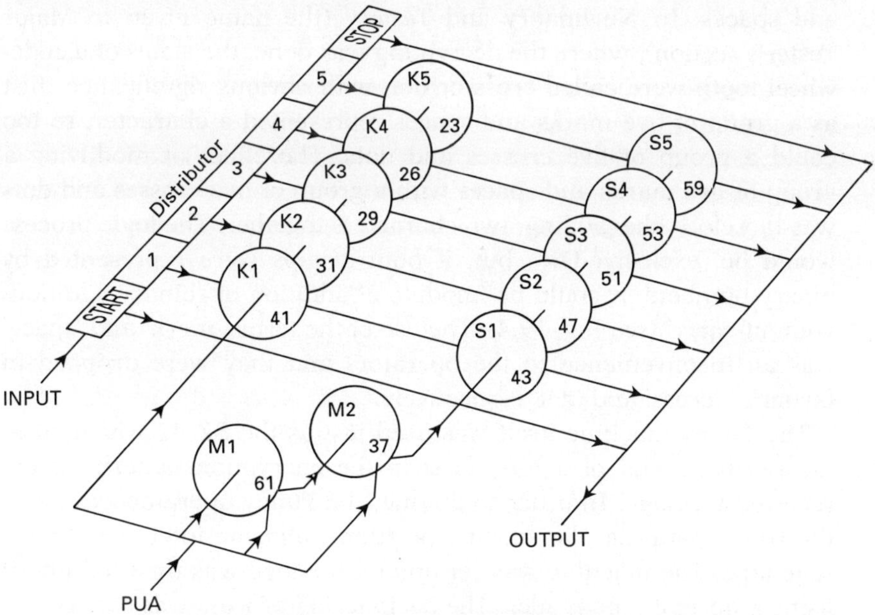

FIG. 20.1. The Tunny machine

up to the pattern specified for the day, and all could be rotated individually to any required position for the start of a message. The first set of wheels advanced one tooth for every character. Two more wheels of a similar type controlled the stepping of the second set of coding wheels and were called (at BP) the motor wheels. The first motor wheel advanced by one tooth for every character, but the second did so only when permitted to do so by the teeth of the first. The second set of coding wheels stepped only when permitted to do so by the teeth of the second motor wheel. Like the character-coding wheels, the motor wheels could be set to any specified tooth pattern and could be made to start from any position.

It was the job of the cryptographers, aided by Colossus, to determine the tooth patterns and starting positions of all twelve code wheels on the SZ 42. The wheel patterns were changed at intervals and once found would apply to all intercepts on that link during the period. The starting positions were changed for every transmission and so had to be broken each time. All this information was needed before the Tunny operators could set up their machines to produce a clear text.

Transmission of the messages was by telegraphy, in which discipline the digits or elements of the character code were called marks and spaces. In Newmanry and Testery (the name given to Major Tester's section), where the decrypting was done, the states of a code-wheel tooth were called cross or dot, with obvious significance. Just as a group of five marks and spaces represented a character, so too could a group of five crosses and dots. The effect of modifying a group of five marks and spaces with a group of five crosses and dots was therefore like 'adding' two characters together. The logic process would be 'exclusive-OR', but, if both groups were represented by binary numbers, it could be 'modulo-2' addition or 'binary addition-without-carry' (see Fig. 19.4). The use of the terms 'mark' and 'space' was an inconvenience to the operators and they were dropped in favour of 'cross' and 'dot' respectively.

The Tunny machine itself was used just as the SZ 42 was used at the receiving end of a link, to strip the encryption pattern off the received message. In order to do that, the Tunny operator was given the wheel patterns, the starting positions, and the intercepted message tape. The machine was set up and the tape was then fed into it using a normal tape-reader. The deciphering process was carried out as a repeat of the enciphering one; it was not a reversal of it. The output was connected to a slightly modified teleprinter, which, if all were going right, would print out the clear message. The modifications to the teleprinter caused the six character combinations which would normally have controlled its functional movements to print symbols instead. This was necessary because, otherwise, it would not have been able to print out the enciphered message or the cipher streams from the code-wheels, all of which contained those characters in places where the functional movements were definitely not wanted.

The operator watched the process carefully (inserting the necessary carriage-return and line-feed operations by hand) and was quick to stop it if the print-out ceased to be clear. That could happen for various reasons, perhaps the most common being that the original signals had been sent over a radio link which, at times, faded. The Tunny operator had then to ensure that, after the bad patch, both tape and Tunny had missed out the same number of characters. In difficult cases, or when the bad patch was a long one, it was necessary for a cryptographer to find a new set of restarting positions for the wheels. The output from the Tunny machine was by means of a page-printing teleprinter which printed in typewriter fashion but on to a continuous roll of paper $8^1/_2$ inches wide. The text was clear in the sense that it was no longer encrypted but it still required a good deal of attention to make it meaningful. It did not contain any figures, because the printer had been modified to print a symbol instead of actually shifting case when letter shift or figure shift was received. The text itself was full of military abbreviations of all kinds and there were other minor character changes which all helped to give the print-out a confused appearance. In this form, however, it left the Tunny room to be cleaned up elsewhere.

The Tunny machine performed the same function electrically as did the SZ 42 mechanically, but physically did not resemble it in any way. Like Colossus, it was designed and built at the Post Office Research Station, Dollis Hill. It was certainly not a machine in the normal sense, but was made from a variety of the components used in the automatic and manual telephone exchanges of that time. Perhaps the most significant items to be simulated were the coding wheels of the SZ 42. In Tunny, their function was carried out by electrically driven switches in which an input wire could be connected to any one of twenty-five output wires in sequence. The output wires were made to behave as the teeth of the coding wheels. Two such switching elements could be wired together to provide fifty outlets and three to give seventy-five. By making them skip over unwanted outlets they were able to simulate each of the coding wheels, the smallest having twenty-three teeth and the largest sixty-one. They were known in Tunny as the 'marker switches'.

A representation of the functions of the Tunny machine is given in Fig. 20.1. The input character consisted of a sequence of seven electrical elements, each of which passed through the machine on a path of its own. The first and last elements were not enciphered, and served only to start and stop the operation. Hence we are concerned only with the remaining five coding elements. For these there were five paths through the machine, each containing two of the electrically simulated coding wheels already described. A timing circuit distributed the five elements of the incoming character, one along each path, where they were acted upon in accordance with the patterns set up on the 'wheels'. The elements, duly changed, emerged in sequence on to a common output wire, and then represented plain text, which was printed out by the teleprinter.

A stepping pulse, PUA, tended to step the wheels at the conclusion of each character. The first set of coding wheels, K1–K5, and the first motor wheel, stepped every time. The second motor wheel stepped whenever the first motor wheel pattern enabled it to do so. The second set of coding wheels, S1–S5, stepped whenever the second motor wheel pattern enabled it to do so. The number of teeth on each wheel is shown, and when a wheel was stepped, it moved on one tooth-space.

There was also a second group of switches, very similar to the markers and working in unison with them, known as the 'chaser switches'. At the beginning of a message, when the markers were set into their correct starting positions, the chasers would follow, each one taking up the same position as its associated marker. As the message went through the machine, the markers stepped just as the wheels had done on the SZ 42, while the chasers remained in their original starting positions. At suitable intervals the operator stopped the process and brought the chasers into the positions then occupied by the markers. This had the effect of providing her with a new starting point, so that, if the print-out ceased to be clear, she need not go right back to the beginning of the message in order to try again.

The setting-up of the code patterns and starting positions was done by inserting plugs into a large array of sockets which represented the teeth on the coding wheels. A similar array of lamps displayed the positions reached by the markers and chasers, thus enabling the operator to see each wheel pattern and her position on all the wheels at any time.

Tunny was a flexible and versatile machine, used not only in the role of a deciphering SZ 42, but also, at times, by the cryptographers to assist them in some of their manual work. It was fabricated almost entirely from Post Office telephone exchange equipment. The multi-contact switches were automatic-exchange 'uniselectors'; the sockets and lamps were those from manual-exchange switchboards and, in addition, there was a large number of the relays (electrically controlled switches) which were to be found in both types of exchange.

The foregoing explanation has been given in very general terms and omits some of the lesser features as well as any detail of the circuitry. More of this is given in a separate description which follows for the benefit of the more technically minded reader. It is perhaps of interest to add here that, complex as the SZ 42 was in its initial state, three subsequent changes were made to it which made it even more formidable. All three were modifications to the way in which the second set of coding wheels was stepped. In one of these, the tooth pattern of the second element of the first group of coding wheels was used with that of the second motor wheel and it was the result of their 'OR' combination which controlled the stepping of the second group of coding wheels. In another, the process was similar, except that the pattern added to that of the second motor wheel was obtained from the first element of the second set of coding wheels. The third was again similar, but this time the additional pattern was that of the fifth code element of the clear text, two characters before the one being worked on. Messages were sent using any combination of these 'limitations', as they were called, but, fortunately, the last one was so dependent on the accurate transmission of the message that its use declined soon after its introduction.

The use of binary form enables an example to be given of the addition of two characters by 'modulo-2 addition' (see Fig. 20.2). The result of adding any character in the first column of the table to any character on the bottom line is the character shown at the intersection of their co-ordinates.

A	7																															
B	G	7																														
C	F	Q	7																													
D	R	T	U	7																												
E	5	0	K	4	7																											
F	C	H	A	6	N	7																										
G	B	A	H	W	3	Q	7																									
H	Q	F	G	X	Y	B	C	7																								
I	S	2	4	K	U	J	M	L	7																							
J	4	L	S	5	R	I	Z	2	F	7																						
K	N	P	E	I	C	5	Y	3	D	6	7																					
L	Z	J	M	3	W	2	4	I	H	B	X	7																				
M	2	S	L	Y	X	Z	I	4	G	Q	W	C	7																			
N	K	Y	5	S	F	E	P	O	R	U	A	V	T	7																		
O	3	E	P	Z	B	Y	5	N	V	W	Q	R	6	H	7																	
P	Y	K	O	2	Q	3	N	5	T	X	B	6	R	G	C	7																
Q	H	C	B	V	P	G	F	A	Z	M	O	S	J	3	K	E	7															
R	D	W	6	A	J	U	T	V	N	E	S	O	P	I	L	M	X	7														
S	I	M	J	N	6	4	2	Z	A	C	R	Q	B	D	X	W	L	K	7													
T	W	D	V	B	Z	X	R	6	P	3	2	5	N	M	4	I	U	G	Y	7												
U	6	V	D	C	I	R	X	W	E	N	4	Y	3	J	2	Z	T	F	5	Q	7											
V	X	U	T	Q	2	W	6	R	O	Y	Z	N	5	L	I	4	D	H	3	C	B	7										
W	T	R	X	G	L	V	D	U	Y	O	M	E	K	2	J	S	6	B	P	A	H	F	7									
X	V	6	W	H	M	T	U	D	3	P	L	K	E	Z	S	J	R	X	O	F	G	A	C	7								
Y	P	N	3	M	H	O	K	E	W	V	G	U	D	B	F	A	5	2	T	S	L	J	I	4	7							
Z	L	4	2	O	T	M	J	S	Q	G	V	A	F	X	D	U	I	3	H	E	P	K	5	N	6	7						
2	M	I	Z	P	V	L	S	J	B	H	T	F	A	W	U	D	4	Y	G	2	O	E	N	5	R	C	7					
3	O	5	Y	L	G	P	E	K	X	T	3	D	U	V	A	F	N	Z	V	J	M	2	4	I	C	R	6	7				
4	J	Z	I	E	D	S	L	M	C	A	U	G	H	6	T	V	2	5	F	O	K	4	3	Y	X	B	Q	W				
5	E	3	N	J	A	K	O	P	6	D	F	T	V	C	G	H	Y	4	U	L	S	M	Z	2	Y	W	X	B	R	7		
6	U	X	R	F	S	D	V	T	5	K	J	P	O	4	M	L	W	C	E	H	A	G	Q	B	B	Y	3	2	N	I	7	
7	A	B	C	D	E	F	G	H	I	J	K	L	M	N	O	P	Q	R	S	T	U	V	W	X	Y	Z	2	3	4	5	6	7
	A	B	C	D	E	F	G	H	I	J	K	L	M	N	O	P	Q	R	S	T	U	V	W	X	Y	Z	2	3	4	5	6	7

2=Letter shift 3=Figure shift 4=Carriage return
5=Line feed 6=Word space 7=All space

FIG. 20.2. Addition of characters

21. Operation Tunny

GIL HAYWARD

MUCH has been written since the Second World War on the subject of the Enigma, a lot less on Colossus, but nothing whatever about the machines which actually deciphered encrypted German teleprinter signals, using the analytical material provided by Colossus. Most popular accounts of Colossus, which should rightly be regarded as the first true electronic computer, give the impression that this machine produced decrypted text in clear German. This was theoretically possible, but Colossus was too valuable a machine as an analytical engine to be allowed to devote time to this.

The German enciphering machine against which Colossus was pitted was called the 'Schlüsselzusatz 40/42', made by the firm Lorenz (see Plate 8). This will be referred to henceforth as the SZ. It had two sets of five rotors, each of which was used to modify the five signal elements of transmitted teleprinter characters, plus two extra rotors which controlled the movement of the second set of enciphering rotors. This machine was an attachment for a standard Lorenz teleprinter and was somewhat smaller and lighter than the other enciphering machine, the Siemens *Geheimschreiber*, known to be used by the enemy, which was a teleprinter combined with a similar type of enciphering mechanism in one unit. Even so, the SZ was quite a heavy piece of equipment measuring about 20" × 18" × 18", and not intended for field use.

In early 1944 the decision was taken to construct a number of machines dedicated to deciphering the SZ traffic, code-named Tunny, at about the time that Colossus I was put into service. It was soon evident that further Colossi were needed and a much improved design was commissioned in March 1944, to be ready by 1 June. Thus the two projects ran concurrently at the Post Office Research Station at Dollis Hill, London, both under the direction of Tommy Flowers.

I was serving in North Africa in January 1944 as an Intelligence Officer, on a project that also had support from Dollis Hill, when I was posted home to join the team to design and construct the deciphering machines, code-named Tunny. Some ten or so Tunnies were eventually made and tested at Dollis Hill and then installed at Bletchley Park in a building adjacent to the Newmanry which housed the Colossi.

The Tunny design team was headed by Sid Broadhurst, who had considerable experience in automatic telephony circuit design, and his concept of the German look-alike machine was based entirely on readily available standard Post Office parts such as 3,000-type relays and uniselectors.

Because a cursory examination of a Tunny machine would show that we knew the sizes and relative positions of the enciphering rotors, all the development and construction work was carried out in one small laboratory adjacent to the Line Transmission lab, and mainly by the design team themselves. It was imperative that no one should know that the make-up of the SZ was known to us, and, as far as I can recollect, no formal drawings or circuit diagrams were ever made. Those necessary for the construction were done freehand in the small office across the corridor from the lab.

The beauty of Sid Broadhurst's design was that orders for our stores would give no hint as to the use to which they were being put. My earlier suggestion that a mechanical model would not be very difficult to produce was turned down on the very good ground that too many people would have to be involved. I privately cherished the idea of building an SZ with Meccano, using standard-sized sprockets with chains having links equal in number to the teeth on each rotor. Although this could not be pursued at the time, the notion of defeating the Germans with a Meccano model had a certain appeal. In the event our electro-mechanical models proved to be more flexible and easier to modify than the SZ machine we were able to examine after the end of hostilities.

A character sent in teleprinter code consists of seven elements, a start (space) element, five signal elements (either mark or space) which carry the intelligence, and a stop (mark) element. The first six are of 20mS (milliseconds) duration, and the last of 30mS. In practice, elements are transmitted either as mark (–80 volts) or space (+80 volts). The start element sets the receive mechanism running and the next five elements set up electro-mechanically the character to be printed. The stop element stops the mechanism to await the arrival of the next character-start element.

At BP we called a mark a 'cross' and a space a 'dot', just as today we use a 1 or a 0 in binary logic. Thus our WRNS and ATS would recognize •X•X• as R and XX••• as A and so on. They soon became adept at reading punched paper tape, holes being crosses and blanks being dots. 'Cross' and 'dot' will be used for the rest of this chapter.

The objective of SZ was to modify the signal elements of each character sent in what it was hoped would appear to be a random, non-repetitive manner. The machine had ten enciphering rotors, each of which had a different number of teeth equally spaced around its periphery. A tooth could be either effective (a cross) or ineffective (a dot). In the actual machine we later discovered that each tooth was pivoted on the circumference and could be left projecting radially (effective) or folded down sideways, parallel with the axis (ineffective), being retained in either position by a spring.

Let us consider the first group of five rotors. Each rotor was advanced by one tooth for each character transmitted, and was associated with one signal element. The enciphering was achieved by a special method of adding the condition of a rotor tooth with the corresponding incoming signal as shown in Table 21.1, an exclusive-OR 'truth table'. This indicates that when the signal element is a dot and the rotor condition is such that the signal will not be changed, then the signal passed on is still a dot. Similarly, with a cross signal and a non-changing rotor position, the passed-on signal is a cross. Conversely, if the rotor position is set to change the signal condition, then an incoming dot leaves as a cross. The use of dot and cross for rotor and signal conditions is similar to today's binary notation, where 0 and 1 are used. In traditional addition, using the familiar scale of 10 and normal 'carrying', the result of adding 5,234 to 6,789 is 12,023. However, with non-carrying addition the result, 1913, is quite different. Applying this to a scale of 2, or binary addition, the result of adding 0101 to 1111 with carry is 10100. The non-carrying addition,

TABLE 21.1 *Truth table*

Signal	Rotor	Output
•	•	•
X	•	X
•	X	X
X	X	•

known in these computer-minded days as an 'exclusive-OR', of corresponding digits, gives the result 1010. The simple rule is therefore, 'If the corresponding digits are the same, the result is 0; if different, the result is 1.' The non-carry aspect of the process also allowed cryptanalysts to work either from left to right, or from right to left—whichever was more convenient.

In 1944 the term 'exclusive-OR' was not used at BP. We knew this process as 'non-carry binary addition', which seems to be a very fair description of the operation. In our machines a timer diverted the serial elements into five separate parallel channels where simple relay circuits performed the exclusive-OR on each element.

The second set of rotors was driven indirectly via the extra pair of rotors already referred to, by movement of the first set, and now processed the elements once more, performing an exclusive-OR of the output of the first set with their own tooth states. The SZ sent the final element outputs to line in serial form in real time. The far-end machine, set up exactly as the sending machine, performed the reverse process, producing a print-out of the original clear text. Tunny, operating in 'local', produced the clear print-out on the teleprinter on which the enciphered message was input, to the delight of our operators, many of whom were linguists and could well appreciate what was coming through. Table 21.2 shows the reversible nature of the exclusive-OR process in enciphering and deciphering the word 'NOW'. The first rotor set was known as the Chis and the second the Psis; the Ks and Ss of Fig. 20.1.

At no time outside BP can I recall seeing the rotor-teeth numbers written down. We were encouraged to forget them as far as was

TABLE 21.2 *Typical enciphering–deciphering process*

Clear	**N**	**O**	**W**	
Input	••XX•	•••XX	XX• •X	1
Chis	X•X •X	•X•X•	••XX•	2
To Psis	X•• XX	•X• •X	XXXXX	3=1+2
Psis	••XX•	•X• •X	XX• ••	4
Output to Line	X•X •X	•••••	••XXX	5=3+4
Chis at Input	X•X •X	•X•X•	••XX•	6=2
To Psis	••• ••	•X•X•	••• •X	7=6+5
Psis	••XX•	•X• •X	XX• ••	8=4
Output	••XX•	•••XX	XX• •X	9=7+8=1
Clear	**N**	**O**	**W**	

practicable, and now, after practically fifty years, the forgetting process is almost complete. I do remember that most of the numbers were primes and that Chi 1 had 41 teeth, and the others were in descending order from this. The actual figures, now confirmed by one of my former colleagues were, Chis: 41, 31, 29, 26, 23; Psis: 43, 47, 51, 53, 59. The two extra rotors, which we called Motor 1 and Motor 2 (M1, M2) were situated between the Chis and Psis and had 61 and 37 teeth respectively.

Standard 25-point multibank Post Office uniselectors were used to simulate the rotors, the active contacts being spaced out over twenty-five contacts for Chi 5, which was no problem, and over fifty contacts for the remaining Chis using single-ended wipers at 180° running on two adjacent banks, the switches being arranged to self-drive over unused contacts. The timing of operations was fairly tight, and long self-drive runs could not be tolerated. For M1 and the last three Psis, each having more than fifty contacts, two uniselectors were used, the drive being switched from the first to the second when the first reached its last contact. When the second reached its last contact the next signal pulse stepped both switches to their first outlets. The active contacts, representing rotor teeth, were wired in sequence to three sets of horizontal rows of standard telephone switchboard jacks arranged across the centre of the machine, which occupied a double width PO rack 7'6" high. The Chi jacks were in the top set, the motors in the second set, and the Psi jacks in the third set. Active teeth (crosses) were made by inserting a brass peg into the appropriate jack. The array thus formed was known as the 'wheel pattern'. The brass pegs were again standard manual exchange equipment, normally being used to 'busy out' a line on a switchboard, and had white ivorine tops with a central red dot. Beneath each row of jacks representing one rotor was another row of the same length into which only one peg was inserted to indicate the starting or home position of that rotor.

Quite a bit of additional equipment was added to the basic Tunny for operational convenience, and this will be described later.

On the receipt of a start signal (dot or +80v), six timer circuits were activated, causing the incoming signal elements to be diverted sequentially into paths containing relay contacts set according to the patterns of the corresponding Chi and Psi pairs of uniselectors, called the 'markers'. The outputs of each path were fed in turn to a polarized telegraph relay, in such a way that, if the Chi and Psi conditions were the same, the telegraph relay put out a signal of the same polarity as the incoming signal. If the conditions were different, the signal output was the reverse of the input. The telegraph relay output was applied directly to the receive magnet of the teleprinter on which the enciphered message was typed.

The wheel-pattern relays had been set to their correct conditions during the transmission of the previous stop signal, locked into that state and isolated from their respective uniselectors. As uniselectors are relatively slow-moving devices, their drive magnets were energized as soon as the timer circuits were set running, and released at the start of the third element of the current character. It must be borne in mind that a uniselector steps on the release of its drive magnet; thus the uniselectors had until the end of the fifth element to step to the next active contact, self-driving over redundant contacts. During the stop element the pattern relays were re-set and locked to the required state for the next character as read from the repositioned uniselectors. As the wheel pattern relays thus held the current pattern whilst the switches stepped to the next position, Broadhurst called them the 'remembering relays'.

I had no time during a brief examination of an SZ taken to BP at the end of hostilities to verify the method used to perform an exclusive-OR of the signal with the wheel patterns, but it was almost certainly not done as in the rather expanded example shown above. As it was a mechanical device, it must have used the same method as used in Tunny, and depended on the fact that the result of performing an exclusive-OR of A with B and the result with C is the same as performing an exclusive-OR of B with C and the result with A. In other words, the wheel patterns could be combined in the exclusive-OR manner in advance of the arrival of the signal, and then combined in the same manner with the signal to give the desired result.

Details of the uniselector stepping-circuits and of the extra operational equipment referred to above are shown in Figs. 21.4–21.8 and are described more fully in the Appendix to this chapter.

The timing circuits shown in Fig. 21.2 were simple RC valve circuits operating four high-speed relays in their anode circuits at the expiration of each timing period. Unlike the standard PO 3000-type relay, the Siemens high-speed relay had but one changeover contact, so that four relays were needed to furnish enough contacts to perform the necessary operations at the end of each timing period.

A simple way of examining the timer intervals was devised using a rather crude instrument called a 'Telegraph Distortion and Margin Measuring Set', which I had found during a rummage in the Dollis Hill Telegraph Lab. It was made of polished and lacquered brass on a mahogany base, and was regarded as rather an antique even then. It consisted of a disc some six inches in diameter, which could rotate at teleprinter speed, and having a radial slit behind which was mounted a neon tube fed via slip rings on the shaft. A housing round the disc was marked off in seven sectors representing the six elements of 20mS and the stop element of 30mS. The disc made one revolution for each start signal applied to its teleprinter clutch mechanism. All our timer circuits were adjusted using this instrument, and because of the unstable components then available it was frequently called into use. The first Tunny constructed had a serial set of timers, each triggering the next in sequence, as shown in Fig. 21.2. This was done for the sake of simplicity, each timer having components of the same value. In practice this proved to be impractical, as a drift in one timer affected all subsequent timers. This system was replaced in later models with a set of timers which all started together but had increasing timing delays from the end of the start element to the end of the fifth element. A drift in one timer did not then affect any other.

Towards the end of 1944 the Germans introduced an amendment to the standard SZ which caused us some confusion, although Broadhurst quickly devised a circuit to simulate this feature. Luckily it seemed to cause as much trouble to the enemy as it did to us, and they abandoned it after only a few months. We called this the 'P5 (2 back)' limitation, and it had an over-riding effect on the output of M2 in driving the Psi rotors according to the fifth element of the clear text two places before the current position. It is not good practice to use any part of the clear output in this way as a corrupted signal will throw the receiving equipment out of step.

In order to keep track of every wheel position as deciphering progressed, strips of telephone switchboard lamps were installed directly below each jack strip on which the wheel patterns were plugged up. As the wheels rotated, the lamp beneath each wheel position was lit. The current to these lamps was more than the wipers on the uniselectors could be allowed to make and break continuously, so a relay circuit was arranged to disconnect all marker and chaser lamps prior to stepping, and to reconnect them when stepping was completed. As a further refinement, another key dimmed all chaser lamps, so that marker and chaser positions could be easily verified, as both were indicated on the same lamp strip. On the rare occasion when Tunny was out of use, another key cut off all lamp circuits. (See also Chapter 20, p. 172, on markers and chasers.) Keys were provided to inhibit movement of the Chis while the Psis stepped, and vice versa, and to allow manual stepping of wheels.

Whilst the above broadly covers the basic enciphering operation of Tunny, together with some of the facilities which were incorporated to ease the task of the cryptanalysts or to prolong the life of certain machine components, more details are to be found in the Appendix to this chapter.

The memory of those days which remains so clearly in mind is one of unremitting application to the job in hand, when a twelve-hour day, or more, was quite usual and cheerfully accepted. Very little served to distinguish one day from the next, and we kept no diaries or personal notes. Some things, however, do stick in the mind and are worth placing on record.

Although I had been working in Intelligence overseas since the autumn of 1940 on a Top Secret project, I was subjected to the full positive-vetting procedure when I joined the Dollis Hill team. This meant that, although I had a desk in the design office, my new colleagues were not able to begin this new project with me until my positive vetting had been completed. Moreover, they were not able to discuss among themselves any aspect of Colossus, on which all of them were also working, in my presence. After two days of this ridiculous state of affairs Sid Broadhurst could stand it no longer, and soon after lunch on the third day he abruptly remarked to the office in general, 'Let's tell him!' With great relief they all agreed, and in less than an hour I had learnt the whole story. By the end of the afternoon I was already engaged on the design of the uniselector bank wiring before producing wiring schedules. I cannot now remember when my positive vetting clearance came through, but by sticking his neck out as he did, Sid must have saved two weeks or more at a time when such a period could have been, and probably was, vital.

When our first Tunny was nearing completion, it occurred to me that we would need some simple routine for testing the thing before its journey to BP. I accordingly devised a certain pattern for plugging up the rotors, and when Tommy Flowers popped in for his daily chat on progress, I asked him to sit down and type into the teleprinter that sentence so beloved of telegraph engineers, 'Now is the time for all good men to come to the aid of the party . . .'. When he had done this he looked at the printed output, and I shall always remember the look of surprise and boyish pleasure on his face when he read, 'I wandered lonely as a cloud that floats on high oer vales and hills . . .'. (Teleprinters have no apostrophe). He then agreed that we should use this rotor pattern as a standard preliminary test, and none of our machines went to BP before it could write two lines of 'The Daffodils'.

The section where our machines were assembled was presided over by a Major Tester, and became known as the 'Testery', just as Professor Newman's section was the Newmanry. One day in the late summer of 1944 there arrived in the outer room of the Testery a US Army Signals Sergeant, one Tom Collins. He brought with him several large crates each about 8' × 3' × 2', and had had strict instructions to guard these crates with his life. He wore a Smith and Wesson 45 revolver, which he frequently assured us was loaded. It took us several days to convince him that no one was going to make off with his precious crates, and that it was safe to move among us unarmed. My maintenance group of young civilian technicians, all 'stolen' from various telephone establishments, initially showed much more interest in the crates than in what they might hold. They were of North American pine in planed planks twelve inches wide and over three-quarters of an inch thick, and eight feet long. None of us had seen such lovely timber for years. A quiet word with the sergeant revealed that he had no instructions as to the disposal of the crates, which he clearly regarded as rubbish, and he readily agreed that we undertake the onerous task of disposal for him. We did. I have never seen such a rapid vanishing trick.

The contents of the crates turned out to be a quantity of telephone racks loaded with relays, and a small side room was allocated for their assembly. The current radio show *ITMA* (*It's that man again*) featured an American sergeant named 'Sam Scram', and our new colleague inevitably became Sam to all of us. Sam took about two weeks to assemble his baby, which was a specialized message-stream comparator, and I well remember when it was first switched on. Most of the two Flowers teams were present, as we were interested to see how the American cross-point relays, which were unfamiliar to us, would perform. Sam duly threaded in a tape and, with a flourish, switched the thing on. I have never heard such a dreadful clatter from any piece of electrical equipment. It sounded like a monster munching its way through thin tin-plate. I do not know how much current these cross-point relays needed, but on the frequent occasions when most of the two thousand or so relays pulled in together, the lights dimmed in time to the clatter, giving a weird disco effect. We immediately dubbed it the 'Dragon', both because of its chomping noises and as its function was to 'drag' one set of taped data past a fixed set in search of coincidences. To give the machine its due, it did work, but only for a few weeks. One morning we met a very worried Sam, who figured something was wrong with his baby. For a while the Dragon made stuttering noises and then fell silent. We found that most of the relay contacts had cut themselves in half, having worn right down to their contact springs. The Dragon was dead. Sid Broadhurst came along to look at the wreckage, and after a brief examination he turned to me with a smile and said in that dry way of his, 'I reckon we could make one, don't you?' So he went away and designed a Dragon using PO 3000 type relays, and in what seemed a very short time our own Dragon was assembled opposite Sam's defunct machine. The day we started it up Sam was late in getting in, and when he arrived, knowing we were starting that day, he said to me in his familiar American way, 'Well, Cappy, when are you gonna run this thing?' I replied that it was already running. I am afraid that for once Sam was speechless. Our Dragon, except for a very faint background pitter-patter, was practically silent. It ran quite happily for the rest of my time at BP. Soon after this Sam dismantled his Dragon, and it was removed, but what in I do not know.

In the pictures of Colossus released in 1975 an IBM electric typewriter can be seen on a tall stand. This printed the results of the analytical operations performed by Colossus, at very high speed. Golfball typewriters, daisywheel or dot matrix printers had not been invented, and on the IBM machine the whole carriage, which was quite massive, moved as on a conventional machine of that time. The carriage-return action was, to say the least, vigorous, and when it was on this high stand, the machine plus stand, if not restrained, moved rapidly away from Colossus. I was sorry to note that the stout pieces of rope used to secure the typewriter to the stand, and to moor the stand to Colossus, do not appear in the official pictures. This would otherwise have given support to Tommy Flowers's description of Colossus as a 'string and sealing-wax affair'.

There were many at Dollis Hill who worked on Colossus without knowing it, notably Dr Eric Speight, Dr Arnold Lynch, and Don Campbell, all of the Physics Group, who designed and produced the rather complicated, and by today's standards, unwieldy, optical scanning system. The punched paper tape moved past a crescent-shaped mask which produced more or less square-shaped light pulses which passed through a projection lens on to a banked array of photoelectric cells. These cells were of the same order of size as a thermionic valve, and as there were more than a dozen of them, a lot of ingenuity was necessary to place them correctly. It has been said elsewhere that what happened to the Colossi after the war has not been revealed. I am able to say that No. 1 was scrapped, as I was one of the scrapping team. All its normal Post Office parts were returned to the PO Stores for reissue or scrap. Its specialized parts such as the tape wheel frames or 'bedsteads', and the projection unit referred to above, were dismantled and removed to Dollis Hill. It is a most remarkable thing that, throughout the entire operation at BP, not a hint of what we were doing ever leaked out.

On 1 July 1987, Harry Fensom, one of the leading lights on the technical side of the Newmanry, organized a reunion at BP of all the Dollis Hill personnel who worked there during the war. There were thirty-four or so of us altogether, and Frank Veale, the Principal of the British Telecom Training College, which later occupied the BP site, and his staff, entertained us most hospitably in the old Manor. Many of us were surprised to see former Dollis Hill colleagues there, being mutually unaware until that moment that each had been occupied on different aspects of the same project.

No trace of the homes of Colossus and Tunny remains. There is now just a large expanse of newly sown grass.

I give here the names of my stalwart team who kept the Tunnies running for twenty-four hours a day for nearly two years, and to whom we all owe a great debt of gratitude: Cyril Barnet, Frank Crofts, Frank Francis, Dave Geary, Strad Graham, John Groves, Ken Halton, Alan Hogben, Eddie Meads, Geoff Ward, Dick Wilson, Colin Woods, Roy Wright, and the never-to-be-forgotten 'Sam Scram', Sergeant Tom Collins, US Army Signals Corps.

Appendix: The Tunny machine in operation

This description, which gives a general outline of the working of Tunny, is based both on Sid Broadhurst's account and on the recollections of Ken Halton. The account describes the first version of the timer, which dates it to no later than March 1944.

The figures follow the usual convention that all relay contacts are shown in the unoperated condition.

In referring to the top section of Fig. 21.1, the Chi marker switches MKA to MKE and the Psi markers MSA to MSE are stepped to their respective start positions on the operation of the START key. Any switch coming to rest on a plugged (i.e. earthed) outlet will cause its associated remembering relay KRA, etc., to operate via an STPA contact, which releases only after all switches have reached their start positions. COA is normally operated so that KRA holds in via its own contact when STPA releases.

The Distributor (see Fig. 21.2) operates on receipt of the teleprinter start signal (+80 v), the stack of relays G, GG, etc., pulling in and locking via contacts GG and FF. The operation of G releases relay STD, which is normally operated, thus inhibiting the running of the timer, and the A relay stack timer operates 20mS after the beginning of the start signal. Contact AA in turn starts the B relay stack timer and so on until the F stack operates at the beginning of the stop element as shown in Fig. 21.3.

The method of deciphering the elements of the incoming signal can now be followed from the lower section of Fig. 21.1. In the idle condition the –80 v from the teleprinter transmitter holds the polarized telegraph relay P via the unoperated A contact to cross. The teleprinter start signal of +80 v changes the polarized relay to dot and sends a start signal to the teleprinter receive mechanism. The relay contacts KRA to KRE and the pairs of contacts SRA to SRE have already been set according to the wheel patterns before the arrival of the current start signal. Thus at the start of the first element, contact A of the first timer stack changes over and routes the signal via B unoperated to the KRA, SRA contact arrangement. It can be seen that, if both the K and S relays are operated, or if both are released, the polarized relay repeats the incoming signal to the teleprinter receive magnet. If either of the K or S relays is operated with the other released, the signal output to the teleprinter receive magnet is the reverse of the incoming signal. At the end of the first element relay B operates and A releases, isolating contacts KRA, SRA, and routing the second element to the next set of remembering relay contacts, and so on. At the end of the fifth element relay F operates and routes the stop signal unchanged to relay P. The polarized relay P is a standard PO model No. 299AN which has a contact transit time of only 0.5mS, which has no noticeable effect on the timing.

As shown in Figs. 21.4 and 21.6, relay PUA is operated during the start signal by one of the G relays and energizes the uniselector drive magnets. One of the C relays releases PUA at the beginning of the third element allowing

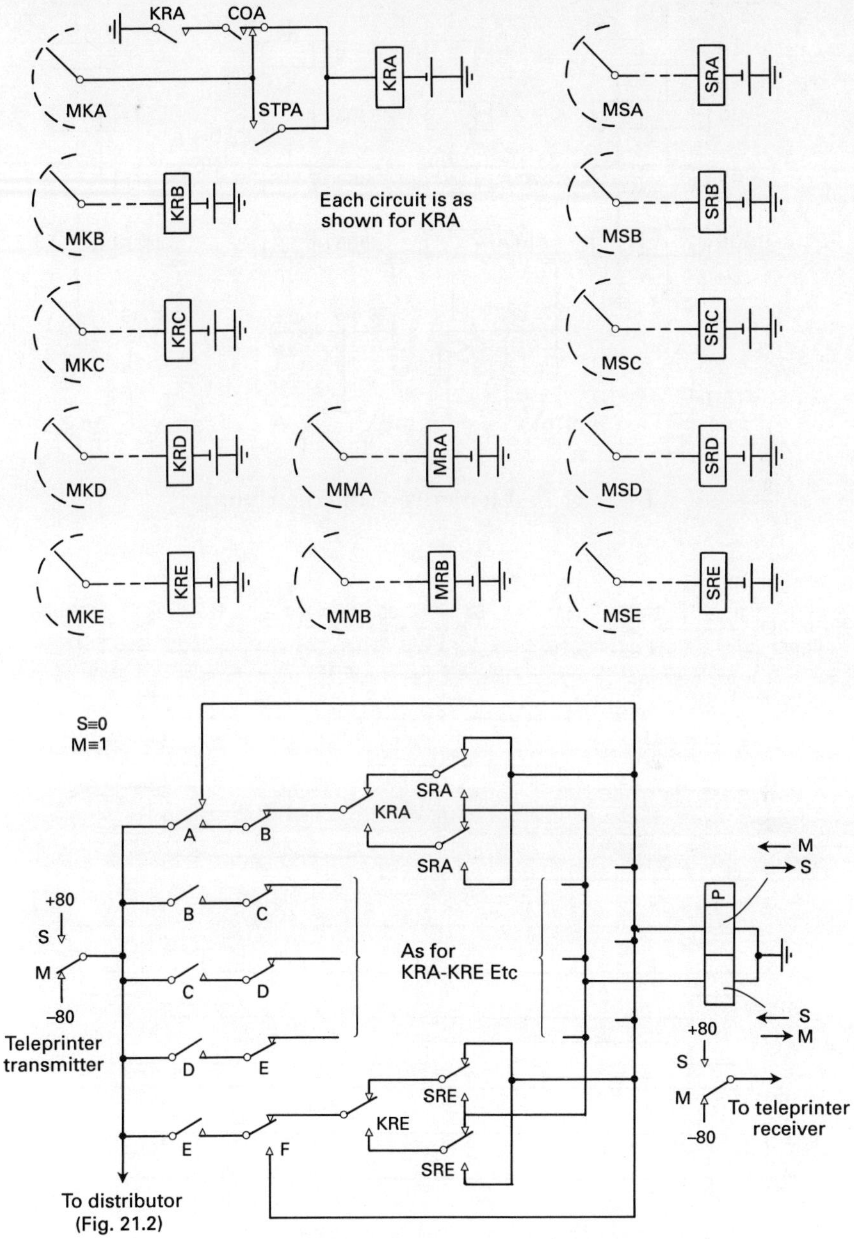

FIG. 21.1. 'Remembering' relays and adder circuits

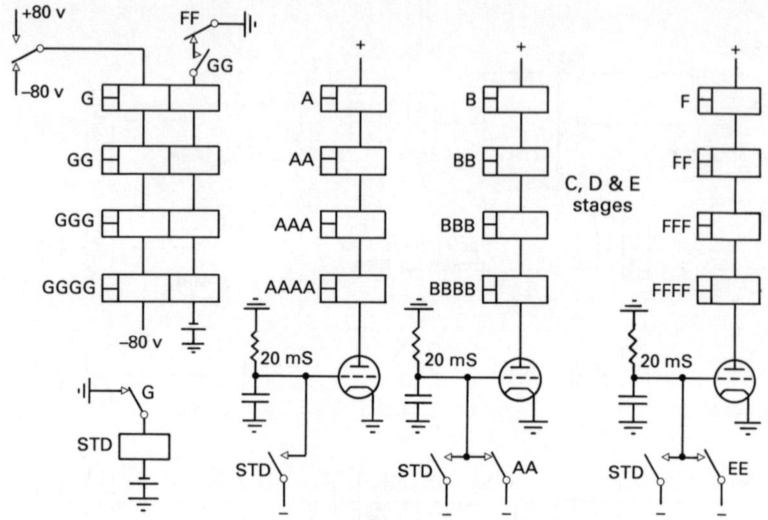

FIG. 21.2. Elements of the distributor

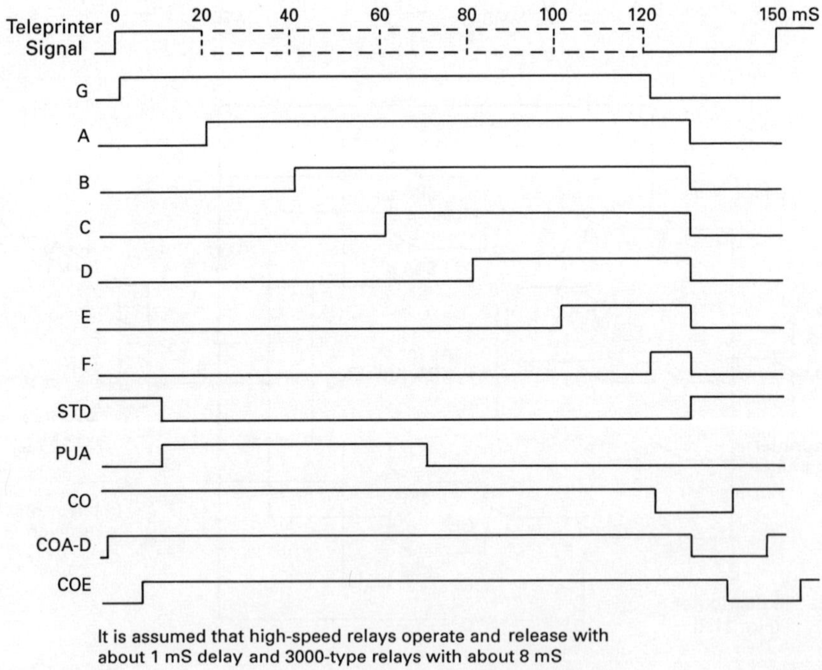

FIG. 21.3. Main timing diagram

the uniselectors to step or self-drive to the next wheel position, which is reached in every case before the end of the fifth element. At the start of the stop element, relays COA to COD release for about 15mS and then re-operate. This allows the remembering relays to pick up the next wheel pattern before once more being isolated from the wheels themselves, leaving the latter free to move during the course of the transmission of the next character.

In addition to the P5 (2 back) limitation already described, a further two limitations were frequently used, and, unlike P5 (2 back) remained in use throughout the war. These were, using Broadhurst's terminology, 'KB (1 back)' and 'SA (1 back)'. These remembered the previous conditions of the second Chi element and of the first Psi element respectively. These conditions were ORed with the output from the M2 pattern (see Figs. 21.4 and 21.7), and thus influenced the stepping of the psi rotors. There is a possible anomaly here, pointed out by Ken Halton in a letter to me:

> A note on Fig. 21.4: There is a known error in the part enclosed in the dotted lines . . . At the end of the para on PV2b the notes say that PDB, KRX, and SRX were in series. They must have had keys to bring them in as required and I can only think that they were wired as I have shown. This arrangement does mean, though, that only one out of the three was used at any one time, or, if not, there was a through circuit only when both (or all three) of the selected ones were operated. This means that they were added on an AND basis.

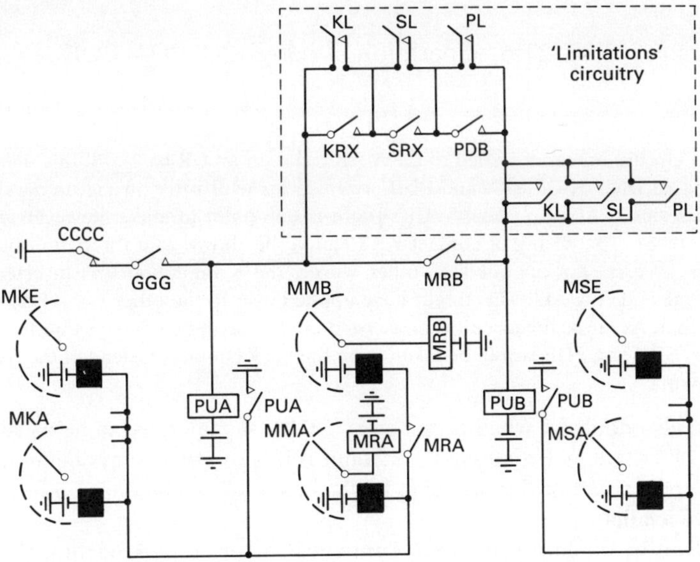

Note: The uniselectors stepped on the release of the drive-magnet

FIG. 21.4. Uniselector drive arrangements

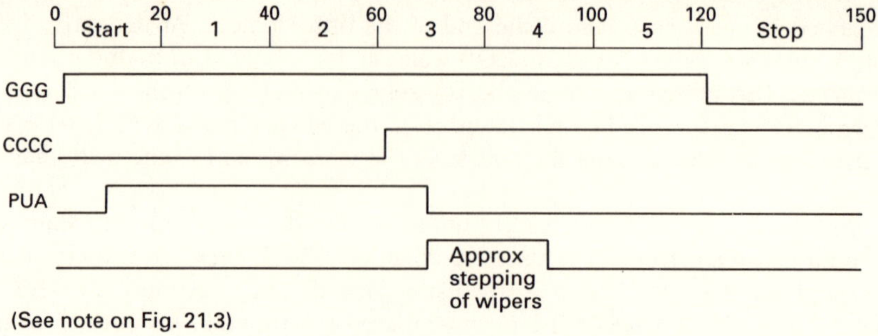

FIG. 21.5. Timing of uniselector stepping

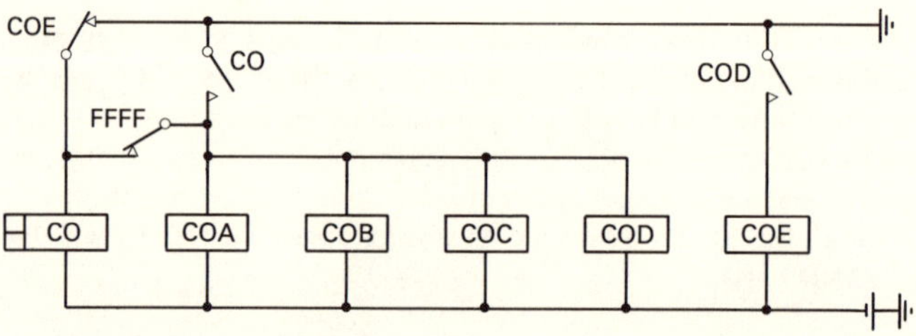

FIG. 21.6. Operation of relays CO, COA–COE

That circuit, however, added to the MRB route on an OR basis. All this seems quite reasonable when KRX, SRX and PDB are in series whilst they are all in parallel with MRB. Series = AND, parallel = OR. There is one point to make, however about the known error. The wiring of contact KRX should be shown as a through circuit when KRX is *released*, not operated. In other words, the K limitation was inverted before being OR added to M2. This might have applied also to the other two—I don't know about that. As far as the circuit is concerned, of course, it only means that the connections to SRX and PDB would be taken from the back contacts instead of the front ones as shown.

It is also doubtful whether the relay STPA was operated quite as shown in Figs. 21.1–21.8 as Broadhurst's account refers to other relays being involved in its operation, but this seems to be the best that can be done with the information available.

Judged by modern standards, Tunny was a very crude machine, but there were at that time no semiconductor devices—the transistor had not been invented. Switching was done electro-mechanically by relay or uniselector, or by thermionic valve, all very power-hungry devices. The only aids to calculation were a book of seven-figure logarithms or a slide rule. I have no

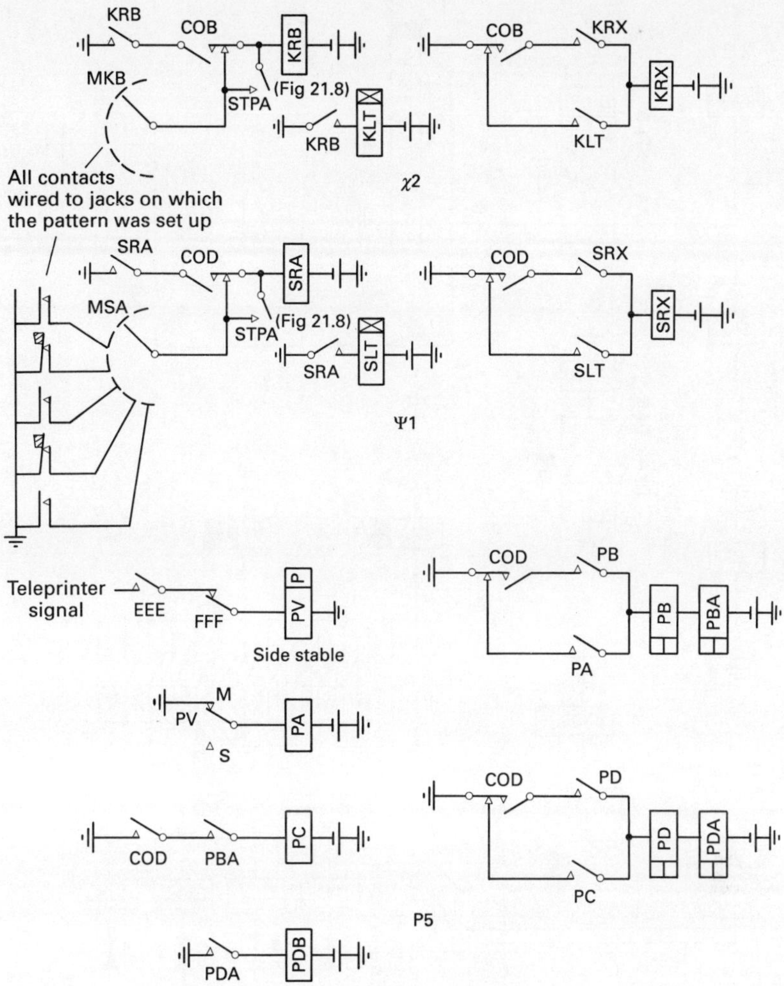

FIG. 21.7. Limitations-'remembering' circuits

doubt that a bright schoolboy of today could build a Tunny using ICs with very little trouble or could write a computer program to run the thing in real time. Technology has come a long way since 1944.

I am much indebted to Ken Halton for producing the diagrams from a study of Sid Broadhurst's account, combined with recollections of his own and of others of our team.

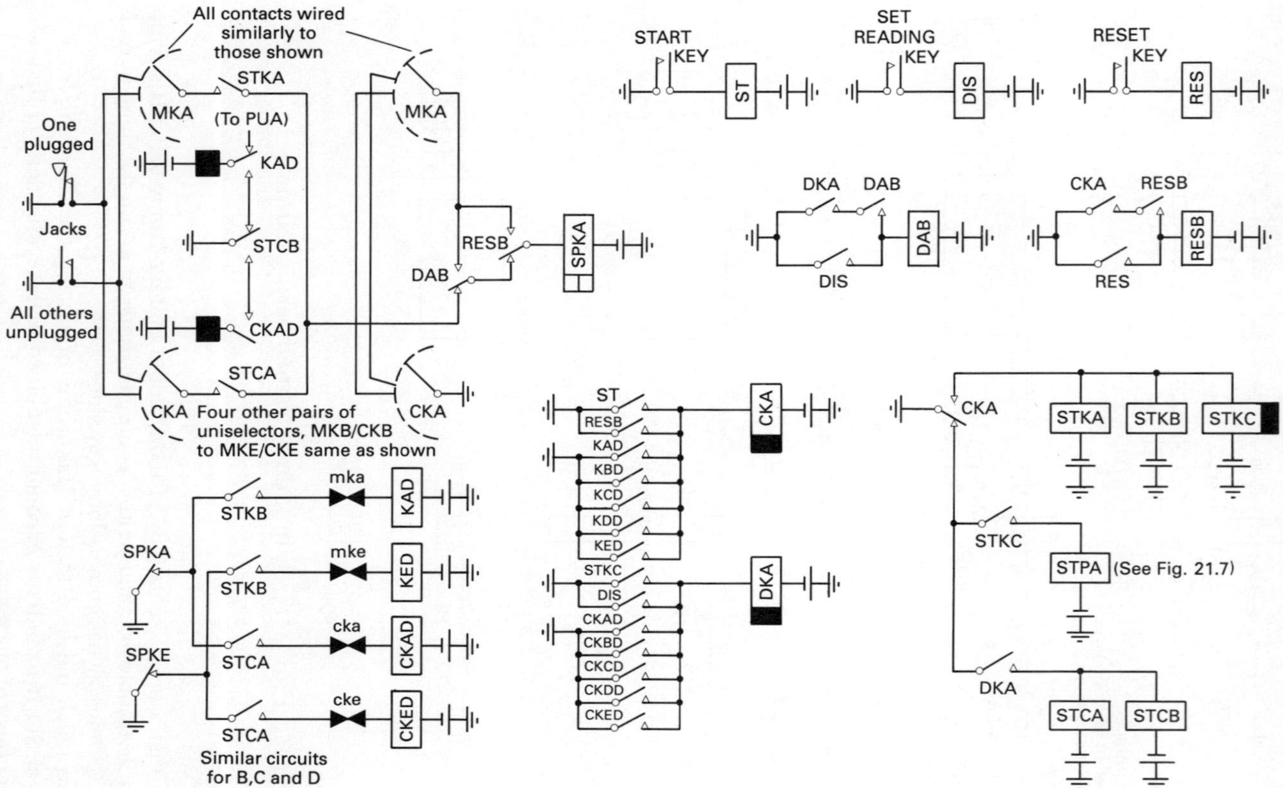

FIG. 21.8. Setting-up circuits for K uniselectors (similar circuits for M and S uniselectors)

PART FOUR
Field ciphers and tactical codes

22. Recollections of Bletchley Park, France, and Cairo

HENRY DRYDEN (also known as 'Pope')

On 15 August 1939 I was one of the members of the Service sections of GC&CS who made their way individually to Bletchley Park, 'in order to test communications', an exercise which had first been carried out at the time of the Sudetenland crisis the previous September. There was in fact widespread scepticism about the likelihood of the country's becoming involved in war. As one cynic put it, 'The Poles are going to be sold down the same river the Czechs were sold down last year.' Certainly none of us foresaw the entry of Japan into any war which might occur, despite the 'Tientsin incident', when the British Consul had his face slapped by a Japanese officer—nor that VJ-Day was exactly six years away.

Indications of a progressive deterioration in the situation in Europe had, of course, occurred since the Munich crisis, but among the rank and file in the Office, as GC&CS was then called, these had had relatively little impact. The Nazi march on Prague in March 1939 was not, as some quarters in Whitehall feared it might be, accompanied by a bombing attack on London. The members of the Military Section were told to keep ten shillings in their pockets, and to be ready, on receipt of a telephone message to the effect that Auntie Flo was not so well, to proceed across country to BP. This turned out not to be necessary, however, and even the Easter invasion of Albania by the Italians, seen as much less significant than the civil war in Spain, merely entailed weekend manning of the Office, although shortly afterwards two members of the Military Section were sent to Malta to speed up exploitation of readable Italian traffic intercepted there. The other precaution, taken later in the summer, was to move the Far East Bureau from Hong Kong to Singapore, but this, though involving much larger numbers of staff, passed almost unnoticed in the London Office. There was accordingly something of a rude awakening when the Soviet–German Non-Aggression Pact was signed on 23 August, and war in Europe suddenly appeared imminent.

My own entry into the (in those days) highly secret world of cryptanalysis resulted from a chance meeting, in Cambridge in October 1938, with the Secretary of the Appointments Board, who produced an application form headed 'Government Code and Cypher School', which meant nothing to me. In December I was interviewed by some fifteen males in civilian clothes, whom I subsequently recognized by degrees as members of GC&CS and the appropriate sections of the Service Ministries.

After several weeks, during which I was presumably being vetted, and which I filled in by teaching French at Marylebone Grammar School, a telegram arrived early in February 1939 at my home in Surrey reading: 'Services urgently required. Report War Office MI 1(b) 1100 next Tuesday.' I duly reported to the War Office, where I was immediately disabused of my assumption that I should be working in Whitehall. The junior of the two officers who received me donned his bowler hat and walked me across the park to Broadway Buildings, opposite St James's tube station. As we approached it, he said, 'All you ever say here is "Third" as you get into the lift. Nobody must know where you work. If you have lunch with someone who insists on walking back to your office with you, you must proceed to the War Office, round the corner to the staff entrance, say goodbye, count 120 and then walk back here.' As I was soon to discover, part of the reason for this secrecy was that the floors below and above the third were occupied by M.I.6, whose Chief was also the Director (senior to the Head) of GC&CS, and who had bought Bletchley two years earlier as the Secret Service war site.

Having been introduced by my escort to Captain (later Colonel) Freddie Jacob, who was acting as head of the Military Section while Captain (later Brigadier) John Tiltman was visiting India and Hong Kong, I met the other members of the section, then about a dozen in number; I was in fact the last of eight graduates recruited in 1938–9 in preparation for the end of peacetime, the management being under no illusion about the likelihood of war.

After lunch I was pitched in at the deep end by being given a 'depth' of Italian messages in a classical book-and-additive system, and an afternoon's explanation of how to recover the book-groups underlying the cipher text. Work on the meaning of the latter was carried out by a linguist, which was just as well, because my knowledge of Italian was limited to terms used in music, art, and restaurants. It was a good running-in job for a beginner, as it was facilitated by the fact that the system had been in use since at least the beginning of the Spanish Civil War, and consequently a large number of book-groups had been established. It was accordingly merely a matter of subtracting a handful of these in turn from the top and following groups in a column of the depth to see whether the artificial key-group thus obtained threw up any other familiar book-groups in the same column.

This continuous process of trial and error was interrupted briefly by the arrival of some German Army cipher keys, obtained by unspecified means and sent to us by our French colleagues. These revealed that the Army medium-grade system was daily-changing double transposition. Traffic using this system would clearly give me the opportunity to apply the knowledge of German for which I had presumably been recruited. The only problem was that, apart from the high-grade Enigma machine traffic, which was being worked on—at this stage unsuccessfully—elsewhere, very little German military material was being intercepted in the first half of 1939.

After the end of the Spanish Civil War in June 1939 I was moved on to another key-breaking job on Japanese Army Air Force (JAAF) material emanating from Manchuria. On the day war was declared, strangely enough, no one in the Military Section was working on German, with the exception of the other 'new boy' who had joined just before me: an Oxford mathematician, who had been detached to work under 'Dilly' Knox on research into the Enigma. The immediate result of the German attack on Poland, however, was a spate of police messages audible in the United Kingdom. A letter-count showed that the system used was transposition, and the originators' habit of sending messages, or parts of messages, of the maximum permitted length of 180 letters provided us with depths for anagramming purposes. This gave John Tiltman, well known already for his remarkable successes against Russian and Japanese material, the opportunity to demonstrate his versatility and practical approach. Having written out a depth—something he always preferred to do himself, because, he maintained, ideas came to him during the process—he cut the texts into vertical strips, numbered from 1 to 180. Using pins and a cork bathmat, he greatly simplified the technique of anagramming enough clear text—in this case about forty consecutive letters—to enable the key to be recovered. Like the Army system referred to above, the keys used were of a standard length of twenty-five. Once this was established, a reasonable knowledge of German and a modest degree of numeracy sufficed to guarantee success.

Our French colleagues were also working on the police material, and we exchanged results through the M.I.6 representative in Paris. To avoid duplication, it was arranged that the two parties should tackle alternate days' traffic. After a couple of months, it was decided that, in the interest of speed, a GC&CS party of three officers and some fifteen other ranks should join up with the French cryptanalysts at the General Headquarters of General Weygand at La Ferté-sous-Jouarre on the Marne. The volume of military material audible in the United Kingdom remained disappointingly small both during and after the Polish campaign, and the period of the phoney war was chiefly notable for the only recorded case of failure by John Tiltman, now commanding what had become No. 4 Intelligence School (4 IS), to break a system he had attacked. The messages were fairly short, and it proved possible to recover some plain texts—stereotyped weather reports—by anagramming, but we never succeeded in reconstructing what were certainly stencils.

While the Army medium-grade and low-grade situation remained frustrating, the first breaks were being made, in collaboration with our French and Polish colleagues (the latter having escaped to France) into the Enigma machine. In January 1940 I became one of the founder-members of Hut 3, engaged in emending and translating German texts—not a very exciting process in itself, because throughout the phoney war the Army radio networks did not, of course, carry operational messages. Nevertheless we had the thrill of knowing that a system which, as became clear later, the Germans regarded as invulnerable, had proved not to be so. An element of cryptanalysis was involved in the emendation of corrupt texts, but I was glad to be selected to relieve the head of the detachment in France.

I joined the so-called 'Mission Richard' in a large villa on the north bank of the Marne. My enduring memories of the two months I spent there have no military connotations, but never, before or since, have I seen such a remarkable display of roses, nor heard so many nightingales singing against each other, nor eaten so much brie in so short a time.

On 1 May 1940 the external indicator system used on Enigma messages being intercepted in the British area changed, and I was bidden to General Gort's Headquarters to examine it. With great diffidence, partly because I was not an expert on the machine and partly because I was a civilian (a fact which did not seem to matter at General Headquarters). I took the train to Arras. As I had expected, all I was able to do was to advise that our radio operators take particular care when transcribing preambles of messages, and that when intercepts were dispatched to the United Kingdom for processing, priority should be given to any showing evidence of misuse or correction of indicators. For a few days I joined the party using captured code-books to decode three-letter messages sent by German reconnaissance aircraft, the only traffic being intercepted apart from the Enigma. Then at about 5 a.m. on 10 May the real war began for the Allies with bombing, chiefly of the airport, though a few bombs fell in the town. An hour or two later an order came from the Director of Military Intelligence, General Mason-Macfarlane: 'Burn that bloody suit of yours, my boy, and get into a battledress.' He added that he was giving me an emergency commission in the field, something which had not been done since Wellington's time, and he had no idea what the War Office would say.

Having brought a battledress and some khaki shirts and been issued with a tin hat, which left me wearing coloured socks and black shoes, I continued to help with processing such German radio traffic as was available. For the most part, this consisted of plain-text messages, because the German advance through the Benelux countries was so rapid that forward units did not bother to encode their reconnaissance reports and requests for Stuka dive-bombers. Thus we were able to provide the Intelligence Staff with an increasingly bleak operational picture. Within a very few days it became clear that the French 9th Army had not reached the Meuse in time to hold up German progress, and that the British force which had advanced into Belgium would have to withdraw. While the General Staff prepared to move into the cellars of Arras, I was sent back to La Ferté.

When the attack actually started on 5 June, we were told that in some sectors of the front so many Germans were being killed that they could not advance over their own dead. Sceptical as we were about these reports, it still came as a shock when, on the afternoon of 8 June, we were told to form up at the station at 8 p.m. for a move by train to an unspecified destination.

In the end, the train (said to weigh 2,000 tons, and to contain the whole of French General Headquarters, plus their wives, mistresses, baggage, poodles, and canaries) left at about 2 a.m. and chuntered via Melun down to Briare, on the Loire south-east of Orléans. We plodded on with our work until 13 June, when the dispatch rider who up till then had brought our raw material from an interception station in the Maginot Line failed to appear. Realizing the implications of this, on 14 June I took off with our driver—having set the soldiers to work in the garden to take their minds off our situation—in the direction of Orléans, in search of news of the British Expeditionary Force. Before long we encountered an RAF dispatch rider in conversation with some nuns, whose lorry laden with children had come to a stop. He told us that all British forces had been evacuated, and that the Germans had marched into Paris at 6 a.m. that morning; so, having given the nuns all the petrol we could spare, we returned to Briare. There was no more cheering.

The next morning we almost missed the train, but found ourselves that evening in Vichy. We spent the following morning, Sunday, stripped to the waist in the cellars of our hotel, burning in the furnace all our material except the keys we had recovered. We were not altogether surprised to learn after breakfast on 17 June that Marshal Pétain had announced that France had asked for an armistice, and also that we would be moving again that afternoon. This time the train took us via Clermont-Ferrand, where we were told by our French friends that they had been ordered to stop. We indicated that we thought we ought to try to get to England, and they immediately gave us a large lorry and advised us to make for Bordeaux. We arrived there via Périgueux soon after dawn on 18 June. Thanks to that uniquely British institution, the schools connection, the oldest member of our party, who had been at preparatory school with him, got in to see the Military Attaché in his bath at 6 a.m., and was given a chit authorizing us to board the cruiser *Arethusa*, then lying at the mouth of the Gironde with the primary task of evacuating the Polish Government-in-Exile and the Czech Intelligence Staff. Embarkation was being supervised by a guards officer, who took one look at our chit and said: 'This is no good. You need a chit from the Naval Attaché.' Recognizing him as a member of what GC&CS called 'The Other Side', with whom I had often shared a lift at Broadway Buildings, I murmured in his ear: 'We're from the third floor.' Fortunately this had the desired effect; having spent the night on board, we sailed, unescorted, on a zig-zag course for Devonport. There we were received by the Women's Voluntary Service with cups of tea such as we had not enjoyed for many weeks.

Back at BP after a few days' leave, I found that Hut 3 had been reinforced to such an extent that I was no longer needed in my previous capacity; instead I was appointed crypto liaison officer, a part-time job, keeping the cryptanalysts in Hut 6 informed continuously of intelligence priorities as seen from Hut 3, and conversely keeping the latter informed of the prospects of solving the various daily-changing keys. This task was supplemented, during the remainder of the summer of 1940, first by key-breaking on the main Vichy French naval cipher, very much simplified by our possession of the code-book, by courtesy of a French cipher officer who had been evacuated from Dunkirk; then by a depressingly unsuccessful stint on Spanish Diplomatic, finally abandoned as one-time pad and therefore unbreakable.

On the personal side, I found that General Mason-Macfarlane's doubts about what the War Office might think of his commissioning me in the field were only too well founded. The net result of my translation into uniform was that for several months I was paid neither as a War Office civilian nor as an officer. When I told John Tiltman that I was becoming financially embarrassed, he promised to investigate, and a few days later produced a sealed envelope containing a cheque for £50, being a loan from the Chief of M.I.6, responsible for administering us until after the war. When I opened the envelope in front of the teller in my bank near Broadway Buildings, I was disconcerted to find that the cheque had been made out to 'Number 37'. The teller, however, was quite unperturbed, and with a deadpan face asked me to endorse the cheque with my usual signature and 'Number 37'. I did not receive my back pay until January 1941.

In the autumn of 1940 I was assigned to assist one of our elder statesmen, Oliver Strachey, who was then working on German *Abwehr* single transposition. This involved writing out messages in columns of overlapping consecutive segments of text in a pattern resembling the gable end of a house (the 'hat' or 'roof' method) and juggling with them until fragments of words began to appear in each line: this was in fact a more difficult operation than anagramming the Police double-transposition 'depths'. After this apprenticeship I moved again, members of 4 IS being regarded as maids of all work, to work for the great Josh Cooper on a three-figure Italian Air Force system. This was intercepted in Cairo, but the material was too voluminous for the local processing resources. Recovery of the 'true figures' of the underlying book-groups would doubtless have resulted in due course, but after a spell of routine key-breaking I was moved again to assist John Tiltman on the German railways Enigma. This was an unsophisticated version of the machine used by the Services, and solution was facilitated by our ability to set up overlapping depths of messages, most of which had standard beginnings.

Although the railways material was producing, throughout the early part of 1941, increasingly valuable information on the transport eastwards of enormous quantities of military material, the arrival in North Africa of German formations under the command of General Rommel, on which Air Force Enigma began to shed light, was of much more direct concern to British forces in Egypt, and, following General Wavell's overwhelming defeat of the Italians, in Libya as far west as Tripoli. Cryptanalytical resources in the former Flora and Fauna Museum at Heliopolis near Cairo had been substantially reinforced in the summer of 1940 by a party under the command of Freddie Jacob, and as Director of the newly established Combined Bureau Middle East he was responsible for the technical co-ordination of the cryptanalytical work of the three Services. There was nobody in the Middle East, however, with experience in breaking German codes and ciphers.

The first contact between British and German forward troops occurred at the end of February, and on 24 March El Agheila was reoccupied by the enemy. At this point, I was 'invited' by John Tiltman to go out to Heliopolis, 'for a month, six weeks at the outside, old boy', to train the Italian experts in breaking German systems. Getting to Cairo, however, proved to be a somewhat less than straightforward exercise. On 4 April I sailed from Gourock in an armed merchant cruiser (a converted 15,000-ton P&O liner), destination Freetown, whence I was to complete my journey by air. Two days later, after a pre-war style lunch, we had just heard on the radio that the Germans had invaded Yugoslavia and that the Afrika Korps was rapidly approaching the frontier of Egypt, when the fire alarm sounded, followed a quarter later by 'abandon ship stations'. The fire, caused by the bursting of an oil-pipe under the boilers, got out of control, and after about two hours the order came to abandon ship.

The following Sunday I got back to BP, soaked in sea water and oil, to be greeted by John Tiltman with, 'Hello, old boy; haven't you gone yet?' About a week later I left the Clyde again, this time aboard a converted anti-aircraft cruiser on her maiden voyage to Alexandria through what Mussolini had designated as 'mare nostrum'. On 30 April I reached Cairo, and on 1 May, the day before the Allied evacuation of Greece was completed, I reported to the Commanding Officer of No. 5 Intelligence School (5 IS).

For about three weeks, in the absence of live material, I had to make up messages for training purposes, but on 20 May the Germans started to invade Crete, and within a few days their communications on the island became audible at Heliopolis. A letter-count showed that the messages were in a transposition system, and application of the methods used from the beginning of the war to solve the police proved that the Army was still using the same system, samples of which we had received from the French two years before. Aided by my 'pupils', I managed to recover a few keys, but too late to provide anything of operational value to General Headquarters Middle East or General Freyberg in Crete.

The intercept station, also located at Heliopolis, was largely engaged in covering high-grade networks, the Enigma messages carried on them being relayed by radio or cable to BP for processing. While I was struggling to get to Cairo, interim arrangements had been made for relevant decrypts, disguised as agents' reports, to be sent to Combined Bureau, Middle East, for distribution to the Services' Headquarters. Because of their sensitivity the messages were shielded from the eyes of the cipher officers by being encoded in a simple substitution before encipherment and dispatch from the United Kingdom. Freddie Jacob and the Commanding Officer of 5 IS, George Wallace, had been taking it in turns, on a twenty-four-hour basis, to decode them before they were sent on in a locked box welded to the floor of a special car. As a high proportion of the messages reached Heliopolis during the night, these officers were glad of the 50 per cent reinforcement I provided until the Combined Bureau Middle East was relieved of the task when the special Ultra network was set up in the summer of 1941. At the opposite end of the cryptanalytical scale, Heliopolis was responsible for backing up the effort in the field on low-grade codes. This had been done very effectively in the case of Italian, in the Western Desert and East Africa, by both 5 IS and the RAF cryptanalysts belonging to what was actually the host unit in the Museum. An erroneous assumption by the latter that all German three-letter material was Air Force had led to the accumulation of a quantity which did not fit the series of German Air Force code-books. When broken into by 5 IS, as it very soon was, the originator of this first batch was found to be the 33rd Recce Unit of Rommel's 15th Armoured Division. It was clear that such codes were eminently suitable for exploitation in the field, and in due course a small combined unit of Royal Signals and Intelligence Corps personnel in armoured cars was attached to 7th Armoured Division Headquarters in time for the second major Western Desert offensive by Allied forces, which opened on 18 November 1941. Speed of decoding and passing of information to the Division's intelligence staff left nothing to be desired, but signals-intelligence operations at this level were distinctly hazardous as well as uncomfortable, and were not repeated at El Alamein. When that battle started on 23 October 1942, so-called Y units were in place at Eighth Army Headquarters and each Corps Headquarters, with others in reserve, in the rear.

Meanwhile two interesting developments of a totally different nature had occurred in the field. The first, which perhaps illustrates the British military mentality, rather than any particular technical aspect of Y work, was a major factor in enabling Rommel to succeed in withdrawing a substantial part of his forces after his defeat south of Tobruk near the end of 1941. An unfortunate disagreement between the Y units with 7th Armoured Division and its Corps Headquarters was resolved by Corps in favour of the 'senior' unit, with the result, we were told, that 4th Armoured Brigade, having pursued the retreating Germans in the wrong direction, ran out of fuel as it sighted their rearguard after being rerouted. It was no consolation to the Desert Rats unit that their version of the vital German signal had been confirmed—too late for the desired outcome to have been achieved.

The second development, a perfect example of a victory by communications security authorities over both Signals and Operations, did not come to light until several months later. In the spring of 1942 the familiar three-letter codes were replaced by three-figure ones. These did not prevent the production of information, except on days when few messages were intercepted, but they took longer to process, as they were reciphered by daily tear-off key sheets. During the German counter-attack from El Agheila, first to the Gazala position and then, in June 1942, towards El Alamein, a German intercept unit was well up with the forward troops. As the Allied retreat accelerated, this unit got a bit too close to our rearguard, which turned smartly round and captured, among others, a number of its personnel and a large quantity of documents. When I was examining the latter, I came across an intercept written in German script, with call-signs annotated '7th Armoured Division' and 'XXX Corps' and a text beginning 'Intercepted message from Rommel', followed by his orders to his divisional commanders, *all in English*. This message had actually been sent, in clear, under a dispensation in the signals-intelligence security rules which permitted such action if the issue of a battle was at stake. A desperate battle was indeed being fought at the time, the outcome of which, as mentioned above, was a victory—but a Pyrrhic one. As far as Y was concerned, the key advantage of being able to produce continuously timely material had been reduced, though the codes remained at least partially readable until fighting in Africa ended at Tunis on 12 May 1943.

Meanwhile, from about 1 July 1941 it became evident that the German Army had adopted a substitution system, a variant of British Playfair: instead of one 5 × 5 box containing twenty-five letters of the alphabet (omitting Y), the Germans were using two different ones. It turned out that the messages were emanating from Salonika and the garrisons of the Aegean islands of Cos and Lemnos, and from Mytilene on Lesbos. Feeling rather smug, we signalled our results to 4 IS, only to be told that they had already solved the system—and had not thought to inform us. Double Playfair remained the German Army's medium-grade cipher until the autumn of 1944, and we continued to exploit it (see Chapter 23). Its successor, a stencil transposition system, was similar to our other main task, a steadily increasing volume of *Abwehr* material from Yugoslavia which was being intercepted by the Radio Security Service, an organization answerable at that time to M.I.5. The cipher gradually became more complicated, and it was not easy for us to keep up with developments. We were gradually receiving high-powered reinforcements, however, mostly from BP, but including a small party from Sarafand in Palestine, who were ordered to stop work on Russian on 22 June 1941, the day the German invasion started. The German agents in Turkey continued to transmit reports in the same easily exploitable single transposition, but the volume of traffic was light, and the contents of the messages trivial. Decrypts, together with the much more interesting *Abwehr* ones, were distributed to the M.I.6 office in Cairo.

Our relatively peaceful existence in Heliopolis, disturbed only by occasional night bombing of Cairo, seven miles away, became increasingly threatened in the spring and summer of 1942. But on the very day that the Cairo Headquarters began burning its records, we were astonished to receive a signal from BP to the effect that we were going to be asked to exploit Enigma material. It was explained to us that an earlier Air Force key was being used, on different days of the month, by Rommel's 'Flivos' (Air Liaison Officers). We were given all the keys which had been previously recovered, and as soon as the first Flivo message had been intercepted it became evident from the external indicator which key-setting we had to apply. Using captured machines, we were able to decrypt all messages received on a given day, and to provide the Cairo Headquarters with some—though less than hoped-for—information on the movements and intentions of German formations. This procedure was much quicker than the normal one, by which intercepted messages had to be sent to BP for decryption, and the decrypts returned to Cairo through the Ultra network, and it continued until the war had receded beyond the range of audibility of German signals.

Before the El Alamein battle started, I was in quick succession promoted to the rank of Major, transferred to 5 IS, to which I had been attached for about eighteen months, and shortly afterwards appointed Commanding Officer of the unit. The first major decision I had to take concerned the deployment of 5 IS personnel. Until then, my predecessor had maintained the principle of retaining all cryptanalysts at Heliopolis, with only occasional exceptions, such as the 7th Armoured Division unit. Now, with a campaign designed to end the war in Africa imminent, and the need for an all-out Y effort pre-eminent, it seemed essential to jettison the principle. Accordingly, I sent nearly all the younger members of both the German and Italian sections up to 8th Army, for further deployment as required.

Once the breakthrough at El Alamein had been achieved, life at Heliopolis became progressively quieter until we moved out in May 1944, and notable incidents were few. The first of these involved the transfer of something over half the staff, under the command of the Commanding Officer of the No. 7 Intelligence School, which since late 1941 had been responsible for traffic analysis, from Egypt to Italy. This was the main result of a visit I had undertaken in December 1942 to Algiers—where I happened to arrive on the day Admiral Darlan was assassinated—for the purpose of finding out why the Y units which had accompanied the north Africa invasion force did not appear to be performing very effectively. The reason was partly the extremely unpleasant weather conditions, but it was also clear that those concerned had not had access to the training material we had been sending back to BP over many months. The second 'incident', which in fact preceded the first one, was the arrival in January 1943 of two companies of ATS, and the third was the transfer of the residue of the combined unit to Sarafand where they remained for the rest of the war.

Having completed my 'month or six weeks, old boy,' in May 1944, I returned to what had become the Military Wing at BP, where it was clear to all that the opening of the Second Front was imminent: in fact, D-Day coincided with the last day of my disembarkation leave. In the absence of any defined job, I instituted a series of daily briefings on the situation in the invasion areas, using both Enigma and other sources. After some four months, when thought was being given to the shape of things after the end of the war in Europe, I was transferred to the Air Section to 'manage' the JAAF section for Josh Cooper. The main task was to organize the training of staff as they became available from other sections, and to build the Japanese Air Force section from less than two hundred to over seven hundred all ranks and all Services. After VJ-Day it became possible to arrange a gradual reverse process, which was extended to all military personnel at BP when I took over command of the Military Wing towards the end of 1945.

Finally, having practically ceased to do an honest (i.e. cryptanalytical) job about half-way through the war, there came the day when I went to Guildford to draw my de-mob outfit. The process was not quite as instantaneous as that on 10 May 1940—I did not report for duty until the next day, 1 April 1946—but as it meant a return to 'honesty' I was content.

Postscript

John Cairncross and I went up to Trinity College, Cambridge, in October 1934, he as a Major Scholar and I as an Exhibitioner in Modern Languages. Whilst we were not close friends, I saw something of him at lectures and supervisions, and once at a cocktail party for the Trinity cell of the Communist Party of Great Britain, which I had just joined. This was a surprise, because he had never given me the impression of being politically inclined. I handed back my CPGB card in January 1935, my brief flirtation having ended in disillusionment.

After graduating we went our separate ways. It was probably in December 1942, whilst on a liaison visit from Cairo to BP, that I ran into him in the passage of Hut 3, having not seen or heard of him since 1936. He was dressed as an Army Staff Captain. He remarked 'This is no place for me', and spoke of being better off in Hankey's office.

He had in fact been Lord Hankey's private secretary from September 1940 to March 1942. Hankey saw all Cabinet papers and exercised a general supervision over the intelligence services, as well as chairing several important scientific committees, but was dismissed by Churchill in March 1942. At all events Cairncross stayed at BP until the summer of 1943, when he transferred to a post in M.I.6.

Our next and last contact was when he invited me to lunch at the Travellers Club in February 1949, when he was back in the Treasury. In the middle of the meal he disconcertingly asked: 'Are we still reading Russian ciphers?' I had no first-hand knowledge of any current work on Russian, though I did know that on 22 June 1941 what work there was had been dropped, and the only off-putting response I could think of, on the spur of the moment, was to shake my head and mutter 'One-time'. He did not pursue this.

23. Army Ultra's Poor Relations

NOEL CURRER-BRIGGS

WHEN you entered the house at Bletchley Park you found yourself in a large, over-decorated hall from which an oaken staircase led to the first floor. Turning to the right at the top of the stairs you came to a suite of three rooms numbered 1, 2, and 3. It was here that Colonel John Tiltman and a small team of cryptographers, of which I was one, laboured to break German double-Playfair military, SS, and police hand ciphers. These differed from the naval hand ciphers described by Morris in Chapter 24, and like him I can only write autobiographically about the period during which I was a member of this team in BP and later in the Mediterranean theatre of operations. Thus what I shall describe suffers from the tunnel vision from which we all suffer and covers the three years from the autumn of 1941 when I first arrived at BP to the autumn of 1942 when I sailed for North Africa with 107 Special Intelligence Section, until the summer of 1944 when, at Castelfidardo in eastern Italy, I went over to breaking Balkan ciphers.

One of the ironies of the cryptographic war was the faith the Germans placed in the security of their military hand ciphers, based on a British system, Playfair, which they themselves had broken during the First World War. Between 1900 and 1914 the British adopted the Playfair cipher, which in its original form was based on a keyword in the first position of a 5 × 5 letter square containing the alphabet omitting 'J', for which 'I' was always substituted. The method of encipherment required the message to be written in bigrams, so that 'come here at once' becomes:

CO ME HE RE AT ON CE

Suppose that the keyword is EDINBURGH, the square, or box of letters, is written down as follows:

E	D	I	N	B
U	R	G	H	A
C	F	K	L	M
O	P	Q	S	T
V	W	X	Y	Z

From this it is apparent that the remaining letters of the alphabet are always written down in strict alphabetical order. For easier understanding, let us take another example, where the keyword might be, shall we say, OEDIPUS. In this case the square would look like this:

O	E	D	I	P
U	S	A	B	C
F	G	H	K	L
M	N	Q	R	T
V	W	X	Y	Z

When it comes to enciphering the message, each pair of letters into which it has been divided is substituted by another pair on a simple principle. Pairs of letters forming two diagonally opposed corners of a rectangle within a Playfair square are substituted by those on the other two corners. Pairs in the same row are substituted by those immediately after them, and pairs in the same column by those immediately below them; a letter at the end of a row jumps to the start of the same row, and one at the foot of a column jumps to the head of the same column. Thus, if we encipher the message with the first square, the first two letters 'CO' are seen to be in the same column. If we encipher on the second square, they are on different rows. In the first square the letters which occur immediately below each of the letters to be enciphered have to be chosen, thus CO becomes OV. In the second square the diagonal letters are chosen, so in this key CO becomes PU. The next bigram, ME, becomes CB in the first key and ON in the second. Thus the rest of this message would be enciphered in the first key as

UN UD MZ ES OU

and in the second as

DG IN CQ EM PS

The whole enciphered messages when written in five-letter groups for transmission by radio, and padded with a dummy letter at the end, when needed, would appear in these two versions as in

OVCBU NUDMZ ESOUQ

and

PUOND GINCQ EMPSL

This cipher gave a fair measure of security so long as the key was changed often enough, but by the middle of 1915 the Germans had completely broken down British Playfair. At the same time they recognized its flexibility and simplicity, and decided that they could make it more secure and adapt it for their own use. Instead of using one 5 × 5 square and dividing the clear text into bigrams in the way I have just described, they used two squares and wrote the message out in key-lengths on specially prepared squared message forms arranged in double lines of a given length. So far as my memory goes, I believe that the key-lengths in use during the Second World War were thirteen pairs of bigrams, but I might be mistaken and they may have been seventeen. The point is unimportant as no matter of principle is involved. The letter X was used to fill gaps between each word and to bring the clear text up to an even number of letters, and the word STOP was used at the end of each sentence. Repeated Xs were used in some cases to bring the clear text to the right number of bigrams to complete a key-length, but this was not always the case. Numerals were spelt out in full.

Let us consider a typical German message to show how the system worked: *An Obergruppenführer von dem Bach, Kiew. Bitte dreitausend Schuss Patronen schicken* ('To S. S. General von dem Bach, Kiev. Please send three thousand rounds of ammunition'). The German was written out on the squared message pad thus, with 'X' to separate words:

ANXOBERGRUPPENFUEHRERXVONXDEMXBACHX
KIEWSTOPBITTEXDREITAUSENDXSCHUSSXPATR

ONENXSCHI
CKENSTOPX etc.

If the Germans used keywords as in the example I have just described, we never discovered what they were, and for all practical purposes this did not affect our ability to reconstruct the letter square they used.

The message, written out in the prescribed fashion, was then enciphered on a key which changed daily at midnight. Since only twenty-five letters were possible for use, and because the German language makes much use of the letter J, and the umlaut accent (Ä, Ö, and Ü) these letters were written down as II, AE, OE, and UE. This greatly assisted the cryptanalysts, as I will show in due course.

The key consisted of two 5 × 5 letter squares set side by side thus:

```
AYKIH  YXUHA
LBMNP  TRKBI
QRCOG  PMCGS
ZXVDS  FDLQV
FWUTE  ENOWZ
  1      2
```

Unlike the original Playfair squares, where the letters were set in alphabetical order following the initial keyword, the German squares were always arranged randomly, so that, in attempting to reconstruct them, we were unable to guess the order of the letters in the squares and their relationship to each other as we would have been able to do had they adhered strictly to the original system.

The second modification was the use of key-lengths. Once the message had been enciphered in the manner described above, the resulting bigrams of upper and lower letters were then encoded in sequence—AH, NR, XE, OR, BX, EV, RO, etc. Because two letter squares were used, the bigram AH was enciphered by taking the letter A in square 1 and the H in square two, and because these occur on the same row, they were substituted by the letters immediately to their right—in this case the Y from square 1 and the A from square 2. The second bigram, NR, was enciphered in exactly the same way and produces in this key PK. The third bigram, XE, is enciphered differently because in this case the X in square 1 and the E in square 2 are on different rows, so now the letters diagonally opposite them are chosen—WF. Bigrams OR, BX, EV, and RO, like the majority of bigrams, are enciphered on the diagonal system. In cases where the letters of a bigram are found at the end of the row, e.g. PI, these are substituted by the first letters of the same row, in this case LT, as in original Playfair.

German message pads were printed so that cipher clerks could write the code letters above and below each bigram:

Y P W N Y S W E Y V E G H P A C H
a n x o b e r g r u p p e n f u e
h r e r x v o n x d e m x b a c h
A K F M R Z C M M N T R N I Z O W etc.

When the message was finally enciphered and ready for transmission is looked like this:

YAPKW FNMYR SZWCE MYMVN ETGRH NPIAZ COHWW
FMANY HZYOG VENTM SRYRO AOOIW HORVO VYMHB
LAOOB CTPTR GZPRW LGFKM

It was a fairly laborious process, needing care and attention to do accurately. Luckily many German cipher clerks, especially when working under stress, were careless or lazy. This led to requests for repeats and sometimes to recipherments when the wrong key had been used inadvertently or the recipient had not received his new set of keys.

So much for the system of encipherment. To ensure the security of any cipher system, the first rule is to avoid as far as possible routine words and phrases. The Germans, being both methodical and courteous, tended to ignore this, addressing recipients with their full rank or title, the name or number of the unit, and where it was stationed. Nearly all messages ended with the name of the sender, his rank and unit. Stocks and other returns were reported in pro forma sets of figures, which when deciphered by the recipient would appear something like this:

1 15 2 5 3 20 4 0 5 736 6 1240 7 0 8 0 etc.

Since such messages had to be written in full, the above would read: *Eins fuenfzehn zwo fuenf drei zwanzig vier null fuenf siebenhundertsechsunddreissig sechs eintausendzwohundertvierzig sieben null acht null*, and so forth.

Even before we knew what these sets of figures referred to, it was easy to spot the *eins, zwo, drei, vier* sequence within them, which told us at once that we were dealing with some kind of routine return of which these were the headings. I cannot, of course, now remember what these numbers referred to, but let us say that 1 = serviceable tanks; 2 = armoured cars; 3 = trucks, and so on. These pro formas were complex and not all units used the same ones, but in the field enough of them did for us to reconstruct them and in some cases to divine their meaning. Occasionally, of course, some pro formas were captured on the battlefield, and these greatly helped the cryptanalysts to break such routine messages when they were intercepted. But, more important, the Germans were in the habit of sending them at the same time each week, so, let us say, we always knew that the message of such and such a length sent out each Friday at about 1600 hours was the weekly ration strength, or something similar.

If the Germans had enforced stricter cryptographic discipline, they would have put an end to our cribs and made life much harder for us. They seem never to have monitored their own traffic, for if they had, they would have quickly spotted offences of the kind I have just described. They never seem to have grasped the danger this led them into, although it is known from decoded Enigma traffic that during the North African campaign their cryptographers were ordered to look at Enigma to find out how secure it was.

Other useful cribs arose from the tendency of German to use long words such as *Panzerlastkraftwagen* and titles such as *Obergruppenführer*. Russian place names like Dnjepropetrovsk (written for encipherment DNIIEPROPETROWSK) and Novorissiisk were most helpful. Cribs, therefore, played a large part in our success, but before we could begin, the intercepted traffic had to be written out in the same way as the German cipher clerks had enciphered it. Although it had been intercepted in the form I have just given (YAPKW FNMYR SZWCE and so on), by the time it reached our desks our ATS clerks had written it out thus:

Y P W N Y S W E Y V E G H P A C H W M N H Y G E T S Y O O I H R O Y
A K F M R Z C M M N T R N I Z O W F A Y Z O V N M R R A O W O V V M

H L O B T T G P W G K
B A O C P R Z R L F M

Our first task was to make a bigram-frequency count of the day's traffic. Using the above key we would find that bigrams FN, YD, WF, HN, TT, FO, WD, IR, and TR would be among the commonest because they stand for the nine commonest clear-text bigrams—EE, XX, EX, XE, NE, EN, XN, NX, and NN—though not necessarily in that order of frequency or in the order I have written their enciphered versions above.

Because the clear text was written in key-lengths, long words tended to 'fold' over themselves or to continue into the next key-length. Starting, perhaps, in the middle of the top line of a key-length a long word would continue on the lower line, or if it began on the lower line it would continue on the top line of the following key-length. Take, for example, the common SS rank *Obergruppenführer*. This might appear as

• • • • • • • • • • • • • • O B E R G
R U P P E N F U E H R E R • • • • •

SS traffic from Russia was especially full of useful cribs of this kind, and none more than returns of prisoners-of-war captured and escaped which were sent regularly to Obergruppenführer von dem Bach-Zaleski by his subordinates, several of whom had useful ranks (cryptographically speaking) such as *Untersturmbannführer* and *Obersturmbannführer*. Furthermore, such returns were certain to contain the words *Kriegsgefangene* ('prisoners-of-war'), *entwischen* ('escape'), *gefangengenommen* ('captured'), and these would be associated with spelt-out-numbers. Combination of these words produced recognizable bigram patterns, as, for instance, where the double 'p' of *gruppen*, the double 'n' of *sturmbann*, and the double 'i' of Dniiepropetrowsk fell above each other in a key length. This, of course, did not happen every time a routine message was transmitted, but when it did, it gave us a most useful break.

Let us suppose that a message containing such a repeated bigram was enciphered in the key I have used above, and that the critical part of the clear text had been written and enciphered thus:

X	T	L	L	F	O	L	T	G	E	B	P	W
r	u	p	p	e	n	f	u	e	h	r	e	r
d	n	i	i	e	p	r	o	p	e	t	r	o
M	O	T	T	N	T	N	W	E	Y	P	N	C

This part of the message would have reached us in this form:

X	T	L	L	F	O	L	T	G	E	B	P	W
M	O	T	T	N	T	N	W	E	Y	P	N	C

The bigram count would have revealed that cipher FN was among the commonest and that it probably stood for EE or XX or one of the other common bigrams I have mentioned. But the tell-tale repeated bigrams LT LT must stand for the repeated 'p' or 'n' in Obergruppenführer or Sturmbannführer and the repeated 'i' in Dniiepropetrowsk. A little trial and error would reveal the clear text of the above twelve bigrams, as follows:

Cipher:	XM	TO	LT	FN	OT	LN	TW	GE	EY	BP	PN	WC etc.
Text:	RD	UN	PI	EE	NP	FR	UO	EP	HE	RT	ER	RO etc.

With this number of bigrams we could begin to decipher other messages and to reconstruct the squares. As already explained, the first letter of each cipher bigram had to be on the same row or in the same column as the first letter of the clear-text bigram in square 1. Thus R and X in square 1 had to be either on the same line in the first square with R to the left of X or in a quadrilateral relationship with M and D in the second square. Thus the XM–RD bigrams had to appear as

```
   1          2
R • • • •   M • • • •
X • • • •   D • • • •
```

or as

```
R X • • •   D M • • •
```

When we examine the bigrams in which E occurs we find out much more. Cipher GE = Clear EP, Cipher EY = Clear HE, Cipher FN = Clear EE, Cipher PN = Clear ER. Since E and F in square 1 are associated with each other and E and N in square 2, they have to be arranged either

```
E • • • •   N • • • •
F • • • •   E • • • •
```

or as

```
E F • • •   E N • • •
```

But we know that Clear ER = Cipher PN indicates

```
E • • • •   N • • • •
P • • • •   R • • • •
```

or

```
E P • • •   R N • • •
```

We have to reconcile the above with the arrangement Cipher LN = Clear FR and the only way this can be done is as follows:

```
E F • • •   E N • • •
P L • • •   • R • • •
```

Cipher GE = Clear EP is the next pair to tackle. Now that we know the two Es are on the same line in each square it follows that this must be a quadrilateral encipherment, so we can add the G and the P thus:

E F • • •   E N • • •
P L • • •   • R • • •
G • • • •   P • • • •

The same can be deduced for the Cipher EY = Clear HE pair. Cipher LT = Clear PI is an interesting and useful pair, for we already know that P and L in square 1 are adjacent, which indicates that this must be a lateral encipherment and that therefore I and T must be adjacent in square 2. But we know more than that; we know that T and P in square 2 are in the same column, so it follows that B and R must be in the same column in square 1. At this stage the reconstructed squares look like this:

• • • E F   • E N • •
• • B P L   I T R • •
• • R G •   • P • • •
• • • H •   • Y • • •

Cipher OT = Clear NP and, as T and P are in the same column in square 2, this must be another quadrilateral encipherment, which means that N and O in square 1 are in the same column. We do not yet know the lateral relationship between N, B, P, and L and between O, R, and G in square 1, so the final order of these two lines cannot yet be established. Cipher TO = Clear UN, Cipher TW = Clear UO, and Cipher WC = Clear RO all help us to make further deductions. These three pairs of bigrams tell us that W, U, and T must be on the same row as E and O in square 1, and that N and D must be on the same row in square 2, but that R and U in square 1 are in the same row and that C and O are in the same column in square 2. This allows us to rearrange the sequence of columns now that we have found all five letters in one row of square 1 (namely, WUTEF), so our reconstruction now looks like this

W U T E F   E N O • •
B • N P L   T R • • I
R • O G •   P • C • •
• • • H •   Y • • • •

and so on, bit by bit until the two squares are completely reconstructed.

Not all keys were as easily broken as those containing the Dnjepropetrovsk crib, but it was not long before we achieved a high degree of expertise in spotting routine messages. This happy state of affairs lasted throughout 1941 and well into 1942.

During the preparations for Operation Torch, the invasion of North Africa in November 1942, it was decided to form a cryptanalysis unit to operate in the field alongside an intercept unit. Originally a group of eight was chosen to man this, including myself and three sergeants who had been working on the preparation of Playfair traffic for us in Room 1. Our 107 Special Intelligence Section, later 7 Special Intelligence Company, was to be attached to 1 Special Wireless Section, Royal Signals, which was responsible for administration as well as for the interception of enemy traffic and our radio links with Army and Army Group Headquarters and with England.

If we were to break Playfair in the field, we had to learn to do this with far less depth of traffic than we had been used to in Room 1, so the five of us were dispatched to a hut in the grounds of BP and fed a restricted amount of traffic intercepted from units in the Low Countries and France. The purpose of this was to simulate field conditions as far as possible. Meanwhile, our colleagues in Room 1 continued to get the full amount of traffic (including, of course, the limited amount we were given) and it was our task to discover how much longer it took to break daily keys. If the experiment showed that it could not be done reasonably quickly, then this would cast doubt on the wisdom of attempting to put a cryptanalytical team into the theatre of operations. We were, therefore, very much on our mettle, and the first time we broke the key before our colleagues in Room 1 was cause for much celebration.

For the next stage of our training we worked on Afrika Korps and *Abwehr* traffic intercepted in the Middle East, sent back to us in BP. This was a much tougher job, for the enciphered German traffic had to be re-enciphered in Typex before it reached us, meaning that much of it was very corrupt. Notwithstanding, we must have satisfied our masters that we could play a useful role in the field, for we were joined soon afterwards by two people from Beaumanor, who were to be responsible for traffic analysis. Towards the end of September we were joined by a small staff of NCOs who were to prepare and index the intercepted traffic and to type deciphered traffic in the original German. Finally we were joined by two sergeant translators.

We sailed for Algiers on 8 November 1942 on the Polish liner *Batory* from Avonmouth. On 20 November the commander received a signal from BP to say that during the past week all German Playfair traffic had become unreadable, and that it was feared a new hand cipher had taken its place. This was a shattering blow, for it placed our future in doubt, but there was nothing we could do while we were still on the high seas but wait until we reach Algiers, where we arrived three days later. There we were met by the advance party of 1 Special Wireless Section and driven to the Jardin des Plantes, where we pitched our bivouac tents under the palm trees. It was not a comfortable night, for the Germans raided Algiers, and we spent it in our tin hats hoping not to be hit by the shrapnel from our own anti-aircraft guns which was raining down all around us.

Next day we were taken to the École Pratique de l'Industrie at Maison Carrée about 10–15 miles outside Algiers. Here we met the rest of the 1 Special Wireless Section advance party, who had already set up aerials on the nearby airfield and had begun intercepting traffic. We were allocated two gin-palaces, the large mobile caravans which did for offices; a third was filled with wireless equipment and a fourth did duty for an administration office.

News from the front was encouraging. We heard that 11 Brigade was approaching Tebourba inside Tunisia, which they captured on 27 November. That day we got orders to follow the Army into Tunisia, and 1 December an advance party left Maison Carrée arriving at Ghardimaou on the 5th some thirty miles inside Tunisia in the mountains above Souk el Arba. Here an advance station was set up.

In his memoirs, General Eisenhower wrote that by 6 December 'we had gone beyond the sustainable limit of air capabilities in support of our ground forces in the pell-mell race for Tunis'. On 2 December 86 Panzer Grenadier Regiment, which we picked up through its call-signs, had landed in Tunis. As if the change in German cipher procedure was not bad enough, there had been a second blow, for at the same time they had stopped transmitting and receiving on single frequencies and had begun to transmit on one and receive on another, thus complicating the interceptors' task immensely. It was at this critical juncture that log-reading and traffic-analysis really came into their own. Without their help and the help of direction-finding we would have been completely at sea. As it was we were able to pin-point the controls of the various units facing us as well as their outstations, which in practical terms meant the

Headquarters of 86 Panzer Grenadier Regiment and later the headquarters of other units as they arrived in North Africa. Sometimes our task was made easier when the German operators sent short messages giving the names of units and individuals in clear, which they did from time to time during what must have been for them a hectic period of consolidation in the new theatre of operations in Tunisia. At least we felt we were not entirely useless.

Ever since we had received the news about the change in ciphers on board ship, we had been examining every scrap of traffic we could get. BP told us within a few days of our arrival in Algiers that all that had occurred was that the Germans were now changing the keys more frequently. Moreover, after we had had a chance to examine traffic intercepted during the early stages of the battle of Alamein, it was clear that the new system, which the enemy had intended to introduce on 1 November, had not been adopted by all units in the field at once. In a swiftly moving battle the new instructions had not reached all units, or if they had, it had not always been possible to put them into effect. The result had been that for about forty-eight hours some enemy units had continued transmitting under the old system. While this caused the Germans much confusion, it gave us a lucky break.

Among the units which had not got their new cipher keys were several squadrons of 164 Light Division. Their cipher clerks kept asking Divisional Headquarters to repeat messages which they said they could not decode. In the end, the commander of 164 Light lost patience and had the messages sent in clear, adding that the new key system would be dispatched as soon as possible. In fact they must have arrived almost simultaneously, for several days' backlog was then retransmitted by the squadron in the appropriate keys, so that we had two versions of about a dozen messages, together with the clear version of another. This was a tremendous help, for it enabled us to study the new system in great detail.

Before long we were able to break the keys almost as quickly as before. What prevented our complete success was the slender amount of traffic during the night, so that there were sometimes keys with insufficient depth to make a break.

The main party of 1 Special Wireless Section and 107 Special Intelligence Section set out for Ghardimaou about 18 December in teeming rain. We spent two uncomfortable nights at Oued Athineni and Guelma, arriving at the Ferme de Mauvas on the 20th. Before leaving England we had gained the impression that we were going to a hot climate, but almost from the moment we landed it rained incessantly. This had a bad effect on operations. Our three-hundred-mile journey to Ghardimaou took three days, largely because the roads were choked with the tanks and trucks of the 2nd Battalion Coldstream Guards, 6 Armoured, and 78 Infantry Divisions, who were moving up to reinforce the flying squads which had got within a few miles of Tunis by 6 December. It was Eisenhower's aim to launch the final attack on that city on 22–3 December, and the battle of Long Stop, near Medjez el Bab, opened on Christmas Eve. The weather was atrocious, which was a strong influencing factor in his failure to achieve this target, and the order to retreat was given on Boxing Day. It then became clear that the campaign was going to be a long one. That day an advance party set out to find a suitable site for a permanent station in which we could work during the winter until the front had settled down. A couple of days later we heard that one had been found at Fort Sidi M'Cid above Constantine, and on 8 January the main party left Ghardimaou on its way back to Algeria. A small party was left behind, for it was decided to leave an intercept station there and to establish a second to the south, so that we could continue to obtain direction-finding bearings on the enemy units facing the 1st Army and the Americans.

In order to maintain continuous cover, a cryptanalyst was left behind, and it was thought necessary to have a cipher in which the main body could communicate with him securely, in such a way that the Royal Signals operator at Ghardimaou would not be able to understand what we were talking about, let alone the enemy. No one had foreseen such a situation arising in which the officers of a special-intelligence unit might be in more than one place at a time and need to keep in touch with each other by radio, so there had been no provision of ciphers. Consequently we had to invent one of our own. We devised what we thought was a very ingenious one, and we arranged to use it if the need arose while the advance party was on its way to Constantine.

The journey was a nightmare. We were the only unit moving westward along a narrow road crammed with eastward-bound traffic, much of it two abreast, and our convoy was often forced off the road for hours at a time to let the oncoming traffic through. The distance between Ghardimaou and Constantine is a little over 150 miles, but the journey took more than two and a half days. As we had expected to do it in less than one, and thus maintain continuous wireless cover on enemy traffic, it became necessary at nightfall on the first day, when we were not much more than thirty-five miles from our starting-point, to let the rearguard at Ghardimaou know so that they could maintain cover and not dismantle the equipment as had been intended. It was therefore decided to send a signal in our patent cipher. We believed it was unbreakable: it was more than that, it was indecipherable! We had thought of so many alternative ways of enciphering our messages, we had quite overlooked the matter of how we were to indicate which of them we had used, and hence how to unscramble the eggs. I sent off a message the first night and a second on the following night, after we had covered about seventy miles. The other party got them all right, but struggled for hours trying to make out what they contained. They never did, until, after a week, they reached Constantine. We were not allowed to forget this in a hurry!

Fort Sidi M'Cid was a Foreign Legion fort in true *Beau Geste* tradition built on the top of a hill above the astonishing gorge which bisects the city of Constantine. It may have looked romantic, but it was the filthiest dump imaginable. One of my most vivid memories of it is cleaning the primitive latrines with the adjutant, since no one else was prepared to take on the job. They consisted of a row of stone holes set in the thickness of the wall over a fifty-foot drop which had to be emptied through an iron door set in the base of the rampart. They were all full. But I recall with more pleasure reading Virgil on the battlements in the intervals of trying to learn Arabic. Hardly typical of military life, but in the true tradition of BP!

Eisenhower's first concern was to get his troops ashore and move them eastwards in time to capture Tunis and Bizerta before the Germans and the rigours of winter prevented him. The weather and the bad roads rather than the enemy saw to it that he failed. It had been expected that Enigma would continue to provide him with the bulk of his intelligence, and, although he received some decrypts, the supply temporarily dried up for, at the same time as the Germans changed their Playfair key system, they introduced many more Enigma keys which took BP some time to penetrate. The planners were, of course, depending on us to produce tactical intelligence, so the key change jeopardized this source as well. With the help of direction-finding and traffic analysis, however, we got our first big breakthrough during the week following our arrival at Sidi M'Cid. On 15 January we got firm news from decrypts that Rommel was retreating from

Buerat and making for the Mareth Line, and during the following week we read most of the traffic we intercepted. This gave us warning of a major Axis offensive in central Tunisia timed for mid-February.

Tripoli fell on 23 January, after which we began to intercept traffic from 10 and 21 Panzer Divisions; thereafter we managed to break their keys with great regularity. During the next three weeks we were able to pinpoint 7 Panzer Regiment, 69 Panzer Grenadier Regiment, 10 and 21 Panzer Divisions, and 5 Panzer Army, and to read the bulk of their Playfair traffic.

Looking back on it now, we can see that this period of relative calm at Fort Sidi M'Cid was fortunate, for it gave us the chance to develop our deciphering techniques in the comparative comfort of a building rather than in the great discomfort of a gin-palace and bivvy tents. Cryptanalysis is not the sort of thing you can do well if your clothes are damp and your mind on creature comforts. Not that the fort was all that luxurious, but we were at least protected from the elements and living a life which left us free to concentrate on the problems that faced us.

On 13 and 14 February Eisenhower visited the central Tunisian front. This coincided with 7 Panzer Regiment's attack on Faid. Farther south, 21 Panzer Division forced the Americans back to Djebel Hamra. We gave warning that 10 Panzer Division had been ordered to reconnoitre towards Fondouk, and that 21 Panzer Division was to get ready to move to Gafsa to join up with Rommel as he retreated from Tripolitania. For a brief spell between 14 and 21 February we lost 10 Panzer, and when we found them again, our direction-finding picked them up near Kasserine. This period of wireless silence proved critical, for we were not able to warn Eisenhower what to expect, or where. On 14 and 15 February the Americans evacuated Gafsa and withdrew to Feriana, followed hotfoot by Rommel. On the 16th the Allies abandoned Sbeitla and 21 Panzer launched a furious attack on the combined US and Free French forces and routed them. The next day Feriana and the airfield at Thélépté were abandoned, but then the weather broke again. The 19th was a drenching day, and the ground, which had been drying out since the previous downpours of early February, turned once more to glutinous mud, which hindered the Germans more than the Americans. On that day, however, we intercepted Rommel's order to advance towards Le Kef and the British V Corps. This told us the direction of his forthcoming thrust, which we were sure he would launch as soon as the weather let up.

That day, 19 February, was important for other reasons, for it saw the establishment of 18 Army Group and the assumption of command by General Alexander. That week also brought the arrival at Fort Sidi M'Cid of Hamish Blair-Cunynghame and a further batch of cryptanalysts and log-readers from Bletchley Park. Though we were unaware of it at the time, this was a vote of confidence in the team which had come out at the start of the campaign, for we had shown that cryptanalysis could be carried on successfully in the field, and that our contribution to the intelligence picture had been great enough to justify further expansion in the future. I think that there can be little doubt that, if we had failed to get to grips with the key changes, we would have been sent home, and that all cryptanalytical effort would have been concentrated in England and maybe Heliopolis and Sarafand, but certainly not so near the front.

The next four days were critical for the success of the campaign. In spite of the weather, but on the strength of a good forecast, Rommel attacked the Kasserine Pass, held by the Americans, and 21 Panzer Division attacked the Sbiba Pass held by V Corps. This provoked a major command crisis, for, while the British held on to Sbiba, the Americans gave way at Kasserine. Luckily the weather forecasters were wrong, for the brief let-up in the rain lasted no more than thirty-six hours, and on 21 and 22 February the heavens opened once more, bringing movements almost to a total stop. The worst was over.

General Alexander had set up 18 Army Group Headquarters to the east of Constantine, and one of his first actions was to order 1 Special Wireless Section to leave Fort Sidi M'Cid and to go to a site nearer him. We left the fort on 23 February and established ourselves at La Verdure the same day. The next day the Allies recaptured Kasserine and two days later von Arnim launched a diversionary attack on the British in the northern sector near Djebel Abiod. Luckily we were able to give warning of this, for we had established the location of the Hermann Goering and 334 Divisions as well as elements of the Manteuffel and Italian Superga Divisions in that sector. The following day we gave warning to General Montgomery that 10 and 21 Panzer Divisions were moving from Kasserine towards Mareth, which enabled him to send forward the New Zealand Division, 8th Armoured Brigade, and 201st Guards Brigade to reinforce his XXX Corps and to invest Medenine. This was a most exciting period for us. Traffic was coming in thick and fast, and we were deciphering it almost as quickly as we had at BP before the change of key systems. We were theoretically working in shifts, but there was so much to do that we hardly ever took time off, and frequently worked when we should have been resting. It was far too exciting to sit by and twiddle one's thumbs in idleness.

During the first week of March Rommel's spoiling attacks round Medenine, in which he threw 10, 15 and 21 Panzer Divisions, failed. How much this had to do with his health is debatable. We knew he was a sick man, and on 9 March he left Africa on sick leave never to return. Two days later, 1 Special Wireless Section was ordered to move to Le Kef, where we established ourselves in another *Beau Geste* fort called Bastion Quatre. Throughout the rest of March we were reading all the German traffic and were able to play a significant part in the battles for the Mareth Line (16–17 March) and Wadi Akarit (28–29 March). On 7 April the 8th Army and II US Corps joined up at Wadi Akarit and broke through the Gabes gap for the final assault on the Axis bridgehead. They reached Sousse on 12 April, and ten days later Operation Vulcan was launched. The British 1st Army attacked 15 Panzer Division on 6 May and the following day the Allies entered Tunis, Bizerta, and Ferryville, leaving a small remnant of enemy forces still holding out in the Cap Bon peninsula. These finally surrendered on 12 May, whereupon hostilities in North Africa came to an end.

Much praise has rightly been lavished on those brilliant men at Bletchley who succeeded in breaking enemy ciphers in the first place, but in my view not enough credit has been given to the hundreds of men and women, all of them privates or junior NCOs, who sat hour after hour snatching from a background of constant static thousands of messages which throughout the war passed from one enemy unit to another. When frequencies and call-signs changed in November 1942 and the traffic upon which the cryptanalysts depended dried up, the interceptors saved the day by their skill in recognizing the sending style of enemy operators. Without this skill we would not have been able to reconstruct the enemy wireless networks so quickly and so thoroughly as we did, and without this our task as cryptanalysts would have been immeasurably harder. These men and women deserve all the more praise because they had very little idea of what happened to the traffic they intercepted, and none of the cryptographic successes we achieved or of the intelligence it produced.

On 16 May we left Le Kef for La Marsa overlooking the splendid bay of Tunis, and two days later took over the Fort El Kebir on a mountain above Bizerta. It was even more filthy than Fort Sidi M'Cid at Constantine if that were possible, and infinitely more windy. We all hated it, though the next two and a half months produced probably the most valuable intelligence ever to be gleaned from medium-grade cipher traffic.

It had been decided at the Casablanca Conference that Sicily should be taken as soon after the end of the North African campaign as possible. We consequently turned our attention to traffic from that island and from Italy. It was a remarkably rapid campaign, lasting no more than thirty-eight days, which makes it sound deceptively simple. It was not, and its success was only achieved by meticulous planning, the largest amphibious operation ever staged up to that time, and an elaborate deception plan. We knew nothing of this deception plan at the time, of course, nor of the crucial role we were playing in it. As General Alexander said when it was all over, the operations in Sicily were less interesting than the preliminary planning because the conventional words were justified—operations proceeded according to plan.

The story of the *Man Who Never Was* has been told by Ewen Montagu in his book of that name, so I need say only that the purpose of the deception was to make the Germans think that the Allies would attack Sardinia or the Peloponnese rather than the more obvious target, Sicily. It is a measure of its success that even we thought we were going to Greece or Yugoslavia when we left Tunisia.

Sitting on top of our mountain overlooking the fine harbour of Bizerta, we worked at full stretch to obtain the enemy's order of battle in Corsica, Sardinia, Sicily, southern Italy, and the southern Balkans. I remember it as a period of great excitement, for things were going right for us. We had thoroughly mastered the new key-system, and, working in the closest relationship with the interceptors and traffic analysts, we poured forth a steady stream of valuable intelligence.

We did not realize at the time, of course, that we were watching the enemy's reaction to the great deception plan. As German documents captured at the end of the war show, Hitler swallowed the bait hook, line, and sinker, for on 12 May he issued an order which downgraded Sicily and stated that measures regarding Sardinia and the

Peloponnese should take precedence over everything else. Within three days of 'Major Martin's' body being found on the Spanish coast, Enigma decrypts from BP showed that the plan had been accepted as genuine. The negative evidence so important in a plan of this kind—knowing what the enemy was *not* going to do—was of the utmost importance. No wonder that Brigadier Airey and General Alexander and other senior officers came to the top of our mountain far more frequently than one might suppose routine inspections called for, and that they hung over us as we were decoding messages like eager schoolboys watching an exciting game of cricket or football! What we were telling them proved beyond all doubt that the way was being opened for the invasion of Sicily that would ensure its success. Between May and 10 July, when the invasion was launched, the Germans made many redeployments. They sent 1 Panzer Division from France to Greece, two divisions were sent from Russia to Greece, Sardinia was reinforced—all of which we reported as it was happening. What we did not detect was any movement of troops into Sicily or to the toe of Italy, for there was none. The only German troops there were old desert friends, 15 Panzer Grenadier Division and the Hermann Goering Division, which we had detected some time earlier. We could pin-point on our maps the exact location of every unit of those two divisions, which posed the old problem—who should share the secret? That, luckily, was none of our business, but it was a hard dilemma, for a too-accurate knowledge might betray the source of our information.

While the landings were taking place, Brigadier Airey spent two days with us 'listening in' to 15 Panzer Grenadier as they moved from one place to another in response to a secondary deception, which led them to believe we would land at Trápani on the western tip of the island where Aeneas had landed and held funeral games in honour of his father, Anchises, after he had deserted Dido in Carthage. On clear days we would see Carthage to our south, while Trápani lay less than 150 miles to the north-east. Meanwhile, our forces were landing at Syracuse and other points on the eastern coast of the island.

We remained on our mountain top at Bizerta until the middle of August, when we were sent to Syracuse. We had covered the Sicilian operations successfully, and now it was time to prepare for the invasion of Italy. Our stay in an olive grove at Avola near Noto lasted no more than a month, and during that time we were joined by new recruits from BP, and, for a short while, by a couple of Americans who came to gain experience of cryptanalysis under field conditions.

The Italians capitulated on 3 September and this was made public on the 8th. The following day the Allies landed at Salerno. Although the Italians were now out of the war, the German reaction was swift and strong. During our brief stay in Sicily we had been intercepting German traffic from the mainland, from which it was clear that at least until 8 September there were few German units south of Rome, and it was not until 6 or 7 September that we were able to detect any major troop movements. Furthermore, we had not only been able to provide a completely accurate picture of the German order of battle in Sicily before our invasion, but we had been able to keep track of all the German units which had been withdrawn into Italy at its conclusion. Throughout the three or four weeks between the end of the Sicilian campaign and the publication of the Italian surrender and our landings at Salerno, we knew that the Germans had not been able to regroup their forces in Calabria or to bring in substantial reinforcements from the north. It struck those of us in the know as strange that so little advantage appeared to be taken of this valuable intelligence. It is now said in defence of the judgement of Generals Patton and Montgomery that a landing at Anzio in September 1943 would have been too risky because of the lack of air support. But, from what Playfair (and no doubt Enigma, too) was telling us, it was clear that the German Air Force did not have enough units in Italy then to do us much harm, and that, while there was undoubtedly *some* risk of landing so far north, it was not unacceptable. There were many among us who felt that, had Patton and Montgomery been bolder then, much of the carnage of Monte Cassino could have been avoided and the Italian campaign shortened by many months.

Sometime early in October 1 Special Wireless Section sailed from Syracuse for Táranto and went to Bitonto a few miles up the coast from the Adriatic port of Bari. This was a period of reorganization to take account of the new situation now that we were in Europe: 113 Special Wireless Section was attached to 15 Army Group Headquarters, first at Sparanise and later at Sessa Aurunca. Elements of 7 Special Intelligence Company were attached to 8 Special Wireless Company at Bitonto, with outstations at Vieste on the eastern tip of the Gargano, and at Benevento high in the Appenines about halfway between Bari and Naples. At this point I was transferred from Playfair-breaking to Exotics.

'Exotics' was the name given to all non-German Balkan traffic—mostly, but by no means all of it, enemy. Those of us in 7 Special Intelligence Company who were taken off Playfair were put to work on ciphers originating in the Balkans. These fell into four main categories—Albanian Partisan, Tito Partisan, Mihailovich Chetnik, and Croat Ustashi.

Although I do not speak a word of either Albanian or Serbo-Croat, I was one of the team given these ciphers to break. It may come, perhaps, as a surprise to learn that one can break a cipher in a language one does not understand, but in fact it is possible where the ciphers in question are comparatively simple and uncomplicated. All we had to know was whether the ciphers were transpositions or substitutions, and about thirty or forty common words. We were told the enciphering method before we began, which makes me believe that work had been done on all this traffic at Heliopolis or Sarafand before we were asked to tackle it. Consequently all we had to do was to apply certain rules and hope to find certain keywords that would establish whether what we were achieving made sense in the language concerned, or was merely gobbledygook. In a language like Serbo-Croat which shuns vowels, words like *crni*, *krk*, and *vrh* can easily be mistaken for the latter. Fortunately we had officers who spoke the languages concerned, who could tell us. All we had to learn were a few common phrases. Many Ustashi personnel would send personal greetings to their family and friends at the end of official messages. These frequently asked the recipient to tell a friend or parent that the sender was alive and well—*ziv i zdrav* in Serbo-Croat—and there were similar phrases like this in Albanian as well.

The Yugoslav traffic was useful in that it complemented the information we were getting from our ability to read the Playfair traffic of the Prinz Eugen Division and other German units who were fighting Tito's Partisans. Long before the British Government withdrew its support from Mihailovich and transferred it to Tito, we were getting evidence from both German and Chetnik sources that Mihailovich was collaborating with the Italians and Germans, often against Tito (who was a Croat), whose Partisans were single-mindedly fighting the Germans and the Ustashi. We were also able to supply evidence of Ustashi atrocities committed against Serbs and Bosnians in the region round Mostar and the Crna Gora as well as in the Dalmatian islands of Pag, Brach, Krk, Korchula, and Hvar.

There can be little doubt that our success in reading this traffic played an important part in the decision to support Tito rather than Mihailovich. Not long after this decision had been taken, a direction-finding station was established on the Partisan-held island of Vis, which lies some fifty miles off the Dalmatian coast south of Split, and which was never occupied by the Germans.

24. Navy Ultra's Poor Relations

CHRISTOPHER MORRIS

'OPERATION Cinderella'. The two words appeared briefly on the door of a room at Bletchley Park during the Second World War. It was the room occupied by one particular party, of which I happened to be a member. The words were at once symptomatic and prophetic. They were symptomatic of the rather low state of morale from which the party suffered on occasion. They were prophetic of the somewhat meagre place which their work now holds in the published annals of Bletchley Park's achievements.

The work in question was work on German naval hand ciphers. But it can, very probably, be regarded as a fair sample of work on enemy hand ciphers in general. In any case, it is the only work of which I can write with first-hand knowledge, although inevitably what I write is bound to have an autobiographical flavour, and bound also to be largely a mere worm's-eye view. It is, however, based on a lengthy memorandum which I wrote at the bidding of my head of section before I left Bletchley in the late summer of 1945; and that memorandum was based on all the relevant documents then available to me, as well as on the spoken or written evidence of numerous colleagues.

Our eyes are still so dazzled by the miracle of Ultra, by the prodigies of mathematical thinking which went into the deciphering of the various German Enigma machines, that very naturally the historians have not noticed and the public have not known that the Germans also made use of rather numerous hand ciphers of varying degrees of complexity. This tunnel vision applies perhaps most of all to naval operations; for the German Navy's Enigma machine was the hardest nut to crack, the last to be broken, and possibly the most important because of its bearing on the U-boat war. Naval Ultra therefore held and still holds a peculiarly dazzling character—so much so that very few people are aware that in the course of the war the German Navy used no less than twenty-seven different hand ciphers, six of them high-grade. The traffic in three of the high-grade ciphers was read, quite often currently, for the greater part of their life spans; and so was the traffic in the majority of the lesser ciphers.

Some at least of the deciphered signals have claims to value or importance—an importance of three different kinds. The signals could be a major source of 'cribs' into *Schluessel* M, the naval Enigma machine, since the same facts or orders were often transmitted in more than one cipher. The signals could contain quite valuable information, occasionally even information of operational importance. They had, too, a certain historical importance because, such was the pessimism of the authorities at the outset, had there not been some early breaks into certain hand ciphers, serious work on German naval ciphers as a whole might never have begun. Something needs to be said under each of these headings.

Signals as a source of cribs

Long after the structure of the Enigma machine became known (and even after a machine was captured), the setting for each successive day had to be discovered. This was not always achieved by pure mathematical analysis nor yet solely by the bombe, the rudimentary computer invented for the purpose. It helped greatly to know the likely content and if possible the exact initial wording of a particular signal. There is indeed no such thing as absolutely 'pure' cryptanalysis. To know what a signal is in German, or that in German E is the commonest letter, or that the signal is on a naval wireless frequency, or that it is likely to be about the weather is, in each case, to have a partial or potential crib. The cryptographer, like all discoverers, must proceed from the known to the unknown.

The German Navy was for a long time quite liberal in providing cribs. Cribs were in fact almost inevitable unless all naval vessels, from battleships to tugs, had been confined to the use of one single cipher. But auxiliaries and small craft did not carry *Schluessel* M, whereas U-boats normally used nothing else. Consequently a storm-warning or a notice that some swept channel had been mined had to be transmitted both in Enigma and in something else—usually in *Werftschluessel* (literally Dockyard Key), hereinafter to be called *WS*. For many months the German cipher clerks took too little care to vary the wording, word-order, or spelling in such signals. Had they but known it, ringing the changes between *fuenf* and *funf* or between *nul* and *null* would have added considerably to our problems.

As both a typical and principal provider of cribs, *WS* deserves a brief discursus. Traffic in it was first detected in April 1940, and the first decipherment from it some months later was produced by fitting on a crib provided in a captured document. After that the signals were deciphered by various cryptographic techniques unassisted by the capture of any keys or tables. 'Cryptographic' was the word used at the time for what is now usually called 'cryptanalytic'. *WS* traffic was read at first retrospectively but by March 1941 as a rule currently, until by February 1945 the traffic had become so negligible both in volume and in content as to be deemed not worth deciphering. The continuous reading of it constitutes easily the long-distance record among German naval hand ciphers. About thirty-three thousand signals in *WS* were read, over thirty thousand of them currently, covering a period of forty-seven months, averaging twenty-three signals a day.

The traffic consisted of five-letter groups, for which the clear text had been written out in vertical columns, each five letters wide, and enciphered by substituting for each vertical pair of letters another bigram taken from a substitution table, using a separate table for each of the five columns.

```
THEPL   ALCOL
AINTE   UMNSF

XTOFT   IVELE
HESIG   TTERS

NALIS   WIDEL
WRITT   IKETH

ENINV   ISXYZ
ERTIC   PQRST
```

There were twenty tables at first and later thirty, a new *Heft* or set of tables being provided at first every two months and later every month. During the cipher's lifetime the cryptographers of German Naval Section had to reconstruct the twenty or thirty tables thirty-eight times.

The substituted bigrams were reciprocal—that is, if AB became XY in one table, then XY in that table would become AB. Moreover, neither letter of any bigram reappeared in its substitute—for example, AB could not become AX or XB, nor yet XA or BX. All of these phenomena, had the Germans but known it, made the cryptographer's task a fraction easier. The cryptographers relied on a reasonable 'depth'—that is, number and length of signals—and on informed or intelligent guesses at the content of certain signals, recognized from external characteristics as likely to be of a routine nature. Cribs were, of course, almost essential when a new *Heft* came into use. It was also possible to exploit repetitions in the same column of certain common bigrams such as EE, EN, NE, and so on. EE occurs twice in the English sample above, as it does in words like

MESSA	BLETC
GE	HLEY

EE is at least equally common in German, as in words like

FREIG	BEDEU
EGEBE	TEN
N	

The beginning of a poem by Goethe may be taken as an illustration of vertical repeats—admittedly perhaps an extreme case:

I	C	H	D	E
N	K	E	D	E
I	N	W	E	N
N	M	I	R	D
E	R	S	O	N
N	E	S	C	H
I	M	M	E	R
V	O	M	M	E
E	R	E	S	T
R	A	H	L	T
I	C	H	D	E
N	K	E	D	E
I	N	W	E	N
N	S	I	C	H
D	E	S	M	O
N	D	E	S	F
L	I	M	M	E
R	I	N	Q	U
E	L	L	E	N
M	A	L	T	

It will be noted that in column 1 IN occurs four times, that in column 3 HE and WI occur twice each, and that in column 5 EE occurs twice.

Once the content of a signal was known or guessed, other vertical bigram repeats could be recognized, even of relatively uncommon letters—for example, the FS in

FEUER
SCHIF
FFLEN
SBURG

To go into further detail might lead me to poach on 'classified' preserves.

Since *WS* was the cipher used by all minor naval vessels in German home waters and, after the fall of Norway and of France, in Norwegian and Biscayan waters (though not in the Channel, no doubt through fear of capture), it soon became apparent that *Schluessel* M and *WS* could and did provide cribs into one another when the same information or instructions were transmitted in both ciphers. Indeed the 'cross-ruffing' between the two was for some time the prize exhibit which Naval Section could display to distinguished visitors, such as Winston Churchill in September 1941.

The heyday of *WS* as a main source of cribs lasted throughout 1942 and into 1943; during this period whenever it was proving difficult to break into a new set of *WS* tables or into a new complication of the Enigma machine, Operation Garden would be set in motion. This meant mine-laying in the known German-swept channels and would invariably provoke *Sperrnachrichten* announcing that such and such a *weg* was *gesperrt* between two specified and numbered points. These furnished ideal cribs, and gardening would sometimes be laid on if the reading of home-waters Enigma was wanted in a hurry, as it would be if an Arctic convoy was about to sail.

Information of operational importance

Other hand ciphers from time to time supplied cribs into one another or into something higher-grade, but *WS* was unrivalled in this field. Nor was its content wholly uninteresting. Any major ship addressing an auxiliary had to do so in *WS*. Consequently almost every German warship from the *Tirpitz* down to destroyers used it on occasion and thereby told us her whereabouts; once, when we had lost track of the *Scheer* for some weeks, she made a *WS* signal reporting on the weather near Danzig. Above all, it was often possible to learn from *WS* that a new U-boat had been commissioned and was exercising in the Baltic. The same cipher could also tell us of the routeing of coastal convoys, of damage suffered by German shipping, of the movements of hospital ships and transports serving the German Army on the Eastern front, and not least the volume of east or west-bound traffic in the Baltic. More than half the *WS* signals deciphered were thought worth teleprinting to the Admiralty.

The longest serving members of the *WS* party were John Barns (later to become a notable papyrologist), Paul Smither (a very promising young Egyptologist who, tragically, had to leave Bletchley early in 1943 to die of leukaemia—but not before he had invented a most ingenious cryptographic device known as the 'key-finder' which greatly expedited the discovery of the five tables used in each signal), Ruth Briggs, now Mrs Oliver Churchill (an excellent young German scholar from Newnham who became probably the party's most reliable all-round performer), Philip Hunt (a young PPE graduate who went later into the Board of Trade), Roland Oliver (still an undergraduate but later to be a professor of African history), and myself. It should be added that whenever more labourers were needed in the vineyard, that is, when a new set of *Hefts* had to be broken, Dr C. T. Carr, later to be Professor of German at St Andrews, would lend his aid, leaving his work on other hand ciphers.

Another high-grade naval hand cipher that was read for a considerable time, from September 1939 to May 1941 (though not currently till April 1940), was *Schluessel* H, known to Naval Section as 'Merchant Navy'. It was used by Merchant Navy ships controlled by the German Admiralty. The cipher in its earlier form consisted of bigram substitution, horizontal or vertical, on a text composed of groups drawn from the International Code of Signals (the Merchant Navy Code-Book). The cipher was broken almost single-handed by Professor W. H. Bruford (a veteran of 'Room 40' in the First World War), largely by analysis, though assisted for a time by the capture of one set of bigram tables. Most signals contained lacunae requiring some ingenuity to complete. After mid-1941 the systems used became so complex as to be deemed unbreakable, at any rate with the labour then available. Since *Schluessel* H provided the earliest naval signals in a high-grade cipher that were read at Bletchley, it caused rather more stir than its normal content really warranted. Indeed in April 1940 the actual workings of two tyro cryptographers (Paul Smither and myself) were sent up to the Admiralty to show what Bletchley's Naval Section could now do. The signal only gave Oxeloesund, Sweden, as the destination of a German merchant ship of moderate tonnage.

The excitement thus engendered can be understood only if we recall the pessimism long maintained in high quarters about the possibility of any deciphering of German naval signals. During the Munich crisis it was noticed that German naval signal traffic had been reduced to a very bare minimum. From this Admiral Sinclair, then head of SIS, deduced that, in the event of war, the German Navy would maintain total wireless silence 'and that therefore this organization of ours is useless for the purpose for which it was intended'. In view of this it may not be wholly surprising that in September 1939 the German Naval Section at GC&CS consisted of precisely two persons, neither of them a cryptographer. For months the Section, even when enlarged to ten or twelve persons, fumbled in gross darkness. The first deciphered signal that ever came its way and threw any light on the German Navy was a police message concerning the punishment of a drunken cook in a *Vorpostenboot*. Since it was not previously realized that ships of that designation existed, the Section realized that it still had much to learn.

Countering official pessimism

But the first feather the Naval Section could put in its own cap was plucked from a strange bird, not really a sea-bird and one whose capture did not involve the highest form of cryptanalysis. This was the virtually self-evident *Flugmeldesignal* reporting enemy aircraft, and enabling us to work out the German 'grid'. Naval officers were said to be impressed by the ability of German Naval Section to say that FLG meant *Flugzeug* ('aeroplane') or that SOT meant *Sudost* ('south-east').

Even after these modest triumphs pessimism continued to prevail. As late as the summer of 1940 I myself heard Commander Denniston, head of GC&CS, saying to the head of Naval Section, 'You know, the Germans don't mean you to read their stuff, and I don't suppose you ever will.' The Section was in fact caught in a vicious circle. It could not get adequate staff without first achieving successes, and it could achieve little success without adequate staff. At first, too, even when potential cryptographers were recruited, for many months they were seconded for more than half their time to other duties such as nocturnal watchkeeping, logging incoming intercepts, learning to interpret wireless traffic from its external characteristics, or commuting to the Admiralty to explain and sell such wares as Bletchley could provide.

Even when some successes had been achieved, the cryptographers laboured under certain disadvantages. An experience of my own will furnish an example. In mid-April 1940 I deciphered a Merchant Navy signal, for which I claim no credit; I was simply doing what Professor Bruford told me and performing an almost mechanical operation. The signal ordered all ships bound for Bergen to report their positions at stated intervals to the German War Office. I was told that ships do not report to War Offices, so would I please correct the error. I had my workings checked and the text remained the same. The ships were of course troop ships, and the signal could have given us advance notice of the invasion of Norway. But I have found no evidence that the signal was ever sent to the Admiralty, and it is certainly unmentioned in the history books. The reason is that hand cipher was on the whole distrusted and graded for reliability well below Enigma—on the grounds that it is human to err whereas the machine cannot lie. Actually, for technical reasons, if a letter has been incorrectly transmitted, received, or copied, it is more easily checked if it is in a bigram substitution cipher than it would be in Enigma. This undervaluing of hand ciphers had quite far-reaching repercussions. As will be shown, it distinctly limited their potential utility and it seriously lowered the cryptographers' morale. But I must first complete my survey of Naval Section's relatively successful work on the enemy's hand ciphers.

One high-grade cipher of considerable value, both for intelligence purposes and for the supply of cribs, was the *Reservehandverfahren* (*RHV*) used by the Germans if and when the Enigma machine broke down, and by some ships instead of the machine. *RHV* involved transposing the clear text through a 'cage' and then applying vertical bigram substitution to the transposed text on four different substitution tables. It was first read, through a captured document, in June 1941 and later rebroken by cryptographic methods. Traffic in it was read, more or less currently, for some forty months, the volume amounting to about 1,400 signals averaging twelve per day; although once, for two days in July 1943, all German North Sea signals (perhaps through fear that *Schluessel* M might be compromised) were transmitted in *RHV*. U-boats carried their own separate *RHV* transposition cages, in case their machines proved faulty or were thought unsafe. This system was known to the Germans as *RHV Offizier*. Only six of such signals were diagnosed at Bletchley with any certainty and all were deciphered (three of them by James Hogarth), two of these giving the current recognition signal schedule.

Prominent among those who worked on *RHV* were J. H. Plumb (later Professor Sir John Plumb the historian), A. S. C. Ross (later to be associated with 'U' and 'non-U' speech), Dr C. T. Carr (already mentioned), Bentley Bridgewater (later Secretary to the British Museum), and James Hogarth (later to be a high official in the Scottish Office). Hogarth arrived at Bletchley as a private. He soon proved too indispensable to be allowed to go to an Officer Cadet Training Unit to become an officer. But, meriting rapid promotion, he ended the war as Regimental Sergeant-Major, although few men have had a less military bearing or physique.

In the Mediterranean the Germans had a separate form of *RHV* known as *Schluessel Henno*, enciphered on the same system but with different transposition cages and bigram tables. It first appeared in May 1943 and work on it was at first unsuccessful and was temporarily abandoned. But in April 1944 all the *Henno* documents were captured in a raid on Mykonos. The Germans must have realized that the cipher was compromised, and they began immediately and rapidly to change transposition cages, bigram tables, etc., one by one. Had they changed all at once they might well have prevented, or at least seriously delayed, any deciphering. As it was, Naval Section was just able to keep pace with them, but shortage of manpower meant that not all current traffic and very little 'back stuff' could be dealt with. The volume of *Henno* signals amounted to over a thousand per month. At one time as many as thirty people were at work on the cipher. It was the Section's most impressive mass attack. Nevertheless the intelligence value of *Henno*, with a few exceptions, proved rather disappointing; and by the end of August 1944, not without a good deal of controversy, work on *Henno* was abandoned.

Invisible exports

No account of the work undertaken by the cryptographers of Naval Section would be complete without some reference to their by-products or invisible exports. These fall into two classes: (1) ciphers which were deemed more suitable for handling elsewhere; (2) ciphers which did not strictly belong to German Naval Section but which the Section's cryptographers worked on in their spare time or in slack periods.

An example of the first class was the *Funkverkehrsheft*, a three-letter book, frequently randomized or 're-hatted' (deliberately jumbled) used by harbour defence flotillas on all German-occupied coasts (especially the Channel Islands). The cipher was partially read from its beginning in mid-1941, partly from cribs and eventually from a captured code-book. The signals included reports of German aircraft crossing the French or Dutch coasts *en route* for the United Kingdom. For this reason relevant decodes were sent to Bletchley's Air Section and/or to coastal stations rather than to the Admiralty, thus constituting an invisible export.

A related cipher *Funkverkehrsheft Kueste* (known as 'K code' at Bletchley), also a three-letter book 're-hatted', was used from December 1942 by coastal batteries and radar stations in the Channel and Mediterranean. As it was an inter-Service code there was some difficulty in getting any one British Service to acknowledge responsibility and pay for the infant's upbringing, but the foundling ended up on Naval Section's doorstep. The decodes were sent to Alexandria and, after D-Day, to the 21st Army Group in Normandy. There is a legend, still unconfirmed, that in the small hours of D-Day the solitary K-code signal from a shore station in the battle area said 'Cancel state of readiness'.

A similar code (three-letter book), simpler because neither frequently nor radically changed, was the *Seenotfunksignaltafel* (*SN*), used and read for three years from July 1940. It was designed merely to delay deciphering and to be very quickly read by its German recipients. Its purpose was to provide a rescue service for aircraft coming to grief in the Channel. In practice, if the aircraft 'ditched' in our half of the Channel, the British 'crash-boat' often arrived on the scene before the enemy's. To facilitate rapid exploitation, the handling of this code was given to Dover Command and dealt with on the spot. Much of the work on all of these ciphers was done by Dr Carr, assisted by Jean Watt (née Donaldson) and later by Sheila Mackenzie.

Other kinds of invisible export arose from quite different causes. The work of the cryptographer can fluctuate. At times the volume of readable traffic necessitates a call for all hands to the pump. But at other periods the traffic may become temporarily unreadable or the stream of traffic, though readable, may dwindle to a trickle. This can easily occur during a night shift. A conscientious cryptographer with time on his hands may turn his attention to someone else's cipher as a work of supererogation. A case in point is that of the cipher known as 'CGG'. This was a relatively simple 'creeping-subtractor' system, used by an enemy agent sitting with a telescope at La Linea and reporting what he saw of our shipping or aircraft. This was deciphered as a sideline by Philip Hunt, one of the *WS* party (and later by myself). The only value of its content was that it provided, for a time, a reliable crib into the GGG Enigma machine used by the German spy network, for which reason it was soon handed over to another section of GC&CS.

Yet another 'sidekick' of the cryptographers of German Naval Section was altogether more interesting and not German at all but Italian. In the winter of 1941–2 there was a considerable dearth of *WS* traffic, and what there was could be fairly quickly deciphered by the *WS* party, which by now had got its eye in. Moreover, the organization of Naval Section was still somewhat fluid, so that manpower could be switched to where it was most needed. At this time the main cipher used by the Italian Navy was the C 38m machine, a Swedish invention commercially and internationally available. It was less problematic than *Schluessel* M but had its own complexities. Every month it was given a new setting which was rapidly broken at Bletchley by three very able young men (one of whom, Colin Thompson, was later to be curator of the Scottish National Gallery). But for a week or so each individual signal had to be deciphered separately by a cryptographic process known as 'rodding'. This was largely and successfully undertaken by the *WS* party. The traffic could be interesting, or even of operational importance, since it might give the routes chosen for transport and supply ships reinforcing Rommel's army.

Credit and criticism of cryptographers

With the manpower available to them, the successes attained by the cryptographers might be called reasonably good. What is less clear and more controversial is how well those successes were exploited. Material learnt from hand-cipher signals was not only graded as less reliable than Enigma material; it was also given a more restricted circulation. I was once on duty at the Admiralty when a *WS* signal about a German ship that was in trouble in the Bight was teleprinted from Bletchley. Both the Admiralty's duty officer and I thought this should be passed to the Air Ministry but it was discovered that the rules forbade it. Again, once on leave I met an old friend who was then in the War Office at the receiving end from Bletchley's Hut 3. His job was to know where and in what strength all units of the German Army were at any given moment, especially on the Russian front. He told me he would give a lot to know how much shipping passed east or westbound in the Baltic every day. At that period I was in the habit of deciphering each morning a *WS* signal from *Wachtschiff Warnemuende* giving precisely this information. I advised consultation with Naval Section through Hut 3. My friend did this and was told that nothing of the sort was known. Such unreliable information could not be passed to the War Office. Sometimes, too, the identification of U-boats in the Baltic from *WS* signals was not sent to the Admiralty until it was confirmed—sometimes days or even weeks later—by the machine.

All this had certain adverse effects on the morale of those working on hand cipher. It brought to a head certain chronic tensions between cryptography and intelligence which were notable at least in Bletchley's Naval Section. It may exemplify the friction between production and sales management that is liable to emerge in any industry. Each party looked somewhat askance at the other. To the intelligence officer, cryptographers were apt to appear as unworldly, absent-minded, eccentric, ill-dressed academics. To the cryptographer, the intelligence officer could appear to be too political by half and often as a shameless empire builder.

Part of the problem was that cryptography, however successful, does not make a good exhibit for showing to a visiting admiral, who is thought to be happier if he is seeing a map full of flags and pins. Moreover, one intelligence officer could and did complain that a certain cryptographer seemed strangely unmoved when told suddenly that the *Scharnhorst* had been sunk. This might well have been due to his having had no means of knowing that the *Scharnhorst* was at sea and/or to his being at the moment immersed in a long bigram count.

Almost certainly a number of intelligence officers had presupposed that cryptography had its own mystique requiring very special mathematical insights amounting virtually to genius. They were then surprised to find that most cryptographers were in fact fairly ordinary if moderately intelligent people and, further, that a good deal of deciphering owed something to the fortuitous capture of some document such as a code-book or a set of tables, not to mention cribs. In other words, they discovered that there was hardly such a thing as 'pure' cryptography. One holder of high office in Naval Section recorded in an official memorandum that 'in this war we have at last been able to call the bluff of cryptography'. Such an attitude, often made fairly obvious, contributed to the cryptographer's *malaise*.

If a cryptographer is unsuccessful, for whatever reason, he tends to be forgotten or possibly misjudged. If he is consistently successful, his work may be taken for granted or supposed much easier than it actually is. This impression was probably heightened in the minds of the higher powers in Naval Section, who were not without a tinge of male chauvinism, by the fact that some of the Section's best cryptographers were women, not least Ruth Briggs.

A very distinguished cryptographer on the permanent staff of GC&CS was once asked what he regarded as a cryptographer's principal requirements, and replied, 'Oh, I suppose a sharp pencil and piece of squared paper.' There is a grain of truth in this view. Except on the really highest slopes, attained only by a Turing, a Knox, or a Welchman, or a Max Newman, where quasi-mathematical genius is required, the cryptographer's main requisites are probably patience, accuracy, stamina, a reasonably clear head, some experience, and an ability to work with others. This last, teamwork, is important but paradoxically can also be a cause of friction, since it tends to make of the cryptographer a natural democrat who may not fit too easily into a hierarchical system, which Naval Section undoubtedly was.

One young lieutenant in the Royal Naval Volunteer Reserve, though able, industrious, and a polyglot scholar, was reprimanded for writing an intelligence report which was critical of Admiral Dönitz. He was told that it was most improper for a lieutenant to criticize an admiral in any way whatsoever.

One set of decisions, taken largely on administrative grounds, contributed not a little to disillusionment in the cryptographic party. This was the deliberate discontinuance of work on three readable German hand ciphers. In each case, admittedly, the intelligence value was diminishing, and in the case of *WS* the traffic itself was dwindling, as was its importance as a provider of cribs. Work on the K code was deemed to have outlived its usefulness once the fighting had moved far inland from the coast, and work on it ceased in August 1944. The decision later in the same month to stop work on the higher-grade *Schluessel Henno* was more controversial. With the staff available it was only being partially read; and the staff allegedly was urgently required elsewhere in the Section. Work on *WS* was continued till the end of February 1945 and, with its demise, the cryptographic part of German Naval Section was virtually wound up. To some of the cryptographers these measures offended against what to them seemed a first principle, namely, that what was worth an enemy's while to encipher must be worth our while to decipher.

The controversy, particularly over the case of *Henno*, may have accentuated the cryptographers' occasional grumpiness. What is certain and must certainly be said is that the cryptographers' morale was never for one moment impoverished in the only sense that mattered. Their earlier discontents were mainly over having to do so much besides cryptography, and their final *cri de cœur* was a lament at having no more cryptography to do. No one who saw them at work, especially in a period after one of their ciphers had changed, could have doubted their zest and avidity for their own job. It might be said that the cryptographers were sometimes, like the British Army, unable to go about their work without swearing. But it will be remembered that the profanity of the British soldiers, though it may have met with frowns from army chaplains, has only once—in the wars against the Maoris—cost them the respect of their opponents. There is no evidence that even Joan of Arc had doubts about the fighting qualities of the 'Goddams'.

Perhaps a brief coda is required because, strictly speaking, the German Navy employed a twenty-eighth hand cipher. When the Germans finally withdrew from France they left garrisons in certain ports with instructions to hold out. Each was given its own cipher. Some used Enigma; others a hand cipher, and only one signal in the hand cipher was intercepted. This one signal came from the Channel Islands. It was self-evidently in a transposition cipher, the plain text having been put through a cage and drawn out so as to form one long anagram. There are relatively simple ways of dealing with this, unless the cage has been complicated by blank spaces or similar devices.

It fell to me to decipher this signal. And it read: *Frankreich ist das bedeutendes Weinland der Welt* ('France is the most important wine country in the world').

25. Tactical signals of the German Air Force

PETER GRAY LUCAS

THE long-range aircraft of the German Air Force communicated with their bases by what was then known as medium-wave and short-wave wireless telegraphy (W/T) using hand-operated Morse. Short-range aircraft (fighters and fighter-bombers) used speech, known as radio-telephony (R/T). Bombers were guided to their target by several different 'beam'-systems and were guided home by radio-beacons. Nearly all of this traffic could easily be intercepted by experienced W/T operators.

The security of messages rested on a code-book containing around a thousand items numbered in sequence. A message was encoded by writing out a list of three-digit numbers, each representing a phrase, word, or character which, when read in sequence, formed the intended message. It was then reciphered by looking up the numbers in a substitution table printed on a card, where for each number a random three-letter group would be found. Messages were deciphered by looking up the three-letter groups in the converse substitution table of random groups listed in alphabetical order, giving three-digit numbers which had to be looked up in the code-book. New substitution tables were issued from time to time. The code-book was in use before the war and was never significantly changed.

It was the substitution tables that brought air-to-ground traffic to Bletchley Park, in accordance with the principle that all codebreaking should be concentrated at GC&CS.

But the rationale of this principle, productive as it turned out to be in so many instances, was of course a great deal simpler than the rationale of events. In air operations they often conflicted. In a different culture, military and civilian bureaucracy could have kept 'correct' but ineffective procedures in place. What the official historians[1] have called the 'creative anarchy' that prevailed at GC&CS allowed people at all levels including the most junior to do what they judged, not always correctly, to be sensible in the circumstances. The results are therefore tinged with irony.

The basic irony, from the point of view of those whose achievement was to maintain rapid access to the code-book, was that aircraft in flight very seldom send interesting messages.

When the war started, the pre-war British arrangements remained in force. The principal intercept station was RAF Cheadle, on the moors between Cheadle and Leek in Staffordshire. A Warrant Officer was in charge of the intercept operators' room, with a telephone line to the three operational Commands to whom, without concealing the source, he passed on such information as could be inferred from German Air Force W/T activity recognized by his operators as they searched the known frequency bands.[2] The operator wrote down everything he heard, including the procedural exchanges. Any formal message was passed into the teleprinter room and sent promptly but without undue haste to Bletchley, where it was decoded, translated, edited, and sent by teleprinter to the Air Ministry in London. In rare cases, it may have been sent on from there to the Commands and perhaps married to the activity report previously received from Cheadle. It was not the practice to pass information back to the Warrant Officer about the messages his operators had taken, though no doubt he gleaned snippets from his friends in the Air Ministry. At first the tables were changed at intervals measured in weeks.

The codebreaking unit at Bletchley, whose job it was to compile the substitution tables, happened to consist of a Professor of Classics from Cambridge, and a Russian émigré who spoke English with an appropriate accent. In December 1939 they were joined by four undergraduates from Cambridge, selected for their proficiency in German. They were called computors with an 'O', a term previously in use for those who did arithmetical donkey-work such as compiling mathematical tables. Their job was to decode and translate intercepted messages, using the substitution tables worked out by the codebreakers. They did this loyally for a few weeks, sitting in a hut at Bletchley.

It was soon perceived that this was not a sensible arrangement. The four computors moved to RAF Cheadle, where they sat at a large table in the middle of the air-intercept room. The operators sat at their receivers ranged round the walls and handed their intercepts to the computors. The messages were immediately decoded, translated, and shown to the Warrant Officer in charge of the room, who passed them to the Commands as he thought fit. A sighting report from a German reconnaissance aircraft, for example, reached Coastal Command almost as soon as it reached its own base. The decoded and translated signals were sent immediately by teleprinter to the Air Ministry. The original signals continued to be sent to Bletchley for the benefit of the codebreakers.

Some time later, the German Air Force began to change the substitution table every day. The codebreakers set themselves to respond quickly. The first breaks would begin to come through from Bletchley by mid-morning, but the computors at Cheadle had not sat idly waiting. The cryptographic task was not difficult. The only permitted elements in a message were the items in the code-book, which were known, and of these only a small proportion were in regular use. (The content of messages could often be roughly predicted, although it was seldom of great interest.) The puzzle was to turn rough guesses into exact fits.

Helped by their daily familiarity with the traffic, and by a North Sea weather reconnaissance aircraft which transmitted a series of almost standard messages beginning at first light, the night-shift computors were well into the day's table before the day shift came on duty. Further traffic, including copious but erratic traffic from training units, was indexed as soon as the operators handed it across, guesses were noted and amended or confirmed, and information from the partial or tentative readings was passed, if the Warrant Officer thought fit, to the Commands. The computors never thought to ask permission to break codes. They did not even know about the principle that all codebreaking should be concentrated at Bletchley.

Eventually the codebreakers in Bletchley gave up and the computors became self-sufficient. A batch of fresh graduates, including young women, joined them in the summer of 1940. Further replenishments arrived from time to time. Some asked to be called up and posted to combatant units. Some were put hastily into uniform and posted to other theatres, including Egypt, to deal with local traffic. One sailed in the naval force escorting the Murmansk convoy PQ 17, to deal with signals from the long-range FW 200 reconnaissance aircraft operating from Norway. He was lost with his ship.

The band of computors remained at Cheadle until the end of the war. The only change the German Air Force made to its air-to-ground communications system, apart from a gradually growing regard for radio silence, was to replace the three-digit–three-letter substitution table with a three-digit reciprocal table, presumably for reasons of efficiency, since one table now served for both enciphering and deciphering. ('Reciprocal' means that if 123 encyphers to 456, 456 also enciphers to 123.) This made it a little easier to reconstruct each day's table.

There is a prima-facie controversy as to where the responsibility for gathering intelligence should lie: with those who need to use it, which implies that it should be dispersed among operational Commands and specialized Services; or with those skilled in gathering it, which tends to imply centralization. The commonsense answer might be that it depends on circumstances; but, since circumstances are not always known and are frequently unpredictable, a general principle may be needed for organizational reasons. The argument put forward by CG&CS had prevailed, and it was not confined to technical aspects of cryptography. CG&CS required full access to centralized exploitation of the intelligence contained in its decrypts to maintain its cryptographic successes. Guessing at the content of messages is as important in high-grade cryptography as anywhere else.

This principle was imperfectly implemented for air-to-ground traffic, no doubt in part because much useful and dependably available intelligence could be derived from it without reading the encoded messages; that is to say, without help from Bletchley. This source was known as traffic analysis (T/A) and was a prolific source of air intelligence.[3]

Signals were read during the land campaigns of 1939–40, but it is unlikely that they yielded any usable intelligence. The only recollection that survives is the excitement among the computors when a corrupt signal that they had rendered as 'harass refugees' was read out in a BBC bulletin, since they had by then realized that their emendation was wrong and should have been 'protect refugees': *Flueqtlinge sqonen* (with 'q' for 'ch' in German signals usage) not, as they had read, *stoeren*. No correction was broadcast.

After the fall of France, German Air Force operations against Britain settled into a stable pattern. From time to time there were changes in strategy, such as the end of attacks on coastal shipping and the end of the Blitz, but no change in what might be called the infrastructure, essentially the communication and command system. The principal feature of this system as regards operational intelligence was that no operation was mounted without interceptable signals being transmitted by a ground station at the home base and by each individual aircraft. Each unit used a different radio frequency. Thus, for example, the number of lines of traffic intercepted during a bombing raid represented the number of units taking part in the raid. In addition there were navigational aids: radio beacons for all operations and beams for the main bombing raids.

This signalling system provided intelligence in two main categories: intelligence relating to intervention in current operations, and intelligence about the strength, operating potential, and disposition of the long-range units of the German Air Force. There was also a third category that was sometimes useful. 'Rogue' signals were occasionally transmitted between ground stations in error or because the normal method of communication had broken down.

When a ground station (base, beam, or beacon) came on the air, this could signify that aircraft were already or were about to be airborne. RAF Cheadle had developed a high degree of skill in recognizing such transmissions and alerting the Commands. Coastal Command received advance warning of operations against shipping, and the night defences received information about the timing of raids and about flight paths and targets. Messages transmitted by aircraft in flight included sightings during operations against shipping and very short signals from bomber aircraft, mostly on passing pre-arranged points *en route* to and from the target or on suffering damage.

The daily report from Cheadle, giving a list of the lines of traffic that had been intercepted, with the number of aircraft call-signs heard, was in effect, after the elimination of training and other spurious traffic, a catalogue of the previous day's enemy air operations, incomplete only to the extent that a few signals could have been missed. This report was of course available every day without fail.

The value of both the pre-operational and the post-operational intelligence would be the greater, to the extent that the lines of traffic could be identified with the correct names of the units. Traffic security rested on frequently-changing frequencies and call-signs. The system for allocating them was never penetrated, but other means of identifying transmissions were found.

A limited amount of information had always been available about the names of units that had taken part in an operation. On approaching their base and preparing to land, aircraft changed to medium frequency and to fixed call-signs, part of the Air Safety Service,[4] but interception was difficult and incomplete. There was, of course, no radar and no air traffic control in the modern sense.

In the reliably interceptable high-frequency traffic, the units identified themselves by means of three-character alphanumeric call-signs. These were drawn from a vast random list which was in Allied hands and had been punched on to Hollerith cards and indexed. Sample call-signs had been studied at Bletchley but without revealing any pattern. It was said that some of them could not even be found. The computors knew why, but as they had been separated from Bletchley they were not drawn into the discussion. Instead they set about solving the problem independently.

The call-signs that occurred in a line of traffic could be seen to have a curiously variable structure, and the computors regarded this as an uncharacteristic idiosyncracy in an otherwise highly regular system. Two of them hit on the idea that these idiosyncracies might themselves be so regular that each unit could be identified by its style. They put themselves on the night shift when there was little air radio traffic and nobody in the station administrative offices. They cleared as much floor space as possible in the largest office, and began sorting the operators' log-sheets for several past weeks into piles with the same style. The piles on the floor showed that the styles were consistent and could be specified. Units could indeed be recognized by their style, but still needed to be named in terms of the known order-of-battle.

The names were gradually revealed through incidents. Mistakes and distress signals, papers from aircraft that had been shot down, interrogation reports, and other chance sources all contributed. Eventually all bomber units were identified, with some mistakes made along the way, and the daily reports were submitted under unit names.[5]

The two computors had heard rumours of a controversy raging in the Air Ministry about the size of the German bomber force. It had been calculated, they believed (correctly, as we now know from the official history[6]), by multiplying the number of known unit-names by a supposed, but actually nearly 50 per cent inflated, establishment of the smallest German Air Force unit, thus producing a figure which was preposterously high. This was known at Cheadle as 'the St Ives estimate', after the nursery rhyme: how many were going to St Ives?

The new method of identification, later inappropriately christened 'foot-printing', allowed the units taking part in a raid to be identified down to the lowest level and sometimes down to the individual aircraft. A chart was drawn up retrospectively and kept up nightly, with a column for each date and a row for each unit or, where possible, each aircraft. Details of call-signs were entered. There were, of course, errors, through not hearing or mis-hearing call-signs, but this chart appeared to give a sound, detailed, authentic, up-to-date representation of the actual strength of bomber forces operating against Great Britain.

The 'official' estimate was revealed by simple statistical calculations, which helped to show that the fighting establishment of the *Staffel*—the approximate equivalent of the RAF squadron—was nine aircraft, and not twelve, as the Air Ministry had hitherto believed. Had management rather than 'creative anarchy' been the preferred way of operating, the project might have been a research project instead of a midnight adventure on the office floor.

All this was going on at Cheadle under permissive supervision from Bletchley. The operational channel for Cheadle intelligence was the Warrant Officer's telephone line to the Commands, followed by daily reports to the Air Ministry. There was little contact with Bletchley over intelligence until the day when the computors decoded a 'rogue' message far longer than normal. It seemed to be the second half of a telegram. It was telephoned immediately to Bletchley, a search was made, and the first half was found. An Enigma machine had broken down in mid-message.

Adaptive as ever, the system responded, despite having coped perfectly with an unexpected incident with no operational significance. There were those who had felt for some time that low-grade and high-grade sources were not being effectively linked. Triggered by this episode, a liaison unit was set up in Hut 3. It consisted of a computor from Cheadle and a member of the Hut 3 staff. Its task was to feed Cheadle intelligence into the Hut 3 system through personal contacts and through the Index. Summary reports were produced daily and duly indexed, but it is doubtful whether there were any significant consequences.

Through making these summaries the liaison unit found itself serving as a 'next-day' review of the computors' 'real-time' operations at Cheadle. Occasionally information, revealed by further study of what the computors had done, was passed back to them. This review and surveillance, for which there had previously been no provision, may well have been the most useful consequence of the breakdown of somebody's Enigma machine.

There were other kinds of low-grade traffic, but none of great moment. A harbour defence command in Antwerp regularly received notice of 'own' aircraft about to fly over. On the afternoon of 14 November 1940 the signal read 'ANGRIFF [attack] KORN', but the computors could not guess at the time and did not learn until later that KORN was the code-word for Coventry.

When the Germans test-fired their V-weapons along the Baltic, the firings and landings were reported between the outstations and the base at Peenemunde in a home-made code so simple that it could virtually be read on sight. Presumably they had escaped the discipline of the normal signals-monitoring hierarchy. These reports may have helped to calm some of the wilder speculation about the size, range, and accuracy of these missiles.

Notes

1. F. H. Hinsley *et al.*, *British Intelligence in the Second World War*, I (London: HMSO, 1979), 273.
2. Ibid. 14.
3. Ibid. 24–5.
4. Ibid. 107–8.
5. Ibid. 319.
6. Ibid. 299–302.

PART FIVE
Japanese codes

26. Japanese naval codes

MICHAEL LOEWE

On 2 February 1942, some twenty young men reported at the showroom of the Gas Company, Bedford, within sight of the statue of John Bunyan that dominated the town. Until that day they had for the most part been engaged in reading for Classical Moderations at Oxford or for the Classical Tripos at Cambridge, where they had also been enrolled in the Officers' Training Corps and were destined for service in the Royal Artillery or other units of the armed forces. But the Japanese assault on the US fleet at Pearl Harbor brought a radical change to their lives and affected the careers of some of them in an unpredictable manner. For it very soon dawned on those who were responsible for organizing wartime intelligence that the services were lamentably short of Japanese linguists. Initially A. D. Lindsay, Master of Balliol, and Martin Charlesworth, President of St John's College, Cambridge, were invited to suggest the names of potential candidates who could be trained to make good the deficiency; and they were expected to name either undergraduates still at college pending call-up, or suitable young persons who were already serving in the forces.

Those enrolled at the Gas Company's showroom on that first day were later to be joined by a few others, including some members of the women's services who had been seconded to the course. This was established as an inter-service project, designed to serve the needs of intelligence units of the Navy, Army, and Air Force, and those of the Foreign Office. It was organized by the Inter-Service Special Intelligence School at Bedford.

Captain Oswald Tuck, RN, who had been trained as an interpreter and retired from the service in 1937, also reported to the Gas Company's showroom on that day, to assume responsibility for giving instruction in Japanese language. In all probability he had no more idea than his students of the nature of the work for which they were to be trained or the type of problem that they would be facing. Intended to last for six months, the course was expected to do no more than leave its students with sufficient command of the language to break ciphers, build up code-books, and translate or summarize Japanese signals traffic into 'Service English'. It was not expected that after a mere six months the students would be able to read Japanese literature, compose Japanese prose, or take part in a conversation in the language. Nor was there scope, in the realistic days of instruction in wartime, for much attention to the niceties of Japanese history or culture. It remained to be seen how far, at the end of six months, the brightest members of the class would be able to read the Japanese press or handle the correspondence of Japanese diplomats. As yet, there were no plans to train interpreters who could comprehend orally delivered messages—for example, from air to ground. The need was limited to that of understanding service messages conveyed by W/T and intercepted in the course of transmission.

At the time, provision for Japanese language-teaching in this country existed almost exclusively at the School of Oriental and African Studies, in London. Without the establishment of regular courses at other universities, and in the absence of language schools, there was no ready-made supply of teaching material on which an instructor could call, particularly for the purposes that were in mind. To introduce the grammar and the script, Captain Tuck had at his disposal, for use by the whole class, a number of copies of Commander Isemonger's *Elements of Written Japanese*; a few copies of Brinkley's dictionary; and one copy of a reasonably recent Sanseido dictionary. These were the tools with which the students were to learn to understand the stack of telegrams, printed in roman letters, and acquired from the Japanese press correspondents' offices when these had been closed down at the outbreak of hostilities.

Isemonger's book was probably the only one of its kind that was available. It presented a student with rows of Chinese characters reproduced in the stark, regular forms used in print, which gave little idea of the grace that a brush and handwriting can impart, and could not serve as models to be copied by hand. Brinkley's dictionary, first published in 1896, hardly set out to cover the language of everyday life, let alone the linguistic needs for the conduct of warfare in the twentieth century. It told a student that *sensui* meant 'an artificial pond, fountain', 'diving', or 'a water-spout'; it did not include the term *sensuikan*, 'a submarine'; *happyō* meant 'making known to the public', 'becoming manifest', 'revealing', 'disclosure', 'discovery'; there was no hint that, in contemporary military parlance, this was the regular word for 'a communiqué'; and all too often, words were defined within the choice and elegant context of Buddhist rituals. In its various Chinese characters *sentō* could mean 'a public bath', 'residence of a retired emperor', 'first scaling the wall of a besieged castle', 'fighting together' or 'scissors'; Brinkley did not hold with *sentōkan*, 'a battleship, or *sentōki*, 'a fighter-aircraft'.

So, when Captain Tuck taught his pupils to grapple with the basic forms of Japanese syntax, the complex system of agglutinization, and the difficulties inherent in a lack of expressly defined person, number, or tense, he had only the barest material on which he could call. Those trained in the Classics felt the absence of such grammatical adjuncts acutely, and the treatises on Japanese language that found their way into the room at some stage were not particularly helpful. But the arrival one day of a series of parcels meant that at last all the members of the class had their own copies of the basic works of reference that they needed; and all gained a new confidence that, with such tools available, they would be able to finish the job.

Distinguished members of the Bletchley Park hierarchy who came occasionally included Colonel Tiltman, never too busy to have a brief word with each student and to enquire about his or her progress; or J. E. S. Cooper, as yet unknown as Josh, who whetted the appetite for future work by telling how RAF officers were being rescued from the North Sea thanks to Bletchley's success in reading German ciphers. For by now the gaff had been blown; on at least one of his visits Colonel Tiltman had left a set of exercises of an entirely new nature: short ciphered texts, whose solution presented little difficulty. The more serious introduction to cryptanalysis which followed at the end of six months' work on language was organized by the Inter-Service Special Intelligence School and lasted for a few weeks.

Lance-Corporal Eric Ceadel, destined later to establish Japanese Studies as part of the Cambridge Tripos, was at this stage detailed to remain in Bedford as Captain Tuck's assistant for the next course. One or two members of the class were posted to Berkeley Street, to work on the diplomatic ciphers, but the great majority shortly found themselves in Bletchley Park. Here they were assigned to separate huts for work on the systems used by Japan's Navy, Army, or Air Force. In time some were transferred to stations that lay closer to the scene of operations, in either New Delhi or Colombo. The present writer was one of six 'boys' who joined the Naval Section; as communication with our colleagues who worked on military or air-force systems was forbidden, and as we were all too well disciplined to disobey such orders, we knew nothing of what went on outside our own immediate business. What follows concerns the efforts made in Elmer's School, Hut 7, and finally Block B.

At Bletchley Park we were overawed by the presence of those whom we saw as experienced professionals, clearly well accustomed to the arcane mysteries of code- and cipher-breaking, and well versed in naval intelligence. The tall and lanky figure of Hugh Foss seemed to look down from a great height on the raw recruits assembled in his office; regular naval officers, resplendent in their gold-braided uniforms, put the young civilians in their place. By way of introduction to the war in the Pacific, we were handed files of our own naval communications to read. These included copies, on pink paper if memory serves correctly, of signals sent from the Admiralty to units of the Royal Navy; the first of these carried the ominous command, 'Commence hostilities against Japan immediately repeat immediately.' The stamped mark of Top Secret which headed these messages could hardy fail to thrill the callow minds of the young readers, proud beyond measure of their university careers and of their ability to handle some Japanese, but woefully ignorant of all matters naval. As often as not we were too proud to ask for elucidation of baffling terms such as CINCPAC (Commander-in-Chief Pacific) with which these papers abounded. This latter deficiency was partly made good for some of us at a later stage, when we were sent to spend a few days on board a minesweeper, or a frigate that was escorting a convoy up or down the east coast.

In the meantime there was little formal training in getting to work with the traffic. This came to us late; there was no question, as there was for the German and Italian sides, of working in immediate response to intercepted messages and affecting the course of an operation. Step by step we became acquainted with some of the different systems that the Japanese were using; with code-books whose groups consisted of four elements of the *kana* syllabary, such as the elusive *ne-no-su-so*, and thus theoretically capable of including 48^4 entries; or code-books formed of four-figure or five-figure groups, and thus more easily amenable to reciphering. We learnt how to recognize the different types of system that were in use; how to identify cardinal features such as the indicators, and how the solution of the ciphering process could be achieved; and we learnt to work out and master the 'garble tables' or other devices whereby the accuracy of the code-groups could be tested.

The present writer can say nothing of the way in which the machine ciphers were broken; the greater part of the work on which we were engaged was that of 'stripping'—that is, recovering and removing the reciphering tables that had been applied to the underlying code-groups—and 'book-building'—that is, recovering the meaning of those groups. Long weary hours of the war were thus spent in subtracting figures from figures, or indexing the code-groups. These were in the form either of four figures, in JN 11, which was used by merchant shipping; or of five figures in JN 25, the main naval code which was used in its varied forms by all ships, including submarines, the four major bases of Yokosuka, Sasebo, Maizuru, and Kure, and the shore stations dotted around the Pacific Ocean. (See also the detailed description of JN 25 in the appendix to Chapter 27.)

New code-books were brought into use from time to time, sometimes with a specialized distribution; the additive tables with which the messages were enciphered were subject to more frequent change. Usually the initial steps in breaking the newly introduced code-books had been taken by our American colleagues, who had had earlier access to the material. For long there was no systematic agreement which determined how the efforts of each party could be used to greatest advantage and with least wastage by way of duplication.

Often the break into a new code-book was achieved by way of identifying the predictable routine messages sent by the Japanese shore stations, framed according to prescribed forms and with recognizable patterns. More rarely, unless memory is at fault, we could be helped by a 'crib' in the form of a message sent twice, once in an old readable system, and once with the newly introduced book. Captured documents, that began to filter in with increasing frequency as the months passed, gave a book-builder an idea of what to look for.

Of its very nature, the process of book-building was cumulative; and it remained true that in all probability the choicest details or the nearly unique features of a message would baffle solution, however long the code-book had been in use. For such details necessarily called on the use of code-groups that had never been seen before in Bletchley Park, and therefore lacked all clues for identification. To this extent a code-book, rather than a cipher or even a machine cipher, could retain a high degree of security, even until it was replaced by its successor. Code-books also possessed one further advantage for the users, in that the fundamental medium for encoding and decoding was that of Chinese character and *kana* syllables; ciphers depended entirely on romanized forms of the language.

Stripping depended on the repeated use of the same sections of the long additive tables with sufficient frequency to make it possible to identify the underlying code-groups; book-building depended on the appearance of code-groups in a series of varied contexts, such that the recovery of their meanings was consistent. Much of the basic investigation on which this rested could be completed quickly by Hollerith punched-card machinery. But naval Japanese was for long the Cinderella of Block B, where the main effort was understandably directed to German and Italian problems. It was only after the defeat of the Italians that such machinery became available with reasonable frequency.

As the months passed the effort devoted to Japanese problems became more and more methodical. Paymaster-Commanders Macintyre and Parsons, and Captain Thatcher, all regular Royal Navy officers, had been engaged in the work in earlier years; and they set about organizing the systematic preparation of the JN 25 traffic. Supporting staff, who were not trained in cipher-breaking or language, kept a register of each message received. They then wrote out, on the special forms that had been printed, the call-signs of the originator and the addressee, with their identification; the groups as received; those groups less the figures of the additive table, which they had subtracted; and, in romanized form, the recovered value of the groups, where known. They also kept the cumulative index of all code-groups. The messages were then brought to the book-builders' room in batches of one hundred, bound together in files designed for the purpose. Bletchley's carpenters even built a few specially designed racks to hold these files; until recently one of these did duty in the Faculty of Oriental Studies, Cambridge, to support the twelve volumes of Morohashi's Chinese–Japanese dictionary.

Every six months saw the addition of newly trained linguists, taught either at Bedford or at the School of Oriental and African Studies. We had also been joined by a few senior men who had served as consular officers. Their knowledge of Japanese was infinitely superior to ours; our know-how of cryptographic procedures was deeper than theirs. These officers included John Lloyd, who at one time ran a course of language instruction in the Park itself, thereby again increasing our numbers.

All in all the value of this work seen in retrospect was highly questionable. The American effort was much larger than ours and their coverage was more extensive. American and British stations abroad maintained direct contact with naval headquarters; our own scrambler telephones, painted green, led to a few high-level offices in the Admiralty, for discussion of policy rather than the immediate conduct of the war. Certainly there were occasions when Block B solved some of the problems, or read some of the messages, before Op-20-G in Washington, the US Navy's Code and Signals Section. From the thousands of messages that were read it became possible to track the growth or decline of some Japanese base units, to extend the knowledge of Japanese naval habits, and to confirm or correct existing ideas of the state of readiness of His Imperial Majesty's ships. Occasionally we could produce a report on a subject, such as radar, in an attempt to show how its use had developed over the months; but necessarily the value of such work was limited, as there was no certain means of assessing what proportion of the Japanese Navy's signals had been intercepted or successfully decrypted.

Memories recall a few personal incidents: the daily issue of meal tickets, when it was sometimes possible to cheat; the illicit supply by one member of the staff of a replacement for that lost cardboard rectangle that served as a pass; the Wrens who decided one Christmas Eve that enough was enough and marched down the corridors of Block B singing carols lustily; the concerts that were given by local talent; and the close of an era that May morning when Nigel de Grey, Deputy Director, assembled us in the open air to confirm that the German war was truly at an end. Some of us remained in the ensuing months; and if we had thought that our knowledge of Japanese language had been improving over the years, we suffered a rude shock one morning in August. Instead of the coded messages reporting the routine arrival of the odd aircraft at a naval station, we were handed a long teleprinted text in plain language—plain doubtless to the operator who had sent it, but barely comprehensible to us. For it was the Emperor's command to cease hostilities, couched in the dignified and traditional language appropriate to so august an occasion. Copies of the much despised Brinkley's dictionary might well have come into their own. But they had long since been abandoned at Bedford; perhaps the odd volume may still be tucked away in one of the cupboards of the Gas Company's showroom.

27. Bedford–Bletchley–Kilindini–Colombo

HUGH DENHAM

TUESDAY, 13 January 1942, just over five weeks after Pearl Harbor. I was 19. I had been at Jesus College, Cambridge, for a year reading Classics, and was expecting to be called up at any time. In fact I had already enlisted voluntarily, and served for 'one day' (actually about a quarter of an hour) as a Fusilier—during which period, the certificate said, my conduct had been 'EXEMPLARY'; they then stand you down until they are ready for you.

At about six that evening I called in on my school-friend Bun (Derek Weaver) at St John's, and chatted for half an hour. As I was leaving he mentioned, as an example of how crazy the world had become, that his tutor, the Revd Martin Charlesworth, had offered him a job in intelligence—six months' course to learn Japanese, then to London or the Far East; like nearly everything else was in those times, it was 'all very hush-hush'. I burst out laughing with him. Then I realized that this was *exactly* what I wanted to do. I immediately called on Charlesworth, who said that he had already put fifteen names forward, but that he would do what he could for me. I spent the next week able to think only of oriental languages and that little sun-drenched intelligence outfit in Malaya (Singapore had not yet fallen). I restlessly called again on Charlesworth as he breakfasted in his dressing-gown, but he of course knew nothing further. Then, within a week, came a letter from Colonel Tiltman, announcing an interview at Devonshire House the coming Friday. It seemed that Friday would never come.

'What are your interests?' the interviewing Board asked.

'Quite varied. At the moment I am teaching myself Hebrew.'

'Are you keen, and prepared to work hard?'.

'Yes'.

Then Colonel Tiltman: 'How is your health?' and 'Do you have any religious scruples about reading other people's correspondence?'

It seemed hard to believe afterwards that the Board would fail me, but I could barely wait for Monday morning's post, and was in despair when it contained nothing. Tuesday's post *did* include a buff envelope for me, the College porter said, but he did not know what had happened to it. Not until midday did it turn up, to say that I was to report to Bedford in six days' time. I was too excited for lunch.

Bedford

We reported at Bedford on Monday, 2 February, and started next day at Ardour House, the Gas Company's corner site; we were in their showroom on the first floor, with the shop in use below. Colonel Tiltman said a few words about the need for secrecy, and then left us with Captain Tuck, RN (retd.). Captain Tuck was an impressive figure, with an impressive white beard. 'When I come into the room,' he began, 'you are to stand up. I shall then say *shokun ohayō*, which means "all you princes are honourably early". You will then reply *ohayōgazaimasu*, which means "honourably early it honourably is". I shall now leave the room and come in again, and we shall do this.' Which we did.

There were about twenty-two of us, mainly classicists, all male but one. Some I already knew. Our hours were to be 9.30 to 12.30 and 2 to 5, including Saturday mornings. Each day everyone was to move back one row, so that everyone had a turn at the front.

By the second week we had learnt the two fifty-long 'alphabets', *katakana* and *hiragana*, and about a hundred Chinese characters, and by the third week we were laboriously translating plain-text telegrams supplied by Bletchley or London. These hand-me-downs, never available in sufficient quantity, were to be our mainstay for the rest of the course, sometimes varied by Japanese newspapers that Tuck produced. Our first textbook was a primer by Isemonger. These arrived early on; lovely volumes with big pages, bound in green; a delight to use. The invaluable Rose–Innes character dictionaries did not come until mid-April, and not until mid-May was Tiltman able to provide us each with the basic Kenkyusha dictionary, specially reproduced and bound for the occasion.

The 2,294-page Japanese-to-English Kenkyusha dictionary is a treasure; a 7½" × 5" × 3½" culture shock; a bedside book in its own right. The dictionary gives the English meanings of some forty thousand Japanese words. In most cases the meanings are illustrated by

Japanese sentences, with English translation. The sentences are often surprising. For instance, the Japanese word for 'supper' is illustrated by the sentence, 'I will meet you after supper outside the brothel.'

The words too can be surprising. There is one for 'rolling up one's sleeves and grinding one's teeth in chagrin' and one for 'trying out a new sword on a passer-by'. *Enkōkinkō* means 'to adopt a policy of befriending distant nations and antagonising neighbours'. And how about the succinct *tōden*—'to make surreptitious use of electricity'?

On 15 June we moved from Ardour House to larger and more permanent premises at 7 St Andrews Road. We proceeded to allocate suitable names to each room—the big one, for instance, was known as the Sign of the Inconspicuous Elephant. But by then the course was beginning to break up. We now knew about a thousand characters, which included those normally used in official and military telegrams, and we could handle texts that were reasonably straightforward. Jon Cohen and Alan Douglas had already been posted temporarily to the Diplomatic Section at Berkeley Street; they went as sample 'products' of the course, and acquitted themselves well; others were working at Albany Road on an undisclosed task. The course formally ended on 27 June.

The experts at the London School of Oriental and African Studies had told Tiltman that no Japanese language course could succeed in less than two years. When, therefore, news spread of the progress at Bedford, we began to receive visitors. In early June Josh Cooper, Head of the Air Section at Bletchley, came to say that we were 'very famous, and much in demand in London'. Shortly after, Admiral Godfrey—Director, no less, of Naval Intelligence—walked into the room, spoke to Tuck, and said to us that the Navy badly wanted us. Towards the end of June Tiltman was able to be more definite. We had reached the point, he said, where we could go abroad without further ado. It would be the standard Bedford cryptanalysis course, a month at Bletchley, and then off; indeed, some of us would be off straight away—the Wiles brothers to Bletchley, and Ceadel, Gibson, Leary, Lloyd-Jones, and Robinson to Captain Kennedy's office in London, which we gathered worked on Japanese military material. The rest were to start the cryptanalysis course on 29 June.

The crypto course was a good one, and stood us in good stead in the years to come. It was also all-absorbing. Even if the task is only an exercise, there is nothing like the exhilaration of the moment when a cryptanalytical problem first 'gives', when you know that the rigid thing is going to crumble; conversely, there is nothing like the demoralization when you can make no progress. At the end, Jon Cohen, Wynn Davies, Johnnie Lambert, Mike Loewe, John Sutcliffe, and I were assigned to the Japanese Naval Section at Bletchley and we arrived on 21 August.

Bletchley

The Naval Section was under Birch. The Japanese part of it, under Foss, was forty strong, and was housed at Elmer's School, a short distance from Bletchley Park proper. There were two Japanese translators already in place, Lieutenant-Commander Keith, and Mr Nichol. Accommodation was tight, but by squeezing up even more tightly they managed to find a small room in which the six of us were installed. We were introduced all round, and then went in to Keith for instructions. He said that there were about a thousand encrypted Japanese naval messages intercepted every day, of which some seven hundred were in the general system, JN 25 (see Appendix to this chapter for details of Japanese naval cryptography). A fraction of these reached Bletchley within days—in fact under forty a day, intercepted at Flowerdown in the United Kingdom. (When we arrived at Bletchley in August 1942 the only available current Japanese naval intercept traffic was that from the station at Flowerdown near Winchester. It must have been forwarded by courier, because it took several days to arrive. In September 1942 we managed to have it teleprinted. Presumably this was done by land-line, unenciphered.) Some of the remainder were in due course forwarded by bag from elsewhere. He said that current material was handled expeditiously at Washington, Kilindini (the port of Mombasa, then the headquarters of the Eastern Fleet), and Melbourne. The Bletchley party had up to that point, he said, achieved nothing. Whenever they began to attack a problem, the solution arrived from another centre and they turned to something else. He said that there was no work in the section for six Japanese linguists.

And so we started. To familiarize us with the material, we were given boxes of messages encoded by a book called JN 4C, with recoveries to date in the 'system' (a body of messages encrypted in the same way was called a 'system'), and we were left to get on with it. The system had become obsolete four days previously.

It would not be profitable to describe our work over the succeeding months in any detail. It was clear that everything that Keith had said was to the point. The Japanese Naval Section had virtually no current messages to work on, and was not in touch with customers. No desk in the section had contact with the operational world.

The section was equally unfitted for research work—that is to say, for studying and solving unsolved systems. Different cryptanalytical problems are tackled in different ways. Some can be worked on *in vacuo* by analysts and mathematicians, but progress on systems like the Japanese naval codes is made in an operational context. For instance, you find a message that has been encrypted and transmitted twice, once in a solved system and once in an unsolved one. Similarly you look for a message which, say, reports 'enemy'—i.e. British or Allied—activity; since you know what we actually did, you know what the Japanese are reporting. This is called 'collateral' information, and it was not available at BP—it took us three months to get so much as a map of the Solomon Islands (where the fighting then was). And even if these handicaps were overcome, the Japanese Naval Section at Bletchley did not possess the tools or the staff. Computers as we now know them did not exist in 1942, but it was possible at that time to handle clerical work by Hollerith punched-card machinery, which was essential to do justice to the task of registering, indexing, and analysing the copious Japanese communications. For whatever reason, Hollerith resources were not made available to the Japanese Naval Section until after the Italian surrender. While we were at Bletchley, we had a limited amount of human clerical assistance; but we spent most of our precious time on tasks of a purely mechanical nature, such as making indexes of the code-groups that occurred in the boxfuls of obsolete JN 4 messages. We were always trying to catch up. Sometimes captured material arrived for translation, but here too translations arrived from elsewhere before we had finished. In contrast, it was reported that the size of the JN 25 party at Washington was already 250 people.

In September the section moved from Elmer's to a new building in the Park proper, and the following February it moved again to Hut 7. New staff continued to arrive, including Lieutenant-Commander Parsons from Kilindini. We arranged a sort of shift system, not because there was anything urgent to be done but because of the cramped accommodation and the limited tools (for instance, indexes). We looked at JN 25 a bit, but spent most of the time on JN 4 and minor codes, producing recoveries of code-group meanings whenever we got our heads above the sea of clerical work and indexing. Quite a lot of effort was spent on editing signals from Washington and sending them on to Kilindini—why this was necessary is hard now to say.

Communications with Kilindini, etc., were by Typex. Typex is an 'off-line' enciphering machine; that is to say, the plain text is keyed in to the machine by hand, and an enciphered text is printed out, which in turn is sent by radio in Morse, by hand. This is clearly a labour-intensive process, and signals to and from the other centres could in fact be delayed by up to four days. It is not practicable to forward large quantities of intercepted cipher messages by these methods; such a requirement calls for a teleprinter link protected by an 'on-line' cipher machine.

As far as I am aware, at that time we did not possess the means of transmitting teleprinter text securely by high frequency. Operational centres for signals intelligence, therefore, had to be near their point (or points) of intercept.

The Japanese Naval Section continued to grow after we left, and after the Italian armistice it absorbed the Italian Naval Section. With one exception, as far as I have discovered, none of those who worked there remembers doing anything useful. In the words of one colleague, 'the recoveries that the section made and circulated were few, tentative and regarded with condescension'. This statement agrees with the impressions which we formed at Kilindini and Colombo. The exception was study of the Japanese cipher machines, called Jade (naval) and Coral (naval attaché), which were only worked on at Washington and in the United Kingdom, and where it is understood that the section at Bletchley made contributions of value.

Kilindini had said they wanted three people, and these were to be Jon Cohen, Wynn Davies, and myself. In anticipation of the posting we had been transferred from the Army pay roll to that of the Foreign Office. As yet we did not know when we would leave, but on 25 February I received a letter from Sir Alexander Cadogan, the Permanent Under-Secretary, signed by an official, to see the official that afternoon. Shortly after two o'clock I was admitted through the barrier in Downing Street, and entered the palatial premises of the Foreign Office. As I sat in the ante-room, the official's secretary made tea and chatted and his typist read a novel. At three o'clock the official returned from lunch, and told me that we would go by sea to Lagos, and then, since we were needed with some urgency, we would fly across Africa to Mombasa and Kilindini.The journey took over seven weeks—from 4 March, on board alongside the dark streets of Liverpool, to the morning of 23 April when our train steamed over the causeway on to Mombasa island, but there is no space here to describe the decimation of the convoy by U-boats, or the exotic days and weeks we spent *en route* in six different African countries.

Kilindini

When in April 1942 Vice-Admiral Nagumo burst into the Indian Ocean with his carriers, sinking anything he found, Admiral Sir James Somerville had withdrawn his scratch Eastern Fleet from Colombo to Kilindini in Kenya. On our arrival at Kilindini we were attached to the Chief of Intelligence Staff (COIS) of this Eastern Fleet. Our unit, HMS Alidina, was housed in Alidina, a requisitioned Indian school on the rocky northern shore of the island. Bruce Keith, recently promoted to Commander (and later to become Captain), had replaced Shaw as officer in command. Freed from the frustrations of the BP Naval Section, he was a new man, and ran a happy, purposeful ship. The senior Japanese translators were Lieutenant-Commanders Barham and Curnock, members of a group of naval officers whom the Royal Navy had had learn the language before the war. (Other members of the group were Macintyre and Parsons, who returned to BP, and Forman, who was sunk and drowned on the way home off Freetown at the same time as we were in harbour there. There were also Merry and Nave at Melbourne.) We were joined by Biggs and Cheke, career diplomats, interned and later released by the Japanese, and a Dutch naval officer, Brouwer. The cryptanalysts at Kilindini were MacInnes, Sharman, Stanton, and Townend, Foreign Office civilians like ourselves.

The 'front line' of the unit was the wireless operators, who intercepted the enemy messages; then the analysts and their staff stripped off the additive key (see Appendix, under JN 11 and JN 25); the linguists established the meanings of the code-groups and translated the texts, for prompt reporting to COIS at Naval Headquarters. At the end of each day we went to the back of the building and supervised the incineration of the secret waste. There was a limited amount of assistance from Hollerith machinery, though much less than became available later on. It was a coherent operation, in a way self-contained, although of course, as the Japanese code-books and key-tables began to change more rapidly, it depended more on the result exported from the large, vigorous party at Washington—normally referred to by us by its cover-name, Susan. However, although our cryptanalytic contribution was eclipsed in quantity by that of Susan, we felt that our recoveries of additives, code-group meanings, etc., were not insignificant, and we prided ourselves on their quality. One of Kilindini's contributions was Brian Townend's break into JN 40, the merchant-shipping cipher in November 1942. The JN 25 party was the main one; we worked in one of the big school rooms, and we spread the additive sheets and the texts and the indexes out on huge laboratory tables, which we pushed together into the centre of the room. With regard to the translated decrypts which went to COIS, we scrupulously distinguished between, on the one hand, what we could categorically guarantee, and, on the other, words or passages where there was an element of doubt—perhaps because of garbled intercept, or uncertain code-group meanings; the bulk of a decrypt would be in the former category, but there were often gaps. When we were unable to provide current decrypts because of a change of code-book or reciphering keys, we used the time to go back over recent material, to squeeze more out of it.

All key and code recoveries and other cryptanalytic information were exchanged between BP, Kilindini, Melbourne, and Susan by signals enciphered by the secure but cumbersome Typex system. (There were also subunits at Brisbane and Pearl Harbor, with whom we were not in regular direct touch.) Intercepted Japanese naval messages were exchanged, as far as possible, by bag. Thus for current intelligence we relied on what we intercepted on the spot. However, if a message was clearly important for the Eastern Fleet but had been intercepted locally in a garbled condition, we would hope to do better when another copy arrived from elsewhere. Garbling, incidentally, is the bane of a cryptanalyst's life. It is hard enough to read what the enemy had intended you not to read, but when you do not know exactly what cipher text he actually transmitted, the difficulties are more severe.

Alidina was small enough for most people to know each other. The clerical staff consisted partly of a group of local expatriate civilians, most of whom found themselves little suited to this, or indeed any, type of work. The rest were some two or three dozen Wrens. Later this total of Wrens steadily increased, reaching perhaps over five times that number. The Wrens, almost without exception, did a superb job. They were young, usually well educated, away from home probably for the first time, living under tight discipline on low pay in austere accommodation, and engaged on routine work of an opaque nature. They did it all accurately, conscientiously, and cheerfully. I remember a draft arriving in Colombo and two of them coming on watch, their first time in a new climate, in a new country, on a new job. At one stage during the night the two were asked to go into the next room, which was empty, and fetch a certain file. They seemed to take a bit of time, but eventually they returned with the required item. Then, five minutes later, with iron self-control, one of the girls asked, 'By the way, what do you do when there's a snake in the filing cabinet?'

The outstanding figure was George Curnock. He led from the front. He was not only a proficient linguist, who inspired and organized; he also produced intelligence. It is one thing to know a language, but it requires special talents to extract sense from a fragmentary text, to assign meanings to hitherto unsolved code-groups, and to recover additive keys. Curnock was not rivalled by those of his contemporaries whom we met. He would, in his own words, 'gin himself up', arrive at Alidina at 6 a.m., and sail through the texts with a momentum that carried him across the gaps. He taught us what could be achieved (gin or no gin), and how to perform our technical duties to a very high standard of productivity and reliability. On the administrative side, he organized amongst other things a proper reporting service for relaying the results to COIS, and probably accomplished much else that we were not aware of. When later he went home on three months' leave, the unit noticably deteriorated, both in efficiency and in co-operation among senior staff. In due course he moved over to head the reporting party. Out of the office he was equally memorable.

We worked long hours, usually seven days a week, with a half day off when convenient. In August two of us took leave to climb to the summit of Mount Kilimanjaro just over the border in Tanganyika. When we returned to Kilindini, Naval Headquarters had returned to Colombo and HMS Alidina was deserted. We followed by warship, and disembarked in Colombo harbour on 14 September 1943.

Colombo

This was now our home for the rest of the war. The unit had become HMS Anderson, and was housed in a range of single-storey buildings on the south-east fringe of town, a mile or so back from the sea. We had felt before that we had been doing a good job, but with the reinforcements that steadily arrived over the next two years I suppose that we must have done better still—more, and faster. The intercept operators and the communications staff had always kept watches. At first at Colombo the 'production' staff worked day and evenings, with a duty officer sleeping on the premises overnight. Then, at the beginning of March 1944, we went over to full 168-hours-a-week watch-keeping, including Christmas Day. The main party was the JN 25 one, handling 150–200 messages a day. Two further parties exploited JN 11 and JN 40. There were other activities on the station manned by naval staff with which we were less closely involved—including a unit under Lieutenant-Commander Colgrave which dealt with Japanese naval air codes. There were also the staff who studied Japanese communications—frequencies, schedules, call-signs, etc.—both to direct the intercept operators and to extract what intelligence the communications themselves provided. For instance, if you could identify the characteristics of individual enemy operators and transmitters, you could track the movement of ships and units. The technique was an advanced one in those days, and was concealed by the name of REB (said, obscurely, to stand for 'Radio Elimination of Bloodstains' but known elsewhere as RFP, 'Radio Finger-Printing'). This room was where some of us saw our first oscilloscope. Last, but not least, was the big Hollerith party, mainly staffed by Wrens, under the eligible Lieutenant Jack Pickup. Jack Pickup, as a former employee of the Hollerith Company at Letchworth, was a professional data-handler.

In October four more translators arrived—Sidney Abrahamson, Peter (Barney) Barnett, Denny Denham (no relation), and Peter Lawrence—having passed through the same Bedford–Bletchley process as we had; they had travelled via the Mediterranean, which was now open, and had been held up for three weeks at Alexandria. There were further arrivals during 1944—Richard Wolfe (a brilliant lad, to die suddenly in Ceylon after the armistice, of infantile paralysis), Johnnie Lambert, Sandy Morris, and George Mitchell. In January 1944 Lieutenant-Commander Alan Merry joined us from Melbourne, a sound linguist who ran the JN 40 party. Also from April 1944 a number of ex-Bedford linguists came commissioned as RNVR sub-lieutenants. Some of these officers joined the JN 25, 11, and 40 parties; the duties of others were more inscrutable, and they would disappear to places like Delhi or Chittagong or Brisbane, or to sea. One of them was John Silkin, later to be Secretary of State for the Environment. Others included Charles Bawden, Maurice Burnett, John Catlow, Eustace Hooper, George Hunter, and Wilf Taylor. Two officers of a placid imperturbable disposition, Sub-Lieutenants Milner and Pond, kept our working data up to date, and their unit was known as the Millpond. Meanwhile Dudley Cheke and Ted Biggs (the ex-consuls) were able to take overdue home leave, Biggs returning to the unit at Melbourne. I myself became doyen of the JN 25 party, which by May 1945 comprised twenty-six service and civilian officers and seven Wrens.

We lived at the St Thomas Wardroom Mess in Colpetty Road. The house was a private one that had been requisitioned, and the garden had been filled with rows of cadjan (woven palmleaf) cabins, with broad shaded balconies. They were quite comfortably provided; no windows of course, just apertures, so that during gales the rain came in not only through the roof but horizontally through the window. Fifty yards away across a railway track was the sea, where you could dive into the phosphorescent water when you came off watch at midnight. In January 1945 a new wardroom mess opened for Anderson staff—Merton House at 41 Guildford Crescent, Cinnamon Gardens—away from the sea unfortunately, but nearer Anderson, and only a few hundred leafy yards from the Wrennery. When we had a few days off, we would travel all over that beautiful island, visiting the ancient cities in the north, or the spectacles at Kandy, or the hospitality of the up-country resorts, where the hills in the centre rise to eight thousand feet.

One thing to record is the priceless sense of community that formed. We were in our teens or twenties, thrown together, Wrens, civilians, and officers, working to a common purpose, sharing unusual experiences. The bonds that then grew have lasted. In the summer of 1991 two dozen of us gathered for a weekend in the west of England. Looking back, I am struck amongst other things by the absence of cliquiness—it was just one group.

What did it all add up to? what effect did HMS Anderson and its predecessors have on operations? This, I am afraid, is a question for a future student. We were not privy at the time to operational decisions, and it would be foolish now for me or my colleagues to attempt a speculative assessment. It can be said that a decrypt *did* provide a timely warning of the April 1942 raid. George Curnock told us how they were working one sultry afternoon in Colombo on a message that described plans for a massive attack somewhere. Then they spelt out the name of the place that was to be clobbered—KO–RO–N–BO; an electric shock ran through the up-to-then relaxed office. This decrypt enabled the Navy and the Air Force and Commander-in-Chief Ceylon to make preparations. Although we did not win the ensuing battle with the Japanese task force, the damage that we suffered was limited, and Nagumo came up against the first opposition that he had encountered in four victorious months. (Our biggest losses were off the north-east Indian coast, where it seems that there was no forewarning.) Also mentioned in the history books is a decrypt that gave the plans for the Japanese withdrawal from the Andaman and Nicobar Islands;[1] the ensuing operations led to the destruction of the Nicobars convoy and of the cruiser *Haguro*, and to the isolation of the Andamans garrison.[2]

We, of course, concentrated on messages that affected the Indian Ocean, and we would see copies of some of the signals that promulgated our results, typically to S4, the commander of the 4th Submarine Flotilla. It seems that, whereas the Public Record Office has released wartime German decrypts for study by historians, the corresponding Japanese material is not available. Perhaps we incinerated it all.

In mid-July 1945 we were visited by Lord Mountbatten, who told us that we were worth ten divisions. At the same time we had a longer visit from Hugh Alexander (later British chess champion), who had made huge contributions to the reading of the German ciphers. He installed time-clock punches throughout the station, to identify where the production line could be speeded up.

Within a month the war had suddenly come to an end. At the time I was on a trip with Harry Field in the jungles of the Tamil north-east of the island, and so missed joining the party that left to assault Penang—a disappointment, although good fortune for my replacement. However, we were back in Colombo in time to splice the mainbrace. Neat naval rum is of a consistency only slightly more runny than boot-polish—to the best of my memory, which for the rest of that afternoon was not particularly clear-cut.

My last technical action was to add a new word to our lexicon. This new word began to appear in decrypts, and was not in any dictionary. By detective work I identified the meaning. Every Japanese service unit at that time possessed a portrait of the Emperor—corresponding to the standard of a Roman legion—which must never fall into enemy hands. Now, all over East Asia, Japanese forces were being ordered to 'burn the imperial portrait', and two suitable characters had been made into an honorific word to indicate this unprecedented ceremony.

Appendix. Japanese naval codes and ciphers

Because the Japanese Navy was so far-flung and because there were no landlines (or, presumably, usable cables), it produced an unusually large amount of radio communications. These were transmitted by high frequency because of the distances, and were by the same token capable of intercept by the allies at a distance.

Like the Japanese Army, the Japanese Navy deployed a large number of cryptographic systems at any one time. But, in contrast to the variety of the army systems, the naval ones were usually based on code-books, unreciphered in the case of low-level systems, reciphered in the case of the high-grade ones. (Note that naval code-books are bulky; whereas an army system often needs to be portable, a naval one does not.) There were one or two exceptions, the most important of which was JN 40. The following list includes the main systems on which our unit worked from 1942 to 1945. The Japanese Naval Attaché systems were different—the main one being the Coral cipher machine; I was not involved in these systems and they do not figure in this account.

In compiling this summary I have had only limited opportunity to find or consult such relevant published material as exists, and the following list does not claim to be authentic or complete. Detailed histories, which we wrote immediately after the armistice, presumably still exist in the official archives.

The JN titles are, of course, names given by the Allies. The Japanese had their own names, such as D for JN 25 and OTSU for JN 4. Bletchley Park seems to have had its own system of K titles (K 35, K 39, etc.).

JN 4

A big code-book, used in tactical situations, unreciphered. That is to say, the user looks up in the book the word or phrase which he wishes to encode and finds the assigned arbitrary code-group; and so on throughout the message. These code-groups, without further modification, are the text which is sent by the radio operator. The receiver of the message of course needs the decode version of the code-book, sorted in code-group order, to decode the text. In the case of JN 4, the code-groups consisted of four *kana* syllables (*kana* syllables are the Japanese equivalent of an alphabet), the fourth syllable being a 'garble check'; by tracking the four syllables through a table you could tell whether the group had been transmitted correctly.

There was no easy way of exploiting JN 4. The code-book was huge. Common words did not stand out clearly, because for each common word the book provided a large number of alternative code-groups. Most code-groups, moreover, had two meanings—what you might call a 'lower-case' meaning and an 'upper-case' one. There were various books—we called them 'green', 'red', 'blue', etc.—changing every few months, so that as you began to accumulate enough messages to interpret the more commonly occurring code-groups the messages would begin to appear from a new book. When we arrived at Bletchley the JN 4C book (successive books were titled A, B, C, etc.) had just been superseded. When we left six months later we were on to JN 4G.

Some books were quite well recovered eventually, but my impression is that we never got much more out of JN 4 than we put into it. Messages in a system like this have a very brief shelf-life. Such decrypts as were produced were not of value to the British fighting services, and I suspect that this was true for the Americans too.

JN 11

A down-market version of JN 25 (see below). Whereas JN 25 was based on five-figure code-groups, JN 11 was four-figure. The system was regularly exploited. Towards the end of the war the additive tables for reciphering the code-groups were replaced by a *ransūban* (see below). The JN 11 *ransūban* consisted of four strips, each carrying a column of (probably) twenty digits, laid side by side to produce twenty four-digit groups of additive key. Each day a new set of four strips was selected from a 'basket' of forty strips.

(Some colleagues remember the existence of a JN 14, later to become JN 147. The description sounds similar to that of JN 11, and I am unable to clarify the position.)

JN (12?)

Transposed *kana*. For plots of minefields.

JN 14 and JN 147

See JN 11.

JN 25

The main system, carrying about 70 per cent of all Japanese naval communications. See under JN 4 above for a description of a big Japanese code-book. JN 25 differed, first in that the code-groups consisted of five digits, not four syllables; secondly, in that the code-groups were reciphered by a 'long additive'. JN 25 code-groups had an attenuated garble-check—all authentic code-groups were divisible by three (which would detect two garbles in three).

The additive recipherment worked as follows. As well as possessing a code-book (both 'encode' and 'decode' versions of course), the clerk had before him an additive book, which consisted of a sequence of eighteen-thousand random five-figure groups. He had to choose a place in this book at random, to act as a starting-point. He then added his first random group to the first code-group of his message, the next to the second, and so on. Finally, he took the page and line of the starting-point that he had chosen, enciphered it on another key-table, and buried the result at a prearranged place in the encrypted message. The recipient of the message of course performed the same functions in the reverse direction and in the reverse order. Before the war the code-book hardly ever changed, and the additive table (the eighteen thousand random five-figure groups) might change once a year. As the war progressed both code-book and additive tables changed ever more frequently, until a book could last as little as three months, and an additive table as little as one or two months. The code-books were titled A, B, C, etc. by the Allies, and the additive tables 1, 2, 3, etc.—for instance, JN 25 L53 (current in 1944).

The following example may help the reader to visualize the process:

Plain text: FROM *KAGA*. ESTIMATED TIME OF ARRIVAL 19TH 2130.

Code text:	21936 from	48222 next group upper case	01905 *Kaga*	38832 stop	87039 ETA	64527 19th	11520 2130	99708 stop
Additive key:	02923	41338	00989	15861	28959	90024	23693	18229
Code plus additive:	23859	89550	01884	43693	05988	54541	34113	07927
Encrypted signal text as transmitted:	23859 07927	89550	01884	*26341*	43693	05988	54541	34113

There are several points to note:

1. All code-groups are divisible by 3.
2. Code-groups exist for dates, times, common phrases, etc.
3. Code-groups exist for names of ships, places, etc. These are usually 'upper case' meanings. Names for which no group exists would be spelt out.
4. Two different variants have been used for 'stop'. For a common element like 'stop' there would be dozens of variant groups.
5. The addition is digit-by-digit 'non-carrying'. For instance 21936 plus 02923 is 23859, not 24859. This is easier for the clerk, and causes no ambiguity.

6. A group has been inserted at position 4 to tell the clerk at the other end where to start in the additive table. There were keys and conventions for doing this, which are not described here; but see the Appendix to Chapter 29 for a broadly similar system.

The task which this system presented to the cryptanalyst is clearly formidable, and could be tackled only with (*a*) an enormous number of encrypted messages to work on, and (*b*) an enormous effort. The Japanese provided the former and the Americans the latter. The problem was not the system in itself. We had been on top of it when the variables changed infrequently, and during the war we became familiar with the lay-out of the code-books, etc., from captures. The problem was the increasingly frequent changes. However, we kept pace, and in the later stages of the war even a simultaneous change of code-book and additive table did not halt production for more than a few weeks. The unit in Washington would begin to produce their first tentative recoveries after two weeks or so, and would be back in business two weeks or so later. Not surprisingly, not all messages were read, and those that were read could be gappy. However, the straightforward material which we read most readily was perhaps the most useful stuff—such as dates and times with latitudes and longitudes for convoys and other ship movements.

Recovery of code-group meanings was called 'book-breaking'. Removal of additive key was called 'stripping', and the ladies and gentlemen who did this were called 'strippers'.

JN 25 came in three flavours—a system for flag-officers, which we never had enough messages to make progress with; a system for administrative communications, more or less ignored by the Japanese; and the main system. It was a US JN 25 decrypt which led to the shooting-down of Admiral Yamamoto Ishiroku in the Solomon Islands area on 18 April 1943 (see Plate 12).

JN 40

Another merchant-shipping cipher. Like the Royal Navy, and equally inadvisedly, the Japanese handed out inferior ciphers to merchant ships. JN 40 consisted of a 100-long substitution table, and a means of 'transposition'.

The user first wrote his message out in *kana* syllables, and substituted two digits for each syllable; the substitution table also included equivalents for roman letters, for digits, and for punctuation. This produced a long sequence of digits. The sequence was then written into a rectangle in one order, and taken out in another, thus changing the order of the digits in a drastic manner. The following simplified example may make the process clear.

Message: ETA: 19TH 2130

The message is substituted through a 7 × 7 square, the two digits showing the row and column of each letter (see Fig. 27.1). (The actual JN 40 square was 10 × 10, to make room for the *kana* syllabary as well as Roman letters, numerals, and punctuation.)

	1	2	3	4	5	6	7
1	A	B	C	D	E	F	G
2	H	I	J	K	L	M	N
3	O	P	Q	R	S	T	U
4	V	W	X	Y	Z	(	)
5	0	1	2	3	4	5	6
6	7	8	9	-	;	/	?
7	.	,	:	○	'	"	

FIG. 27.1. Substitution square for the JN 40 system

Plain text:	E	T	A	:		1	9	T	H		2	1	3	0	•
Intermediate text:	15	36	11	73	77	52	63	36	21	77	53	52	54	51	71

This 'intermediate' text is written downwards into a (in this case) 6 × 5 rectangle according to the key on the top (see Fig. 27.2), and is taken out horizontally according to the key down the side. (The actual JN 40 rectangles were large than this, and there were arrangements for messages that did not fit in exactly.)

	3	6	1	5	2	4
5	5	4	1	5	1	6
1	2	5	5	3	7	2
2	6	1	3	5	3	1
4	3	7	6	2	7	7
3	3	1	1	5	7	7

FIG. 27.2. Transposition square for the JN 40 system

Cipher text as extracted from
rectangle: 255372 613531 311577 376277 541516
Text transmitted in five-figure
groups: 25537 26135 31311 57737 62775 41516

The JN 40 transposition keys changed daily, but once the basic system had been solved the daily keys did not hold us up much. Unlike the decrypts we produced from JN 25, etc., the JN 40 decrypts were without gaps and free from conjecture (no code-groups to surmise the meaning of); also they tended to be produced more promptly.

JN 40 was solved at Kilindini in November 1942. The solution came from a situation which normally occurs only in textbooks. The Japanese sent a message that accidentally left out an easting and a northing in the plain text; they then re-enciphered the correct complete text using the same keys. Comparison of the two cipher messages permitted the enciphering method to be diagnosed and solved.

JN 166

A fairly simple naval air/weather code, meant to change every two months. Also used for signalling practice.

WEWE

For obvious security reasons the Japanese assigned arbitrary call-signs (the groups showing the originator and addressee of a message) to their units, and these changed regularly. To encipher addresses to which a call-sign had not been allocated they used a simple *kana* substitution system, which they called *we-we*.

Ransūban

Towards the end of the war the distribution difficulties facing the Japanese were such that in some cases they replaced the additive tables used in JN 11 and JN 25 by what they called *ransūban* ('random number boards'). The clerk had a *ban*—i.e. a board—into which he inserted strips in a prearranged order; each strip carried an arbitrary column of digits, and from the resulting array he took the additive with which to recipher his code text. The selection of the strips and their order on the board were assigned by the (say) daily key-table.

There were many minor codes, such as:

JN 153. A naval three-symbol air code.

K 23 (name used at BP; 'JN' title not known). A simple code for reporting direction-finding results.

555. A personnel code.

There seems to have been no transmitted plain text, except, of course, for voice.

Notes

I would like to express my gratitude to the many ex-colleagues who ransacked their memories to answer my questions. These include Charles Bawden, Maurice Burnett, John (Nobby) Clark, Jon Cohen, E. W. (Denny) Denham, Hubert (Eustace) Hooper, Sandy Morris, Tony Phelps, Duncan Poore, and Leslie Yoxall. I have been able to confirm some of the details from a box of diaries and letters that I tracked down in the loft.

1. E. Gray, *Operation Pacific* (London: Leo Cooper, 1990), 225.
2. J. Winton, *Sink the Haguro* (London: Seeley Service/Leo Cooper, 1979), *passim*. See also A. Stripp, *Codebreaker in the Far East* (London: Cass, 1989), 68–9.

28. Japanese military codes

MAURICE WILES

It was at breakfast in the Hall of Christ's College, Cambridge, that I read of the Japanese attack on Pearl Harbor. I was in fact still at school, and only in Cambridge to take a scholarship examination in Classics. The coincidence of those two very different events was soon to have a significant influence on my life that I could not then have foreseen.

The Japanese attack found Britain ill-prepared in many ways, not least in people proficient in the language. Most of those who did know it were emphatic about the difficulty of learning it. But Colonel Tiltman was not one to be deterred by such pessimism. Having taught himself enough of the language to get some feel of the problem, he was convinced that it could be done and must be done. He found his one crucial ally in an unexpected quarter. Captain Tuck, a retired naval captain who had learnt the language during his time in Far Eastern waters, undertook to give a basic training in the language to people with no previous knowledge of it in a six-month course.

How were the members of the course to be selected? Classics tutors in Oxford and Cambridge were asked to suggest names of recent classical scholars, now serving in some non-specialist capacity in the forces. Sidney Grose, classical tutor at Christ's Cambridge, put forward a number of names, including that of my elder brother Christopher, who had twice won the Porson prize for Greek verse in his abbreviated time at Cambridge just before the war. The family connection prompted him to add my name also, even though I was still at school and known to him only through that scholarship examination. There followed a brief interview in London probing my interest in the three Cs—Classics, chess, and crosswords—and then, just two months after Pearl Harbor, I left school earlier than planned and embarked the next day on a very different kind of learning experience.

We worked hard, and after five months (a month before the ending of the course) three of us, my brother Christopher, Bobby Robins, and myself (all, as it happened, products of the same school), were sent to Bletchley to work under Colonel Tiltman, so that he could judge whether his experiment had worked and we were likely to prove of any use to him in opening up the field of Japanese intelligence.

It was now the summer of 1942. Tiltman, the man who had had the courage to set up a course to train Japanese linguists from scratch, had recently brought the process of reading the Japanese Military Attaché (JMA) code to the point at which a greater linguistic knowledge than he had the time to acquire was needed for the next and final stage. And that stage was being largely handed over to us. We felt pretty ill-equipped. Knowledge of the language was essential to the task assigned to us, but it was no straightforward matter of translation; as yet there were no texts on which to exercise our newly acquired translation skills. None of the thousand or so characters that we had so painstakingly learnt were there on the page before us. Something more was needed, for which we had no specialist training—an approach to problem-solving that our initial interviewers no doubt hoped had been ingrained in us by our interest in chess and crosswords. Fortunately it was not the most difficult of codes, but it took time for us to figure out what was going on and how to tackle the problems it posed. It was a two-letter code in which the basic *kana* syllables (ka, ke, ki, ko, ku, etc.), used for the phonetic rather than the ideographic element in Japanese writing, stood for themselves, and other two-letter groups stood for common words and phrases. All were written in a complicated pattern inside a grid. Since a two-letter code has room for only 676 different encoded forms, many more words had to be spelt out in full in *kana* than would normally have been the case, thus often providing enough context for us to determine the meaning of the other two-letter code-groups that represented full words or phrases. It was important to the users of the code that errors in transmission should not lead to misunderstandings and mistakes; for example, all numerals had to differ in both letters of their encoded form to make sure that a single-letter error in transmission did not give rise to an unsuspected numerical confusion, and this was done by encoding them on a patterned basis: AK = 1, BL = 2, CM = 3, etc. Once such a pattern was recognized, there would be a rapid step forward in decoding. Foreign names were normally spelt out in *kana*. Until one got used to them, they were not always easy to recognize: CHI–YA–A–CHI–RU does not obviously spell Churchill to the untrained eye. But, once the principle was mastered, they offered plenty of entertainment as well as a quick guide to the subject-matter.

Looking back a little later with the experience of a year or more's work on JMA and other codes, it felt as if we had made heavy weather of it. But we had had a lot to learn as we went along, and we got there in the end. JMA continued to be read, with some hiccups, throughout the war. Some of the traffic it carried related to the personal concerns of embassy staff, but much dealt with issues of political and military significance coming both from Germany itself and from centres, like Lisbon, where the collection of intelligence was a specialized activity. Some of this was hard information; much was embassy gossip. All of it was passed on for others to evaluate. Some items, like the Berlin attaché's account of the Normandy defences, were of obvious value; others, like the reported rumour of a nuclear explosion in Europe, caused a rare reaction of interest from those unknown figures to whom our translations were passed on—but it was indeed no more than rumour.

The three of us who had been the advance guard working on JMA were soon split up to go our separate ways. Christopher Wiles stayed on as the JMA expert, Bobby Robins went off to London to teach the language to others, while I was transferred to work on the Army Air Force code (3366) that was next in process of being broken at Bletchley. It was to be my task for the remainder of the war.

The 3366 system was a much tougher proposition than JMA.[1] It was a four-figure code, which meant that there were fifteen times as many code-groups to be solved. Moreover, the code was reciphered, so that, even when those hidden miracle-workers had solved the problem of the setting of the messages received, so that the starting-place of each message in the cipher-book was known and messages using the identical section of the cipher-book could be brought together, the process of working out one by one the series of random four-figure groups that constituted the cipher-book was a slow and laborious business. At first the number of messages that could be made available to us in their deciphered but still encoded form was pretty limited. But progress was steady and the trickle built up into a regular flow. The main work of decoding was shared by four of us. Alexis Vlasto, one of the very few who came by a route other than Captain Tuck's courses, presided over the operation with quiet humour and with unfailing grace and wisdom. George Ashworth and Mervyn Jones were the powerhouse of the operation. Theirs were the natural gifts indispensable to the codebreaker's art. But such gifts were not sufficient in themselves. Not even George could remember all the past occurrences of all the different code-groups. With no computers to sort and index them, a vast and often tedious job of indexing was needed. At the start we did it ourselves. It was one way of making sure that we attended to and had some chance of remembering precisely what was there. But it soon called for an extended empire of assistants. The key figure was Elsie Hart, whose combination of high intelligence, dedication to the task, and unfailing good humour, made 'Elsie's index' the hub around which the activity of the section as a whole revolved. Every day more code-groups were solved, and at 5 p.m. each day the latest set of solutions (classified as certain, probable, or possible) were collected together and sent by cable to our opposite numbers in Washington. We never met them. But there is a sense in which they were for us the 'enemy' against whom we were working, the spur to more vigorous endeavour. Solutions to code-groups, with which we had been struggling unsuccessfully, when provided by cable from Washington, helped us on our way, but were also greeted with a feeling of failure and self-reproach; times when we could show that they had got something wrong were occasions of unconcealed glee. To find the solution and tell Washington before they informed us was always a powerful incentive. Much later, when we had broken most of the code-groups that were in at all common use, a complete copy of the code-book was captured in the Solomon Islands. The Japanese officer had buried it, but sent in to Tokyo a certificate of destruction by burning which we decoded and read. For the most part it was happy confirmation of what we had solved, and a few outstanding puzzles were cleared up. Seeing it, added a sense of reality to our activities. An actual code-book meant actual users of the book. There really was an enemy against whom our wits had been pitted, other than our opposite numbers in Washington.

Breaking the code-book had been our primary task. But we also had a role in what went before and what came after. Coded messages could only reach us as the cipher-book was broken step by step. A little way down the corridor in Block F cryptographers were working away at that task under the capable direction of David Nenk, whose efficiency and sharp wit earned him widespread respect, even if not always putting people at their ease. On the basis of frequently recurring sequences they would guess what the next code-group of the encoded message was likely to be and test whether their guess would provide plausible sequences in the other messages known to be using the same section of the cipher-book. If it did, one more group of the cipher-book was solved, and one more group of all the messages using that part of the book could be deciphered. And so the process would continue. All this they did with remarkable success, with no knowledge of Japanese or of what the coded sequences might mean.

With our knowledge of the language and increasing ability to read the code, we could often make suggestions that had escaped their statistical approach. It was a happy co-operation—especially for us who could come in and play the fairy godmother for a while without having to wrestle indefinitely with cases that continued to prove intractable.

The routine translation was done mainly by people coming straight from the Bedford courses to work for a relatively short time at Bletchley before moving on abroad. Their role had little of the fascination that we enjoyed.[2] They were not with us long enough to build up the necessary experience to contribute much to the breaking of either cipher or code. The messages themselves did not make very exciting reading. They dealt mainly with the movement of units or of individual personnel, reports of raids, and requests for supplies. Nor were the messages current; there was always a gap between the happenings they recorded or foretold and the time when we were able to read them. So we did not have the stimulus of knowing that the fruits of our labour were of immediate importance in the conduct of the war—something which, we dimly realized, characterized the work of some of those in other sections, even though internal security was sufficient to ensure that we had little idea how true those surmisings were.

The end to our work came with unexpected suddenness. Just as two months after Pearl Harbor had seen me move from school to the world of Japanese intelligence, similarly two months after Hiroshima was to see me begin life as a Cambridge undergraduate.

Notes

1. For more detailed information on these two codes, see A. Stripp, *Codebreaker in the Far East* (London: Cass, 1989), 72, 77–9, 88, 89–92 (6633 described by Stripp was a variant form of our 3366).
2. For a much more positive reaction of one such translator to this aspect of the work, see ibid. 21, and Chapter 29, this volume.

29. Japanese Army Air Force codes at Bletchley Park and Delhi

ALAN STRIPP

SEVERAL of my Cambridge colleagues, some then unknown to me, have already described the typical route into Japanese signals intelligence: the first year of a Classics course, the suggestion from my tutor at Trinity, Kitson Clark, and the interview: 'Do you play chess? Do you solve crossword puzzles? Which? Can you read an orchestral score?' Were they recruiting for a military band? If so, where did chess come in? In retrospect it makes sense: all these rely on visual patterns and memory, useful attributes for budding codebreakers. But that point was not mentioned; only 'Would you like to learn Japanese?' This came out of the blue; but almost anything was preferable to further square-bashing, Bren gun dismantling, and 'purposeful PT', which between them occupied two mornings a week. I agreed, and later was accepted for the Bedford course at £5 a week with lodgings found. It lasted six months, and Eric Ceadel, one of the high-fliers of the first course and after a similar background to ours in Classics at Cambridge, had now joined the venerable Captain Oswald Tuck as assistant instructor.

We were in good hands; Tuck and Ceadel taught us well. Through the week and on Saturday mornings we studied the language and translated Japanese war communiqués and diplomatic telegrams, first in romanized form, later in typical character-plus-*kana*-syllable form. Later still we graduated to a textbook on the principles of flight, full of technical terms. Every evening and weekend we memorized more characters, complete with their meanings and pronunciations, which cannot be deduced from sight but have to be learned by rote.

A colleague has pointed out that we finished the course with a wide inter-service vocabulary (advance, submarine, aircraft-carrier, independent mixed brigade, commander-in-chief, and the like) but never learnt the Japanese for 'you' and 'me'. Absurd as this could be for orthodox students, it made good sense for us. Personal pronouns rarely appear in army, navy, or air force signals nor in captured documents, all of which normally take the form of reports, requests, or orders. Courses in spoken Japanese were conducted in London and were intended for our counterparts who could become interrogators. Other courses, for example in Arabic, were going on elsewhere in Bedford; and it must be remembered that crash courses, of a type unthinkable in peace, were commonplace during the war. Near the end of ours we were given a codebreaking exercise, based on the *kana* syllabary and completely regular in structure—the opposite of normal cryptographic randomization. Later it seemed elementary; then it called for hard work.

Towards the end of the course thirteen of us left for the Intelligence Corps Depot near Rotherham to spend several weeks forgetting what we had just learnt, and to drill, polish, blanco, and memorize Bren gun parts yet again. Eventually the other twelve departed for Brisbane by air, having leapt from Private to Company Sergeant-Major overnight—a remarkable transmogrification even for the Intelligence Corps and the cause of chagrin to our Lance-Corporal instructor—while I, the youngest of the squad, left for Bletchley Park.

The place was unusual in every way. Civilians and personnel of all three services, British and Allied, rubbed shoulders almost regardless of age, rank, and background. Such discipline as was needed sprang naturally from the job rather than from being imposed from above. If the eight-hour shift was too short to complete an urgent task, it was too engrossing to leave. Even BP's astonishing record of secrecy rested more on its obvious necessity than on Draconian edicts. Is it possible to believe that in six tense wartime years not one of the many thousands talked about the nature of the job to a wife, husband, lover, parent, or friend? Yet the secret never emerged. Presumably we were bright enough to see that it mattered.

The twenty or so in our room, presided over by Alexis Vlasto and Maurice Wiles when guidance was needed, got to know each other well and worked well together; nearly all were Classics undergraduates like me. From time to time we met people in adjoining rooms whose work had something in common with ours; if I had stayed longer I might have found out what it was. I assumed at least that all of Block F was devoted to Japanese signals intelligence. Only in 1987 did I learn that the people in the next spur were the 'Testery', Major Tester's team working on the German Fish signals. Equally, at least two other Japanese sections were housed in other buildings.

Our concern was with Japanese Army Air Force (JAAF) traffic. We newcomers began by translating the more straightforward signals which had already been decrypted elsewhere: routine reports of fuel and ammunition stocks or of fit and unfit aircrew, requests for spare parts, and reports of Allied (mostly RAF) air attacks, transmitted from airfields in Burma and Thailand. Then there were orders from headquarters in Rangoon or further afield, including Singapore, Saigon, and Manila, containing small but useful details: 'Captain Hitomura is to proceed to Pitsanulok [a large air base in Thailand] immediately.' I will return to that innocuous signal later.

Many of these routine messages added only crumbs of information to what was already suspected or known. Cumulatively they painted a remarkably true picture of the Japanese position: where their squadrons were and what tasks (fighter, bomber, reconnaissance) they performed; whether they were up to strength; how far their reports were confirmed or denied by our own information—though that was someone else's job. If the RAF claimed to have destroyed three aircraft in a raid on an enemy airfield, it was important to know if the Japanese reported the same loss to their headquarters; if we had lost no aircraft, had they claimed to have shot any down?

But at BP we were too far from the action to get much feedback from our efforts. Even so, a rumour circulated that in September 1942 our colleagues working in Australia had been instrumental in predicting and thus preventing a full-scale Japanese landing at Milne Bay, near the south-eastern tip of New Guinea, which would have given them a well-placed springboard from which to attack the long, exposed, and thinly held coast of Queensland, with fearful consequences. This story was confirmed long after the war.

An odder affair was 'The Divisional Ghost-Pacification Ceremony', which caused raised eyebrows wherever it was mentioned, but was never properly explained. We could only presume that it was some bushido or Shinto equivalent of our Last Post. The two characters for 'division' (*shidan*) were of course in the code-book, but not the others, which were identified through the Chinese Telegraphic Code (CTC). CTC was not a secret code in the cryptographic sense, but a booklet, available commercially, which classified ten thousand characters under the traditional 214 radicals and identified each by a four-digit or a three-letter group. The four-digit series fitted perfectly into the four-digit pattern of the code-book that the Japanese Army Air Force (JAAF) was using; the appropriate CTC number, e.g. 8354, was sandwiched between the groups which effectively meant 'open CTC' and 'close CTC'. I believe 1637 stood for both, and the fact that fifty years later this is the only group that I remember, shows how commonly it occurred. It is important to realize that codebreakers—in the widest sense—soon learn a large number of common code-groups by heart.

This cumbersome system is needed for Japanese even more than for Chinese telegrams; the language has very many homophones (syllables with identical pronunciation) but, unlike Chinese, lacks the different tones by which to differentiate them. Mandarin, for example, has *mai* (falling–rising) for 'buy' and *mai* (falling) for 'sell'—a common cause of confusion for the stranger. Japanese *kansen* has six meanings: main-line, warship, sweat-gland, infection, government-appointed, witnessing a battle—indistinguishable in pronunciation though often clear from context. It will be seen that, if there are six two-character homophones, single-character homophones can run to a dozen or more. Hence the CTC.

After six months I found myself commissioned and posted to Delhi. Bletchley Park's outstation at Delhi went under the cover-name of Wireless Experimental Centre (WEC). It was housed in the buildings of Ramjas College, a former part of Delhi University, and the security area was perched on an isolated hill, Anand Parbat, 'the hill of happiness', some miles outside the city. The Mess and the long bungalows where most of us had single rooms (Majors and above had two) were at the foot of the hill. WEC in turn had two large outstations: Western Wireless Sub-Centre at Bangalore, inland from Madras in south India, and Eastern Wireless Sub-Centre at Barrackpore near Calcutta. A large US signals intelligence unit, generously staffed and provided, was also at Delhi. Small intercept units of both Army and RAF moved forward as the Burma campaign at last swung in our favour, and we were linked with the wider network which took in BP and its US equivalent at Arlington, Virginia, as well as Australia and New Zealand.

But WEC felt very different from BP. Although it was barely a fifth of its size, and was entirely devoted to Japanese signals traffic, it had little of 'the friendly informality verging on apparent anarchy', in Lord Dacre's happy phrase, 'which enabled [them] to develop their talents and carry out their work'. There were no civilians; I do not recall any women. Although orthodox military routine did not obstruct our work, there was a sense of rigidity and hierarchy which did not help it; too often administration relied on authority rather than professionalism.

I was in C Section, which again dealt with the breaking and translating of Japanese signals; next door to us was B Section, which collated and evaluated signals intelligence and compiled the enemy order of battle. I discovered only forty-five years later that they had a map room that could have solved any number of problems for us. When the place name KA-BI-EN, spelt out in *kana* syllables, meant nothing to us since it was not on our small maps, their large resources could at once have identified it as Kavieng in New Guinea, near Guadalcanal, the scene of such bitter fighting. They in turn had no idea that we were stuck.

Nevertheless at Delhi we were closer, and felt closer, to what was going on not only in Burma but in Thailand, the Philippines, and further afield in the Pacific. Some news filtered through to us via the informal grapevine of General Headquarters India Command, although its organization seemed archaic and overweight. Indeed its sleeve-badge was un-heraldically described as 'The Star of India falling through red tape into a sea of ink'.

WEC worked mainly on 6633 (see Appendix) and on other army and army air force systems such as ABC (a low-grade affair used for weather reports, 'enemy-aircraft-spotted' reports, and 'estimated-time-of-arrival' reports) and BULBUL. Among other things BULBUL revealed the work of the Air Route Departments (*kōkūrobu*), whose function was 'to dispatch, control, service, and maintain aircraft, and supervise their crews, whilst *en route* to each Air Army area'. A specifically important function of theirs was the ferrying of replacement aircraft, particularly now that Japanese losses in Burma began to mount just when some units were being transferred away eastwards to meet what was perceived as a growing US threat to Japan itself. The WEC *kōkūrobu* unit identified the main staging route along which these aircraft were ferried: from Thailand through Tenasserim to a dozen or so airfields in Burma. Naturally the RAF was kept closely posted and intercepted many of these flights.

The 6633 and other signals broken by us and by other Allied centres, and worked up into joint intelligence summaries, produced by late 1944 a virtually complete order of battle for the JAAF. It showed not only where almost every *hikōsentai* (Air Regiment, nominally of forty-eight fighters or thirty-six bombers, plus one aircraft for the Commanding Officer) was stationed, but how many of those aircraft were serviceable, what type they were, where they had served since 1942, where their base unit in Japan was, and often what the full name of the Commanding Officer was.

This is where, as well as collateral reports, the Index came in. Every reference to a unit or a person went into it. Our Captain Hitomura, posted several pages back to Pitsanulok in Thailand, had an interesting history. Little was so far known about the small unit which he had commanded in south Burma, though the aircraft were thought to be twin-engined Kawasaki 'Nick' night-fighters. Signals to and from this unit had included some new and indecipherable code-groups which were believed from context to refer to electrical equipment. Before being promoted from Lieutenant and sent to command this unit, Hitomura had spent some months in Japan.

His move to Pitsanulok was interesting. Several night raids on the air base there had met unexpectedly prompt and well-planned night-fighter defence. One experienced RAF pilot and his crew claimed that only radar could explain it. The Japanese were known to have been slow in developing radar; this posting suggested that photographic reconnaissance should be laid on, to see if any radar aerial arrays could be spotted. Could other postings to Japan, and back again to other such units, perhaps similarly equipped with 'Nick' night-fighters, form a pattern? What else could we learn? Meanwhile one or two of those new 6633 code-groups could be very provisionally labelled 'concerned with radar?'.

The 6633 decrypts also warned us of Japanese attempts to break Allied signals. Helped by poor Chinese cryptographic security, they penetrated traffic between Mountbatten and Chungking, from the British 36 Division, and from the V Force patrols which gathered information from behind the Japanese positions in Burma. They also eavesdropped on incautious conversations between US Army Air Force pilots, based in south China, and the control tower, before they took off to raid Japan. The volume and timing of these characteristically breezy exchanges enabled the Japanese to make rough estimates of the probable scale and target of these raids. Each service had its own signals-intelligence organization; Plate 11 identifies three common types of JAAF signals-intelligence unit.

More urgently, signals from or about JAAF units in and near Burma now began to show where they were pulling back—and something more. Ground troops operate *progressively* over a combat area, whereas in the Second World War aircraft other than helicopters could fly only from a few *specific* airfields, especially in a country of swamps, jungles, and mountains like Burma. Every time a squadron was ordered to move its base back from X to Y, it gave a strong clue to other Japanese intentions, not least because the Japanese Army Air Force worked closely with the Army. As always, signals intelligence was combined with other information gathered from captured documents, aerial reconnaissance, and the interrogation of prisoners, however few they were in this theatre of operations.

The bushido tradition meant that at first no Japanese were captured alive. As the fortune of war turned, so the once inexorable rule of *seppuku* (commonly but wrongly known as *harakiri*, another reading of the same characters) began to be ignored, particularly by young conscripts and a few who had studied or lived abroad before the war. Even they often assumed that our treatment of prisoners might be as barbaric as theirs, and after several days of captivity in quite normal conditions, treated as we treated our own troops of similar rank, they were still living in a dream world.

Those who had worked in our field were usually flown back to Delhi and housed in the Combined Services Detailed Interrogation Centre in the Red Fort; in a perfectly clean and cheerful building that had once been the elephant stables. 'Detailed interrogation' means simply what it says; no Gestapo-like techniques were used. I learnt something of the art from Robin Gibson, of the first Bedford course, whom I accompanied to the Interrogation Centre several times. His quiet approach put them at their ease—but still they could not believe what was happening.

First, they were alive and well treated. Secondly, all these foreigners *appeared* to be speaking their language, something well known to be impossible—an attitude still often found in Japan and China today. The CSDIC officer already known to them spoke it really well. Now these others, who spoke a more stilted form, knew all about Japanese code procedure—this was the third unbelievable fact.

We treated them as colleagues talk to each other at an international conference today, exploring the subject from the inside. After a casual conversation about codes in general, and mentioning several that they did not know about, as well as those they did, so that they understood us to be colleagues in some sense, we would innocently ask: 'Let me see—was that when we began to encipher the discriminant?' and they would generally obligingly agree or courteously correct us. The word 'we', not 'you', was all-important. The veil of secrecy, as familiar to them as to us, actually brought us together as co-specialists, and we always tried to direct the conversation where the prisoner was happiest to talk, steering it only gently. In consequence all but one major, whom Gibson could not persuade to utter until he met him again in Singapore after the war was over, talked.

The 6633 decrypts carried early Japanese reports of the second Chindit incursion under Wingate, which carried nine thousand airborne troops hundreds of miles inside Japanese-held territory in Burma, and within a few days had anti-aircraft guns and even Spitfires established there to protect them. A colleague still remembers one signal as showing 'an offended punched-in-solar-plexus-anguish' at this enterprise, quite without precedent in the area.

The victory in Burma, a triumph above all for General Bill Slim and his forces, was clinched by the capture of Rangoon in the first week of May 1945, three months before Hiroshima. The atomic bombs in turn brought a new phrase into Japanese signals: *mujōken kōfuku* or 'unconditional surrender'—though we must note even in those words that other pairs of characters pronounced *kōfuku* can mean 'good fortune' or 'school uniform'.

After that I spent almost a year at a tiny outpost at Abbottabad, in the North-West Frontier Province near Rawalpindi, after a one-man crash course in that elegant language Farsi. There all five of us were soon invited to apply for permanent posts 'in the racket'. The others did, and were accepted; unlike them I had no degree, and felt too that a lifetime spent doing a job which I could neither reveal nor discuss with anybody else was a different matter from a merely temporary Top Secret job in wartime. By October 1946, being in any case in the longer queue of Far Easterners, waiting for their turn to be brought home and demobilized, I was in Singapore half-way through yet another crash course, in Russian—the Cold War was beginning to concentrate everyone's mind—when I heard that I had been given a Class B release to return to Cambridge for my belated second year reading Classics.

Appendix. The 6633 System

The 6633 system was well planned, perhaps gaining from experience with 3366, described by Maurice Wiles (see Chapter 28). Like 3366 and Denham's JN 25 (see Appendix to Chapter 27), it had a two-part code-book (*nibun ryakugō*), one volume each for encoding and decoding, and it used 6,000–7,000 of the 10,000 possible four-figure groups. Each of these represented a word, phrase, sentence, numeral, personal or place-name, foreign word, punctuation, *anything*—the great virtue of a code-book. It was, of course, compiled so that the allocation of code-groups to meanings was absolutely random, as shown in Plate 11.

When the cipher clerk had encoded the message group by group to form the code text, he turned to his key-book (*sūji angō*). This too had 10,000 random four-digit groups, and we named each period of its use after a colour, like the Enigma keys. He opened it at random, chose a starting-place at random, and wrote down one key-group under each code-group, up to the end of the message. If his starting-place was on page 38, column 5, row 4, he wrote down this indicator 3854 at the head of the message, or buried it deeper for the benefit of his colleague at the receiving end:

Code text:		2671	8453	6967	5129	0813 etc.
Key text:	(3854)	9814	5205	7348	3682	4987 etc.

Thus far the process tallied with that used for 3366 and JN 25, but for 6633 the key text was not added to the code-text. Clearly the Japanese wanted to make life more interesting for our team. Instead, a third element in the system now came into play: a square substitution-table (*ransuhyō*) of 100 boxes arranged in ten columns and ten rows, each containing the figures 0–9 in a different random order. It appears that these tables should have been 'Latin squares' in which no figure is repeated in the same column or row. Not all of them were of that pattern, and that fact gave us a small toe-hold in key-breaking.

Fig. 29.1 shows a typical substitution square. The procedure was as follows. The upper line (code text) denoted the columns in the substitution square; the lower line (key text) denoted the rows. Each pair of co-ordinates thus indicated a digit, which the cipher clerk wrote down to form a third line, continuing the process throughout the message to form the reciphered text. The indicator 3854 was prefixed to this text, or buried in it, or otherwise disguised, and the signal was ready to transmit, given the usual procedural preambles.

Despite the cumbersome process, the advantages are obvious. Non-carrying addition always gives the same answer; so does non-borrowing subtraction. Code-books reciphered on admittedly shorter and over-repeated additive keys were regularly broken during the First World War for this reason. Moreover, with an additive key, 3 above 4 *or* 4 above 3 add up equally to 7. In 6633 each denotes a different box, usually containing a different figure.

Rows shown by key text \ Columns shown by code text	0	1	2	3	4	5	6	7	8	9
0	4	7	3	0	5	9	2	6	1	8
1	9	5	1	8	3	0	6	2	7	4
2	5	0	7	4	2	1	8	6	9	3
3	3	9	2	7	4	6	0	1	8	5
4	2	3	8	0	9	7	0	4	1	5
5	7	2	0	1	3	5	9	8	4	6
6	0	1	9	3	8	4	7	6	5	2
7	1	8	6	4	2	7	5	0	9	3
8	6	1	9	5	7	2	3	8	0	4
9	8	4	7	2	6	3	1	5	7	0

which gives:

	2671	8453	6967	5129	0813	etc.(columns)
	9814	5205	7348	3682	4987	etc.(rows)
(3854)	7323	4291	5508	6193	2714	etc.(signal text)

FIG. 29.1. Substitution square for the 6633 system

The beauty of the square, from the user's point of view, is that each new one creates a new arithmetic.

The square, occupying less space than a crossword-puzzle frame, can be changed easily easily and often, and in practice was changed roughly once a month until after the Imphal and Kohima battles, when the Japanese retreat began to cause them distribution problems.

Most of us took turns sooner or later at key-breaking—'stripping', as others have called it, I think following American usage. With an additive system like JN 25 or 3366, key-breaking can be done when you have broken or captured the code-book but lack the key (perhaps because it is new), provided you know how the indicator is used to show the starting place in the key for each message

With 6633 the principle was the same, but you needed to have both code-book and key-book to break the current square (substitution table), or else code-book and square to break the key. However many layers a reciphered code system has, you can normally break one layer only if you know the others.

With only one message our task is too hard; all is conjecture. Occasionally that is sufficient: in a signal 'Lt Fujiwara' (one group missing) 'to Captain', obviously the missing group means 'is promoted'. We see what code-group is needed and work backwards, through the square, to see what key-group gives that code-group, and very tentatively pencil it in. A non-Latin square may offer a choice of digits or no digit at all; the latter means an error somewhere.

A wider gap is clearly harder to bridge, but if several messages straddle the gap it can still be done. If even two of them make sense we can hardly be wrong. The process is called 'building a depth', which entails using several signals to bridge a gap of unsolved key. You write out the cipher texts one under another at the correct 'offset', so that in any one column all the code-groups will have been reciphered with the same key-group: this pattern will have been shown by the indicator, as explained earlier. Often the depth will be only two or three messages deep. The process, first described by Kerckhoffs in 1883, was designed to solve additive keys, but its underlying principle holds good also for the more complex structure where a substitution table is used.

In the following typical example we know the code-book and have solved the current square. A depth of three messages has been set up and some of the key has been recovered, leaving a gap of five missing key-groups which we now have to restore:

1.	Yesterday	evening	—	—	—	—	—	RI	NU	
2.	. . . small bombs	3708	—	—	—	—	—	856,	litres	22330
3.	. . . the enemy	will	—	—	—	—	—	river	shortly	
			1st	2nd	3rd	4th	5th			
			(missing key-groups)							

(Oriental scholars may object that this is not in Japanese word-order; I trust that most readers will put up with this for the sake of clarity.)

Message No. 1 is inscrutable. No. 2 is clearly a routine report of stocks held. No. 3 offers no help yet. If we try 'large bombs' for the first missing key-group in Message No. 2, the key needed to produce it gives 'our' in No. 1, and 'advance' in No. 3. We are in business. But we are unlikely to spend hours going through all possible numerals to continue No. 2 unless there is a very special reason.

To cut a long story short: for the second missing key-group, 'towards' in No. 3 gives 'troops' in No. 1, and '545' in No. 2. For the third, 'incendiary bombs' in No. 2 gives 'were forced to' in No. 1, and 'Mandalay' in No. 3. The fourth is harder: the obvious guess 'abandon' (or a synonym) for No. 1 produces nonsense, but if we assume that one digit has been garbled in reciphering, transmission, or interception—a common phenomenon—it works, giving '2250' in No. 2 and 'intending' in No. 3. Finally, 'delayed-action bombs' in No. 2 gives 'TI' in No. 1 and 'to cross' in No. 3. The sense is clear in Messages No. 2 and No. 3. In 1, 'TIRINU' is confirmed with a reluctant General Headquarters (it can be easier to get one's information from the enemy) as 'TILIN', a village in the Gangaw Valley which an advance party of 4 Corps captured two days before. The full texts are:

1. Yesterday evening our troops were forced to abandon TIRIN . . .
2. . . . small bombs 3708, large bombs 545, incendiary bombs 2250, delayed-action bombs 856, litres 22330 . . .

3. . . . the enemy will advance towards Mandalay intending to cross the river shortly.

The reward often lies not in the content of these messages but in the closing of one more gap in the key-text, which will help with many other messages, still to be sent, spanning the same gap. Newly broken key-groups will be passed on, at least once a week, to colleagues at other Allied cryptanalytical centres. In this case the content too was rewarding. The rest of Message No. 3 showed the Japanese identifying the advance of 33 Corps towards Mandalay as the main threat—as Slim hoped they would. In fact it was the wide outflanking movement of 4 Corps, hinted at in Message No. 1, leading to the capture of Meiktila eighty miles *south* of Mandalay, which sealed the fate of the main enemy forces and opened the way to the capture of Rangoon some five weeks later, and thus to the effective end of the campaign just as the monsoon arrived, three months before Hiroshima.

30. Recollections of *temps perdu* at Bletchley Park

CARMEN BLACKER

Most of my time at Bletchley was spent in NS VI, a division of the Naval Section which specialized in the provision to cryptographers of 'equivalents'. When technical terms, for which there was no entry in any dictionary, turned up in a deciphered message, NS VI undertook to provide the nearest English equivalent of the term, be the subject-matter W/T, navigation, or the newly invented radar, and be the language German, Italian, or Japanese. The section was directed by Geoffrey Tandy, who, by dint of gathering as many people as possible into his section and never letting anyone out, quickly rose to the rank of Commander in the RNVR. He was familiarly known to his subordinates as 'Six'. My job in NS VI was to look after a small library of 'pinches', or captured documents likely to yield useful equivalents, indexing all the promising words on cards.

My recruitment to BP was effected by Mr John Rideout, a scholar of Chinese, tall and thin with prematurely grey hair, who had acquired enough Japanese to enable him to read the Japanese commentaries on the Chinese classics. In 1942 he was doing his patriotic duty by helping out with the teaching of Japanese to the miscellaneous crowd of new students at the School of Oriental and African Studies in London. It was he who informed the Foreign Office that I was a promising student of Japanese, and who arranged for me to be interviewed with the prospect of 'an important job'. This job was highly secret, and nothing about it could be divulged to me; but it would enable my rudimentary knowledge of Japanese to be put to good use in the emergency.

I was accordingly interviewed at Grosvenor House by a Miss Moore, a formidable woman, compared with whom Miss Buss and Miss Beale were puny wraiths. Of course, she said, she could tell me nothing whatever about the work I should be doing, further than to say that the pay would be low, the hours long, and the possibility of night work strong. Why had my father been born in Paris? That might well count against me in the final selection . . . I dared to ask why night work was necessary, to which her withering reply was, 'You *want* this job, don't you?' I was tempted to reply, 'Not at all, but I was given to understand that you wanted *me*.' But, alas, years of indoctrination not to 'answer back' to elders and betters inhibited me.

I was soon told that I must undergo a special course of training for the new work that lay ahead, and must present myself every morning at the School of Oriental and African Studies. The teacher was to be Mr Rideout himself. Whatever was to be the nature of the mysterious future work, his method of instruction and preparation was curious. Without a word of any kind he would spend twenty minutes or so writing on the blackboard a transcription into roman letters of a leading article from an old Japanese newspaper, the *Asahi* or the *Mainichi*. I and the Wren officer Mrs Tate, who was my only fellow-student, had to copy what he wrote into our exercise books. His writing was extraordinary, and it was by no means easy to make out the tiny chalk-grey words on the dusty board. The copying finished, Mr Rideout lit another cigarette and left the room. The session was over. I would go straight back to Waterloo, thence on a slow train to Guildford, thence on a slow bus to Shamley Green, whence I walked the remaining mile to our house, arriving about 3.30.

The rest of the day would be spent in wrestling with the translation of the text, which was made ten times more difficult by the fact of its being in roman letters. Numerous words in Japanese which sound the same, but when written with their proper Chinese characters are instantly recognizable, were reduced to flat meaninglessness in roman letters. I would spend hours wondering whether the word *tai-sei* meant 'completion, accomplishment', or 'a downward tendency', or 'the general drift of the situation', or 'the reins of government'. Or whether the word *kōsei* had meant in its leading article 'justice, equity', or 'correction, revision', or 'resuscitation, revival', or 'composition, constitution', or 'an offensive operation', or 'a stentorian voice'. The next morning I would repeat the journey to the School. Mr Rideout would spend a few minutes pointing out the errors in Mrs Tate's and my translations, and the silent transcription would start again.

When I finally found myself at Bletchley, and before being sent to NS VI, I was sent for a few weeks to translate decoded messages from the Japanese merchant shipping code known as JN 40, I realized that none of the laborious course that Mr Rideout had devised was of the smallest practical use for the work before me. It was of even less use in NS VI.

My pay was £2 a week, and it was explained to me that, if this seemed low, it was partly due to my age, 18, and partly to my being a woman. I should always remember, too, that there were many girls at BP who were paid only thirty shillings a week. From this sum £1 would be deducted for my billet, three shillings a week for my transport to and fro in a khaki bus, and half a crown for my lunches. This left exactly fourteen shillings and sixpence a week (72½p) to cover everything else.

In my first billet in Wolverton there was no heating in the bedroom, and in the sitting-room downstairs the Forces Programme was on all day long on the wireless. One hot bath a week was allowed. I was anxious to learn more Japanese, so in the evenings would sit on my bed wrapped up in a blanket, putting out a hand from time to time to turn a page.

Eventually I moved to a much nicer house in Newport Pagnell occupied by an old lady and three cats. Here I paid thirty shillings a week to have my own sitting-room where I could work in peace, but had to supply and cook all my own food. This left only four shillings and sixpence a week (22½p) to cover food and all other necessities. In the summer I saved three shillings a week by bicycling the eight miles each way to and from work. The road, which led through the villages of Willen, Woolstone, Woughton, and Simpson, was as flat as a table, and there was of course next to no traffic. I usually accomplished the journey in under an hour. When I worked the evening shift, from 4 p.m. to midnight, this regime meant that I got home by 1 a.m. But the next day I had until 3 p.m. for walking, studying, or exploring the countryside.

Certainly, had my parents not been able to give me an allowance, I should not have been able to make ends meet. Today I marvel at the trust the Foreign Office placed in people's uncomplaining sense of patriotism in daring to risk such low pay for such highly secret work.

My first duty on arriving in NS VI was to ransack all the cupboards in the Naval Section to see if any Japanese captured documents had by chance been left there. Some cupboards revealed piles of photostat copies of old code-books, sent months before by the Americans.

In others I found manuals of call-signs, likewise photostatted and out of date. There also came to light a photostat copy of a handwritten Radar Manual, a little volume entitled *Kūshū* or 'Air Raids', a book on the Type 93 Echo-Ranging Set, and the Japan Nickel Review.

I was instructed to make accession lists of all these items, and then to read the Radar Manual, the book on Echo-Ranging, and the Japan Nickel Review, and to put on to cards, with correct page reference, any words likely to turn up in a decoded message. Hence the 'research party' of the subsection, which consisted of Frank Taylor, an exile from the John Rylands Library in Manchester, and Pam Griffiths, and of course anyone in another subsection engaged in translating decoded messages, could consult my index in the event of any of the words turning up.

So from 9 a.m. to 6 p.m., when I was on the day shift, and from 4 p.m. to midnight when I worked the greatly preferable evening shift, I read these baffling books and committed their vocabulary to cards. Needless to say, had the books been written in English I would have had no more notion of what they were about than when I read them in Japanese. But it was easy to see that, when the Japanese terms for the temper-brittleness of steel turned up, or acid open-hearth furnaces, or face-centred cubic lattices, or eutectoid points, or heterodyne oscillators, or even transmitter-oscillator-buffer-amplifiers, on to cards these had to go.

I think I am correct when I recall that not once was any useful purpose served by my index. Frank Taylor used dutifully to consult it from time to time, but the words I had gleaned from the arbitrary rag-bag of Japanese 'pinches' that had come our way, were never the words he needed. My index grew week by week until it filled a whole drawer—until it expanded into a second drawer. But not once did any researcher or translator ever profit by it.

It was a very different matter, needless to say, with German and Italian captured documents. On 11 June 1944 I came into the office to find the tables piled high with books, charts, letters, and maps captured after the Normandy landings, and Six gave us a short lecture impressing on us that men were risking their lives to capture these documents. And a few days later he congratulated the German part of the section on their work; the speed with which BP was intercepting, deciphering, translating, and dispatching to the Admiralty the German messages was 'something phenomenal', and the part NS VI was playing in providing equivalents was a vital one.

On 4 June Six gave a demonstration to the whole section of the captured Enigma machine. It was the most ingenious device that I had ever seen.

The German side of things was sizzlingly hot, urgently intense, subject to constant harrying from the Admiralty for more accession lists of the latest captures. But for Japan no such excitement could be roused. The library and the resulting index was a backwater. The main thrust was far away on the other side of the world in American hands.

Not even when the code of the Japanese Naval Attaché in Berlin was broken, who by all accounts was taken by his German hosts on a tour of the rocket bases and doodle-bug factories, and who had sent detailed descriptions home of everything he had seen—not even then did my index prove useful.

By January 1945 I was utterly bored with the work, which seemed to contribute nothing to the war effort, and my morale began to weaken. On one of my leave days in London I met Arthur Waley, who said, 'Why don't you learn Chinese in your spare time?' Why not indeed, and when, after three or four hours plugging away at the Japan Nickel Review, flesh and blood could stand it no longer, I used to substitute another book, which no one else in the office could distinguish from the first, in which the poems of Li T'ai Po or the magic stories in the *Liao Chai Chih I* were set out with Japanese translation and commentary. On the evening shift, when things were quieter, and when there was no possibility of Six suddenly appearing from the next room with some alarm or excursion, demand or reprimand, the temptation to spend more time on these delectable books than on the Type 93 Echo-Ranging Set was less resistible. My derelictions grew more unconscionable.

On another of my leave days in London I called on Professor Eve Edwards, who was in charge of the crash courses in Japanese for service students at the School of Oriental and African Studies, and told her of my predicament. I could not, of course, tell her what I was doing, further than that it seemed a complete waste of time. 'We would be glad of extra help with the teaching here', she assured me; 'I will see if I can get you transferred.'

I naturally informed Six of what I had done, only to be met with a blank refusal. 'No one will leave this section', he pronounced. 'You can resign yourself to staying here until the end of the war.' I was bitterly disappointed, but saw no alternative to resigning myself to a longer wait.

In February 1945 I contracted an old-fashioned red-flanellist complaint known as a quinsy, known to most people only from its mention in Sherlock Holmes's *Case of Identity*. My throat swelled up so alarmingly that I could hardly swallow. After massive doses of the drug then called 'M and B' I was sent home on sick leave to recuperate. During this period the telephone rang, with the message that, at the request of one Sir Theodore Adams, I was to be 'released' and transferred *forthwith* to the School of Oriental and African Studies. There I was to act as Special Lecturer in the intensive courses to teach Japanese to soldiers, sailors, and airmen.

I had to go back to the office to collect my dictionaries and other paraphernalia, and was prepared to bid everyone a cheerful farewell. At Bletchley station I was met by Enid Reid, who with the greatest kindness had slipped out of the office on purpose to waylay me. 'I must warn you', she said, 'that everyone in the office has been forbidden to speak to you. We have been told that you have done no accession lists for several weeks, and that you have got out by underhand means, and hence must be sent to Coventry. Don't be surprised if no one says a word to you.'

How grateful I was for the warning. People I had taken for pleasant acquaintances cut me dead, and Six's Number Two, Flight-Lieutenant Baghino, known as Bags, summoned me to his office to tell me to pack up my things and leave with the least possible delay, so as not to disturb the office.

I discovered later that the situation had been exacerbated during my absence by the fact that a girl called Peta, a talented artist, had circulated a picture of Commander Tandy, dressed as an oriental potentate in a turban, sitting cross-legged on a cushion. Before him crouched a figure which was apparently me, in an attitude of supplication. Out of Tandy's mouth came a balloon, with the legend 'What, you want to go away and do useful work? Never heard such nonsense!' It was rumoured that I had put Peta up to drawing this scurrilous picture. It was, of course, a far more daring and imaginative gesture than I could possibly have conceived at the time, and the charge was quite unfounded.

But this last incident did nothing to lessen the relief and jubilation with which I gave up my pass at the gate and for the last time walked out of this top-secret place, where such wonderful and scarcely credible intellectual feats had been accomplished, where many people had spent their finest hours, but where I do not honestly think that I served any purpose useful in shortening the war.

APPENDIX

How the Bletchley Park buildings took shape

BOB WATSON

WHEN the war broke out I was living in Fenny Stratford. Later I got married and lived in Bletchley Park for twenty years. I still live within sight of BP, where the RAF camp guardroom used to stand.

My trade was carpenter and joiner and sometimes locksmith, and I worked at BP and the outstations for nearly forty-five years. There were twenty-five building tradesmen and four gardeners in the section, and we got on well together except when two bricklayers had a difference of opinion and one hit the other over the head with a four-foot spirit-level. Our boss was a local builder, Mr Faulkner, and I got on with him very well because I had known him from boyhood. He was fond of cars and hunting, and rode with the Whaddon Chase Hunt. He also helped some of the poorer people of Fenny Stratford without many others getting to know about it. He used to visit the site at Bletchley Park once or twice a day, arriving in all his hunting glory if he was going hunting later. You knew when he was viewing the site because his dog Laddy always arrived first. This is my story of how the buildings of Bletchley Park took shape and how we fitted them out.

The Bletchley Park estate can be traced back as far as the Domesday Book, when it was part of Etone Manor. In 1882 it was bought by Herbert Samuel Leon, a London stockbroker, who was created baronet in 1911. He too was a great local benefactor. He had the mansion built in the grand style. It has a large copper dome, and one of my grandfather's jobs—he was foreman carpenter for a Fenny Stratford builder—was to make and fit all the supporting woodwork for it.

Sir Herbert died in 1926 and Lady Fanny ran the estate until her death in 1937. Their son, Sir George Leon, decided to sell the whole estate, consisting of the mansion, outbuildings, two entrance lodges, twenty-eight cottages, and 581 acres. The mansion and grounds went to a local syndicate, of which Mr Faulkner was chairman, and there were plans to sell the land as building plots, with Mr Faulkner's own house on the lawn by the lake.

After the sale some of the stable block was taken down, the apple store was converted into a large bungalow, and the mansion was got ready for demolition. Then all work suddenly came to a stop, because GC&CS had taken an interest in the site. Why Bletchley Park? Some people say it was because of the good communications. Bletchley was at the intersection of railways running north, east, south, and west, as well as the Watling Street to London, now the A5.

During the Munich crisis of 1938 GC&CS had a practice occupation of the mansion. It went well, so plans were put in hand to develop the rest of the site. A new approach road from Church Green Road had already been laid, with houses down one side; it was named Wilton Avenue. Some of the road inside the Park was relaid with concrete, and a new water main was laid from Little Brickhill reservoir to serve the Park and the camps which were built later.

New electricity cables were laid, as well as GPO land-lines into the mansion, terminating in what had been the Leon's billiard-room. It also contained the small telephone exchange until a large blast-proof one was built outside the ballroom. It was only taken down in 1991, and took four men two months to demolish. Teleprinter lines were also installed.

The mansion has a small tower, within which are two large slate water tanks above a small room. This was soon made into a wireless room (Station X), and an aerial array was erected between the high chimneys and the top of a tall tree (*Wellingtonia Sequoiadendron Giganteum*) in the centre of the lawn. (In the late 1980s the top of this tree was blown down, revealing the old aerial strap grown into the trunk.) Later four very tall trees had their tops cut off, and Royal Navy riggers fitted aerials from them to what became Hut 1, making it in turn Station X, the BP wireless station. After a very short life it was moved again to Old Whaddon Hall, some six miles from Bletchley. After the war the section was moved to Hanslope Park and became the Diplomatic Wireless Service. So Hut 1, a mere forty feet by sixteen feet, was its birthplace.

These early huts had brick 'sleeper' walls with the floor, sides, and end roof-timbers of Canadian pine. The outside covering was shiplap boarding or asbestos cladding. Once the outside frame was up, Mr Faulkner used a lot of local carpenters to fit up the insides. These buildings took shape as if they were on an assembly line. Apart from Hut 1 I have not given many hut numbers because they have changed several times since 1939. People who worked in BP over the years still get confused as a result.

These ordinary huts were followed by several larger blast-proof buildings, one of which was for the *bombes*. The largest was about ninety-five feet by thirty-two feet, the main Teleprinter Room in E Block. In 1957 it was converted into an assembly hall for the Bletchley Park Training College, opened by Princess Alexandra on 29 November 1957. It is now the Princess Alexandra Hall in the Civil Aviation Authority's section of Bletchley Park. On 19 October 1991 it was used for the Bletchley Park reunion which marked the fiftieth anniversary, almost to the day, of the letter to Churchill from Turing, Welchman, Alexander, and Milner-Barry. This resulted in his famous 'Action

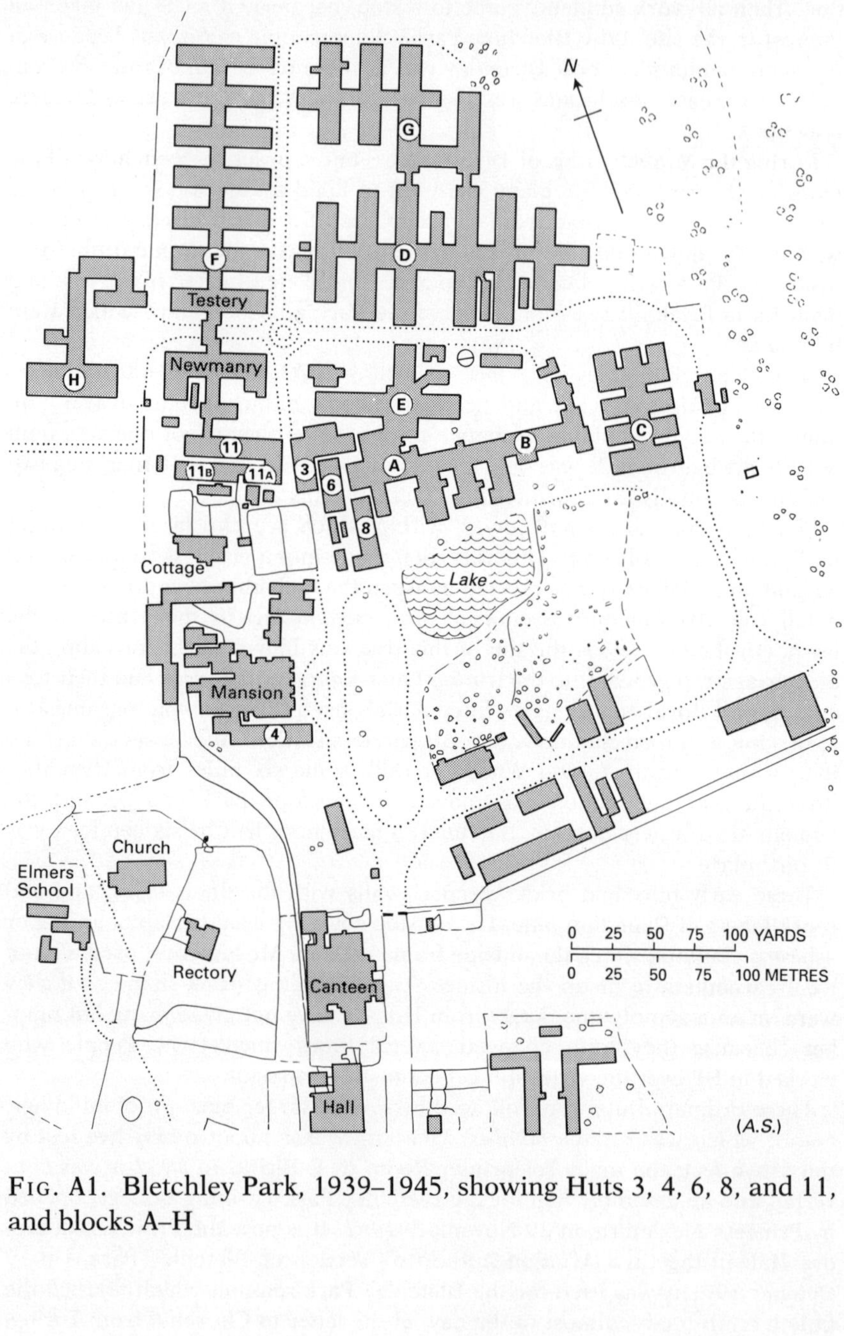

FIG. A1. Bletchley Park, 1939–1945, showing Huts 3, 4, 6, 8, and 11, and blocks A–H

this day' note to General Ismay, ensuring that the codebreakers got the extra staff they urgently needed 'on extreme priority'.

All the huts had wooden black-out shutters and it was the porters' job to look after them night and morning. Most also had blast walls built round them, originally eight feet high but reduced to some five feet high in 1944. They also had Army tortoise stoves or oil stoves fitted—apart from Hut 3, which had a Victorian greenhouse heater, still in use today—but as time went by central heating was installed.

Phase Two followed in 1942 with A and B Blocks, two-storey steel-and-brick buildings on the north side of the lake, and C and D Blocks, single-storey buildings beside the main teleprinter room and the east–west centre road. While this was going on, Price and Co. were laying roads, most of which had to be widened to two lanes later, with water and electricity mains under the roadsides. All the electricity cables were run in loop rings, so that, if one failed, the other came on. Later it was realized that BP needed a stand-by electricity supply, and two very large diesel engines from ships came to hand at just the right time.

Across the north–south road (e.g. in Hut 11, the Newmanry, and H Block) was the home of the Robinson machines and Colossus. These buildings had a steel frame and brick wall, and three pairs of double doors eight feet by six feet. To see one taken down about 1990 was one surprise after another. I measured one of the concrete footings with a steel foot in it; it was four feet square by over five feet high. Even with giant wrecking machines it took a long time to knock it down. There followed F Block, originally with only ten spurs (with four more added later) and a bridge over the road, G block between D Block and the north boundary, and H Block on the west (see Fig. A1).

An air-raid shelter was built for staff working in the mansion, in the lawn to the south of it, with a main passage about fifty feet long and arms each twenty feet long, fitted out with bench seats. After the war the top was removed and the passages filled in.

The Bletchley Park Fire Brigade had eight men on site, two of whom also looked after the fire-fighting equipment, and in the north-west corner of the lake was a hut with a very large electric pump feeding six hose outlets. At one stage they were called to fight a fire in the Colossus building. The bitumastic floor was alight, as well as wooden racks containing Colossus spares. In the south-east corner of the lake was a small jetty. One day two labourers were sent to remove it. Ted slipped off the end of the jetty. Charlie went to pull him out and got stuck up to his knees in mud, leaving a third man to rescue them. After booking out so many pairs of wellington boots, they never lived that episode down.

The BP Home Guard unit had three huts near the gate and could be seen drilling most lunch breaks. They had a rifle range in the woods.

The Transport Section from London brought cars whose chauffeurs lived in upstairs back rooms in the mansion. As the staff increased, so did the number and variety of vehicles, filling the Park roads whenever the shifts changed. They ranged from small cars to buses, bringing in people from billets all over Buckinghamshire and Bedfordshire and taking them back, and there were trains every day between Bletchley and Cambridge, calling at Bedford, for Bletchley Park personnel only.

On the left of Wilton Avenue is the Assembly Hall, fitted out for lectures and films, and also used for concerts, both by BP staff and by visiting musicians.

Just outside the boundary to the south-west was Elmers School, a former country house converted into a private school ten years before the war. GC&CS used part of the house, the stables, and the laboratory. On the night of 20 November 1940 some bombs fell nearby. The first was in Rickley Lane, the next on the Elmers stables and laboratory rooms, which had to be repaired or rebuilt. The next fell in the Park, in a high soft earth bank densely covered with trees, about twenty feet from the extension end of Hut Four. The bank and the York stone retaining wall took most of the force, but the small building moved slightly and was jacked back into position. The next bomb landed in another earth bank but did not explode, so required the attention of the Bomb Disposal Squad, and others landed in fields near the railway.

There were large RAF camps for BP personnel, built in the fields south-west of the Park, with over two hundred buildings in all. The main entrance was at the end of Rickley Lane, with a side entrance into the Park down a private road, Park Gardens, with a Military Police post at the gate. After the 1940 bombs but before the camps were built, a number of anti-aircraft guns were moved in between Shenley Road and the railway. I am pleased to say that they never had to be fired.

We did all sorts of woodwork jobs inside the Park and in the outstations. One day we were told to make a tunnel connecting Huts 3 and 6, to take a sliding office tray, which we did. The hut people brought us the tray and we asked how it was to be moved. They put two cup-hooks into it with a string attached, and called 'OK, your pull' or 'OK, my pull'! Later they used broom handles. After some time we had to fit sliding doors over the opening to stop the draught. You could still see the place where the tunnel was, fifty years later.

To speed up the flow of message slips, four-inch steel tubes were laid between some huts, under the road and into the brick buildings, using a high-pressure pneumatic system to carry message capsules. The distribution room was at the bottom of the stairs in E Block, near the teleprinter room. There was also a conveyor belt running under the road from here to the main corridor of D Block, and from there to the receiver room at the far end.

Another job that stands out in my memory is of one day when I was given a rough drawing and some used parts that looked like suitcase fittings, and told to make a case as shown in the sketch. The case had a long lid with a hinge at the back and a hinged drop-down front. When it was complete I handed it in and asked what it was for. I was told 'a typewriter'. 'Ah yes,' I said to myself, 'some typewriter.' After all these years and seeing pictures of the Enigma machine I now know what it was for.

Index of codes, ciphers, and cryptanalysis

General index

Entries in **bold type** refer to chapters written by the person named.